Eve's Proud Descendants

Eve's Proud Descendants

FOUR WOMEN WRITERS
AND REPUBLICAN POLITICS IN
NINETEENTH-CENTURY FRANCE

Whitney Walton

STANFORD UNIVERSITY PRESS
STANFORD, CALIFORNIA

Stanford University Press
Stanford, California
© 2000 by the Board of Trustees of the
Leland Stanford Junior University
Printed in the United States of America

CIP data appear at the end of the book

For Tom

☞ Acknowledgments

It is a pleasure at last to have an opportunity to thank the many friends, colleagues, and acquaintances who helped me during the long process of researching and writing this book. Many thanks to those who listened to my half-formed ideas and contributed to a clearer direction for this project, including Ruth-Ellen Boetcher-Joeres, Sally Hastings, Judith Stone, and Melinda Zook. Several individuals read parts of the project and offered helpful suggestions; I am grateful to James R. Farr, Rachel Fuchs, Ellen Furlough, Nancy Gabin, Robert May, and Michael Smith. At various stages of my work I was fortunate to be invited to present my findings to several groups: Tuesday Lunch at Denison University, International Studies Seminar at Denison University, the New York Area French Historians Seminar, and the New Biography Seminar at Santa Clara University. Comments from the participants in all these groups were encouraging and constructive. I am very grateful to Mary Louise Roberts, who generously supported the project at a critical moment, and I am deeply indebted to those extraordinary individuals who read the entire manuscript and offered valuable criticism—Jo Burr Margadant and Karen Offen. Many other individuals too numerous to name also offered encouragement to this study in a variety of ways—at conference sessions, over coffee, in written communications, and in casual conversation—I thank you all. Any errors that remain are entirely my own. Finally, I wish to thank my partner, Tom Brush, for his love and sense of humor. This book is dedicated to him.

Contents

Illustrations follow pages 2, 86, and 224

Eve's Proud Descendants

1 ☞ Introduction

In a work first published in 1847, Marie d'Agoult (under the pseudonym of Daniel Stern) rewrote the Christian creation story to cast Eve as striking the first blow for human freedom. In her version, God is a tyrant who threatens Adam and Eve with death if they eat the fruit of the tree of knowledge. "Man resigns himself to this inactive and unconscious happiness," d'Agoult writes, "but woman, listening to the voice of the spirit of liberty within her, accepts the challenge. She prefers sorrow to ignorance, death to slavery. At great peril she seizes the forbidden fruit with a bold hand; she leads man with her in her noble rebellion." D'Agoult then narrates the familiar consequences: God punishes Adam and Eve by banishing them from Eden, sentencing them to mortality, and condemning women to bear children in travail. But instead of viewing Eve as a corrupting influence on man, morally weak and inciting man to evil disobedience, d'Agoult presents Eve as the true hero among the three figures in the story. According to d'Agoult, Eve deserves to be honored and cherished as an immortal revolutionary: "Eve remains forever, for her sad and proud descendants, the glorious and cursed personification of the emancipation of human genius."[1]

D'Agoult's unusual and innovative refashioning of this well-known story suggests that women are leaders in the struggle for intellectual and political liberation, that they seek knowledge at any cost, and that they promote freedom against oppression. As one of "Eve's proud descendants," d'Agoult was herself an intellectual and a professional writer, and, in 1848, although initially apprehensive about revolution, she enthusiastically supported the republic it inaugurated. Both her work and life raise important questions about women, gender, writing, and politics, since in her time most people, including her fellow, male republicans, considered women ill suited for literary endeavors and especially for political engagement. By contrast, d'Agoult claims for women a rational and political capacity despite laws premised on female irrationality that excluded women from politics. In her own thoughts and actions regarding republicanism, as in this new interpretation of the biblical Eve, d'Agoult rescripted masculine stories about sexual difference, gender relations, and political power to endow women with admirable qualities and a leadership role. She, along with three other women writers, adhered to a vision of republicanism in which women were men's equals, yet they did not immediately contest men's exclusive claim to political rights. This stance has cost its protagonists a prominent place in the history of republicanism and of feminism in nineteenth-century France; indeed, they appear only fleetingly, if at all, in histories of France.

Scholars pondering the problem of the relationship of women to politics when they lacked political rights offer two main interpretations for France in the nineteenth century. The first is that a minority of women acted as feminists and claimed for all women the rights denied them and granted to men; the second that a majority fulfilled the roles of citizen wives and mothers set forth during the French Revolution, devoting themselves to domestic occupations while men alone attended to politics. Scholars agree that politics was explicitly a male pursuit with the formation of the first French Republic in 1792, but there is some debate about the nature and implications of the republican exclusion of women from politics. Was it logically irrefutable, or historically contestable? Were there any alternatives to women's either claiming political equality with men or abiding by the ideal of republican motherhood? This book argues that four women writers did contest the republican exclusion of women from politics, but they constructed an alternative position for women between the two poles of feminist equality and republican motherhood.

These four women writers were George Sand (1804–76), Marie d'Agoult (1805–76), Hortense Allart (1801–79), and Delphine Gay de Girardin (1804–55). (See Figs. 1–4.) In varying degrees and in different genres, they were all successful authors in the same Parisian literary milieu at roughly the same time, starting in the 1820s and continuing through the 1870s. Additionally, they each enacted a republican politics that was neither a claim for political equality nor an acceptance of political exclusion. In distinctive ways each figure wrote herself as a republican woman, as a female individual with certain public capabilities,

Lith. de Thierry Frères.

MME G. SAND

FIG. 1. Jules Boilly, *Mme G. Sand* (1837). Paris, Bibliothèque nationale de France, Cabinet des Estampes. Photo Bibliothèque nationale de France, Paris.

FIG. 2. Henri Lehmann, *Mme la comtesse d'Agoult* (1839). Paris, Bibliothèque nationale de France, Cabinet des Estampes. Photo Bibliothèque nationale de France, Paris.

FIG. 3. Sophie Allart Gabriac, *Hortense Allart* (1829). Paris, Bibliothèque nationale de France, Cabinet des Estampes. Photo Bibliothèque nationale de France, Paris.

FIG. 4. Hersent, *Delphine Gay, Mme Emile de Girardin* (1824). Paris, Bibliothèque nationale de France, Cabinet des Estampes. Photo Bibliothèque nationale de France, Paris.

and as a model for other women. They also rewrote the republican script regarding family relations, positing egalitarian alternatives to the patriarchal family of male republicanism. Although ostensibly they did not challenge exclusive male possession of political rights, in both their lives and their works Sand, d'Agoult, Allart, and Girardin undermined its foundation in the gendered separation of spheres.

This book is both a biographical study of the four women and a historical analysis of French literary and political culture, especially during the July Monarchy (1830–48). Its premise is that individuals construct their lives and their identities out of the culture that surrounds them. That is, people make meaning of conditions and experiences through the language, ideas, values, and beliefs available to them. In the process they may change the culture, as, for example, Sand, d'Agoult, Allart, and Girardin changed republicanism when they engaged in republican writing and politics. Both literary and political culture were dominated by men at that time, and the representations of women who participated in them were notoriously unflattering. Yet these four women shared the distinction of making good in the competitive world of letters and of creating a new model of republican womanhood. How they accomplished this says as much about a formative period in publishing and politics as it does about the talent, ingenuity, ambition, and luck of Sand, d'Agoult, Allart, and Girardin. The careers of these four reveal both the power of the gendered separation of spheres on the public imagination and the limitations of such a fiction constructed out of nothing more than imaginings about gender.[2]

I first became acquainted with Sand, d'Agoult, and Girardin when I was searching for evidence of French women's consumer tastes and habits in the nineteenth century. I was struck by their professional success at a time when most middle-class women married, becoming mothers and housekeepers. Looking further I learned that many other women had aspired to and even had made careers of writing in nineteenth-century France, but my interest gradually focused on Sand, d'Agoult, Girardin, and Allart because, in addition to challenging ideas about femininity through their lives and work as authors they also shared a fascination with and commitment to republicanism as a political ideal. The similarity of their life choices, political allegiances, and self-constructions suggested that they were more than eccentric, exceptional figures. They fashioned identities for themselves as independent, successful, political women that appealed to many of both sexes and that resonated with the public. Although hardly exempt from criticism, ridicule, and even hostile condemnation, the four women nonetheless broadened the possibilities for feminine behavior and activity and articulated a less rigidly gendered, even feminine, ideal of republicanism. Thus they impelled me to reconsider the nature of femininity, feminism, and republicanism in early-nineteenth-century France.

Why study these particular individuals as a group, and why these four among the numerous French women writers of the nineteenth century? First, there is strength in numbers. A biography of any one of these figures could help explain the construction of republican womanhood in the landscape of postrevolutionary France, but the fact that four individuals, in unique ways, all contributed to the same model enhances the credibility of this historical interpretation. Second, these four women's literary and political identities directly interacted, and that leads to consideration of the commonalities that unite them. The four were almost the same age, experienced the same events and conditions, came from similar social backgrounds, knew one another, circulated in the same literary and political milieu, and they were all republicans. All were born within a period of four years, between 1801 and 1805, and all came from the upper bourgeoisie or the aristocracy. Political changes brought uncertainty, insecurity, and occasionally even hardship to them and to their families from the time they were children. Shared literary interests and acquaintances led them to meet one another by the time they were young adults. Girardin and Allart were publicly acknowledged authors in 1822; Sand made a stunning literary debut in 1832, and d'Agoult dated the start of her career in letters from 1841.

To be sure, the July Monarchy was a particularly flourishing period for women writers, including Louise Colet, Virginie Ancelot, Madame Tastu, and Flora Tristan, to name only a few.[3] But Sand, d'Agoult, Allart, and Girardin formed a cohort of female authors and shared a common circle of friends and acquaintances. Relations among them were variously amicable, jealous, intimate, distant, critical, and supportive, but for good or ill their lives and identities were intertwined. They were positive examples for one another, proving that women could succeed as writers and thus providing hope and validation for the fulfillment of their aspirations. But they were also negative models, individuals with distinctive characteristics and writing styles that threatened to become stereotypes of women writers. In seeking to avoid identification with stereotypes, each of the four cultivated literary genres and a personal style often deliberately in contrast with those of the others.

Moreover, the four writers were all interested in politics, and in varying degrees and forms they all supported the republican cause. Republicanism following the Revolution of 1830 was an amorphous and capacious ideology and an energetic but divided movement. Republicans agreed on few things, but they shared a mistrust of monarchy and aristocracy, a belief in meritocracy, adherence to representative government, and support for electoral reform. Beyond this common ground, however, republicans differed considerably in their visions of a future French republic. For some, moderate reforms such as the expansion of suffrage and the sovereignty of Parliament were the main goals. For others republicanism entailed nothing less than democracy for all adult men and a complete restructuring of social and economic relations through the state.[4] Sand, d'Agoult, Allart, and Girardin anticipated that there would be both political and social reforms from republicanism, but they distinguished themselves from most republican men in their fundamental expectation that a republican government would improve the civil condition of women and reform the family to make it egalitarian rather than patriarchal.

These four authors were not the only women to support republicanism, but literary success and social class, among other things, separated them from other women involved in politics and favoring republicanism—namely, the socialist feminists. Although Sand and Girardin occasionally wrote for middle-class feminist publications, all four authors were as much concerned with politics and republicanism as with feminism—a fact that set them apart from the socialist feminists.[5] Espousing many of the same ideas as socialist feminists about social transformation and the improvement of women's condition, these four upper-class authors adopted different, literary styles of political engagement—in contrast to feminists' all-female organizations and newspapers—and they differed on the subjects of gender and family relations and the positioning of women in politics. Sand's republicanism was socialistic and democratic, as was that of the socialist feminists; d'Agoult and Girardin could be described as liberal republicans; Allart was elitist, sometimes bordering on authoritarian. Each saw herself as a distinctive individual, even an exceptional woman, who could not ignore the prejudices and barriers against her development as a female literary and political figure. In their writing and republicanism they sought to diminish the legal, social, and cultural limitations on the achievements and contributions of women. In the process they transformed republicanism into a less exclusively masculine movement and ideology.

George Sand was and is the most famous French woman writer of the nineteenth century (possibly excepting Germaine de Staël). In texts and images of her time she was idolized as a literary genius, but also demonized as immoral, unnatural, and dangerous. Those who knew Sand participated in the creation of her complex public image. Hortense Allart, for example, referred to Sand as *la Reine* ("the queen"), from a statement of 1834 by the songwriter Pierre-Jean Béranger that Sand was "the queen of our new literary generation."[6] Marie d'Agoult's representation of Sand was more ambiguous, reflecting popular discomfort with Sand's behavior, writing, and politics. D'Agoult asserts that "a thousand byronic stories" were told about Sand, whose novels were "a revolt against society" and "the cry of woman against the tyranny of man," and whose lifestyle was exotic, mysterious, and subversive. According to d'Agoult, Sand "wore men's clothes and smoked; intrepid amazon, she traversed wild scenes and forests; she was also rumored to conspire; she frequented republican cabals. Was she a man, a woman, an angel, a demon?"[7] Several scholars have analyzed the myth-making, often malicious, that surrounded Sand and that extended to women writers and women in politics more generally, emphasizing the lack or distortion of feminine qualities in women with literary or political aspirations.[8] Such representations were important in the ongoing self-creations of Sand, d'Agoult, Allart, and Girardin, for the women engaged with and transformed them in the constructions of their identities. However, before analyzing the lives that these four individuals made for themselves, some basic information about them is necessary, even though it is impossible to separate interpretations of a life entirely from the "facts" of that life.

Sand was the daughter of an aristocratic military officer and a poor woman who had had other lovers before she met Sand's father. She was reared by her mother and grandmother after the death of her father when she was four years old. Married at the age of eighteen to the illegitimate son of a baron, Sand soon became a mother of two children, but she grew depressed and discontented with her marriage and with her life on her country estate. In 1830 she arranged with her husband to spend part of the year away from home, pursuing a literary career in Paris—and taking a lover. With the overnight success of her first single-authored novel, *Indiana*, in 1832, Sand became a celebrity. Her penchant for wearing men's clothes (an economizing measure and a professional necessity, according to Sand)—but especially the content of her novels, featuring illicit passion, indeterminate gender identities, cross-class relationships, and revolutionary, working-class heroes—contributed to Sand's notoriety. Moreover, Sand was among the higher-paid novelists of her time, an unusual, perhaps unique, position for a woman. She won a separation from her husband in a well-publicized trial in 1836, engaged in several other love affairs, and became an ardent socialist and republican. In 1848 she spent about ten weeks working in various ways for the Second Republic before abandoning public service and retreating to the countryside to continue writing. For the remainder of her life she wrote persistently, being a mentor for younger writers such as Gustave Flaubert, and spent much of her time in the countryside and involved with family and friends.

Sand's literary and political career was both a model and a burden for other women, notably for Marie d'Agoult, who was an intimate friend of Sand's from 1835 to 1839. Born of an aristocratic French father and bourgeois German mother, Marie d'Agoult led rather a luxurious life in both France and Germany as a girl, even after her father's death when she was fourteen. She made a suitable marriage to a count in 1827, had two daughters, and hosted a fashionable salon in the royalist *quartier* of Saint-Germain in Paris. In 1835 d'Agoult left her husband and surviving daughter to flee to Switzerland with her lover, the musician Franz Liszt, with whom she had three children. D'Agoult learned about republicanism during the years with Liszt, and when that relationship deteriorated she returned to Paris, established a new, increasingly republican salon, and began to publish articles and books—art reviews, fiction, histories, and philosophical, political, and literary essays. Like Sand, she supported the Second Republic in 1848 and considered herself a keeper of the flame of republicanism in her salon and in her writing following the regime's demise in 1852.

Hortense Allart won the friendship and respect of both Sand and d'Agoult for her defiant lifestyle, erudite writing, and selfless loyalty. Allart came from the middle class; her father lost his position with the downfall of Napoleon in 1814. Orphaned at the age of nineteen she stayed with family friends and started publishing books, determined to make a name for herself in letters. Pregnant at twenty-four she traveled alone to Italy to deliver the baby, whom she raised, along with another child born thirteen years later, by herself. Allart had several lovers and was married in 1843, but she left her husband after one year. She published many books, including works of fiction, but her main interest was history and philosophy, especially as they related to politics. Initially hopeful for the Second Republic, she drew lessons from its downfall regarding the strengths and weaknesses of popular activism and elite statecraft that she incorporated into subsequent works on history and politics.

Allart and Delphine Gay de Girardin were first cousins, but they appear to have had no contact with one another as adults. Girardin's parents, like Allart's, were middle class, and they, too, suffered a reversal of fortune with the downfall of Napoleon. Widowed at the same time that Girardin first won acclaim for her poetry, Girardin's mother promoted her daughter's literary inclination so that Girardin could provide for the two of them with her poetry readings and publications. At the relatively advanced age of twenty-seven Girardin married a successful newspaper entrepreneur and aspiring liberal politician. She hosted a brilliant salon, occasionally entertaining Sand and d'Agoult, and she became an immensely popular newspaper columnist and a moderately successful playwright. As a couple the *salonnière* and the newspaper editor exercised tremendous influence in the enmeshed society of letters and politics, and their writings were increasingly critical of the government of the July Monarchy. They, too, welcomed the Second Republic in 1848 but fell afoul of different leading factions. After the revolution Girardin retired from journalism and wrote a few more plays before succumbing to stomach cancer in 1855.

Even these selected facts about Sand, d'Agoult, Allart, and Girardin suggest that they led unorthodox, independent, and public lives, and for this reason they have attracted numerous biographers. But with a few exceptions, these biographies are primarily concerned with presenting an exceptional woman rather than analyzing a life as a historical construction. Many biographies focus on Sand, d'Agoult, Allart, and Girardin as essentially literary figures, and as remarkable chiefly for the famous men who were their lovers and friends. More recent biographies of Sand and d'Agoult have examined their writings, and especially their behavior, to determine to what extent each woman was a feminist—usually according to 1970s understandings of feminism.[9] Without diminishing the distinct identities of these four individuals, I present them as creating themselves in interaction with the same surrounding culture, a culture that, among other things, defined femininity in restricted terms and generally discouraged women from literary endeavor, passionate love, and political engagement. Thus I analyze Sand, d'Agoult, Allart, and Girardin as creating themselves in a historically specific, gendered context. Several feminist scholars have developed this approach and applied it to selected texts by the four authors (as well as other women writers) to argue for a feminist content.[10] In general I find this work persuasive, but I wish to analyze a far larger body of text as a manifestation of a life. My analysis is based almost entirely on a wide variety of texts and genres by the four authors—letters, personal narratives, fiction, poetry, drama, journalism, essays, and histories. From my perspective, these are all documents that represent their authors or their ideas for public consumption; even letters constitute a self-representation to the reader, if not to a broader public. To a far lesser degree I include texts and images from other sources about these women, for they are useful as cultural responses to the four lives, to which Sand, d'Agoult, Allart, and Girardin often responded in turn. Like literary scholars, I discern a feminist content in much of the four authors' literary productions, but unlike them, I see this as part of a larger feminist politics in the context of early-nineteenth-century French republicanism.

Historians, in contrast to literary scholars, are more hesitant to label these four women writers as feminists, largely because they eschewed working-class feminists.[11] Moreover, historians rarely even consider Sand, d'Agoult, Allart, and Girardin political figures at all, and they almost completely ignore the huge cache of writing they produced as a source of material for the understanding of French history in the nineteenth century.[12] More than simply restoring them to the historical narrative, however, I intend to show through their lives how fluid and experimental were postrevolutionary literary and political cultures, and how women writers used ideas and conditions—such as romanticism, a publishing boom, political turmoil, socialism, republicanism, and feminism—to subvert restrictions on femininity. Historical scholarship on reading and writing tends to accept contemporary denigration of women writers without investigating the possibilities that women themselves exploited, much less the alternative models of women writers that they projected to the public and that further encouraged aspiring female authors.[13] Political histories, and notably histories of republicanism, adhere to a similar assumption; since only men had political

rights, and politics was part of the masculine sphere, women were simply not part of the story. Some acknowledge the masculine gendering
of republicanism, but only a few explore its processes and contentions.[14]

There is no disputing that, starting with the writings of Jean-Jacques
Rousseau and playing itself out initially in the French Revolution, the
majority of revolutionary and republican men denied that women had
the capacity for, or the right to, political participation, but different
scholars offer different accounts and interpretations of that late-eigh-
teenth-century masculinization of politics. Lynn Hunt maintains that in
the process of eliminating one form of government (absolute monarchy) and erecting another (constitutional republicanism), revolutionaries constructed these radical political developments using images
and language that were familiar to them—namely, those of family relations. In Hunt's account the prevailing family romance that defined the
French Revolution was that of educated, white, mostly professional
men who styled themselves as destroying a tyrannical father (Louis
XVI) and a corrupt mother (Marie-Antoinette) in order to establish a
new government of equal and virtuous brothers (republicanism). After
Hunt persuasively presents the visual and textual evidence for this interpretation, she admits that other family romances might also have
structured the revolutionary republic, and that the exclusively masculine, fraternal republic was by no means inevitable.[15]

By contrast, Carole Pateman and Joan Scott argue that republicanism was inherently patriarchal and masculine, consciously based on a
theory of male authority—patriarchy being simply redefined to paternal authority in the home and fraternal authority in the state—and female dependence—predicated on "natural" sexual difference. According to them, the foundation of republicanism (and contract theory or
rights theory) in sexual difference causes enormous difficulties for feminists who must either deny palpable physical differences between
women and men or get entangled in a paradox of arguing for equality
on behalf of all women, which simply reinforces the difference between
them and men that they are trying to overcome.[16]

Although republican notions of sexual difference were often presented as "natural" and empirically provable, inconsistencies and con-
tradictions remained. Indeed, Geneviève Fraisse posits that no real theory lay behind the exclusion of women from politics, but rather male
"phantasms" that complicate the theorizing and countertheorizing of
the practice of excluding women. Here then was a wedge with which to

prize open the shutter against women in republican politics. Women who could undermine the masculine gendering of specific republican and political attributes—notably the capacity for sustained rational endeavor and its public presentation—thus initiated the process of challenging the exclusion of women from politics without a head-on, confrontational demand for political equality between the sexes. Fraisse asserts that the French Revolution, by uncoupling knowledge and power, allowed some women to seek knowledge without power and therefore to establish themselves as independent individuals, an accomplishment that would ultimately serve as a precondition or as a sort of bridge to organized feminist demands for equal rights.[17]

All of this scholarship contributes to a better understanding of how politics, and especially republican politics, assumed a masculine guise in the modern era, and how feminists challenged this gendering. For the most part, however, these works address the issue on a theoretical and abstract level. To be sure ideas and language were important to Sand, d'Agoult, Allart, and Girardin, who, after all, made a living from them. But politics is a practice, a network of power relations, as well as a body of theory, and the meaning of political terms and gestures changes over time. My study analyzes how four women writers changed the meaning of republicanism by transforming its underlying assumptions about sexual difference, separate spheres, and the family. Only by examining their lives as constructs and performances is it possible to comprehend how they did this. Sand, d'Agoult, Allart, and Girardin created independent existences for themselves through their intellect and, in the process, elided the boundary between the private and the public. Moreover, the transformations they proposed and enacted in gender relations, marriage law, child-rearing, education, and family relations threatened the very bedrock of republicanism, since they would eliminate the dependent, ignorant, domestic wife and mother who was the justification for the independent, educated, republican patriarch and citizen.

Numerous contemporaries of these four authors did, in fact, assert political equality for the sexes. Socialist feminists such as Jeanne Deroin, Eugénie Niboyet, and Claire Démar, to name only a few, were articulate and courageous proponents of equal rights, and they have been the subject of several perceptive analyses of their feminist republicanism.[18] These works, however, tend to dismiss the contributions of Sand, d'Agoult, Allart, and Girardin because the four authors rejected the socialist feminists and their demands. But that is only part of the story. Sand, d'Agoult, Allart, and to a lesser extent Girardin engaged in a separate struggle to integrate feminist issues into republican concerns, a mostly genteel struggle waged in salons and in the pages of books and newspapers that circulated among a predominantly, though not entirely, elite audience. Their common enterprise was to transform cultural attitudes toward women and to improve women's civil status as necessary precursors to the acquisition of equal rights. Although their ideas about republican strategies and state forms varied, their suggestions regarding women and the family nonetheless formed a coherent alternative to republican motherhood and to complete sexual equality.

Chapter 2 examines the families, family relations, and childhoods of the four women. It argues that they, like their male contemporaries, were "politicized" at an early age simply because they and their families lived through significant political changes that affected their lives directly—notably the vicissitudes of the Napoleonic wars, the downfall of the First Empire, and the establishment of the Restoration. It accounts for the ways that Sand, d'Agoult, and Allart constructed their childhoods according to the republican beliefs they adopted as adults. The chapter also charts early suggestions of subsequent literary and political identities through the parents' class backgrounds and political affiliations, child/parent relations, education, sexual awareness, literary awakenings, and gendered child-rearing practices.

Chapter 3 follows the chronology of the four lives to address courtship, marriage, sexuality, and love, and how these experiences contributed to the four women's defining themselves as writers. Coming of age at the height of Romanticism, all four were deeply concerned with spiritual love and sensuous passion, but they had to reconcile such notions and feelings with expectations for females regarding marriage, obedience, and maternity. Sand, d'Agoult, and Allart all had extramarital affairs, and writing was a means of explaining them, even justifying them, to themselves and to a larger public. Although Girardin did not follow the same path, she was no less concerned with the relationship between writing and heterosexual love for a woman, perhaps even more so, since it is likely that her early success in literature impeded her quest for married love. This chapter analyzes the different modes that each author devised for the literary expression of sexual desire and heterosexual love during a time in which most such articulations came from a masculine point of view through male-defined Romanticism.

Textualizing love and desire for women was a major impetus in these four women's literary identities, especially in the early stages. Additionally this chapter explains the meaning of pseudonyms as new "marriages" for Sand, d'Agoult, and Girardin, and as a rebellion against marriage for Allart.

As published authors, Sand, d'Agoult, Allart, and Girardin had to come to terms with the negative stereotypes of women writers; indeed, their very success contributed to the proliferation of such satirical, often hostile representations, in both words and images. Chapter 4 analyzes their accounts of prejudice against women writers and how they responded to it. It argues that the four authors engaged with the stereotype of the bluestocking and attempted to undermine it by creating alternatives, including their own self-representations. Additionally, their relations with one another contributed to the variety of alternatives to the bluestocking. Sand, d'Agoult, Allart, and Girardin invoked and elaborated upon classical figures of intellectual and political women, such as Aspasia, Sapho, Diotima, Cassandra, Cleopatra, and the amazon, not only as models for their own self-creations but also as models for all women.

The next two chapters address the articulation of the four women's republicanism. Chapter 5 analyzes the different ways in which Sand, d'Agoult, Allart, and Girardin understood republicanism and supported it as women writers. It begins with a general explanation of the varieties of republicanism in the July Monarchy and follows with accounts of how each woman came to embrace republican ideals. This chapter then lays out the contours of each individual's republicanism, her position on democracy, freedom, representation, and the social obligations of the state. In addition to developing different meanings of republicanism that somewhat corresponded to the variations among republican men, Sand, d'Agoult, Allart, and Girardin devised unique modes of expressing and furthering that ideology—as ongoing quest, culmination of progress, cultivation of statecraft, and satire and family romance. Chapter 6 shifts to the different ways in which Sand, d'Agoult, Allart, and Girardin transformed republicanism by proposing sweeping changes in gender and family relations. Analyzing their ideas about marriage, divorce, education, love, and the family, this chapter argues that these authors created the image of the republican woman in contrast to the republican mother. Moreover, it explains how they lived the ideal of republican womanhood. Sand, d'Agoult, and Allart established households without men, in which they combined work and family, sociability and intimacy, home and politics; the Girardin marriage offered the possibility of a true partnership and egalitarianism. In writing and in action the four women challenged assumptions about dependent females, separate spheres, and the patriarchal family that underlay the republican exclusion of women from politics, thus introducing the possibility of political equality in the future.

Chapter 7 explores the four women's rendering of the 1848 Revolution and the Second Republic. Enthusiastic about the revolution that toppled Louis-Philippe and promised the fulfillment of their republican dreams, they quickly became disillusioned with the nitty-gritty of power politics. This chapter traces each individual's changing responses to different phases of the republic, and explains their dismissal of socialist feminists' call for women's political equality. Noting male politicians' poor handling of republican government, Sand, d'Agoult, Allart, and Girardin considered the time not yet ripe for addressing even their own, feminist demands. Nonetheless, they continued to write about and to support a vision of republicanism that included republican women. Politics discouraged them, but a republican ideal remained; they "rewrote" the revolution after 1848 to represent a more successful republican and feminist vision.

Marie d'Agoult rewrote the story of Eve to create a positive model of a revolutionary, intellectual, and political woman. In similar fashion d'Agoult, Sand, Allart, and Girardin created a model of republican womanhood through their many literary productions. This republican woman exposed the fiction of the separate spheres ideology that presumed to bar women from public life and to make men heads of the households to which women were supposed to be confined in their own best interest. The model resembled the four authors themselves, who were independent women, earning a living through writing, engaging in politics in conversation and in print, and, except for Girardin, running a household without men. Privileged backgrounds and literary success allowed these four authors to lead such lives, but their writings propagated the possibility that all women could be family members and public figures, mothers and intellectuals, lovers and politicians. From their perspective the reforms that would make this possible, including changes in marriage law, legalization of divorce, improved education for women, and the amelioration of the conditions of the working class, could come about only through republicanism.

2 ⌒ Growing Up Female in Postrevolutionary France

At the age of eight, Aurore Dupin (the future George Sand) dreamed of rescuing Napoleon and his armies from the Russian campaign of 1812–13. There had been no news of the imperial forces for fifteen days, and this dreadful mystery concerning the whereabouts of thousands of soldiers and their leader who were trying to return to France weighed on Aurore's childish mind. She dreamed that she acquired wings, flew to the steppes of Russia, and found the lost troops. In the dream she guided the men back to France, and she claims that "when I regained awareness, I was tired and in pain from the long flight; my eyes were blinded by the snow, and I was cold and hungry, but I felt great joy at having saved the French army and its Emperor."[1] A few years later, after Napoleon's final defeat at Waterloo in 1815 and his imprisonment on a British-controlled island off the western coast of Africa, sixteen-year-old Hortense Allart fantasized about joining Napoleon on Saint Helena, "to care for the emperor in his dreadful exile, to live near him and for him, and, who knows? What didn't I imagine in my girlish dreams?"[2]

Napoleon loomed large on the contemporary scene of early-nineteenth-century France, and even young girls from the elite classes were not immune to his influence. Both the little Aurore and the adolescent Hortense were much taken with the emperor (or with the stories they heard about him), and they wanted to help him during his times of trial. Hortense even hints vaguely that she might provide erotic or sexual comfort to Napoleon. But in their autobiographies both Sand and Allart took pains to identify this attachment to Napoleon as strictly childish or adolescent fantasy deriving from patriotism or power worship, rather than as a portent of political allegiance. "Since then," Allart wrote, "I judged the emperor more correctly, as did everyone; and I hated war."[3]

Sand indicates that even as a child she tempered her imagined rescues of Napoleon with rational doubts about his motivations. She claims that during the Hundred Days she daydreamed of carrying him through space, setting him on the dome of the Tuileries, and confronting him with her questions and her judgment:

> If you prove to me by your answers that you are an ambitious, bloodthirsty monster, as people say, I shall hurl you down and dash you to pieces on the steps of your palace, but if you can vindicate yourself, if you are what I have believed you to be—a kind, great, just Emperor, a father to his people—I shall restore you to your throne and defend you against your enemies with my flaming sword.[4]

According to Sand, Napoleon answered her questions well, admitting that he had made mistakes resulting from his excessive love for fame but promising henceforth to seek only the happiness of the French people. For this he was rewarded with a touch of Sand's flaming sword on his body to guarantee his success.[5] In this fantasy Sand resembles Joan of Arc, trying to save her leader and her people from defeat at the hands of the English. But Sand's vision goes beyond Joan of Arc's fighting for her king to an even greater empowerment, because Sand passes judgment on her leader. She imagines herself to be an avenging angel setting straight a wayward emperor. For all his power—and clearly this was part of the attraction of Napoleon for Sand, as well as for Allart—Napoleon was subject to the even greater and more mysterious power and authority of the fantasizing girl hero. Sand suggests to her readers that already as a child she had a clear notion of political justice and efficacy, and that she tried to implement it in her fantasies.

Politics affected the four women writers' lives from the beginning. Born under the Consulate (1799–1804) or the Empire (1804–14), Sand, d'Agoult, Allart, and Girardin felt the shadow of Napoleon over their childhoods. For good or ill their families' fortunes were tied to those of the emperor, and the experiences of his rule, his downfall, and the restored Bourbon monarchy marked these women just as much as they did the men who came of age during that period.[6] The four were very young during these upheavals, and naturally they did not fully comprehend their political significance. Far more immediate to these girls were the material manifestations of the Empire and its collapse, such as a father's lost position, family emigration, the presence of soldiers, and economic insecurity. Marie d'Agoult, for example, associated Napoleon with the end of her childhood innocence and security, inasmuch as his return to France from the island of Elba caused the temporary breakup and emigration of her family: "His conquering sword . . . drew me abruptly from this first golden dream of the morning, started by the child in the night of the maternal womb."[7] Still, as adults reflecting back on the early years of their lives, three of the four women writers constructed childhoods that foreshadowed their mature political formation. And politics entered into Girardin's young life, even though she did not leave an autobiographical account of it. This chapter will chart and analyze the childhood experiences of Sand, d'Agoult, Allart, and Girardin, focusing on their family relationships, education, preparation for becoming writers, and political formations. It relies much on autobiographical works by Sand, d'Agoult, and Allart, reading these texts as feminist self-constructions.[8] This reading also puts the personal narratives of the three authors, along with biographical data on Girardin, into historical context—notably the changes in family law that occurred during the French Revolution, and common childhood experiences of the time. First, however, brief biographies of the early years of the four authors will provide a useful background.

Childhood

Aurore Dupin (the future George Sand) was born on 5 July 1804, just one month after her parents were married in a civil ceremony. Her father, Maurice Dupin, a French officer of noble lineage in the Napoleonic army, had struggled for years to reconcile his doting mother to the woman he loved: Sophie Delaborde, a camp follower of the popular classes. With Sophie's pregnancy just a month from term, the couple finally married in Paris, still withholding those facts from the older Aurore Dupin, after whom the infant girl was named. After four more years of military service, including a stint in Spain, Maurice brought his family (including a newborn boy who died after only three months of life) to his mother's estate of Nohant in the Berry region. This was little Aurore's first memory of her grandmother and of the home that became her own. Aurore's mother and grandmother, radically different in personalities and background, managed to get along for several years in the same house, even after the death of Maurice in a riding accident in 1808. But throughout Aurore's childhood and adolescence the two women competed for her affection, although Sophie allowed Aurore to live with her grandmother after her own removal to Paris.

Aurore grew up at Nohant with her half-brother, Hippolyte, the child of Maurice and a household servant. The two were educated by Deschartres, their father's former tutor, until Aurore entered the convent of the English sisters in Paris to complete her education. She left the convent when she was seventeen and returned to Nohant, where she nursed her grandmother through a fatal illness and then lived with relatives until her marriage in 1822 to Casimir Dudevant, the illegitimate son of a baron.[9]

Marie de Flavigny (later Marie d'Agoult) started life in 1805 in Frankfurt, the home of her rich German Protestant mother. Her aristocratic father, Alexandre de Flavigny, a French Catholic, took the family to France in 1809, where they lived for the most part in Touraine and where Marie enjoyed the company of her older brother, Maurice, when he was on vacation from school. In 1815 Alexandre sent his wife and daughter back to Frankfurt to ensure their security while he fought with the royalists against the resurgent Napoleon. Marie went to boarding school in Frankfurt and then returned to France in 1816, where she was educated at home by her parents and a host of specialized tutors. Baptized Protestant, she took her first communion in the Catholic Church as the socially expected thing for an aristocratic girl in France to do. Her father's sudden death when she was fourteen led to yet another return to Frankfurt; a year later Marie was back in Paris to attend the convent school of Sacré-Coeur and to finish her education. In 1822 Marie's mother took her out of the convent, and during the next five years Marie received and rejected numerous marriage proposals until she accepted that of Comte Charles d'Agoult in 1827.[10]

Delphine Gay was born in Aix-la-Chapelle in 1804. She was the youngest of the five children (four girls and one boy) of Sigismond and Sophie Gay. Life was good for the family at that time. Sigismond held the position of receiver general in the imperial finance administration, and Sophie was a popular *salonnière* and occasional writer of fiction and drama. However, in 1811 Sigismond was dismissed from his post, perhaps in revenge for an insulting remark made about another official by Sophie. He then ran a bank in Aix, and Sophie turned to more writing. Delphine's mother somewhat encouraged her interest in literature and writing, and the girl's studies at home were oriented toward preparing her to be a poet. Delphine's first literary triumph came when she was seventeen, the French Academy awarding her a special recognition for a poem she had submitted to one of their competitions. That same year

(1822) Delphine's father died, and though Sophie tried to support herself and her daughter from her writing, the real breadwinner became Delphine. Delphine recited her poetry in the most fashionable aristocratic salons and on several important state occasions during the Restoration. Sophie worked hard to get Delphine married well, as she had succeeded in doing for her older daughters, but Delphine had no fortune. None of her marriage prospects panned out until her wedding with the newspaper publisher Emile de Girardin in 1831.[11]

Delphine's aunt, Marie Françoise Gay, was married rather late in life (at the age of thirty-three) to a financier and dilettante, Gabriel Allart. Their first child was Hortense Allart, born in 1801 while the couple was on business in Milan. Hortense and her younger sister were raised in comfort and among imperial high society. At a young age Hortense began reading voraciously, and she gained much of her education through her own endeavors. With the fall of the Napoleonic Empire in 1814 Gabriel lost his lucrative position. He was in the process of reestablishing himself in finance when he died in 1817. Marie Françoise turned to writing for income, as she had supported herself and her younger siblings before her marriage. But Marie Françoise died in 1821, and Hortense was taken in by a family friend. The following year Hortense published her first book, a historical study, and met her first love, who was not among the several eligible men she might have married. Pregnant by this lover in 1825, when she was twenty-four, Hortense traveled alone to Italy, where she gave birth to a son in 1826.[12]

It might be informative here to group the four women writers into pairs, in terms of class background, political experience, and orientation to writing. Sand and d'Agoult were both affiliated with the noble ranks of France, and, despite the upheavals of the revolutionary and imperial eras, they grew up with financial security, modest in Sand's case and substantial for d'Agoult. In fairly typical fashion for the aristocracy, their families generally spent the winters in Paris and summered in their country estates, and for both Sand and d'Agoult the experiences of childhood in the countryside were happy and important parts of their lives. The two authors reveal a romantic appreciation for nature in their writings, and they also describe rich, imaginative worlds they created for themselves as children living in a rural milieu. Moreover, the adult women indicate that as girls in the country they often played with peasant children, an experience that serves as foreground for their later commitment to progressive social policies and democratic

political ideologies. Sand and d'Agoult were similarly educated at
home by a host of tutors and masters, and they both attended convent
schools, living, however briefly, in a feminine community and under-
going a phase of intense Catholic piety. Although both Sand and
d'Agoult "chose" their marriage partners, they were steeped in the lore
of arranged marriages that were the norm for girls of their class.

In contrast to Sand and d'Agoult, Girardin and Allart were decidedly middle class, downwardly as much as upwardly mobile. Their
fathers' careers succeeded on the basis of their financial acumen but
foundered in imperial court intrigue, the end of empire, and early
death. The mothers of Girardin and Allart were notably resourceful,
particularly in making money from writing, and, in the case of Allart,
also from translating. Much less information is available on Girardin's
and Allart's childhoods than on the early years of Sand and d'Agoult—
on their relations with family members, on youthful experiences and
imagination, and on their education. Unlike Sand and d'Agoult, they
knew reversal of fortune and economic insecurity as adolescents and
young women, and, as their mothers did before them, they turned to
writing early in their lives to secure a livelihood. Lacking fortunes, Girardin and Allart did not have marriages arranged for them, and they
spent more time as single women (before marriage) than did Sand or
d'Agoult. Girardin had nearly resigned herself to spinsterhood before
she was married at the age of twenty-seven, and Allart did not marry
until she was forty-one.

Family Relations

A notable feature of the parents of all four authors is that they married
for love, and that the authors' mothers exercised independence and
even rebellion in their selections of a husband. The geographical dis-
placements of the revolutionary wars led to two of the matches, since
both Maurice Dupin and Alexandre de Flavigny met the women they
would marry while on military campaigns. And it is conceivable that
new laws and new ideas about the family during the French Revolution
contributed to the cultivation of affection within the families of the four
women writers.[13] Perhaps the example of love matches and, apparently,
relationships of mutual respect, even of equality, inspired Sand,
d'Agoult, Girardin, and Allart to seek similarly loving and satisfying
relationships in their own lives. To do so, three of the four violated so-

cial and legal codes of female respectability, but their autobiographies suggest that there was a precedent for defiant behavior in their own families by women acting as agents in the pursuit of love.

Sand represents her parents' relationship as truly a love match, to the point that Maurice deceived and defied his adored mother in order to secure his alliance with Sophie. Sophie had been the mistress of a rich man when she met Maurice, but she committed herself utterly to the poorer man, following him to Nohant when he visited his mother and accepting Maurice's decision to hide the truth of her presence from the jealous Madame Dupin. Indeed, Maurice hid much from his mother about his relationship with Sophie until after their marriage and the birth of little Aurore. From Sand's perspective, Sophie was pure and honest in her love for Maurice, despite her history of prior sexual relations, because Sophie's "youth had been delivered up to frightening hazards, owing to the force of circumstances." As far as Sand was concerned Sophie's youthful transgressions were absolved by her devotion to Maurice: "One fact remains before God: she was loved by my father, and apparently she deserved it, since her mourning for him ended only with her life." The faithful love of Sophie and Maurice redeemed Maurice as well, according to Sand, compensating for the heartbreak he caused his mother. Sand, interestingly enough, does not bother to excuse Maurice for fathering a child by a servant before he joined the army, or from considering his early sexual relationship with Sophie as a passing affair. Was Sand so enamored of the memory or the fantasy of her father that she could not find fault with him? Or did she simply accommodate the double standard by which such behavior by men was considered acceptable, while the same actions by women brought down harsh condemnation? In any case, Sand suggests that her parents led virtuous lives in their marriage. Sand recalls her parents' home life as blissfully loving and harmonious—"They found themselves happy only in their little household"—and perhaps Sand's numerous affairs sought to reproduce this ideal of marital love and mutual regard.[14]

D'Agoult, too, made a point of conveying the voluntary and passionate origin of her parents' relationship, and especially the daring on the part of her mother. Marie-Elisabeth Bussmann was a young widow when she met Alexandre de Flavigny, who was part of the royalist, émigré French forces in Frankfurt in 1797. According to d'Agoult, Marie-Elisabeth's mother, "the old Mrs. von Bethmann," prohibited the marriage, considering Flavigny nothing more than a fortune seeker and

disdaining his Catholicism and his impoverishment, as well as his being a nobleman and émigré. To ensure the end of the infatuation the
Bethmanns used their influence to get Flavigny imprisoned for an al-
leged irregularity of his passport. But the imprisonment of her beloved
only enflamed Marie-Elisabeth's passion and steeled her determination. She visited Flavigny in prison and stayed for a scandalously long
time. According to d'Agoult, when Marie-Elisabeth returned to her
home, she confronted her family thus: "'Now,' she said to her mother
and to her older brother, with a boldness that no one suspected hereto-
fore beneath her shy demeanor, 'do you still wish to prevent me from
marrying him?'" The only way for the family to redeem her reputation
and their own was to permit the marriage. For d'Agoult this singular
act of defiance and passion by Marie-Elisabeth was her mother's finest
hour, and she admired equally the same behavior on the part of her
half-sister, Auguste Bussmann, who also boldly "arranged" her marriage to the poet Clemens Brentano against her family's wishes and
then divorced him three months later.[15] D'Agoult thus sets the stage in
her autobiography for her own act of rebellion and passion, though it
would occur after her marriage.

Allart, who writes very little about her parents in her autobiography, also asserts that they married for love: "My father had married her
for love some years after his break with the actress." The actress refers
to one of many liaisons Gabriel Allart enjoyed before his marriage to
Marie Françoise Gay, when she was thirty-three years old and supporting herself and her siblings by translating English novels into
French.[16] Gabriel must have found Marie Françoise admirable in many
ways to have wed her and presumably given up his bachelor habits. For
Marie Françoise's part, Gabriel represented the possibility of married
status, prosperity, children, and a home of her own, despite his rakish
reputation. Marie Françoise and Gabriel were mature individuals with
considerable experience of the world when they married in 1798. Similarly, it is likely that Girardin's parents also married for love, since her
mother, Sophie, had already married and survived one husband before
she married Sigismond Gay. Moreover, one biographer indicates that
both Sophie and Sigismond had lost fortunes before they married, so
that presumably neither entered the union for the other's money.[17]

In a period when arranged marriages among the upper classes were
the norm, and stories abound of mismatched couples and unloving relationships, the love and independence of these four sets of parents are

notable. The examples of the Dupins, Flavignys, Gays, and Allarts suggest that the disruptions of revolution and war, to say nothing of the legalization of divorce from 1792 to 1816, contributed to marital practices much in contrast to those of the Old Regime, and not necessarily to marital breakdown.[18] The limitations of such changes, however, are manifested in the marriages of Sand and especially d'Agoult—unions that were arranged, unloving, and ultimately terminated by Sand and d'Agoult, who sought more satisfying relationships.

Sand and d'Agoult describe their family relations in considerable detail, and they include in their autobiographies genealogies of their maternal and especially paternal ancestries. They are both conscious of their mixed parentage and its effect on their own personalities and identities. Sand, whose lineage was both aristocratic and common, says that her "birth . . . straddles, so to speak, two classes" and contributed strongly to her "socialist and democratic instincts."[19] D'Agoult's mixed parentage was cultural as well as social; she was the child of a French aristocratic father and a German bourgeois mother, and she maintains that for that reason she always felt a bit different from those around her: "As far back as my memory goes I see myself as I remained all my life, simultaneously German and French by blood and by physical and mental nurturing. . . . I never felt entirely French or German, but apart, isolated, a little foreign . . . also a little foreign, on many occasions, to myself and to those who loved me."[20] Both Sand and d'Agoult felt marked in some way by their mixed parentage, and it perhaps contributed to doubts about their identities, their difficulties in personal love relationships, and their progressive politics.

The two authors also shared the trauma of witnessing their fathers' early deaths and thereafter growing up in female-dominated households. Sand and d'Agoult adored their fathers. The second paragraph of d'Agoult's autobiography attests to his centrality in her early life: "Above all else in the world I loved him, I admired him, and it is toward him, with the greatest tenderness that all the emotions and all the happy imaginings of my happy childhood are directed."[21] Pleasing her father and being allowed to accompany him on hunting and fishing expeditions were among the greatest pleasures of d'Agoult's childhood. In d'Agoult's rendering, Alexandre de Flavigny represented the best of human qualities—honor, loyalty, intelligence, and a certain amount of modesty manifested in a simple lifestyle—simple, that is, by the standards of the French courtly aristocracy. D'Agoult was utterly grieved when her father died unexpectedly of a fever, and no doubt it was easier to recall his perfections than his flaws, as his death was so untimely.

Moreover, after Alexandre's death d'Agoult's brother Maurice took over as head of the family, but from d'Agoult's perspective he never adequately replaced her father. D'Agoult was devastated by her father's death, and she recalled that she immediately submitted to her brother's authority: "I vowed . . . to transfer to this older brother all the filial piety, all the respect and all the love that I had had for my father." But according to d'Agoult, Maurice de Flavigny, the new household head, did not adequately appreciate his sister's unspoken pledge of obedience. And in a footnote to this section of her memoirs d'Agoult writes that in the final years of her brother's life Maurice spoke with her about this disillusionment and suggested that both their lives might have been better had their sexes been switched to match their differing characters. She recalls Maurice as saying "that nature apparently made a mistake in making him the brother and myself the sister. Had the roles been changed, he added, all would have been for the best, no problem would have followed, and both of our destinies would have been perfect."[22] D'Agoult implied that since her brother failed to fulfill his responsibilities as father substitute, her subsequent acts of insubordination might be excused.

Sand was only four years old when her father was thrown from his horse and died of a broken neck, so she knew her father only from her grandmother, her mother, and, later in life, from the many letters her father had written as a youth and young man to his own mother. She was explicit that his early death contributed to his being "a shining apparition" in her memory, that he was more an object of Sand's fantasy than a remembered individual—precisely because Sand hardly knew him. In a remarkable passage Sand suggests that her own self-creation was inseparable from her imagined memory of her father: "My being is a reflection—weakened no doubt, but rather complete—of his. . . . had I been a boy and had I lived twenty-five years earlier, I know and I sense that I would have acted and felt in all things like my father."[23] Sand not only idealized her father; she also identified herself closely with Maurice's character, values, and behavior.

It may appear that d'Agoult and Sand in writing their autobiographies are still seeking their fathers' approval for themselves with their extremely one-sided assessments of their fathers' characters. But they are also constructing their fathers in their own images, fashioning ideal beings according to their own criteria of human and manly goodness. They write their fathers as men who would approve of the characteristics and accomplishments of their daughters, no matter how unorthodox. And it is fathers who act publicly and have political beliefs—hence who could understand and appreciate the public lives and politics of Sand and d'Agoult. By contrast, their mothers eschewed public life and devoted themselves to family and home, which became increasingly a confining ideal for women as the nineteenth century progressed.

Sand, in a sense, had two mothers—Sophie, her father's wife, and the elder Madame Dupin, her father's mother. The two women were complete opposites in temperament and background; according to Sand they were "the two extreme types of our sex." Sand describes her grandmother and her mother thus: "One fair, blond, serious, calm and dignified in her behavior, a real Saxon of noble race, with grand manners full of ease and benevolent kindness; the other dark, pale, intense, shy and awkward in the presence of high society, and always ready to explode when the storm raged too forcefully within, a Spanish nature, jealous, passionate, angry and weak, mean and good at the same time." Sand portrays Madame Dupin as highly refined, rational, formal, sociable, and very much in the mold of an Old Regime *salonnière*. Though Sand loved her grandmother, she truly appreciated her only when she was in her teens and her grandmother's health was failing. Sophie, by contrast, was artistic, hard-working, adept with her hands, a competent housekeeper, imaginative, and a little mad. She was loving but mercurial, and though she often lashed out verbally and physically at her daughter, Sand found her fascinating and adorable. Sand seems clear-sighted in her descriptions of these two women who reared her, suggesting that despite the emotional difficulty of their competition for her affection, she benefited from their different qualities and abilities. Sand never lacked for love when she was growing up, and she remembers her childhood as a "golden age," "a vanished dream to which nothing can be compared later on."[24] But she does not worship or identify with her mother or her grandmother as she does with her father.

D'Agoult presents a generally unflattering portrait of her mother, though she credits Marie-Elisabeth for her audacity in procuring the marriage with Flavigny, and for teaching music—serious musical understanding, rather than the superficial accomplishment common for girls at that time—to the child Marie. For the most part, however, d'Agoult disdains her mother for being materialistic and conformist.

And she is blunt about how, in contrast to her overwhelming attraction to her father, she felt quite the opposite for her mother: "I did not like my mother [ma mère . . . ne me plaisait pas]. . . . her presence was not at all to my liking; her conversation did not keep my intellect awake. . . . She had no hold over my thoughts."[25] Did d'Agoult really dislike her mother so much, even as a child? To be sure, d'Agoult had serious disagreements with her mother, particularly over her affair with Liszt, but these were adult controversies. Given her idealization of her father, presenting him as possessing only good qualities, it is possible that d'Agoult constructed her mother equally one-sidedly, but as possessing primarily negative characteristics.[26] It is probably no coincidence that the values and characteristics d'Agoult attributes to her parents are the same ones that she associates with different regimes, political ideologies, and societies. That is, Marie-Elisabeth's materialism, conspicuous consumption, anti-intellectualism, and bourgeois snobbery are precisely the features of the July Monarchy and Second Empire that d'Agoult despises. By contrast d'Agoult contorts her father's ultraroyalism and smattering of Enlightenment learning into rational, judicious, progressive republicanism.

Father-worship was far more muted in Allart. She does speak favorably of Gabriel Allart, whom she describes as "tall and with a nice face," and who, "by his competence had created for himself a very important financial enterprise [un cabinet d'affaires très-important]." She claims that she learned from him a healthy religious skepticism, and "heroism in private life"—that is, how to endure stoically the reversal of fortune that assailed Gabriel and his family. Allart maintains that, had Gabriel lived longer, he "could have inspired in me the elevated friendship that Laure subsequently inspired," and that her life would have been very different because Gabriel would have found her a good husband: "He wanted to marry me very early, and since he understood love, he would have made me a pleasant, intelligent, and perhaps long-lasting match." Allart's account of her mother is even briefer, describing her as a woman with "much virtue, merit, and wit, and who was very pretty" and having written a very fine book.[27]

Even George Sand was puzzled by Allart's reticence about her parents and her family when she first read Allart's autobiography in 1872. Writing in the preface to Allart's book that Allart "does not seem to have felt much sorrow over losing her parents," Sand then speculates: "I doubt whether she was reared with much tenderness." Although

Allart maintains that "my sister and I were reared in pleasures and prosperity," until her father lost his position, she also suggests that she might have been a lonely child. "One hears a great deal about the pleasures, the memories of childhood; I hardly tasted them. I was of delicate health and should have benefited from a stay in the country, but I knew of existence only through reading, living outside of myself." Perhaps, indeed, Allart was often left to her own devices as a child, while her father worked at his business and her mother "assisted him well in doing the honors of his house." Perhaps, too, her father's economic failure may have bothered her more than she admits, despite her effort to "maintain that equilibrium of soul that the ancients call for in reversal and in prosperity." Significantly, Allart describes in great detail and exalted language a close friend of the family who took care of her after she was orphaned at the age of twenty—Laure Regnault de Saint-Jean d'Angély. Of Regnault, who had lost her fortune, social position, and husband around the time of Napoleon's fall, Allart writes: "She had suffered especially for glory and patriotism; nothing small or shabby was in her. She was a great soul, worthy of antiquity; but this lofty character was united with incomparable generosity."[28] If Allart worshiped anyone from her childhood and youth, it was Regnault and not her parents. As I will explain below, Allart created a "surrogate father" in the form of Regnault.

Because there is so little evidence, it is difficult to assess the relationship between Girardin and her father. Girardin indicates that she was happy as a child: "I had only sweet moments in my childhood."[29] But much suggests that Girardin's relationship with her mother, rather than that with her father, was of primary importance in her life.[30] By all accounts Sophie Gay was a dynamic, sociable, and outspoken woman, and after she was widowed, mother and daughter formed a couple for nine years and remained close until Sophie's death in 1852.[31] Shortly after Sigismond died, Delphine wrote a poem entitled "A ma mère" that contains some references to Delphine's desire to assuage her mother's grief through her poetry. The poem refers to a dream in which love comes to Girardin, and Sophie shares in her joy:

> And my heart lost itself in this enchantment.
> Smiling, you were contemplating my torment,
> With a look both maternal and complicit.
> God! How happy I was! . . .

But then Girardin saddens when she realizes that her own happiness in love only highlights her mother's loss, and she remembers her own grief over her father's death:

> God! How happy I was! And yet, . . . I wept
> And this happiness seemed to increase your regrets.
> He for whom we weep was not part of our joy.
> For I no longer hope that a dream can return him to us;
> A dream can create a softer future,
> But it cannot lift the weight of a memory.

The poem focuses as well on the relationship between Delphine and her mother regarding Delphine's decision to become a writer:

> In vain does your prudence try to stop me in my transports;
> Mother, it is too late: your tears have made me a poet![32]

Thus the poem tries to console Sophie for the loss of her husband, and it also addresses issues related to women writing and to the relationship between Sophie and Delphine. These subjects intimately engaged daughter and mother, but they had little to do with Sigismond.

Other questions about the four authors' childhoods remain. For example, there is no indication of whether or not the infant girls were breast-fed or wet-nursed. And sibling relationships, though addressed by Sand and d'Agoult, are hardly mentioned by Allart and Girardin. Sand records her parents' heartbreak at the death of her small infant brother, and she also lovingly describes her half-sister Caroline, whom she visited frequently during her childhood, despite her grandmother's original objections to this association. More immediate in Sand's early life was her half-brother Hippolyte, with whom she grew up at Nohant. Hippolyte, several years older than Sand, was her playmate and school chum; she loved him, but his rowdiness and sense of humor appealed to only part of Sand's character; she felt there was much she could not share with her brother. Additionally, since Hippolyte was illegitimate, he appears never to have challenged Sand's primary position in the heart or inheritance of her grandmother. Sand writes of her grandmother that "sometimes, while watching me play, she would have a kind of hallucination, call me Maurice, and speak of me as her son."[33] Sand records no such identification between Hippolyte and Maurice in the eyes of Madame Dupin.

D'Agoult loved and respected her older brother Maurice, but she was also intimidated by him. Six years her senior, Maurice was usually away at boarding school or traveling abroad while d'Agoult was growing up. "I regarded him as a being way above me," she writes, referring to his more extensive knowledge and experience, as well as to his greater age. Maurice deigned to play with his little sister when he was at home, but he took over their games. D'Agoult recalls that one of her amusements was to construct miniature gardens on a table, inside the house, something that struck Maurice as "a girl's game." Maurice masculinized it by building life-sized gardens that d'Agoult appreciated but that were no longer her own: "It was indeed very beautiful, but I don't know why, these real gardens did not appeal to me as did the fictive ones, and I soon lost interest." D'Agoult interprets this incident as manifesting the fundamental difference between herself and her brother: "the unbridgeable difference between realists and idealists." D'Agoult suggests in her autobiography that her realistic, prosaic brother helped her define herself as his opposite—imaginative, idealistic, and perhaps even rebellious.[34]

In some ways, d'Agoult, as an adult, resembled and perhaps identified with her older half-sister, Auguste Bussmann, more than her brother Maurice, for both young women defied their families in love and politics. And Auguste was kind and loving to d'Agoult during d'Agoult's convent days. D'Agoult never, however, had even heard of Auguste until she was eleven years old: "Never did anyone speak of her in my presence. Our mother, despite her own memories that should have made her indulgent on this point, would not forgive her daughter for marrying without her consent." Only when Auguste remarried, to a man acceptable to her mother's family, did d'Agoult learn that she had an older sister.[35]

In contrast to d'Agoult's and especially Sand's extensive accounts of sibling relations, Allart mentions her younger sister Sophie as part of her childhood only once in her autobiography, asserting that the two of them "were reared in pleasures and prosperity" until their father's ruin. Sophie Allart was, apparently, a talented painter who studied with Ingres, exhibited in Paris salons, and went to Rome to pursue her career. In Rome she met a French businessman whom she married. The marriage ended Sophie's professional career as a painter, and she also seems to have adopted more conventional values and behavior than her sister. Allart wrote to d'Agoult that, following the birth of her second illegitimate child, Sophie refused to communicate with her: "My sister has not written to me since I had a baby." But in just over one week the two sisters were reconciled.[36]

Girardin's relations with her sisters and brother are still more difficult to discern. As an adult she was extremely close to her oldest sister,
Elisa, who became Madame O'Donnell in 1817. Madame O'Donnell
was herself a *salonnière* and informal literary critic of high repute
among the intelligentsia, and she reportedly assisted Delphine with social tidbits and literary insights for the regular newspaper column she
wrote, *Courrier de Paris*. Elisa O'Donnell nursed Delphine through a
near fatal bout of smallpox, and, before she married Emile de Girardin,
Delphine wrote several stories for her nephews, since she considered
herself then a spinster aunt. Yet there is no account of her childhood
sibling relations, and only one biography even mentions that Delphine
had a brother.[37]

Another elusive subject from the formative years of the four authors
is child and adolescent sexuality. Despite, or rather because of, Sand's
notoriety for advocating promiscuous sex, her autobiography contains
almost no mention of sexual relations and feelings. Sand does mention,
however, that sexuality was a forbidden topic in her childhood, and she
implies that this was because she was female: "To understand botany
(which is not at all a science considered to be within the purview of
young ladies) it is necessary to know about the mystery of procreation
and the role of the sexes; . . . As you can well imagine, Deschartres
made me skip over that issue."[38] Even Allart, who as an adult flaunted
the sexual gratification she enjoyed from her lover Henry Bulwer,
mentions nothing of sexual awakening in her youth. Only d'Agoult offers a hint of the intimate details of pubescent sexuality among nineteenth-century girls. When she was about ten years old she attended a
day school in Frankfurt with a slightly older cousin, Cathau Boode. According to d'Agoult's description, Cathau was a mature and lively
young teen who welcomed the attention of her many young male ad-
mirers. D'Agoult explains that she hardly understood what was going
on between the older girl and the boys who surrounded her, but that
she felt it was something both desirable and dubious: "I vaguely felt
that between these young persons of the two sexes was something very
appealing and a little secret that would be sweet to know." This inde-
scribable awareness was heightened by an incident at the school. Several girls were taking religious instruction for their Protestant first
communion when suddenly the young, male theologian who was
teaching them was dismissed from the school. The prettiest of the girls
who had been his pupils was in tears over the teacher's departure, and

rumor had it that she, too, was to be sent away to her parents. Older girls seemed to understand what was going on, but when d'Agoult asked her cousin Cathau, she received only this elliptical reply: "It is a novel."[39]

This association of eroticism, secrecy, and fiction was common in d'Agoult's account of her childhood. She writes, for instance, of discovering novels kept in a special cabinet in a room off the salon. Secretly, d'Agoult says, she spent about six months reading works by "madame Cottin, madame de Genlis, madame Riccoboni, and Anne Radcliffe that disordered my poor little brain," until suddenly she found the cabinet locked. D'Agoult was never punished, and no one ever spoke of the matter; d'Agoult's fantasies, however, were enriched by romance. "I continued to live outside of myself in the company of beautiful princesses, in enchanted groves sighing over love; I dreamed only of ravishers, white palfreys, and faithful shepherds. I knew from then on that perfect love was to see a handsome knight at one's feet, who pledged his love for the rest of his life." D'Agoult even fancied that she was in love with a poor, local aristocratic boy, but the love existed only as a secret, so she never once discussed it, much less acted upon it.[40] Female authors provided this forbidden fruit of romantic imaginings, but did women in the family actually discuss sexual matters?

Sand, Allart, and Girardin never mention puberty or menstruation, and d'Agoult asserts that first communion was the public marking of girls' passage from childhood to adolescence. The silences regarding puberty suggest that it was not a subject of public, or perhaps even of much private, discussion.[41] But d'Agoult is generally more attentive to her body than are the other authors, at least in print. She notes that when she entered the convent at the age of fifteen she stopped menstruating, and she refers to menarche as "the crisis by which girls' bodies complete their preparation for maternity." She explains that she felt no pain or discomfort, and that the nuns refused to discuss the matter, as they refused to discuss anything related to physicality. As soon as she left the convent and returned to her mother's house, "all returned to normal." However, d'Agoult interprets this change in her body as a form of rebellion: "What was this arrestation of life that happened in me? A revolt of physical nature when moral nature obeyed? A protestation of persistent instinct against persuaded reason?"[42] D'Agoult's relative openness about sexual curiosity and puberty is unusual among the four writers, but what is common among Sand, d'Agoult, and Allart is their preoccupation with faith and skepticism during their adolescence. Perhaps religious concerns prevailed over or masked sexual concerns for young adolescents in Restoration France. Perhaps the language of religious questing was the only language available to them to explain changes in their bodies and in their identities. And perhaps d'Agoult's linking of sexuality with novels, romance, and women writers prefigured her career, and those of her peers, as a sexual rebel and author.

Despite the great interest scholars have shown in the family and childhood since Philippe Ariès's path-breaking book on that subject (original French version, 1960), there is still remarkably little known about the history of family relations and early childhood.[43] Indeed, historians rely heavily on the autobiographies of Sand and d'Agoult, among others, to reconstruct the experiences of childhood and to assess the historical influences of family, culture, and community on the developing personality.[44] My focus here has been on factors that might have influenced Sand, d'Agoult, Girardin, and Allart in their sexual transgressions, their becoming writers, and their republican politics. All four apparently came from loving families and parents who encouraged the young girls to be themselves and to follow their inclinations, particularly regarding intellectual pursuits. Love as the primary foundation for marriage was a lived model to the four women and may have contributed to their own pursuits of heterosexual love in and outside of marriage. The fact that in all four cases the fathers died prematurely is, I believe, significant. For Sand and d'Agoult the early death of their fathers allowed the daughters to (re)create their fathers in their own image and express a greater attachment to this masculine, public figure than to feminine, domestic mothers. And even though Allart and Girardin lost their fathers when they were older (when the girls were in their late teens), that loss at the very least diminished their marriage prospects.

Moreover, d'Agoult is the only one of the four who had a brother of any importance in their personal narratives, and perhaps that accounts for the lack of much gender difference noted in their upbringings. To be sure, Sand grew up with her half-brother Hippolyte, whom she mentions often in her autobiography and to whom she always remained close until his death in 1848. But Hippolyte was illegitimate; he had a different last name than Sand and was not treated as a legitimate son would have been. Girardin, too, had a brother (who died in 1837), but he is hardly mentioned in the biographies, and Girardin's relationships with her mother and her four sisters, especially Elisa Gay O'Donnell, appear to be her most significant family relations. By contrast, d'Agoult asserts that she adored her older brother Maurice almost as much as she adored her father, and that she transferred all of her affection and obedience to Maurice when Alexandre died. It is clear that Maurice became the new head of the family and that he had considerable influence on decisions about Marie's life (when and where she should go to boarding school, the acceptability of her suitors). Overall, however, Maurice was absent more than he was present. All told, Sand, d'Agoult, Girardin, and Allart do not seem to have been much constrained in their upbringing, and their childhoods appear to have been relatively untroubled, despite the financial reverses of Sigismond Gay and Gabriel Allart. Yet education was a matter that they looked back upon with much thought and some criticism, for given their adult decision to become writers, education was crucial to their self-creations.

Education

Female education was a contested issue throughout the nineteenth century, and the four authors did not escape the controversy over how much education was appropriate for a girl and to what end. The conventional view starting with the French Revolution and solidifying during the nineteenth century was that girls should be educated in order to fulfill domestic duties successfully, including the early education of children.[45] Yet certain conditions of the four authors' families allowed them to receive at least some of the classical background that was the foundation of male education. The literary mothers of Girardin and Allart contributed in some measure to their daughters' preparation for literary careers, and Sand and d'Agoult received a broad, if not deep, education at home and from a wide variety of teachers.

Sand first learned writing and reading from her mother, and music from her grandmother. Around the age of seven she began to take more or less formal lessons, at home, in literature, arithmetic, geography, history, and Latin, and in addition she acquired a smattering of Greek and botany. Her teacher was Deschartres, the former tutor of her father and manager of her grandmother's estate. According to Sand, Deschartres was "a tyrant by nature," and though "he was always able to control himself with the people he liked," including Sand herself, he exercised his tyranny and pedantry with less restraint on Sand's mischievous half-brother: "He was as calm and patient with me as he was rough and brutal with Hippolyte." When Sand's grandmother moved the household to Paris for the winter Sand took lessons with the mother of a girlfriend, and special teachers of dancing, music, drawing, and writing also came to the Dupin apartment. Although Sand presents herself as a fairly willing pupil, she writes, "The only subjects I really liked were history, geography . . . music, and literature." She felt that she gained little expertise from the many private lessons she took in the so-called social graces: "On the whole, all these lessons were more or less a waste of money. They were too superficial to really teach us any art." And she proposed an alternative approach to education that would address the individual child's interests and talents: "It would have been better to test our abilities and then to keep us working at a specialty we were capable of acquiring."[46]

Sand developed strong views about education, and in her autobiography she criticized the prevailing pedagogy of her time, which employed a method of dry, rote learning and forced children to learn subjects for which they had no aptitude or use. Instead, she believed that education should be more personalized, and allow children to focus on their abilities and interests: "Can we not then set up a system in which the intelligence of ordinary children is not sacrificed to the needs of a select few?" In particular Sand found Latin dull and useless, and ultimately detrimental to her development as a writer. "It was my misfortune that Deschartres, who shared the prejudice underlying masculine education, believed that to refine the use of my own language, he should teach me Latin." Sand regretted the time she spent on Latin at the expense of French: "The time I wasted not learning Latin might have been much better employed studying French, at an age when one learns better than at any other." In retrospect she wished that Deschartres had taught her French grammar, which she needed later in life as a writer, and which she had to teach herself as an adult: "Purity and correctness are still what my mind craves today more than ever." Because Sand, unlike many girls, did, indeed, learn some Latin, she may well have found from experience that this part of her education was useless in terms of helping her to master French. But it is also possible that Sand is responding implicitly to criticism about her writing by asserting that a masculine education does not necessarily guarantee good writing in French: "Fortunately, I stopped studying Latin quite early, with the result that even if I do not know French very well, I know it better than most men of my generation. ... You will also find that women of twenty to thirty, who have had some education, usually write French better than men, which in my view is the result of their not having wasted eight or ten years of their lives learning dead languages."[47]

D'Agoult's education was similar to Sand's in terms of the initial instruction by parents and then the hoards of private tutors. But d'Agoult extols the learning she acquired with her father and associates it with the most progressive pedagogy of the Restoration. She writes that her father's favorite authors were "Horace, Ovid, Rabelais, Montaigne, La Fontaine, and above all Voltaire," and that he selected passages for her to copy from these works, and never from religious texts. Moreover, lessons with her father took place near a window overlooking the garden. Alexandre took care never to overtire little Marie, and Marie was completely motivated by the desire to please her father and be rewarded by a fishing or hunting expedition with him.[48] The notion of rewarding children for achievement was part of the so-called Lancaster method of teaching, newly imported from Britain. D'Agoult took classes in Paris from a Lancaster adept, the abbé Gaultier, who met once a week with pupils and asked them questions about what they had learned. Boys and girls were rewarded with chits for each correct answer, and at the end of the session the chits were tallied and prizes distributed to the best pupils.[49] D'Agoult considered her classes with her father and with Gaultier as far superior to any other instruction of her childhood and youth. The Lancaster method, and, implicitly, her father's method, were very progressive for the time; they were Socratic, coeducational, and equal, in the sense that girls as well as boys studied Latin, French grammar, sacred and secular history, geography, and elementary mathematics.

Both d'Agoult and Sand attended convent schools in Paris to "finish" their educations. The Sacré-Coeur, which d'Agoult attended, was the most prestigious of such institutions in terms of the social status of its pupils, and the convent of the English nuns was selected by Sand's grandmother on the same basis.[50] D'Agoult claims that she was a model pupil, so docile and obedient that the sisters invited her to join the elite coterie known as the Children of Mary: "The medal and ribbon of the Children of Mary ... were honors accorded for good conduct and that conferred certain rights, with great moral authority in the school." However, d'Agoult refused the honor because she considered this group to be merely informers for nuns seeking to punish girls who disobeyed the rules: "To belong to a police of any sort, no matter how saintly, repulsed me; the thought of betraying my schoolmates, even authorized, encouraged, and rewarded by the nuns, inspired me with real horror."[51] By contrast, Sand describes herself as willfully unruly during her first year in the convent, joining a group of rebels out of scorn for the idiocies of religious ritual: "I wished nothing more than to submit to the general discipline. But when I saw that this discipline was so stupid in a thousand ways and so nastily administered, I cocked my hat and resolutely enlisted on the side of the 'devils.'"[52] Despite their different behavior, both d'Agoult and Sand found the convent education useless in terms of serious learning; its only purpose was to impart social graces to girls preparing for marriage. "What emptiness, what impoverishment, what dearth of elevation and seriousness," d'Agoult said of the teaching of all subjects in the convent.[53]

Nonetheless, Sand and d'Agoult went through a phase of intense religious piety during their stay in the convent, and they gained an appreciation for the companionship and security of an enclosed, feminine community. Sand even claimed that in the convent she "came to be happier than [she] had ever been in [her] life," and that she "spent three years there without longing for the past or dreaming of the future."[54] For Sand the convent was a refuge from the expectations of her grandmother, the capriciousness of her mother, and the struggle between the two women for her loyalty. With her conversion to piety Sand gained the support of the nuns, and she consolidated her popularity and friendship among the other pupils: "I was a friend to everyone, the mentor and master of all revels, idol of the youngsters." She seriously contemplated taking vows, and she was heartbroken over leaving the convent. Sand writes that, when her grandmother decided to remove her from the convent, "that news hit me like a thunderbolt right in the midst of the most perfect happiness I had ever felt in my life. The convent had become my earthly paradise. I was neither a student nor a nun, but something in between, with absolute freedom, in a space that I cherished and left with many regrets, even for a day."[55] Similarly, d'Agoult, despite her revulsion at the poor hygiene and injustices practiced by nuns and pupils, found a certain comfort and identity among the girls of the convent. D'Agoult befriended a much maligned retarded girl, Adelise, in the convent, and she saw in her friendship with that unfortunate pupil a manifestation of her willingness to defy convention and combat injustice. D'Agoult writes of Adelise: "She would have revealed to me from then on, if I had been capable of such self-observation, one of the persistent characteristics, one of the hazards of my life: the eagerness to brave 'what will people say'; the challenge imprudently made [jeté], and without figuring my strength, to the injustices of opinion or of fortune."[56] Although d'Agoult stayed in the convent for only one year—unlike Sand, who spent three years without vacations in the convent—she found herself unexpectedly sad when the time came for her to leave. At her mother's anticipation of all the entertainments Marie would enjoy after leaving the convent, d'Agoult wanted to burst into tears and beg to stay there forever. She could hardly articulate the source of her sadness: "I saw before me only promises of the sweetest existence. And yet I was afraid, afraid for my youth, afraid of life!"[57] D'Agoult knew that by leaving the convent she entered into a new phase of her life—waiting for indissoluble marriage with some unknown man.

Allart and Girardin never knew the horrors and wonders of convent life. Apparently the two were educated entirely at home and to a large extent on their own. Allart, like d'Agoult, claims to have learned skepticism from her father. Gabriel, after seeing Hortense and her sister kneeling in prayer and reading the Bible for several years, finally told their mother to let the girls read the correspondence between Voltaire and the King of Prussia. From that point on Allart maintains that she abandoned reading the Bible, but that she always believed in God.[58] Another point that Allart makes about her education was the inconsistent, even hypocritical attitude of a male physician toward adolescent female learning. Allart asserts that her health was delicate and that she suffered some kind of ailment that hindered her studies when she was twelve or fourteen. Indeed, in a letter she wrote as an adult, Allart recounts: "I did not have very good health when, as a young girl, I fell in a faint . . . [and] Bourdais (a great doctor) wanted to burn my notebooks, and then later, worried about another condition, he told me to read a lot."[59] Despite these setbacks, she asserts, "I took great pleasure at that time in literature and in history. I especially studied the history of England. I began to study Latin."[60] Girardin, too, appears to have studied much on her own, but also under her mother's guidance. Her biographers indicate that, following Sophie's advice, she was influenced by, perhaps even studied informally with, authors who were friends or acquaintances of her mother—namely, the critic François Villemain and the poet Alexandre Soumet.[61] Additionally, Sophie's cultivation of Delphine's literary proclivities increased in inverse proportion to the family fortunes following Sigismond's death.[62]

For the rest of their lives Sand and d'Agoult deplored the deficiencies of female education, both on a personal level and in general. D'Agoult deeply regretted that she did not learn from the truly great thinkers until she started teaching herself as an adult during the years she lived with Liszt: "Minds of truth and of life, Homer, Sophocles, Dante, Shakespeare, Spinoza, Herder, Goethe, and yourselves, Bossuet and Pascal, in whom faith is grand and nourishes masculine virtues, what would you not have been for me had I become acquainted with you earlier, when the vigor of my mind was still free and proud . . . !"[63] The reference to "masculine virtues" is hardly by chance; education and the texts given to boys and girls were indeed gendered, and only as an adult did d'Agoult seize the opportunity to study "masculine" texts. And both d'Agoult and Sand believed that female education should be reformed to be equal to that of male instruction, and even that education should be coeducational (see Chapter 6). Allart, who studied continuously throughout her life and who regularly describes the authors she read in her autobiography, complained less about her own education but echoed Sand's and d'Agoult's call for improvements. For Allart and especially Girardin economic constraints limited or prohibited formal instruction. Moreover, Girardin appears to have been pressured to write at an early age to support herself and her mother, and Allart, by her own admission, possessed a driving ambition to make a name for herself as a writer at a young age. Thus the issue of education, part of a preparation for a writing profession, segues naturally into that of writing itself. In what other ways did Sand, d'Agoult, Allart, and Girardin anticipate their careers in letters?

Anticipating Women Writers

Nineteenth-century critics were wont to describe writing in gendered terms; an obvious example is that moral writing and much poetry were considered feminine, while texts dealing with abstractions and tragedies were deemed masculine.[64] There were far more subtle shadings as well, and female writers were made aware of them at an early age. Indeed, if this third-hand account is correct, Girardin learned about women writing and about writing like a man from her mother, Sophie

Gay. Girardin's biographer cites an acquaintance of Victor Hugo's as the source for some advice that Sophie gave her when she determined to become a writer:

If you want to be taken seriously, you must be an example; study the [French] language profoundly, not approximately, and demonstrate this to those who have studied Latin and Greek. And then, in your appearance avoid all the eccentricities of bluestockings; look like other [women] in your dress and distinguish yourself [among women] only by your wit. In short, be a woman in your role and a man in your grammar.[65]

Sophie Gay apparently appreciated what Sand said of Deschartres's principle regarding male education; the study of Latin and Greek was supposed to improve the understanding of French grammar. One biographer indicates that Girardin learned Latin, and most biographers concur that she did assiduously study French literature and contemporary writing.[66] Biographers of Girardin and Girardin's own writings suggest that Sophie was not, at least initially, terribly keen on her daughter's devoting herself to a career in letters. After all, Sophie knew from experience the rewards and the tribulations a woman writer could expect. The death of Sigismond Gay might have marked a turning point in the disagreement (if there was one) between mother and daughter over Delphine's commitment to writing.[67] In the poem "A ma mère" Girardin begins with an epigraph taken from another female poet, Marceline Desbordes-Valmore, lines suggesting that writing, though maligned (especially when done by women) also assuages sorrow and brings comfort of many sorts:

> Why consider my taste for writing verse a crime?
> The prestige of it is so sweet for a saddened heart!
> It lifts the weight of sorrow that oppresses me;
> Like a tenderer mistake it has its sensuous pleasure.[68]

Girardin then writes that her mother's concern for her daughter's welfare has failed to brake her ambition to become a poet; indeed, Delphine writes poetry out of a desire to console her mother. "For such a desire why would you wish to see me punished?" Girardin queries. She goes on to suggest that she is not a genius, and that even if she achieves greatness it will be for her mother's sake only. And she concludes from this that she would be exempt from the envy and resentment with which other writers might assail her.

> The evils that you predict are associated only with genius;
> To such illustrious ills I have no claim:

What cry could be raised against a feeble voice?
Does one ever see the song of a pious muse
Arouse clamors of envious hatred?[69]

This poem suggests that Sophie has warned Delphine frequently of the dangers of becoming a poet, especially a woman poet, and that Delphine has decided to follow her inclination despite these well-intended cautions. Shortly after this poem was written Delphine won the special recognition from the French Academy for her poem on the French nuns ministering to the sick in Barcelona. Sophie realized that if she and her daughter were to survive on writing, it would be Delphine's, not her own, that would be successful. From that moment on, Delphine earned her living by writing.[70]

Allart, too, came to writing at an early age, although she presents this as resulting entirely from ambition and choice rather than economic necessity. Allart is unusually forthright about her desire for fame and success, unlike many female autobiographers, including Sand and d'Agoult, who express ambivalence about their own ambition, or who even deny it as a motivating factor in their writing careers.[71] Allart asserts that she first considered becoming an actress but that her friend Regnault discouraged her from pursuing that goal. Starting life as a retiring child of delicate health, Allart maintains that she developed into a gregarious, outgoing, almost reckless young woman during her stay with Regnault and as a result of the influence of yet another *salonnière* and *merveilleuse*, her godmother, the duchess Hortense de Raguse:

I was, from that moment, ambitious, adventurous, pleasant, and thus in danger. I would not have wanted [to lead] an obscure life. I loved literature and I put all my hopes in it. Far from being afraid of life, of society, they vividly attracted me. I thrust myself toward the future with enthusiasm.[72]

By this time Allart had written and published her first book, on Protestantism and freedom in history, which she read first, in manuscript, to Regnault: "She listened with interest, gave me good advice and much encouragement."[73] Allart reveled in the encouragement and guidance she received from Regnault, and she credits Regnault with instilling in her a passion for life, as well as with making available to her the benefits of her worldly wisdom and sociability. At the age of twenty-one Allart was launched in her career of letters.

Sand and d'Agoult came to writing later in life than did Girardin and Allart, but they suggest in their autobiographies the personal characteristics, activities, and occurrences that foreshadowed their entry into the writing profession. Sand's imaginative life as a child speaks for itself. Her fantasies, games, fears, and dreams easily persuade a reader that their author is a born story-teller, a creator of vivid and emotional fictions. Sand indicates that long before she learned to write she had babbled "interminable stories that my mother referred to as my novels." In a refreshingly self-deprecating and humorous manner, she links this childish practice with her adult profession. Sand indicates that her mother "declared [her stories] phenomenally boring because of their length and the extent to which I developed digressions. This is a defect, they say, I still suffer from; I admit I take little notice of present reality, and have today, exactly like when I was four, an insuperable lack of restraint in that genre of creation."[74]

Sand's account of how she learned to write is suggestive also of the creative novelist she became, and it sheds further light on her views regarding the education of children. Sand relates how she quickly became bored with the penmanship exercises her mother gave her, and she developed her own system of "writing" with images resembling hieroglyphics. Her grandmother found Sand's "writing" droll: "She claimed it was marvelous to see how I had succeeded in expressing my little ideas with such primitive methods, and she advised my mother to allow me to scribble by myself as much as I wanted. She said, rightly, that one wastes a lot of time trying to teach children beautiful handwriting, instead of thinking about the purpose that writing serves." Eventually Sand learned to write in the conventional manner, but she claims that she had learned the fundamentals of grammar and generally correct spelling on her own with her self-devised system: "When, later, Deschartres taught me grammar, it took only about two or three months, since each lesson only served to confirm what I had already observed and applied." For Sand, writing preceded reading: "It was while learning to write by myself that I came to understand what I was reading."[75] Sand's narrative of her early story-telling and writing suggests her lifelong engagement with and appreciation for the creative process and for language.

D'Agoult's account of her childhood experiences with writing are more self-consciously foreshadowings of her ultimate awareness of herself as a professional writer. A major episode for d'Agoult as a child was an encounter with Goethe during one of her stays in Frankfurt. Goethe, an august occasional visitor to the Bethmann family house, was introduced to Marie by her uncle. D'Agoult recounts their most minute actions as laden with portent—she was intimidated by him, he took her by the hand, she looked up at him, he returned her gaze, and so forth. When he took his leave from the family, Goethe, according to d'Agoult, "put his hand on my head and left it there, caressing my blond hair; I dared not breathe. It would not have taken much for me to kneel. Did I feel that in this magnetic hand there was for me a benediction, a tutelary promise?"[76] D'Agoult is uncertain if she understood this interaction as a "benediction" during the moment it occurred, but she recalled it as having a beneficent effect on her throughout her life.

D'Agoult asserts that creative impulses manifested themselves in her at an early age in her fabrications of miniature gardens. She says that she experienced "the wonder of poetic creation" with these projects, and, as we have seen, they showed her how different was her artistic and idealistic temperament from her brother's realism. She did not care for the real, life-size gardens that Maurice made: "Wasn't it precisely because there was too much reality in them, because art was too mixed up with nature, because imagination no longer had a major role in our pleasure, and because, instead of a free invention, we had before us only a reduced reproduction of the objects that surrounded us? Isn't the entire secret of art here [in this contrast]?"[77]

For d'Agoult and Sand, early instances of artistic imagination were not necessarily gendered. The two authors suggest that these tendencies were neither particularly feminine nor transgressively masculine. Similarly, Allart presents her childhood love of reading and study as unremarkable from the perspective of gender. Only with Girardin is there at a young age any indication of limitations on female intellectual endeavors, and the evidence suggests that this understanding came when she was in her mid to late teens and when she and Sophie had to consider writing for a living. Was this freedom of imagination typical of most girls, or even of most children under the Empire and early Restoration? Or were these three figures exceptional in the freedom and encouragement they received from their parents and caretakers? Secondary sources and prescriptive literature from the early nineteenth century suggest more rigid gender differentiations in child-rearing than appear in the narratives of Sand, d'Agoult, and Allart. Early-nineteenth-century French discourses on the family and the function of the head of the family in perpetuating gender roles provide a significant backdrop to the female authors' accounts of their families and their parents' exercise of authority, as well as issues of gender and politics.

Republican Daughters

Conservative and liberal theorists of the family in early-nineteenth-century France could hardly conceive of a family without a father. For them, fathers dominated wives and children by a natural right, similar to the natural authority of the king or state. The family mediated between the individual and the state, and the function of the father was to control the individual on behalf of the state, preparing children to become citizens themselves. Although liberals allowed that paternal authority ruled in the best interest of family members, analogous to representatives who governed in behalf of voting and nonvoting citizens, both conservative and liberal family models adhered to rigid gender roles. That is, individual development in the family was limited by sex. A girl's future was to be a wife and mother devoted to domestic concerns, while boys would become men who represented families in the public realm as well as dominating the private life of the home.[78] These positions were clearly spelled out in the Civil Code of 1804, in which male authority over wives and children and the gender separation of spheres were articulated.[79]

Yet women writers' portrayals of their families do not conform to this discourse. Their remembered or imagined fathers appear as liberators of the authors' independent identities rather than as authority figures molding their daughters for a domestic career. Sand, d'Agoult, and Allart honored their parents, and especially their fathers, in their autobiographical narratives. In this way they diminished the transgressive nature of their own characters and life choices and legitimized themselves as daughters and as family members. However, Sand and d'Agoult constructed fathers who, in a sense, authorized their daughters to be independent individuals, who even constituted models of values and behavior for their daughters to emulate. Allart constructed an alternative "father" in the person of a female friend; Girardin focused on her mother, who wanted a conventional and loving marriage for her youngest daughter but also taught her to be a poet.

Almost the first third of Sand's autobiography is devoted to her family history: the life stories of her grandmother, her mother, and especially her father. Sand presented her father not as an authority figure or an upholder of gender divisions of labor but as an ideal being who liberated Sand from the domestic destiny of females, allowing her to adopt his masculine characteristics, including his independence of mind and action. Implicitly, Sand's republican politics, egalitarian values, and quest for love were sanctioned by her father. Maurice Dupin, according to Sand, supported the republic, believed in a meritocracy, and married a woman for love, despite her low social origins and the bitter opposition of his mother. Sand created a father who was herself, and the qualities she admired in him were thus admirable qualities in herself.

Sand viewed her father as reflecting the most important historical developments of his day. "I see him summarizing in himself, without being aware of it, during every period of his life, what was happening in public life; and his reaction to it seems to me . . . to have had serious consequences not only for me [but also for] everyone [else]." And this "reaction" was to support the revolution despite the hardship it caused him and his mother. When Maurice was in his teens, his mother, Aurore Dupin, was arrested for contributing money to the cause of the comte d'Artois. Madame Dupin spent more than eight months in prison, before being released in August 1794. Sand insists that her grandmother unfailingly supported the principles of the republic, and that Maurice did as well. "Suffering because of the Revolution to the depths of his being, knowing that his adored mother was threatened by the guillotine, I never see him curse those ideas that gave birth to the Revolution; on the contrary, I see him approve and give his blessing to the downfall of the privileged classes."[80] Out of her aristocratic background Sand created for herself a republican heritage. She offers little hard evidence of Maurice's particular republican ideology, but, significantly, she portrays Maurice as living out his political beliefs in his private life.

Specifically, Sand asserts that Maurice's marriage to her mother was a political act, implementing a fundamental republican principle:

He will marry a daughter of the people, which means he will carry on and apply the egalitarian ideas of the Revolution in the intimacy of his own life. He will struggle in the bosom of his own family against aristocratic principles and the world of the past. He will break his heart, but he will have fulfilled his dream of equality.[81]

Sand is the product of this egalitarian union, and she claims that she is practically identical to her father. In the same chapter that begins with her assertion that she would have been just like her father had she been born male and twenty-five years earlier, Sand also says that "assuredly" she would have been a Jacobin had she lived during the revolution.[82] Sand is simultaneously constructing a political identity for her father and for herself. By doing so Sand does not appear to be presumptuous in asserting a political position, nor is she demanding the right to do so either for herself or for all women. Rather, she casts herself as fulfilling her father's desires and ideals. Sand's political allegiance thus becomes a measure of filial piety rather than a violation of patriarchal, and, one could say, republican, law.

D'Agoult did not go so far as Sand in erasing the difference of gender between herself and her father. But she, too, claimed a republican heritage on her father's side. Like Sand, d'Agoult also provides a long genealogy of her family, and among the Flavignys of the past she describes in some detail a sixteenth-century royalist with republican sympathies. In a book that Charles de Flavigny published in 1594 on the kings of France, d'Agoult detects a note of "heresy" in his devotion to the French monarchy. According to d'Agoult this ancestor admired "the constitution . . . of the Helvetic Republic" and declared that had he "been Swiss, and had a Burgomeister infringed on the sovereignty of [his] country, [he] would take a thousand lives, if [he] had them, to uphold [his] popular freedom." D'Agoult considers her ancestor's independence of mind a typical trait of a cultivated and true gentleman, and she asserts that this characteristic is evident in other Flavignys imbued with "good taste and the gift for literature."[83] She identified with her father's aristocratic background, which for her embodied values of honor, disinterestedness, and reason. As an adult d'Agoult violated family codes of honor by abandoning her husband and by becoming a republican. But at the same time that she defied aristocratic tradition she turned other aristocratic qualities—namely disinterestedness and reason—to her advantage. "Rocked in my cradle to stories of the Vendean wars, linked by family ties to the elder branch of the Bourbons, . . . impartial study of ideas, and not personal hatreds, led me to opinions that differed from those of my people."[84] D'Agoult maintained that her father's family was actually less prejudiced regarding class than her mother's, so that, paradoxically, she "inherited" egalitarianism and belief in meritocracy from her aristocratic background; she furthermore disinherited herself from the bourgeois legacy of snobbery and status-consciousness.[85] D'Agoult constructed her father as a symbol of qualities she admired and adopted, even to the point of linking her republican politics with aristocratic values. Like Sand, d'Agoult recast her father in such a way that she could cast herself as a dutiful daughter, ex-

ercising her birthright of "heretical" republicanism even within an ul-
traroyalist family.

While Sand and d'Agoult constructed fathers to conform to their
personal republican ideals, Allart created a female authority figure as
her surrogate parent. Allart began her autobiography by describing her
relationship with Laure Regnault de Saint-Jean d'Angély rather than
her childhood or family background. She even said that Regnault was
her first love, and that her "birth" occurred at Regnault's country home:
"In this place I was truly born, if being born means feeling, loving,
knowing a passionate friendship." Although Allart praises her parents,
she writes of Regnault: "I wanted to be her daughter [*J'aurais voulu être
sa fille*]." This may be related to a later section of the narrative in which
Allart regretted that she and Regnault had not discussed matters of
love and marriage, because she thought that Regnault's vast experience
and worldly wisdom might have tempered her infatuation with the
man who made her pregnant at the age of twenty-four. In Allart's narrative Regnault assumed more authority than either parent. Indeed,
after Napoleon's death in 1821, when Allart and Regnault were com-
miserating at the loss of their hero, Allart writes that "it was she [Regn-
ault] who became my emperor." Although Allart remembered her father fondly, she portrayed as limited his significance in her life and in
the development of her character, describing her mother as having had
even less influence. Regnault, by contrast, embodied the characteristics
that Allart most admired, appealing to Allart through an erotic combination of power and emotion: "Surprised at her authority, more seduced up to this point by qualities of strength than by those of feeling, I
saw this woman in the union of sensibility and heroism, awaken my
tenderness by the qualities that had most seduced me."[86]

Instead of worshiping her father, Allart worshiped Regnault. Regnault was beautiful, kind, generous, intelligent, strong, and political—
all qualities that describe Allart herself. It was from Regnault that Allart
sought and received guidance and encouragement for writing. And it is
likely that Allart "inherited" her love of politics from Regnault as well.
Regnault was no republican; she was an unswerving Bonapartist, and
Allart shared this enthusiasm in her youth.[87] However, Allart would
later become a republican, and her ideal of republican womanhood
would be the exceptional female of Plato's republican philosopher
kings and queens. In Allart's eyes, Regnault was one such exceptional
woman, and she, more than Allart's father, authorized her young pro-

tégée to become a writer and a republican, to become herself an exceptional, and, in the context of the nineteenth century, unconventional woman.

Girardin found her model and authority for writing and politics in her mother, Sophie Gay. Indeed, according to Lamartine, "Mme Gay herself constructed her daughter's pedestal," and in Delphine "she saw herself reborn." Sophie Gay ardently desired good marriages for all her daughters, but she also recognized Delphine's literary talent and had at least two reasons for cultivating it. First, Sophie Gay was a writer who had enjoyed some renown for her dramas, and she vicariously enjoyed her daughter's greater fame. Second, Sophie and Delphine were destitute after Sigismond's death, and they needed the money and the social benefits that would result from Delphine's literary success. Moreover, Sophie had the literary connections to capitalize on Delphine's talent; her friendship with Juliette Recamier, for example, probably prompted the invitation to Delphine to read her poem "Le Dévouement des médecins français et des soeurs de Sainte-Camille dans la peste de Barcelone" in Recamier's salon in 1822.[88]

However, Girardin's poem "A ma mère" suggests that it was no easy feat to satisfy Sophie's ambivalent and contradictory ambitions for her daughter. The poem defends Delphine's commitment to writing poetry and asserts that whatever glory she obtains will be for the sake of her mother: "You will bask in its reflection." The poem also claims that poetry is merely a means to attract love, to fulfill Sophie's goal that Delphine marry. But this eventuality is problematic because it threatens to compete with Sophie's love:

> Ah! if heaven would deign to unite me with him one day! . . .
> But no, go away, seductive chimera;
> In disturbing my peace you are offending my mother;
> As long as she loves me, what else could I desire?
> Nothing . . . such a great happiness forbids me from hope![89]

Girardin expresses considerable ambivalence and confusion in this poem, but ultimately she professes her devotion to her mother whom she will resemble in many ways—a successful writer, a brilliant *salonnière*, a woman of strong character, and a republican.

Sophie ultimately became a republican, perhaps more out of convenience and nostalgia than conviction. The heights and depths of the Gay family fortunes might well explain her pragmatic political allegiances. Sophie renounced her loyalty to the Empire when her pleas for a new position for Sigismond were ignored. Girardin's biographer, Georges d'Heilly, claims that she became a legitimist and was among the first to welcome back the Comte d'Artois to France with the Restoration of 1814. And given that after he became Charles X this same d'Artois saw fit to provide Delphine Gay with a state pension, Sophie's switch to legitimism appears most reasonable and expeditious. Yet, at the same time that Delphine was praising the French king in her poems, she also supported the cause of Greek independence by writing a poem and raising money. D'Heilly suggests that Sophie never forgot her glory days under the Directory, and that she looked with favor upon a republican form of government—a position that Delphine shared under the July Monarchy and in 1848.[90]

Conclusion

These accounts of the families of Sand, d'Agoult, Allart, and Girardin suggest the existence of little, if any, paternal authority while the four women were growing up. In the authors' renditions, fathers, a surrogate authority, or a mother represented the possibilities for public life that their daughters eagerly and dutifully explored. The fathers that Sand and d'Agoult imagined were as much projections of their own identities as remembered parents, and Allart "chose" her model parent and authority in the person of Regnault. The three women writers constructed their "fathers" in such a way as to make themselves appear to be loyal daughters, adopting characteristics similar to those of their fathers. And Girardin ultimately adhered to her mother's tutelage in the creation of a public identity. These parents promoted their daughters' individual development and did not confine them to expectations of strictly domestic careers.

As young adults Sand and d'Agoult were seemingly headed for conventional domesticity—married at eighteen and twenty-two, respectively, to men who were their social equals and who were more or less acceptable to their families; they both bore children within a year or two of wedlock. Had their fathers lived, perhaps they would not have deviated from that direction. But in the absence of living fathers Sand and d'Agoult created fathers who implicitly supported their ventures into adulterous love and sexuality, and their careers as writers. Girardin was a "girl poet" from her late teens through her late twenties, supporting herself and her mother from her writing, her public performances, and her pension—but a woman cannot remain a girl poet forever. And Allart, under the aegis of two former *merveilleuses*, probably envisioned herself at the age of twenty-one as a future, unmarried Madame de Staël, having just published her first book and ambitious for literary renown. These four women were on the brink of personal and professional transformations that would bring them to the forefront of French literary and political culture in the revolutionary age of the July Monarchy and the Second Republic.

3   ☞   The Erotics of Writing

Affective Life, Literary Beginnings, and Pseudonyms

Hortense Allart's autobiography of 1873 opens with the following lines:

Only distinguished talents are worthy of public attention; only superior beings are permitted to speak of themselves. But I thought that true feelings expressed naturally might be of interest. I believed that since women's lot is sometimes so unhappy, readers would like to see one woman who freely followed her heart, and who placed love and independence above all in her destiny.[1]

Allart's confession claims to reveal the truth, even if, or perhaps precisely because, she is not a person of distinguished talents. She might also be suggesting that indeed, she is a person of distinguished talents inasmuch as she deems her story worthy of public attention. Moreover, she identifies herself as a woman who is unlike other women. That is, Allart disassociates herself from the masses of women who are made miserable by the constraints that law and society place upon them. She, by contrast, has flouted rules and conventions by "freely following her heart," for she reveals in the narrative that she had numerous love affairs with men and bore two children out of wedlock.

"Freely following her heart" entailed not only amorous generosity and sexual freedom but also a quest for independence that often conflicted with heterosexual passion. Independence for Allart meant living on her own, controlling her time and her space so that she could devote as much time as she chose to her profession of research and writing. Allart loved learning as much as she loved men, and those two desires coexisted, tensely but productively, throughout much of her life. That is the truth she promises to reveal in her autobiography—her experiences of love and independence that are the source of her happiness.[2]

Allart, d'Agoult, and Sand became public figures coincidentally with or following their fulfillment of sexual desire outside of marriage. To some extent their writing was a vindication or defense of that transgression, contextualizing it within the rigid laws, inhumane social practices, and cultural hypocrisy that made marriage a trap for women especially, and offered no other outlet for the expression of their erotic passion. Girardin, unmarried until she was twenty-seven years old, suffered the indignities of spinsterhood and perhaps frustrated love or desire until she wed Emile de Girardin in 1831. Evidence regarding Girardin's erotic feelings and sexual experiences is much skimpier than that available for the other three women, but her writings suggest that she, too, found fault with the many limitations on female expressions of desire.

Sexuality in the nineteenth century was ideally confined to and regulated by marriage.[3] Female sexuality in particular was discussed publicly as existing appropriately only in the context of domestic and marital privacy. Although various experts and commentators acknowledged the existence of female sexual desire and pleasure, they regarded it either as less intense than male sexuality or, in contrast, as dangerous and frightening in its strength.[4] Hence, elite women who desired or had sex outside of marriage were highly transgressive. Women who wrote for publication were also transgressive, so is it any wonder that these four women writers were doubly transgressive—through sexuality and through writing? Yet in the discourses of the time such transgressions threatened to masculinize the women who committed them; women writers especially were caricatured as unfeminine, unnatural—in short, as less than women. Female authors might appropriately write about love, but in muted and bland though highly spiritual terms. Writing about erotic passion was already dubious, and explicit physicality quite beyond the pale—even for male authors.[5] The problem was to write, and to write about sexual transgression, while still remaining "women."

The four authors lived and wrote at a time when Romanticism flourished, including the notion—projected in works by René de Chateaubriand, Charles-Augustin Sainte-Beuve, Alfred de Musset, and others—that, for men, passionate love was an essential experience. Illicit desire in particular forced the male literary hero to know himself as a unique being through the contrast between his erotic feelings and desires on the one hand, and social convention and religious morality on the other. In fiction, then, male romantic writers ennobled sexual desire by presenting their heroes' passions as motivated by idealism rather than by lust, and being sometimes unconsummated.[6] But whereas love was only a part, though an important one, of men's lives, many romantics believed that it was the essence, the only component, of women's lives.[7] This meant that for women writers, writing competed with love as a defining feature of existence. Intellectual pursuits, associated with writing, both conflicted with and coincided with love and sexual desire.

This chapter explores how the four women writers experienced love and sexuality, how they came to writing, and the significance of pseudonyms in their self-creations as women writers. I begin by analyzing accounts of love and especially of sexual desire in writings by the four authors. The emphasis is on autobiographical narratives, but, especially in the case of Girardin, who left no autobiography, other works are included as well. Love was something that all four authors valued and sought, and like many male romantic authors they articulated transgressive love and desire as spiritually uplifting and as an essential part of self-development and creation. But they cast love and desire in distinctive ways, to accommodate other experiences and desires, including the abandonment of husbands and families, childbirth and motherhood, spinsterhood, and professionalism. Love and desire are significant in the writings of the four authors, but they are also combined with other aspects of their lives, rather than being the sum total of them. Moreover, the satisfactions, frustrations, and transgressions of the four women writers' experiences of love and desire would ultimately inform their feminist critique of women's civil status in France and their republican politics.

A central part of their self-creation was as writers, and the second section analyzes the beginnings of their literary careers. Writing for these authors when they were young often assumed an erotic quality, and in particular instances writing even replaced heterosexual love and desire. Finally, the chapter ends with the establishment of the four authors in Parisian literary culture and the authorial identities they constructed, notably through pseudonyms.

Love and Desire in the Youth and Young Womanhood of Women Writers

Marie de Flavigny married Comte Charles d'Agoult on 16 May 1827. D'Agoult suggests that she agreed to this match because she had already rejected several suitors, and, what is more important, she had, by her own timidity, lost a suitor whom she truly esteemed and might have loved. D'Agoult berated herself for this loss: "With what bitterness, for many years, I blamed myself and repented of failing to listen to the voice of my heart." Refusing to confide in anyone, she turned instead to romantic fiction: "In a sort of frenzy I plunged into the reading of novels: *Werther, René, Adolphe, Manfred, Faust,* that in exciting my feelings, inoculated me with a poetic and unhealthy disgust with life." Her family consulted doctors and tried to distract d'Agoult with gifts, balls, and carriage rides in the Bois de Boulogne. Finally, d'Agoult asserts that she was simply tired of dealing with the endless marriage proposals, and that she asked her mother and brother to make the decision for her: "One day, I can't really say how it happened, I firmly resolved to put a stop to it. I went to find my mother, and expressed to her the extreme repugnance I felt for the role assigned to me in the preliminaries of an act that I viewed as nothing more than a duty to be accomplished; I begged her, at the next offer, to consult with my brother and then say yes or no without discussing it with me." D'Agoult says not a word about her feelings for her intended before the marriage. She describes le comte Charles d'Agoult in the terms by which her family evaluated him: "He did not have a fortune to equal mine; but, being a valiant soldier, . . . [and] a close relative of the most intimate friend of the next queen of France, he was sure to advance rapidly. . . . It was on all counts a fine match."[8] Following the marriage the d'Agoults had two daughters, Louise, born in 1828, and Claire, born in 1830.

On the surface this was an ideal marriage, matching two well-born individuals who abided by the social conventions of the legitimist aristocracy and who, through Marie's salon, contributed to the luster of this social circle. Nonetheless, d'Agoult found little satisfaction in her family and less in her devoted husband. A suicide attempt and a brief stay in an institution for the mentally ill marked the year 1832, but those two occurrences were carefully concealed by the family.[9] In her autobiography d'Agoult does not mention them, but she describes the despair she felt in her marriage: "From the day of my wedding I had not one hour of joy. The feeling of complete isolation of heart and mind in the new relations created by conjugal life, a sorrowful surprise at what I had done in giving myself to a man who inspired in me not an iota of love, cast a moral sadness on all my thoughts." She is generous enough to exonerate her husband from any personal fault, aside from being simply incompatible with her. And d'Agoult knows that in terms of material and social circumstances, her marriage was perfect; her husband was decent and honorable, she had two lovely children, she was rich, and she enjoyed a wide variety of entertainments. But according to d'Agoult these circumstances only masked an unhappy heart: "How little my intimate existence corresponded to this brilliant facade!"[10]

Although d'Agoult always maintained that her husband's behavior was above reproach, in her fiction she suggests that marital sex could devastate a young and ignorant bride. In the story "Valentia" the heroine of the same name is married off to a known womanizer who drugs her and rapes her on their wedding night. Valentia wakes up the next morning feeling ashamed and humiliated but without knowing why. When she sees her husband, she thinks she should have killed herself or attacked him: "Instinct alone signaled to me that I needed to avenge an unpardonable insult."[11] Ultimately, Valentia achieves her justifiable revenge through a love affair with her husband's nephew. "Valentia," like much of d'Agoult's writing, including her autobiography, is a scathing critique of the institution of marriage and the way it inhibited love, especially for women.[12]

In her autobiography d'Agoult portrays the haplessness of her husband and especially of herself, locked in a union that each had innocently and unknowingly entered into simply to satisfy laws and social convention. She emphasizes her own unhappiness, and asserts that even the delight she experienced from her children was tinged with melancholy.[13] Although d'Agoult's salon was brilliant, aristocratic *salonnières* had lost power with the 1830 Revolution and the establishment of the July Monarchy, and Charles d'Agoult's prospects for social and political advancement also disappeared. In addition to being somewhat bored with salon life and dissatisfied in her marriage, d'Agoult was losing her Catholic faith, replacing it with Romanticism and a vague social idealism.[14] This backdrop is important for understanding her affair with Liszt.

D'Agoult recalls that when she first saw Liszt in December 1832 he appeared to her as an apparition, an unworldly figure who affected her as no other person had before or would again. According to d'Agoult's description, Liszt was the image of the Romantic figure: "Tall, excessively thin, pale face, with great sea-green eyes that shone like agitated waves, a suffering and powerful physique, an undecided walk that seemed to skate above rather than touch the earth, a distracted and worried air, as of a ghost waiting to be called back into the shadows—

thus I saw before me this young genius."[15] D'Agoult felt immediately that she and Liszt had much in common; they had both suffered from the tyranny of public opinion, he as an artist and she as a woman. He became an habitué of her salon, they saw one another frequently, and they finally declared their love. D'Agoult presents this scene in highly romantic terms, with Liszt at her knees, begging her pardon for a careless word that had hurt her: "This forgiveness, in the burning clasp of our hands, was an explosion of love, a consent, a mutual pledge to love one another, to love undividedly, without limit, without end, on earth and for as long as the skies lasted!"[16]

The two consummated their love in a small apartment, but this secret affair reached a crisis with the illness and death of d'Agoult's daughter Louise in late 1834.[17] D'Agoult contends that the sad event further alienated her and her husband, and that in her numbed grief only Liszt brought her to life. For months during the child's illness and after her death Liszt had not seen d'Agoult, departing Paris to stay with the Abbé Félicité-Robert Lamennais at La Chênaie in Brittany. But on his return Liszt met with d'Agoult. According to d'Agoult she succumbed to Liszt's exhortations that they flee France together, and that this escapade was somehow divinely inspired. D'Agoult maintains that Liszt assured her that there was no God but love: "The unknown God, the strongest of gods, took possession of us and of our destiny."[18] Love purified d'Agoult of sin and weakness and exonerated her from the pain and unhappiness she would cause her family. As she wrote in *Nélida*, the remorse felt by the unfaithful young wife was itself a weakness, a hindrance to the brave and powerful love that she felt for her lover, Guermann, which was beyond human laws: "She persuaded herself that all sacrifices, including that of conscience, were yet a small price to pay for discovering such a love."[19] Ideal, romantic love, according to d'Agoult, prompted her to abandon her husband and child in May 1835 and travel to Switzerland, where she met Liszt as they had arranged.

D'Agoult presents her first and probably only experience of openly acknowledged passionate love (in the summer of 1835) in terms of the glorious natural beauties of the Swiss mountains in summer. The tall mountains, steep valleys, and dark evergreens isolated the lovers from society and laws, from the civilization that they had to escape in order to revel, free from guilt, in their pure, natural love.

Triumph of love, how you were complete and magnificent in us! . . . Bulwarks of granite, inaccessible peaks that you raised between us and the world, as if to hide from its view, hidden valleys, black pines that enfolded us in your shadow, the murmur of lakes, the hollow rumbling of steep overhangs, arresting and gentle rhythms of alpine sites that gave to our drunkenness of one day a kind of feeling of eternity.[20]

Although d'Agoult and Liszt had fulfilled their sexual desires long before the flight from Paris, d'Agoult suggests in her novel, *Nélida*, that nature "divinely" opened the heroine's body to life, happiness, and love: "The invigorating sighs of the pine forest, the healthy mountain air, the sweet smell of rich pastures, entered into all her pores and made her blood circulate; ... physical well-being acted vigorously against moral sadness."[21] For d'Agoult nature helped awaken the senses, particularly for a young woman suffocating in an unhappy marriage and bound by social mores. And expressions of sensuous feelings in response to natural beauty were less controversial than descriptions of sexual passion by a female author. Moreover, nature served as a fortress protecting the lovers from outside influences. In the sparsely populated mountains and valleys of Switzerland, d'Agoult and Liszt could indulge their passion, momentarily free of responsibilities and public opinion. But the romantic idyll could not last. With hindsight d'Agoult notices that as soon as she and Liszt left the mountains to settle in Geneva for the winter, the pure love and exclusive devotion she thought she was experiencing proved to be illusory. When Liszt invited the "world" that they had sought to escape into the apartments and the lives of the exiled couple, the relationship changed and ultimately deteriorated.

For d'Agoult love simply did not exist in her marriage, and she represents love as a positive, divine force that is sometimes above the law of human social interaction. The only other love relationship that d'Agoult describes with anything like the intensity of her attraction to Liszt was her love for her father. The relationship with Liszt provided d'Agoult with the fulfillment of her Romantic ideal of spiritual union, mutual devotion, and physical satisfaction. Three children issued from this liaison, but they hardly figure in d'Agoult's account of that period in her life. Frequently the couple left the children in the care of wet nurses, friends, or relatives, and d'Agoult writes of them in her memoirs more often when they are older and after she and Liszt had parted ways. D'Agoult wrote extensively about marriage, love, and maternity in her various works, and these will be addressed in Chapter 6 as part of an analysis of her politics and feminism. When d'Agoult sought a replacement for Liszt in her affections, it was not with her children, or with other men, or with female friends. Liszt's love had provided identity and fulfillment for d'Agoult; with him she had lived her ideal of passion and exclusive devotion. She was his artistic muse, and he encouraged her to read, think, and write about philosophy, art, and politics. But after his departure heterosexual love was no longer d'Agoult's goal or ideal. Instead, she found identity and fulfillment in writing.

In contrast to d'Agoult, Allart experienced her first love affair while she was a young, unmarried woman and had already committed herself to a writing career. Allart asserts that in her early twenties, perhaps earlier, she aspired to a profession rather than to love, and she insists that she refused several marriage offers because she did not love the suitors.[22] But at this time, too, from 1822 to 1824, Allart developed a passionate attraction to a young Portuguese and Irish aristocrat, Antony de Sampayo, whom she had met at the house of her friend and surrogate parent, Laure Regnault de Saint-Jean d'Angély. According to Allart, Sampayo appealed to her because of his intelligence and cultivation, in addition to his Mediterranean good looks and northern, distanced temperament. She was flattered by Sampayo's willingness to discuss politics and history with her, and she mentions in particular that he had her read Adam Smith. Intellectual, emotional, and physical stimulation coalesced in Allart's infatuation with this young man, who was supposedly training for the priesthood: "We discussed frozen things and politics; however, I loved him without admitting it to myself. He was a god to me, his mind and his virtue, his youth and his beauty combined to make him the most seductive I could ever meet." Allart indicates that she was willing to enter into a sexual relationship with Sampayo long before he would have considered it, even it if meant adultery: "I thought of making some ordinary marriage that would allow me freedom, and devoting myself to pleasing him, to making him sensitive [à le rendre sensible]. This plan would have horrified him in his virtue, so I did not dare give over to it."[23]

With hindsight Allart suggests that she wishes Regnault had put a halt to this romance. She laments that during their many intimate conversations Regnault never warned her about the feelings of desire that awaited her: "Oh! Since then, how I have regretted that we never talked about passions." Allart was convinced that had Regnault been her mother, Regnault "would have wanted me to triumph over my heart that was already taken. . . . Her prudence would undoubtedly have saved me from the beginning." Allart reproduces a letter from her youth that suggests that even at that time she worried about the consequences of her passion, because the letter makes the case that women *should* act upon their feelings, despite social restrictions. Allart invokes Madame de Staël and argues that if sensibility (*la sensibilité*) is the source of genius, then is not following one's emotions, even to do wrong by society's lights, justified? Allart's descriptions of Sampayo's passion for her and the mixed agitation and exultation it aroused in her fill many pages of the autobiography. Allart celebrates her love for Sampayo, declaring that it elevated her intellectually and spiritually: "I think that being loved by you raises me to the highest moral elevation that is possible for me to attain."[24] She presents a struggle between their mutual desires, his morals, and her self-control.

One night Sampayo accompanied Allart to her house, and she went into her room. Ambiguously, she states that she could not abide being there by herself:

I felt inside of me a violent pressure, a torment both moral and physical, and a great trouble, a mind in turmoil. A man of sober genius prey to a thousand different impressions, had just seized me and covered me with his own anguish. Such was then the nature of this passion, capable of transforming me in his hands and making me feel the torments that he felt himself. I saw around me only shadows and fright, horror and disorder. A thousand ideas assailed me; but I pushed them away to remain mistress of myself. I feared finding myself ill and losing all control over my character.[25]

Allart seems to have resisted her desire for intimacy with Sampayo at this time, but she was profoundly unhappy for that reason. She claims that she felt morally uplifted by the love she shared with Sampayo. The two, however, experienced doubts and insecurity about the other's commitment, for, at this point, they refused to consummate their love. Love was suffering, for both Allart and Sampayo, and they both exalted in it.

Allart then left the house of the Bertrands, for whom she had worked for two years. She wrote that Madame Bertrand, who had treated her with great kindness, guessed everything. What did she suspect? That Allart was leaving her in order to live alone and entertain Sampayo in her Paris apartment? That Allart was already Sampayo's lover? In any case Allart did live alone after leaving the Bertrands, and she published her second book, on Madame de Staël, in 1824. Throughout 1825 she received many male visitors, including Sampayo, and she

suggests indirectly that she shared her bed with Sampayo, that they experienced sensuous pleasure—*la volupté*.

Allart followed Sampayo to his country retreat, knowing that his
father was away and that the two would be alone. They met in a forest,
and Allart wrote, "We lose ourselves." Sampayo told her the entire
history of Greece, and on leaving her very late one night he said that he
was her slave.

After a three-week separation Sampayo saw Allart in Paris, and
they realized that she was pregnant. Allart determined to travel alone
to Italy, allowing herself to decide whether she will return to Sampayo
or end their relationship. They parted cordially, with Allart insisting
that she was by no means an unfortunate victim in this love affair—
"But this virgin whom he left a mother, was still in some ways a virgin,
since his austerity and his scruples lent a seldomness and a chastity to
the moments of abandon for which he reproached himself."[26]

Allart had several subsequent love affairs, and like the one with
Sampayo, each is inseparable from writing and intellectual pursuits.
Intelligence, conversation, great ideas, ambition—all were erotic
stimulants for Allart. She describes her passion for Guglielmo Libri, a
young physics professor committed to the cause of Italian nationalism,
who was very attentive to Allart at the time that she gave birth to her
son Marcus in Florence in May 1826. According to Allart, Libri inspired
her with passion because he represented Italy: "Except perhaps for
voluptuousness, he had all [Italy's] gifts. He had its fire, eloquence,
ambition, talents, generosity, greatness, beauty." Allart also became the
lover of the aging Chateaubriand, first in Rome, where they met, and
then after she followed him back to Paris. Allart is honest that he flattered her about her writing in order to attach this young and beautiful
woman to himself—Chateaubriand was over sixty in 1829, while Allart
was not quite twenty-eight. In Paris they met routinely at a trysting
house near the Austerlitz bridge where they would drink champagne,
dine, and sing songs. "In this condition," Allart writes, Chateaubriand
"was more amorous, more lively; he told me that I provided him with
the most charming pleasures, he called me seductress, and so on, and in
this isolated place he did what he wanted."[27]

The best lover Allart knew was Henry Bulwer, an English aristocrat,
politician, and diplomat whom she met in London in 1830. From the
start Allart was as much attracted to Bulwer's political career as to his
person. She writes, "He asked me to live with him in England as his

wife, in the political occupations of Parliament, and in the domestic affections of his country." Indeed, she accepted his invitation to live with
him as his mistress because she viewed that as perhaps the only means
by which Allart herself might be involved in politics: "Didn't he offer
political research, the art of orators, this ambition—all of which were so
dear to me? As a woman, could I have access to them otherwise?" Allart returned to France and explained the situation to Chateaubriand,
who chided her for having three lovers (he must not have known the
full count), especially one who was English. After breaking with Chateaubriand on amicable terms she collected her son and headed for the
coast to meet Bulwer again, experiencing for the first time the mysterious pleasures of sex that she had never known before: "Up to this time I
had known an intellectual love, where the senses, turned away and resisted, had languished unawakened. Today, I reached the Venus of antiquity, the sacred Venus, or rather I reached this sacrament of love that
the priests had made the sacrament of marriage." Allart waxes eloquent on the pleasures she knew with Bulwer, despite their disagreements, and she credits him with great skill at arousing the senses of a
woman. Once, when he was about to leave her for an urgent return to
Parliament, she describes the particular attentiveness he showed her as
a lover. "It was, in a way, a feminine tenderness that I blessed a hundred times; really, an extraordinary and perfect man, he knew profoundly the flirtatiousness and the exquisite art of love. From him I understood the sublimeness of the senses carried so far away by the
struggles and the exaltation of the moderns."[28]

Allart's words suggest that she unabashedly enjoyed sex, and that
she also intellectualized it, describing the pleasure she experienced
with Bulwer as resembling some lost, ancient rite. Allart was a scholar
and admirer of the ancient Greeks and her analogy of sexual pleasure
with antiquity was consistent with her eroticization of intellectual pursuits, and her intellectualization of eroticism. Sensuous pleasure and
pleasure of the mind are characteristics of the exceptional woman, according to Allart: "The superiority of woman almost always manifests
itself in the violence of her passions . . . [but] woman no more than man
is made for love alone . . . the superior woman needs action or intellectual pursuits [des lettres]."[29] During her brief marriage Allart missed
the intellectual and sexual stimulation she had enjoyed during her days
as a single woman. In a letter to Sainte-Beuve written approximately

three weeks before she left her husband, Allart recalled fondly the many lovers she had known, and she contrasted those pleasures with the isolation she felt in marriage: "Oh, my lovers, my agreeable [*aimable*] lovers, lovers of one day or of ten years, lovers of the imagination, lovers of the heart, how charming is the memory when one lives alone and oppressed."[30] Sex and ideas were so inseparable for Allart that Sainte-Beuve wrote a poem to her, suggesting that she was unique among women in accompanying embraces and kisses with philosophical and political discussion:

> Here is the stoic with his masculine wisdom
> In return for a sweeter present:
> It has to be Aspasia or you,
> To think of such names, the evening of a caress
> Or the morning of a tryst.[31]

Delphine Gay was twenty years old when her first collection of poetry was published in 1824. By that time she was well known in Parisian literary circles, regularly reciting her latest works in salons such as that of Madame Récamier. The young poet also wrote and recited verses for public occasions, including the coronation of Charles X and the opening of the Ste. Geneviève Church (during the French Revolution and under subsequent regimes, the Pantheon). Delphine Gay was a noted blond beauty, as many of her contemporaries attest. Marie d'Agoult, who first met Delphine Gay in 1826, described her as "tall and slightly heavy, her head proudly resting on a neck of classical beauty, aquiline profile, clear and luminous eyes, she had . . . the air of a sibyl."[32] Alphonse de Lamartine, writing after her death of his first meeting with her in 1825, used the same adjectives and analogies as d'Agoult; he finds her blond hair blowing in the wind similar to that of the sibyls, and her profile aquiline and proud.[33] And Théophile Gautier claims that all the romantic and rebellious youth who attended the riotous opening of Victor Hugo's *Hernani* in 1830 were so struck by Gay's beauty that they applauded her from the floor.[34] But even such beauty as hers could not overcome on the marriage market the disadvantages of lack of fortune and excess of talent.

During this time several marriage opportunities presented themselves to Delphine Gay, but none of them worked out. A baron de Lagrange and a Roman prince paid court to Gay, but no engagement resulted. At one point the poet Alfred de Vigny was a possibility, but his mother refused to allow him to marry a penniless commoner. Perhaps the most fantastic scheme was one concocted by court ladies of a morganatic marriage between Delphine Gay and the comte d'Artois, who would later become Charles X; this was thwarted by the king's indecision and his commitment to a dead mistress.[35] It is difficult to discern how Delphine Gay felt about these various men, but she wrote a poem dedicated to Alphonse de Lamartine in 1828 that suggests a deep attachment to the poet. Lamartine was married when he met Gay, and in the poem she writes, "Why am I so unhappy about his leaving? / I have not the right." She then probes the nature and meaning of her feelings for Lamartine, suggesting that she feels more than friendship, but something that is not love either. Rather, she proposes that she feels for him a kinship based on their shared poetic sensibilities:

> One speaks to a friend of earthly sorrows;
> One confides to love a momentary secret;
> But, to the beloved poet, one says without mysteriousness
> What only God understands![36]

Gay, of course, was writing poetry throughout this period, and many of her works address the subject of love, a not uncommon theme. Poems including "Magdeleine" (1822–27), "Elgise" (1825), and "Le dernier Jour de Pompeii" (1827) are historical, addressing, respectively, Mary Magdelan's conversion from heterosexual lust to Christianity, an English farmgirl's brief infatuation with King Alfred disguised as a shepherd, for whom she sacrifices her love when she realizes he is the king, and a confession of love between a priestess and a soldier at the altar of Apollo as Pompeii is covered with volcanic ash. But it is her short, seemingly more personal poems that address the subject of love in more prosaic and critical terms, less idealized and glorified than in the epics.

Several poems describe the pleasures and anxieties of young girls awaiting love, and there is often foreboding and despair regarding the transience of feminine beauty and the fickleness of masculine affection.[37] Girardin expresses some frustration with the social expectation that young women must make themselves attractive to please potential suitors, while there is no guarantee that such effort will bear fruit:

> What a lot of tedious duties to be beautiful for an evening!
> Is [being] sparkling a goal? Is pleasing others an obligation?
> How I hate the futile importance of grooming!
> The attire so long in concocting . . . and perhaps useless![38]

In addition to lamenting the tiresome chore of looking beautiful, and the uncertain benefits of such work, Girardin also describes a tension between a young woman's talent for writing poetry and her desire for love.

Girardin's poem "A ma mère" (1823) argues that there is nothing wrong in her becoming a poet, and that the love her mother has for her is more than sufficient to her happiness.[39] "Corinne aimée" (1828), however, analyzes the conflict experienced by the heroine of Madame de Staël's book between her desire for love and her ambition to create. At the beginning of the poem Corinne claims that being loved inspires her poetic genius, and that she wishes to win poetry competitions and honor her lover with her triumphs.

> I am still a poet—and I want the world
> To guess my happiness through the ray of my verse
> I want to sing of it, giddy with harmony
> To the fire of his love to ignite my genius.
> Yes, I want to reach my rivals in the race
> And justify his choice with new successes.[40]

The poem indicates that Corinne has suffered, but she is finally happy since she has found a man who understands her and who is not put off by a woman of talent: "He alone could love a woman's glory!" She claims that her lover is great and generous enough not to feel threatened by Corinne's artistic accomplishments. But then Corinne reconsiders. She berates herself for her ambition and vows that being loved is triumph enough for her; she will enjoy glory, success, and happiness through her lover, and only through him. Her joy, however, will always be tempered by sorrow—the sorrow of having waited so long for love? Or the sorrow of abandoning poetry?

> And so, my joyful heart likes to remember
> The sorrows for which one word could console me;
> And, finding sad charms in this memory,
> It dares believe in happiness—at the cost of so many tears![41]

In de Staël's story Corinne loses Oswald's love to her more conventionally feminine half-sister. She then loses her capacity for poetry and dies. But in Girardin's poem Corinne sacrifices her art and ambition for Oswald's love. In the poem Corinne does not die, but she pays a high price for the joy of being loved.

Other poems from this period of the 1820s and early 1830s address thwarted desire for love, and the limits as well as satisfactions of literary accomplishment and renown. Girardin was crowned for her poetry at the Capitol in Rome in 1827, just as was Corinne, and several poems imply that a female poet and a beloved woman are mutually exclusive. This understanding seems to have been a source of distress for Girardin, who had cast her lot with writing at an early age and who feared that her literary success might prevent her from enjoying other pleasures, such as love and motherhood. Yet she does not entirely trust love either. She writes in "A ma mère":

> At the foot of the altar [of love] I will break my lyre;
> But should I desire this dangerous happiness?[42]

Ultimately, with her marriage to Emile de Girardin, Delphine Gay was able to pursue her literary career within the framework of a union of mutual esteem if not passionate love. Girardin's poem "Mathilde" and her story "Le Lorgnon" both focus on figures that closely resemble Emile de Girardin, a figure presented as intelligent, honorable, determined, melancholy, and extremely attractive to women. Was this a love relationship, or one of convenience? Delphine Gay had a greater literary reputation than Girardin when they married, but fame did not guarantee Delphine and her mother a secure living or future. Emile de Girardin, the illegitimate son of an aristocratic officer, did not even get to use his father's name until 1828, when he was twenty-two and published a successful novel entitled *Emile,* the plot of which bore great similarity to his own life. He determined that literature, and specifically journalism, were the keys to his success, and he had already started two newspapers when he began frequenting the salon of Sophie and Delphine Gay.[43] Whatever else they brought to the relationship, Delphine Gay gained the respectability and promised security of marriage, and Emile de Girardin gained entrée into the toniest salon society. Professionally the two gained far more than this in their union.

Girardin's poems written in the early 1830s address feelings of disillusionment and despair rather than marital bliss or even satisfaction. In "Désenchantement" (1834) Girardin suggests that early success as a female poet later on becomes a burden, when the author fears she has lost her talent because of unhappy or unrequited love. The poem asserts that the disillusioned poet is unable to respond to love or friendship, and so her despair and isolation are worsened. Similarly, "Aux jeunes filles" (1835) claims that the author, too, was once a girl with innocent hopes and fantasies, including the ambition to be a poet, which was fulfilled. But the author explains that adulthood dashes these youthful ideals, and she advises young women never to grow up, and not to put on the airs of mature women:

> At last, in the promised happiness
> I found only bitterness and disgust, even deep sadness;
> And I would gladly exchange all this worldly success,
> These favors that others envy and that must be purchased,
> For the naive pleasures that you wish to abandon.[44]

These poems suggest that youthful beauty, talent, and public acclaim are no guarantees of lifelong happiness. They explicitly state that talent and fame *in a woman* are the source of the problem, that they preclude the happiness of sustained literary creativity and satisfying love: "Oh, the brilliant success of poet and woman, a success both permitted and prohibited!"[45] Girardin suggests that a woman poet is a violation of a feminine ideal, and that she pays the price for her achievement with unhappiness.

The early years of Girardin's marriage might, indeed, have been trying in a variety of ways, though a letter from Sophie Gay to her daughter Euphémie asserts that "Delphine is very happy being loved as she wishes by an intelligent and good husband."[46] For several months the young couple shared an apartment with Girardin's mother, Sophie Gay, but in 1832 Emile and Delphine moved into their own, much nicer lodgings. This was devastating to Sophie, who was thus separated from a much-loved companion; she also lost the star attraction of her salon.[47] Additionally, in 1833 Delphine suffered a serious bout of smallpox, from which she recovered with no disfiguration. But it is likely that the death wish she expresses in "Désespoir" (1834) was, if only momentarily, sincere, and related to her inability to bear a child. Biographers indicate that because of his own struggle with his illegitimate identity, Emile de Girardin desperately wanted a legitimate son. At some point Emile introduced Delphine to his illegitimate son, whom Delphine accepted and to whom she even left a legacy upon her death.[48] Still another source of personal unhappiness and marital tension might have been an incident in 1836 in which a young dandy, smitten with Delphine de Girardin, committed suicide after she refused to flee with him. One biographer claims that this circumstance caused an irreparable rift between husband and wife.[49] All of these personal difficulties—competing claims on Delphine's love by her mother and her husband, serious illness, childlessness, jealousy—might have strained even the most loving relationship. Moreover, Delphine went through a major transition in her literary career between the time of her marriage in 1831 and 1836, when she became a journalist. Gradually abandoning the writing of poetry, Delphine wrote a novel and a few short stories from 1832 to 1836, perhaps, as her poems suggest, out of lack of poetic inspiration, or perhaps because as a mature and married woman she felt a need or desire for a new literary identity or challenge. In any case fiction never became a major genre for Girardin, but journalism and drama did.

Girardin had ample opportunity to seek love or sexual satisfaction beyond marriage. As the center of one of the most brilliant salons in Paris during the July Monarchy, Girardin associated with and influenced a host of leading male writers and politicians, and she routinely received intimate friends such as Gautier, Balzac, Victor Hugo, Eugène Sue, and Lamartine in her bedroom while her husband was away at work at *La Presse*.[50] Girardin well knew of Emile's infatuation with Marie d'Agoult, whose salon rivaled her own in the distinction of its habitués, but she publicly passed off this affair with a witticism. D'Agoult wrote to Liszt that Girardin reportedly said: "My husband is flirting with Mme d'A[goult], but I am not worried about it. It is not risky with intelligent women; it is only with stupid women that men go too far, since they have nothing to say."[51] There is no evidence that Girardin ever took a lover, though she lived surrounded by the literary and political male elite of Paris. The Girardin marriage, for all its difficulties, was a partnership, and a poem of 1839 by Delphine de Girardin suggests a profound attachment to and respect for her husband. Emile had twice been elected to the Chamber of Deputies but was subjected to humiliating doubts about the date and place of his birth, regarding, first, whether he met the age requirement, and second, the nationality requirement for election to office. Girardin defends his patriotism and affirms her strong support for him and his career:

> A man grew up in the midst of a sordid struggle.
> He possessed nothing but the love of a woman;
> But both of them well-armed, holding each other by the hand,
> They followed in life a perilous road.[52]

George Sand's sexuality has long been an object of intense interest and investigation. Her love affairs with men have been a continuing source of fascination since Sand's own time, and scholars have also debated whether Sand was frigid, and whether she had a lesbian relationship with the actress Marie Dorval.[53] Sand's autobiography is reticent on the subject of her personal love relationships and experiences of sexual pleasure, probably because much of the general public found her fictional representations of love and sexuality shockingly explicit and transgressive. The autobiography is Sand's means of creating her own public legend, of revising and recasting her image from adulterous and immoral to maternal and responsible. "Therefore, scandal lovers, close my book. It is not made for you," Sand writes.[54]

According to Sand her marriage with Casimir Dudevant was based on reason rather than love. She asserts that Dudevant frankly told her during their "courtship" that he was not a loving or passionate man: "He never spoke to me of love, he admitted to being little disposed to sudden passion, or enthusiasm." According to Sand, Dudevant offered her "peaceful domestic happiness" in the form of marriage, and she maintains that, at the time, this suited her perfectly: "I think that at that time in my life, just as I was emerging from such great indecision between convent and family life, a suitor's sudden passion would have terrified me." With the encouragement of her friends, who functioned virtually as foster parents to Sand following the death of her grandmother, Sand introduced Casimir to her mother, who very nearly prevented the marriage. Sand maintains that her mother's often irrational ravings against Dudevant actually made her more determined to marry him, and eventually, with many stipulations, Sophie Dupin agreed to the match. Sand and Dudevant were married in 1822.[55]

Not long after the birth of Maurice, in 1824, Sand fell into depression, and in her writings she bemoaned the lack of love in her marriage. She explains in her autobiography that she and Dudevant were totally incompatible, and that although she tried to understand him and attend to his needs and desires, her own character and her inexperience militated against any mending of their fraying relationship. Dudevant did not share Sand's tastes for music, literature, and philosophy, preferring to hunt and drink heavily with Sand's half-brother Hippolyte and to consort with the female servants at night. Sand claims to have found some solace in an unnamed "invisible man," but she protests that this relationship was entirely platonic and romantic in the sense of being cerebral, idealized, and conducted largely through letters. It is precisely at this point that Sand breaks her narrative to address accusations that she is immoral. Although she casts this section as a discussion of her religious faith, it bears implicitly upon her personal and fictional rebellion against the institution of marriage. "Some sanctimonious characters have . . . declared me to be without principles, from the beginning of my literary career, because I allowed myself to challenge purely human institutions which it pleased them to look on as God-given."[56] Some scholars think that Aurélien de Sèze, the "invisible man," or Stéphane d'Ajasson de Grandsagne was in fact the father of Sand's daughter Solange, but according to Sand, this "absent being" sought elsewhere the sexual gratification that he could not find with Sand herself.[57] He "was tired of my superhuman aspiration to sublime love," Sand writes, and it seems that she, too, got over this "rapturous friendship" to move on to the beginning of her career as a writer.[58] Sand speaks no more of her personal feelings of love and eroticism in the autobiography, claiming that she owes discretion to those with whom she had intimate relations. But she does address love in the abstract and as a necessary foundation for marriage, for reproduction, and for self-realization (see Chapter 6).

In 1830, after discovering Dudevant's will, in which he harshly maligned Sand, Sand determined to free herself, at least part-time, from this oppressive master of the house and of her. She arranged, with Dudevant's acquiescence, to live in Paris for part of the year. And for a time she shared her Paris apartment with Jules Sandeau, her lover and another aspiring young writer from the Berry region with whom Sand collaborated on a novel. Although several of Sand's love affairs, including the one with Sandeau, are not recorded in much detail in Sand's letters, her sensual feelings for the lawyer Michel de Bourges are expressed in a letter she wrote to him following her trip to Switzerland to visit d'Agoult and Liszt. Sand spends a lot of time reassuring the jealous Michel that she has not even looked at another man since she left him, much less had a sexual relationship, and then she declares how she is sexually aroused by the thought of Michel when she is contemplating the beauty of the Swiss landscape:

I've suffered a great deal from my chastity, I admit; I have had very enervating dreams. The blood has mounted to my head a hundred times, and, in the middle of the day, in the heart of the beautiful mountains, listening to the birds sing and breathing the gentlest (*plus suaves*) fragrances of the forests and the valleys, I am often sitting alone, to the side, with a soul full of love and knees trembling with voluptuousness. I am still young, even though I say to other men that I have the calm of the elderly, my blood burns, in the midst of nature that instills drunkenness with its beauty, love boils in me like the sap of life in the universe.[59]

The relationship with Michel de Bourges continued for a few more months, but eventually Sand could no longer tolerate his jealousy and his tyranny. His version of love required Sand's self-abasement, which she finally rejected. And it is not surprising that Sand should then articulate to another correspondent her view that marital love can be based only on complete equality between male and female partners.[60]

Sand experienced love and passion for several men and lived seldom without a male companion. Even after she won a legal separation from Dudevant in 1836 she continued to believe in an ideal of marriage that included physical gratification and spiritual love, but she also believed that inequality between the sexes prevented true marriage, for herself personally and for her society generally. Sand's novels are filled with love relationships that critique social hierarchy and patriarchal authority, and that, alternatively, represent her ideal of mutual love, trust, and esteem. Sand's fiction tends to represent love in more spiritual than sensual terms, and sensual feelings are often problematic. For example, in *Indiana* the most erotic scene describes a love in which the partners are not equal; the Creole servant Noun seduces Raymon with her "wild tropical lust," overcoming his love for her mistress Indiana, who is "her more cultured sister." And *Lélia* focuses much on a woman's struggle to control her passions and thereby to exercise domination over men through their sexual desires.[61] Love and marriage were intensely political for Sand because she held both up as shining ideals that social mores and men's laws corrupted, degraded, and denied. Hence, her writings about these topics were far more than an affirmation of or justification for personal rebellion; rather, they were calls for social and political transformations that would allow women and men to love freely, devotedly, and as equals.[62] Indeed, writing itself was a sort of love affair for Sand, as she wrote in March 1831: "I am more than ever resolved to pursue a literary career. . . . I feel that the life I lead is fulfilled. I have a goal, a task, let us even say, *a passion*."[63]

From Love to Literature

It is highly contrived to separate love from writing in the lives of d'Agoult, Allart, Girardin, and Sand. The love affairs of d'Agoult, Allart, and Sand set them apart from "respectable" women, as did their writing and their independence—all of which were closely connected. And Girardin perhaps feared for a time that writing precluded love in her life, until she combined them, to some extent, in her union with Emile de Girardin. In writing about sexuality and authorship all four women are conscious of its transgressive nature, coming from the pens of females. However, for d'Agoult, and perhaps for Girardin, writing is a substitute for the love of a man, a surer means of identity-creation than the relative existence of mistress or wife, and a far more generous outlet for self-expression. Even Sand, and especially Allart, who managed for many years to combine love and writing, describe conflicts between these two aspects of their own lives, and they write about this tension in the lives of fictional female characters. Writing allows the four authors to be independent, and although part of that independence is defined by the freedom to love whom they wish, love occasionally threatens that independence, which is why Sand, d'Agoult, and Allart were, for much of their lives, unmarried women. Writing is the means by which the four authors articulate this problem and seek to resolve it through legal, political, social, and cultural change. Writing fulfills both personal and political needs and desires.

In her autobiography D'Agoult tells the story of the end of her love relationship with Liszt and the beginning of independence and a writing career. Looking back she identifies the first indications of the deterioration of their love with Liszt's cultivation of other acquaintances in Geneva, while d'Agoult, in part because of her awkward position as mistress (and perhaps because of her pregnancy), and because of her belief that she and Liszt could be everything to one another, stayed home alone in the apartment. What really bothered d'Agoult was the commitments made and actions taken by Liszt without consulting her. She was astonished at her own acquiescence to Liszt's will: "I remained confused at what I had done and had allowed to happen. ... I had fallen so low in lacking presence of mind, wit, sincerity! It was unbelievable."[64] As d'Agoult charts the slow dissolution of her relationship with Liszt, she also marks the rise of her intellect and self-confidence. Despite the sorrows, difficulties, and quarrels of this illicit relationship, d'Agoult eventually came out of it with self-determination, purpose, and, ultimately, personal success. Significantly, her memoirs hardly mention the three children born of this union. Rather than filling the void left by Liszt with their children, d'Agoult recovered herself through writing. And in this d'Agoult was aided by several persons, including Liszt himself, Delphine Gay de Girardin and her husband, Emile, Hortense Allart, and George Sand.

D'Agoult spent much of her time "in exile" developing her mind and her writing skills. She read widely, conversed with intellectual men, studied paintings, and rearticulated Liszt's ideas about art, the artist, and society into reasoned articles that were published either under Liszt's name or anonymously. Her friends and associates, including Liszt, encouraged d'Agoult in these enterprises, urging her especially to write and publish, presumably on her own account. As much as the affair with Liszt unleashed d'Agoult's passion and freed her from an unsatisfying marriage, it also liberated her intellect and provided her with a purpose beyond that of being muse and mistress to a genius.[65] Equally important, however, in aiding d'Agoult's writing career was George Sand.

Liszt had met Sand in 1834 through Alfred de Musset, with whom Sand was involved in a tempestuous love affair. And through Liszt, d'Agoult and Sand met in the early months of 1835. Their friendship began largely through correspondence, for d'Agoult left for Switzerland in May of 1835, and she did not see Sand again until September 1836, when Sand, having successfully won a separation from her husband, traveled with her children to Chamonix to meet Liszt and d'Agoult for a mountain excursion. D'Agoult expressed gratitude to Sand for the inspiration that her works provided for her (as for many of her readers), and for Sand's personal encouragement of d'Agoult's writing. What d'Agoult does not mention in her memoirs is that Sand encouraged her to write specifically about women, as this letter from Sand to d'Agoult on 15 December 1836 reveals: "Write then. Write about the condition of women and about their rights; write bravely and modestly as you know how to do." Sand goes on to mention Allart's recent publication on women and democracy, which she finds meritorious in substance but rather poorly written. The implication is that d'Agoult could write better, serious nonfiction than Allart, and, Sand modestly suggests, than herself, for she writes: "I am too much of a dunce to write anything but stories, and I haven't the energy to educate myself."[66] Thus, Sand generously suggests that d'Agoult has the learning and analytical skills to write nonfiction, and that Sand will never compete with d'Agoult in that genre. Moreover, she goads d'Agoult with the reference to Allart, who has successfully published a work but who is "pedantic" and "unpleasing."

At this time Sand and d'Agoult were friends, but during Sand's stay in Majorca with Chopin in 1839 the two had a falling out; it was due to the interference of a third party, who counseled Sand to break with d'Agoult, claiming that d'Agoult was saying slanderous things about Sand.[67] Whatever the reasons for the cooling of this friendship, and many interpretations are available, d'Agoult ultimately followed Sand's suggestion by writing about women, among other subjects, and by writing primarily nonfiction. Only too aware of Sand's towering influence in Parisian literary circles, d'Agoult determined to be a woman writer distinctly *not* in Sand's image. In her own account of Sand and of their friendship, d'Agoult emphasizes the revolutionary and feminist orientations of Sand's writing, and the mysterious, androgynous aspects of her character, rather than her talent as a writer and contribution to literature. She also emphasizes Sand's desire to meet, correspond with, and visit d'Agoult. D'Agoult carefully qualifies her admiration for Sand, indicating (with hindsight) that she aroused apprehension in d'Agoult as well as attraction: "Was she a man, a woman, an angel, a demon? Like her Lélia, did she come 'from heaven or hell'?"[68] D'Agoult portrays Sand as exactly her opposite, in appearance, temperament, and mental qualities. She suggests that Sand was very much at ease in her masculine clothes, displaying "a certain grace of youthful virility," implicitly in contrast to d'Agoult's elegant femininity. She also describes Sand as too Catholic, too much a being of imagination, unlike d'Agoult, who prided herself in being skeptical and rational.[69] D'Agoult constructed herself to be Sand's opposite, and indeed Sand assisted her in this process by helping d'Agoult to discover her own, individual artistic personality: "She made me examine myself, plumb the mysteries of my heart far more deeply than I had yet done. She helped me to know myself, to analyze myself."[70] Despite the infamous break between Sand and d'Agoult, the two women shared many values and goals, including republicanism, and d'Agoult gratefully sought and received from Sand the reassurance and self-confidence to write under her own name and thus break yet again, though far more publicly, from the role of aristocratic matron.

D'Agoult and Liszt parted more or less permanently in 1839, and d'Agoult returned to Paris, where she was welcomed back into society by Delphine Gay de Girardin. Girardin introduced d'Agoult to major literary figures of her own salon—Lamartine, Victor Hugo, Théophile Gautier—and to her husband. It took d'Agoult a while to establish herself socially and materially, and then to put pen to paper. And competitiveness with other women was as much a stimulus to her writing as positive encouragement. She was piqued into action by the fact that her sister-in-law, Mathilde de Flavigny, was publishing a book on Christian education for mothers of young children. "Honestly, I can't get over it and I feel ashamed. I must get to work and I don't know how to begin."[71] Several months later, in December 1840, Emile de Girardin asked d'Agoult for a review of Sand's latest book, *Le Compagnon du tour de France*, which d'Agoult resisted, claiming that she wanted to work on a story.[72] But d'Agoult changed her mind, and the review appeared in *La Presse* on 9 January 1841 under the authorship of "An Unknown." D'Agoult deemed her hard criticism of Sand's book a success, and she enjoyed the controversy over both the review and the author's mysterious identity. She earned further success almost a year later with the publication of a series of art reviews that were published under the name of Daniel Stern. D'Agoult's satisfaction with herself is unmistakable; writing to Liszt on 10 January 1842, she asserts: "You must have received my three masterpieces. They are very much talked about. The salons debate over them. My name has been mentioned, but I deny it. They are praised to the skies. It is a success to arouse the jealousy of *L'Enfance chrétienne* [the book by Mathilde de Flavigny]."[73] D'Agoult had found the way to a literary career, for Girardin was eager to publish works by authors who caused a public stir and thereby sold newspapers.

In her autobiography d'Agoult then briefly analyzed the articles and stories that immediately followed these first publications, which also appeared in *La Presse*. She admits that the single novel she wrote, *Nélida*, was flawed, and that her writing talent was by no means for fiction. But she confesses the need she felt in 1846 to see this work published and establish herself in literary society and intellectual circles and to escape from her tendency to depression.

I had a perhaps blind but irresistible need to emerge from an isolation of heart and mind that had already several times left me prey to thoughts of suicide. I needed to get out of myself, to put into my life a new interest that was not love for a man, but an intellectual relationship with those who felt, thought, and suffered as I did.[74]

Writing thus liberated d'Agoult more completely than did the affair with Liszt, although Liszt helped d'Agoult reach this point of self-emancipation. D'Agoult sought public approval for her work, and by extension for her existence. Additionally, writing consolidated d'Agoult's political interest in reforming "everything" through republicanism, as she and Sand agreed in 1837.[75] As d'Agoult said of the character Nélida that she created in the book of the same title: "I wanted to portray a woman possessed of the feeling of the ideal; thinking to find it in marriage, then in free love, she is mistaken and she *should* die, but she lives. She will love again, but no longer a man (for no man is worth being loved as she loved). She will love *all those who suffer*, she will act, freely and strongly from this point on; she will extend her hand to the oppressed."[76]

While writing her memoirs in the 1860s d'Agoult viewed herself as a woman who had led a remarkable life, and who had affected the literary and political culture of her time through writing. "It would be mistaken," she writes in the introduction of her autobiography, "to believe that only men can exert a serious influence outside of private life." D'Agoult asserts that manly activities of soldiering or statesmanship are not the only means of exercising a strong will, and that an exceptional woman, one who does not abide by the conventional social rules, acquires virile responsibilities of public influence. "Such a woman who kindles the imagination, excites the mind, and instigates a re-examination of received opinions will influence her century . . . perhaps as much as a legislative assembly or an army captain."[77] D'Agoult goes further in her justification of women entering into public life, implicitly as writers. She claims that as a result of their oppressed position women understand better the problems that afflict society, and their articulation of such issues promises the beginning of improvements. "Submissive or rebellious, humble or famous, the daughter, the sister, the lover, the wife, the mother has suffered—much more than the son, the brother, the lover, the husband, the father, in her more delicate sensibility and in her more subjected condition—the dissension of a world that no longer has any faith, traditions, respected habits, and where nothing stands upright, not even lies."[78]

Thus, at the same time that d'Agoult asserts her own exceptionality as a justification for writing her autobiography, she also claims the right for all women to write generally. The point of her own personal suffering and that of all women is to render them suitable for instigating social change. Scorned by and marginalized from a society that d'Agoult considers to be materialistic, dishonorable, and unprincipled, women are, according to d'Agoult, uniquely positioned to criticize and transform that society. D'Agoult had thought initially that she could perform this transformative function as lover and inspiration to Liszt, but ultimately writing, not love, fulfilled this desire. Similarly, Allart, who thought she might influence politics by being involved with political men, found that writing was a more satisfying means of achieving that end.

Hortense Allart published her first book in 1822 when she was just twenty-one years old and under the tutelage of Laure Regnault de Saint-Jean d'Angély. According to her autobiography Regnault offered constructive criticism and encouragement on Allart's historical novel, *La Conjuration d'Ambroise* (1822), a work "in support of Protestants and freedom."[79] The appearance of her book in print, and the enthusiasm for life that she gained from Regnault, combined to make Allart optimistically commit herself to a career in writing. "I was, from that moment, ambitious, adventurous, pleasant, and thus in danger. I would not have wanted [to lead] an obscure life. I loved literature and I put all my hopes in it."[80] This love and hope were not misplaced, for, fortunately for Allart, literary pursuits did not betray her as men did.

Although sex and intellectual pursuits were closely connected in Allart's heterosexual relationships, she also found that she had to uncouple them on occasion in order to maintain her independence. A notable instance of this was when Allart and Bulwer were living together in England in 1830. Bulwer spent so much time in Parliament and away from home on political business that Allart pined away in their London apartment, separated from her friends and miserable in the dreary English weather. Moreover, it became clear to her that marriage to Bulwer was impossible; he risked losing a substantial inheritance from his mother by marrying Allart. In addition, by 1835, if not earlier, Allart knew that Bulwer was unfaithful.[81] For years Allart remained attached to Bulwer, visiting him frequently and receiving him in turn, enjoying their physical relationship, and concerned about his health until he finally married in 1848. But she left him to resume her independent existence. Bulwer could understand this because, according to Allart, "his ardor took violently to two things: love and ambition; ambition won over him, but since he felt that love, too, could have won him over, his ambition was so afraid of it that ambition triumphed in advance." Allart knew this because she was ambitious also, and ambition led her to put her writing career above her love relationships. She asserts that later she realized that Bulwer was better off without her: "I often thought afterward that he had found [other women] one hundred times better than I was, women who die of love and who do not write books."[82]

Ultimately, study and writing were the primary sources of Allart's happiness, even above love. In her story "Marpé," included in the autobiography, she describes the heroine, who is momentarily separated from her lover, Remi: "When I return to these studies, when I see myself in my garden, with my books and my child, I find myself the happiest woman in the world, I think of leaving Remi, of not delivering up to him a life so happy and so easy. I escape from a revisiting of mad passion."[83] For Allart the pleasure of the senses is inseparable from the exercise of the mind, but the exercise of the mind actually improves when freed from "mad passion." To be sure the experience of love was precious and valuable, enlarging Allart's understanding of human nature and relationships, and bringing her closer to some ideas and to politics than she might have been otherwise. She continued to have both sexual relationships and intense friendships with several men, including Bulwer, the critics Charles-Augustin Sainte-Beuve, Charles Didier, and Niccolo Tommaseo, and a politician, Jacopo Mazzei, who was the father of Allart's second child.[84] But love for a man also had the potential of subordination for women, something that Allart realized pointedly after her brief and failed experiment with marriage. She claims that in the late 1840s her old friend and lover Libri thought Allart had missed a great chance by failing to commit herself to him: "Libri told me several times that in not wanting to tie myself to him in our youth, *I had missed my life*. I did not reply to this, but his domineering character did not suit me. After these conversations with him I returned calm, amused, happy and without regret to Herblay."[85]

In the long run independence and writing provided greater security and happiness to Allart than did love and sexual pleasure. At about the age of forty-five Allart writes: "Youth and its unbearable turmoil had passed. One had only to enjoy writing and one's independence. Was the age of passions finished? I think not, but where was an object to inspire them?" Allart says that she did have an alternative "passion" in her heart, and it was wisdom [*la sagesse*]; "I attained it in all its sweetness." Allart had tried to become involved in politics through her relationships with Bulwer and with Méritens, but since these had failed, she devoted herself solely to letters: "I was as ambitious as ever. What to do? When I saw that I could not attain a political life through marriage, I occupied myself only with writing. Guided by my taste and by my pleasure, I read a great deal, I studied, I was assiduous."[86]

Sand, too, worked relentlessly at her writing, even amidst the most wrenching of personal and family crises. Her passions, though numerous and intense, seem to have hardly affected her literary productivity. But unlike Allart and d'Agoult, who justified their writing on the basis of their exceptionality, Sand claimed that she came to writing simply as a form of gainful employment. She asserts that in the beginning of her marriage she was perfectly content to be a housewife and a mother, and that she never disdained housework. But she maintains that financial problems at Nohant, plus her concern about the bad influence of her drunken half-brother and husband on her children, prompted her to seek "useful work." Sand enumerates the many remunerative tasks she tried, including translating, portrait drawing, sewing, and painting ornamental objects, but for a variety of reasons she was not good enough at any of them to make a living. She suggests that writing was something she felt she could do, though she denies any ambition or aspiration to writing in particular.[87] Sand maintains that freedom and honest labor were her primary objectives in becoming a writer:

To be an artist! Yes, I had wanted to be one, not only to escape from the material prison where property, large or small, closes one in a circle of odious, trivial occupation, but also to escape the control of public opinion [sic] insofar as it was narrow, stupid, egotistical, weak, provincial; to live outside the world's prejudices insofar as they were false, outdated, arrogant, cruel, impious or dull, but moreover and above all, to reconcile myself with myself. I could not bear to be idle and useless, leaning, in my position as master, on the shoulders of the workers.[88]

Sand here reiterates the romantic ideal of the artist who is beyond financial concerns and bourgeois conformity. The statement also reflects Sand's socialist sympathies, which she acquired in the mid-1830s, with her refusal to live off the labor of others. However, Sand's correspondence suggests that a desire for personal independence and artistic fulfillment, and for a means of supporting her children, were the main motivations for launching a writing career.[89] Additionally, this move expanded and consolidated her relations with like-minded, artistic, and bohemian men, in contrast to the boorish, unimaginative menfolk of Sand's household.

Sand's stories about her literary initiation are amusing and lighthearted, but at the same time they reveal the difficulties that a woman confronted in the quest for a career in letters. Sand maintains that crossdressing was necessary for her to gain access to a broader swath of public experience than was available to a respectable lady. Sand felt that as a provincial and as a female she needed to educate herself in art, politics, and urban life as part of her training in artistic and self-creation. Sand writes:

My character was taking shape and real life was opening before me, dressed as I was in men's clothing, which allowed me to be enough of a man to see a milieu that otherwise would have remained forever closed. . . . I contemplated the spectacle from every point of view I could—the wings and the stage, the loge and the pit. I climbed to every floor—from clubroom to studio, from cafe to attic.[90]

Sand acknowledged that her dress and behavior were objectionable to many, and that some accused her of satisfying base desires rather than learning to be an artist. But as Sand asserts, male clothing gave her a liberating anonymity; it was more practical and less expensive than female dress, and it allowed her to roam the streets, go to the theater, visit museums, and enter clubs—activities that her male friends engaged in constantly but that were impossible for a woman dressed in delicate shoes, long skirts, and little velvet hats. In her gray frock coat with matching trousers and vest, gray hat and wool tie, Sand states, she "flew from one end of Paris to the other. . . . My clothing made me fearless. I was on the go in all kinds of weather, I came in at all hours."[91]

Cross-dressing allowed Sand to overcome some of the limitations on female access to the public sphere, but she also sought mentors and contacts to give her entrée into the competitive and male-dominated literary market. Regional affiliations brought Sand into a circle of Berrichon writers headed by Henri Delatouche, and Sand also claims to have obtained literary advice from Honoré Balzac and the critic Jules Janin. But the theories and principles that these literary mentors offered were mutually contradictory, and ultimately, Sand asserts that she wrote *Indiana* (1832), the first book she produced without a collaborator, by ignoring all advice and by following her own instincts. *Indiana*, a novel about a young, romantic woman married to an older, brutish man, who tries to escape her "incarcerated" condition through a love affair, was an immediate success, both popular and critical. Sand consolidated this achievement with subsequent novels that further enhanced her reputation and that provided her with the financial independence, self-confidence, and network of friends and legal advisors to successfully sue her husband for a legal separation in 1836. Sand's enormous energy allowed her to maintain a grueling writing schedule for most of the rest of her life, while simultaneously attending to her children, households, lovers, and friends, along with patronizing a host of worker-poets and contributing to a variety of literary and political causes.[92]

Love remained a central concern for Sand as both a person and an artist. Indeed, she describes her theory of fiction as consisting of an idealized passionate love framed by "real-life" settings and characters. "In sum, the idealization of a sentiment yields the subject, leaving to the art of the storyteller the care of placing that subject within a situation and realistic framework that is drawn sensitively enough to make the subject stand out."[93] In the process of configuring and reconfiguring the love ideal, Sand explored various possibilities of sexual identity and erotic relations in her fiction, including androgyny, transvestism, incest, lesbianism, and misalliance or cross-class love. Although Sand remained a popular writer throughout her life, some of her works provoked criticism for the sexual transgressions they described or suggested, and for the challenge to the institution of marriage that they represented.

Girardin's love life and her writing about love were less transgressive than those of d'Agoult, Allart, and Sand. However, she engaged in a unique writing experiment that suggests erotic undertones, if not overt sensuality. In 1845 *La Presse* ran a serial novel entitled *La Croix de Berny*, referring to an imagined horse race in which riders must confront various obstacles as part of the race course. This was a literary race, however, among four riders/authors; each would write a letter and construct obstacles of character and plot to which the others responded in turn. The four "gentlemen riders" in this case were Théophile Gautier, Joseph Méry, Jules Sandeau, and vicomte Charles de Launay, a.k.a. Delphine Gay de Girardin. Each writer of a letter, all good friends, became a character in the story: Gautier was Edgard de Meilhan, Méry was Roger de Monbert, Sandeau was Raymond de Villiers, and Girardin was Irène de Chateaudun. The four form a complicated love entanglement, but basically the three men fall in love with the same woman. Chateaudun is engaged to marry Monbert, but she mistrusts his love, and she disguises herself as a grisette, Louise Guerin, to test his devotion. As Louise, Chateaudun meets Meilhan and Villiers, both of whom fall in love with her. Chateaudun sees Monbert at the theater in the company of two floozies, and she feels entitled to break their engagement. She then witnesses Meilhan drugged on hashish and with a beautiful black woman at his feet, and she also feels released from his protestations of love. Chateaudun returns the love of the idealistic Villiers, and they marry. But Villiers knows his happiness is short-lived and that his two [former] friends Monbert and Meilhan will punish him for stealing the woman each man loves. Sure enough, Meilhan kills Villiers in a duel, and Monbert seeks Chateaudun to report his death. He finds that Chateaudun herself is dead. There are no winners in this steeplechase.[94]

Chateaudun is more interested in a marriage of minds than of bodies, and she takes the opportunity early in the story to berate aristocratic men in general for their pretense of education and superiority, which they betray by associating with unworthy women. Or rather, they seek inappropriate female companions *because* of their flawed character: "They are proud, and the proud enjoy themselves only with those whom they despise." Before she meets the exceptional and good Villiers, Chateaudun swears off marriage to men of her class because she does not want her fortune "to be distributed as an encouragement to all the miserable courtesans of Paris."[95] Although the sentiments Chateaudun expresses are only mildly subversive, the writing of this collaborative story is suggestive of erotic possibilities, not the least of which is Girardin's literary competition with three of her male peers.

The ideal of love and of sexual desire that Sand, d'Agoult, and Allart promulgated in their fiction and essays closely resembled that of male Romantic writers. Yet writing about it as women aroused a different, usually negative, response from the public and from other, male writers. The love affairs, learning, ambition, and independence that marked the male Romantic writer, and his hero, as individuals and artists, contrarily served to divest women authors of individual identity, and to stereotype them as sexually promiscuous, ignorant, pretentious, and unfeminine. Paradoxically, women writers' use of male pseudonyms was a move that contributed to their self-creations as autonomous individuals and as women.

Pseudonyms and Women Writers' Identities

Sand, d'Agoult, Allart, and Girardin all used pseudonyms at some point in their writing careers. Sand and d'Agoult, like their famous English contemporaries George Eliot (Marianne Evans), Charlotte Brontë, and Emily Brontë, launched their first publications under male pseudonyms. It is possible to interpret this act as a denial of personal identity in order to get unbiased reviews from critics who considered writing an inappropriate activity for women and generally expected little of serious art in writings by women. However, Sand and d'Agoult asserted other motivations that suggest that a pseudonym was a means of establishing or multiplying identities, for both women indicated that bearing their husbands' names required them to adopt pseudonyms as authors.[96]

Sand recounts how she reassured her mother-in-law that their common Dudevant name would never appear in public on the cover of a book.[97] And d'Agoult remembers on the eve of publishing her first article (at least, the first article for which she claimed sole authorship and to which she put a name) that she felt unable to use her married name, which "did not belong to [her] alone," and that she did not wish to seek permission from her husband to do so. Moreover, she asserts her independence by saying, "If I must be criticized in the newspapers, I want no one to feel honor-bound to defend me."[98] Neither of these women felt that their married names were their own, and they chose to publish under names fashioned by themselves. In becoming George Sand and Daniel Stern, these two women were effecting the divorces from their husbands that they could not legally obtain in France in the 1830s and 1840s, when they started publishing. Indeed, Sand writes of the creation of her pseudonym: "It was a contract, a new marriage, between the poor apprentice poet who I was and the humble muse who had consoled me in my hardships."[99] The pseudonyms represented the assertion of a public identity, chosen consciously by the women themselves and not assumed by law and social convention, as were their married names. Sand was especially protective of her pseudonym when she feared that her early collaborator and lover, Jules Sandeau, might publish a work under the name of J. Sand, the pseudonym they had used for their first and only joint publication. Having made the name of Sand famous and profitable, George Sand asserted her exclusive possession of it: "I earned [it] myself, after the event, by my own toil."[100]

Allart's case is different. Her first several works were published long before she married, and most were published under her birth name, or with an added "de Thérase," probably to elevate her social status.[101] However, after her brief, year-long marriage, Allart added part of her husband's name (Napoléon-Louis-Frédéric-Corneille de Méritens de Malvezie) to her own, forming Hortense Allart de Méritens, even though she broke completely with the man, asserting that she joyously threw his wedding ring out of the window of her carriage as she left his house forever.[102] Even when she did use a pseudonym with the publication of her autobiography in 1872—Madame P[rudence] de Saman [l'Esbatx]—the name was female. It was a contrivance, however, that employed additional names of her husband—Saman et l'Esbatx— and the first name of Prudence seems to have been chosen deliberately and playfully to correspond with the title of the autobiography, *Les Enchantements de Prudence*.[103] Allart's self-representation is quite the opposite of "prudent," with her literary ambition, love affairs, and illegitimate children. Yet Allart also maintains that after she passed middle age her "enchantments" consisted of study, reflection, and writing— which might indeed be considered "prudent" for a mature woman.

Allart seems to have been more brazen than her peers in publicizing herself steadfastly as a female and in appropriating her husband's names after she left him. Perhaps the additions and the pseudonym represent Allart's effort to assume aristocratic status with the noble particle *de*. Perhaps by assuming her husband's names after she left him Allart was taunting the authority he exercised so tyrannically over her while they lived together. It is possible, too, that Allart anticipated the furor that her autobiography would in fact cause because of the frank revelations of her many love affairs with prominent men, and for that reason chose to hide the name—Allart—that her two sons bore.[104] In any case, Allart's name changes do not seem to be fundamental denials of her feminine or authorial identity. Even the pseudonym came very late in Allart's life—when she was seventy-one years old—and effected a new lease on her authorial life, as many of her previously published works were reissued under the titles of *Les Nouveaux Enchantements* and *Derniers Enchantements* by Madame de Saman before her death in 1879.

Girardin's use of names and pseudonyms represents yet another trajectory of a woman writer negotiating the intricate path of publishing and literary culture. Girardin, of course, was a "child" poet, publishing her first works under her name of Delphine Gay when she was still in her teens. Poetry was considered a suitable, feminine genre, so the girl and her mother probably felt no need to publish under another name.[105] Moreover, Sophie Gay and her sister-in-law Marie Françoise Gay had already established the Gay surname in connection with their fictions, dramas, and translations, and, still more important, the phenomenon of a "girl" poet, and later *la muse patriotique*, undoubtedly helped book sales. Thus, for the first part of Delphine Gay's literary career, the use of her given, feminine name was probably a great advantage. In 1836, however, when she started her innovative news and gossip column in her husband's newspaper, *La Presse,* Delphine Gay de Girardin signed her articles vicomte de Launay. The use of aristocratic names was common in newspaper writing, and Girardin was competing with men in the decidedly masculine culture of the popular press.[106] This journalistic venture was a great risk, and a significant departure from the poetry on which Girardin's literary reputation was based. And now she was a married woman—married, indeed, to the owner and editor of the newspaper for which she was writing. There were thus a number of good reasons for Girardin to adopt a male pseudonym for her column, *Courrier de Paris.*

Girardin played with her identity as vicomte de Launay; she was the man-about-town, strolling the streets of Paris; attending performances, art openings, and balls; charting the social seasons and the latest fashions; reviewing books and commenting on politics. From the start Girardin's tone and approach in the *Courrier* were playful, witty, and satirical. This included satirizing herself, an interesting process, since she had two identities—the male, aristocratic vicomte and the female, middle-class Madame de Girardin. Girardin also wrote a few novels and stories, and she wrote several plays that she signed with her married name, Madame Emile de Girardin. Thus, she had a separate name for almost each genre in which she wrote.

None of the pseudonyms fooled anyone for very long; within a matter of weeks, at the most, after the first publication, critics and other literary folk apparently learned who was the female author behind the unknown male name. Still, women writers enjoyed the short-lived deception. Sand, for example, was amused that a review of *Indiana* asserted that a woman must have occasionally guided the pen of the male author G. Sand.[107] The pseudonyms did, however, serve their purpose of allowing the authors to experiment with new identities, and even to play with their multiple identities and to play with readers' prejudices about women writers. Indeed, women writers constantly combated the stereotype of themselves as bluestockings—simultaneously adulterous and sexless, studious and unlearned, and neither masculine nor feminine. The adoption of a pseudonym was only the beginning of a long process of individual identity assertion and a broader challenge to the belief in female intellectual incapacity, and female inferiority generally.

4   ▶ Cassandra, Diotima, Aspasia, and Cleopatra

Challenging the Bluestocking Stereotype in Literary Culture

In 1842 the satirical newspaper *Le Charivari* published a caricature of George Sand that represents her dressed in men's clothes and standing in a cloud of smoke, apparently generated by the cigar she holds in her left hand. Beneath her right elbow and her right hand, which holds a quill pen, are the titles of some of her novels, but also political statements that Sand never made—calling for a chamber of female deputies and a chamber of mothers. A few lines of verse at the bottom of the illustration read, "If the Georges [*sic*] Sand of this portrait leaves you a little perplexed, it is because genius is abstract, and is, as we know, unsexed." (See Fig. 5.) While this caption might refer to Sand's cross-dressing as "perplexing" and as suggesting an ambiguous sexuality, it also seems to deride Sand's literary accomplishments through association with "extreme" feminist political stances. Sand's feminine body very clearly defies the attempt at masculinization through cross-dressing; the vest stretches tight across her breasts and the trousers strain at her crotch from the breadth of her hips. So the quip about genius and sex seems to focus more on questioning Sand's genius than her sex.

In contrast to Sand's willfully feminine body defying her male dress (and perhaps also her feminine sex betraying her pretense to male genius), another caricature printed two years later suggests that writing defeminizes women. Honoré Daumier did an entire series of caricatures on intellectual women, entitled *Les Bas-bleus* (the bluestockings) and in one image, an extremely thin, even scrawny bluestocking dressed in her underclothes preens before a mirror. "It's strange how this mirror flattens my figure and slims my chest," she says to herself. "But what do I care?

Mme de Staël and Mr. de Buffon have declared that genius has no sex."
(See Fig. 6.) Here the figure's silly pretension suggests that her talent as an
intellectual is highly doubtful, but equally questionable is her femininity,
for she is portrayed as notoriously lacking in even the most basic of feminine attributes—breasts and hips, to say nothing of beauty or even attractiveness. In both the particularized portrayal of Sand and the generic representation of the intellectual woman, the combination of being a woman
and a writer (or an intellect) is portrayed as puzzling, ridiculous, improb-
able, or impossible. Both caricaturists deride the axiom "Genius has no
sex" by suggesting that females who cultivate their minds or contribute to
literary and intellectual production are fated to sexual ambiguity, extreme delusions, and, in most cases, dismal failure. The anxieties about
women writers that these two images typify arose precisely because so
many women were, indeed, writing and getting their works published.

During the July Monarchy publishing flourished in France. Tech-
nological innovations in printing and print reproduction, cheap newspapers with paid advertising, reading rooms and subscription libraries,
and a growing reading public contributed to a flood of newspapers, pe-
riodicals, and books.[1] Both female and male authors benefited from this
boom, and at least one scholar views the 1830s as a golden age for
women writers, since so many saw their works in print.[2] But along with
the opportunities came fierce competition, and, notably in the 1840s,
men were wont to scapegoat women, attributing a decline in literary
quality and increase in literary commercialization to the contributions
of female authors.[3] The figure of the bluestocking became the pejorative
for any and all women who aspired to intellectual ability and pursuits.

In both texts and images the bluestocking embodied a collection of
stereotypes, often mutually contradictory, of women writers. The bluestocking connoted an intellectual woman generally, but increasingly it
satirized the woman author or would-be author. In both verbal and
visual caricatures the bluestocking is almost always ugly; lacking in
feminine attributes such as breasts and hips; sexually promiscuous; ne-
glectful of household, uxorial, and child-rearing responsibilities; and
ridiculously proud of her presumed artistic genius. The bluestocking
often smokes little cigars, and she dominates her husband. The caricatures suggest that women writers are bourgeois and that they have
violated bourgeois ideals of femininity: beauty; submissiveness; devotion to husband, home, and children; and the cultivation only of social
graces rather than of the intellect or of professional skills.[4]

For example, another caricature by Daumier in the bluestocking series shows a pregnant woman smoking a cigar and speaking to her husband while he dries a dish. In the text below the woman says, "Tell me, husband, I have a good mind to call my play *Arthur* and to entitle my son Oscar . . . but no, on second thought, I will decide nothing until I have consulted with my collaborator." (See Fig. 7.) Is the woman writer's literary collaborator also the father of the unborn child? So Daumier implies. All the stereotypes of woman writers are manifested in this caricature—an ugly, adulterous woman smokes a cigar and thinks about literature, while her henpecked and cuckolded husband submissively does the housework. From Daumier's perspective women writers cause complete disorder in the household; indeed, they are disorder itself. So unnatural are women writers that they even lose their maternal instinct, as Daumier suggests in another image from the same series, in which a woman writing at her desk (with a wastepaper basket filled with her discarded literary attempts) shouts angrily at her bewildered husband, who is holding a baby: "Take that thing away; it is impossible to work in the midst of such an uproar. Go take a walk and when you come back buy some new baby bottles in the passage Choiseul! Ah, Mr. Cabassol, it's your first child, but I swear to you it will be your last."[5] (See Fig. 8.) These highly disagreeable female characters appear to have no talent whatsoever as authors, and worse, they have no feminine qualities beyond the capacity to bear children.

Throughout their literary careers Sand, d'Agoult, Allart, and Girardin encountered various forms of prejudice against women writers, and they dealt with it in different ways, both publicly and privately. To be sure not all men succumbed to the bluestocking myth, or at least many of them separated out individual women writers from the mass of "bluestockings." Individual literary men helped each of the four female authors in the same ways that they helped other men—by being loyal friends and supporters, offering constructive criticism, providing recommendations to publishers, procuring part-time employment, writing favorable book reviews, and actually publishing manuscripts. Yet these four women writers could hardly forget the public disapprobation they incurred by being women and by writing, and many of their works reveal efforts to combat the stereotype of the bluestocking and to construct an individual and personal identity—and thereby a more positive image of women writers in their diversity and individuality.

Si de Georges Sand ce portrait
Laisse l'esprit un peu perplexe,
C'est que le génie est abstrait,
Et comme on sait n'a pas de sexe.

FIG. 5. A. Lorentz, *Miroir drolatique* (1842). From *Le Charivari*, 5 August 1842. Washington, D.C., Library of Congress Rare Books. Photo Library of Congress.

C'est singulier comme ce miroir m'applatit la taille et me maigrit la poitrine! Que m'importe?... Mme de Staël et Mr de Buffon l'ont proclamé... **le génie n'a point de sexe**.

FIG. 6. Honoré Daumier, *C'est singulier comme ce miroir m'aplatit la taille . . .* (1844). From *Le Charivari*, 30 January 1844. Washington, D.C., Library of Congress Rare Books. Photo Library of Congress.

Dis donc... mon mari... j'ai bien envie d'appeler mon drame **Arthur** et d'intituler mon enfant **Oscar**!.. mais non.. toute réflexion faite, je ne déciderai rien avant d'avoir consulté mon collaborateur !....

FIG. 7. Honoré Daumier, *Dis donc ... mon mari ...* (1844). From *Le Charivari*, 1 February 1844. Washington, D.C., Library of Congress Rare Books. Photo Library of Congress.

FIG. 8. Honoré Daumier, *Emportez donc ça plus loin . . .* (1844). From *Le Charivari*, 2 March 1844. Washington, D.C., Library of Congress Rare Books. Photo Library of Congress.

This chapter analyzes the four authors' accounts of male prejudice against women writers, along with their responses. It argues that these women writers consciously engaged with the bluestocking stereotype and attempted to undermine it. In addition to creating themselves against male stereotypes, these four women writers also created themselves in contrast to one another. The network of relations between Sand, d'Agoult, Allart, and Girardin was a significant component of literary culture under the July Monarchy, whether those relations were cordial or mistrustful. In addition to providing delectable grist for the gossip mill, this network also established the boundaries and differences between the four artists. Often in private and occasionally in public women writers appropriated the classical learning that bonded literary men with a shared cultural heritage, to ascribe to themselves names like Clio, amazon, Aspasia, Sappho, Diotima, Cassandra, and Cleopatra—all female figures from ancient history and literature. They countered the ludicrous and denigrating bluestocking image with precursors and models from classical culture who were intelligent, erotic, and powerful women—indeed, who were teachers of men. Literary culture, in its various exclusions of women and notably in the form of the bluestocking, contributed to the feminism of these four authors. Conversely, these four authors created alternative conceptions of women writers as individuals to be reviewed and criticized on their own artistic or scholarly merits rather than as members of a (marginalized) subgroup. Often accused of antifeminism precisely because of their individualism and lack of solidarity with other, socialist feminists, these women writers nonetheless promoted a feminist project of claiming women's right to and ability for intellectual endeavor.[6] Some facts of their literary production and personal circumstances provide a necessary foundation for the analysis of these women writers' place in and contributions to literary culture.

Writing Careers under the July Monarchy

With the publication of *Indiana* in 1832, George Sand became a famous author. Apprehensive and hopeful about her first novel written without a collaborator, she indicates in her correspondence that she aspired to only as much success as was necessary for her to make a living. But the success of *Indiana* was immediate and overwhelming. Just a month after publication Sand was receiving letters and visits to her Paris apartment from all manner of persons seeking to pay homage, obtain patronage, or beg for handouts.[7] Sand followed up this triumph by publishing *Valentine* later that year, another story about the tyranny of men and of society over women through the institution of marriage. *Lélia*, published in 1833, brought Sand more renown as well as controversy. In this novel the sisters Lélia and Pulchérie represent opposite sides of female character—the first is austere and virginal, seeking spiritual certainty and a better society; the second is all sensuality, committed to a life of pleasure and sexual freedom. Neither conforms to a middle-class ideal of domestic femininity, and some critics accused Sand of advocating free love and immorality.[8]

Nonetheless, from this point on Sand was an established author. Until her break with the editor Buloz in 1841–42 over the leftist opposition politics of her novel *Horace*, Sand regularly published her fiction in the prestigious *Revue des deux mondes*. But even after this disagreement Sand never lacked for publishers, and she was among the better-paid writers of her day. Her output was astonishing, comprising some eighty novels; numerous plays, short stories, and essays; various autobiographical works; and a huge correspondence that in its recently published form fills twenty-five volumes. Sand's fiction was diverse in its content and form, but always idealistic—that is, upholding ideals of love, faith, gender equality, and social justice. She became a patron of worker poets in the 1840s, advising aspiring writers from the working class on their writing and helping them get their works published. This coincided with her commitment to socialism and republicanism that also manifested itself in the content and characters of her stories, and in her involvement with the founding of a journal and of a newspaper supportive of the working class. Sand's stature in the world of French letters during her lifetime was widely acknowledged. Her fiction was frequently collected and reprinted, and critics seriously reviewed her work. But even before Sand took French literary culture by storm in 1832, she acknowledged the precedence of both Girardin and Allart as published female authors.[9]

Girardin's fame as a poet in the 1820s, though anchored in legitimist salons and literary circles, spread beyond to a wider public. D'Agoult frequented some of the same salons, and it was there that she met Girardin for the first time. Sand mentioned her with awe, as a literary great, in a letter she wrote shortly after her arrival in Paris in 1831. With the marriage to Emile, Girardin distanced herself from the Paris literary scene for a while, spending portions of the year at their country estate but continuing to write poems and stories. Balzac encouraged Girardin to develop her fiction-writing and to produce a major novel, but although her stories were successful Girardin chose a different genre for her next literary incarnation. In 1836 Girardin made a comeback in a new guise. Instead of the girl-poet, she became the vicomte de Launay, aristocratic man-about-town who reported on high society, literature, theater, fashion, politics, and urban customs in a column entitled *Courrier de Paris* printed approximately every two weeks in Emile de Girardin's *La Presse*. According to her intimate friend Théophile Gautier, Girardin was the originator of the society and urban news column. For the next twelve years, with occasional lapses, Girardin produced her *Courrier de Paris*. Simultaneously, she hosted a brilliant salon, the gathering place for the major (mostly male) figures in literature and politics of the time. But Girardin broached yet another literary genre in this, her prime of life. As early as 1839 Girardin rendered her experience of journalism and her views of male journalists into dramatic form in the play *L'Ecole des journalistes*, which was simultaneously satire, comedy, and tragedy. Although this first play was never performed publicly in Girardin's lifetime, her subsequent plays were indeed staged, usually with success. Her first tragedy, *Judith* (1840), failed, but the next was better received, and the comedies were highly successful, especially *Lady Tartuffe* (1853). Although it is impossible to know precisely how large a readership existed for any single author in Paris during the July Monarchy, it is reasonable to assert that Girardin and Sand were the most widely read female authors of the time.[10]

Hortense Allart gained her first literary recognition in the same year as Girardin—1822—but the trajectories of their careers diverged. Allart's first publications were a historical novel and a literary critique of Madame de Staël, and by the time Sand wrote her first novel Allart had also published three works of fiction. Allart's works were reviewed positively, but the reviews were small, anonymous, and not often seen in the prestigious journals. No less an authority than Chateaubriand encouraged her writing at this time, but, according to Allart, he suggested that she focus on nonfiction rather than fiction. By and large, Allart followed this advice. Although she did write a few more novels and stories, she wrote several essays, and her major works were two histories, one of the Florentine Republic and the other of the Athenian Republic. Her final works were autobiographical and also served as vehicles to reissue her earlier fiction. Allart viewed herself as a researcher as well as a writer, as a student of literature, politics, and history. Although her early book on Madame de Staël was her only published work of literary criticism, Allart contributed to literary analysis through her correspondence with Sainte-Beuve, who frequently lifted ideas and entire passages from Allart's letters for his own reviews and essays—without attribution. In terms of income from writing and literary renown, Allart was probably the least successful of the four women writers, but her accomplishments should not be depreciated on the basis of the august company around her.[11]

Marie d'Agoult joined the ranks of women writers relatively late, in 1841. To be sure she had already published works under Liszt's name or anonymously, but she came into her own as Daniel Stern after considerable preparation and encouragement from Sand, Girardin, and Allart. D'Agoult started her literary career as a critic of music, literature, and art, although later on nonfiction would be her genre of choice and her source of greatest satisfaction. She wrote one novel and a few stories, but she prided herself on her rationalist bent and considered her works of history and political philosophy to be her greatest achievements. In 1847 she published *Essai sur la liberté* and in 1849 the *Esquisses morales*, both of which outlined d'Agoult's ideas on political freedom and improvements in women's condition. In 1848 she published a series entitled *Lettres républicaines*, a counter to Sand's more populist reports on the Revolution of 1848 and the early Second Republic. *L'Histoire de la Révolution de 1848*, published in three volumes between 1850 and 1853, rated high acclaim and consolidated d'Agoult's reputation as a serious and accomplished writer. It is probably no coincidence that d'Agoult's main writings were in the genres of nonfiction, the same as Allart, and in contrast to the genres of fiction, poetry, journalism, and drama in which Sand and Girardin excelled. D'Agoult's personal skills and proclivities prompted this choice, and she also faced less formidable competition in those areas.[12]

These brief and incomplete lists of literary output by the four authors imply considerable talent, determination, hard work, and luck on the part of these women. Each was successful in terms of getting her work published and earning a living as a professional writer at a time when unknown numbers of women and men who aspired to the literary profession never got their manuscripts published or were unable to sustain lifelong careers in letters.[13] Additionally, Sand, d'Agoult, Girardin, and Allart contributed to literary culture by means other than writing. Girardin and d'Agoult were renowned *salonnières*, hosting gatherings in their homes that included both leading literary lights and ambitious young hopefuls—almost all male. Works of literature were read, discussed, occasionally even produced in these salons, and the salons were also one of several means by which women like Girardin and d'Agoult tried to promote their favorite authors to election to the prestigious Academy. Sand and Allart did not hold salons on the same scale or with the same regularity as did d'Agoult and Girardin, but they did socialize with many of the same persons. Moreover, Sand maintained an extensive correspondence with publishers, critics, and fellow authors through which she shared ideas, counseled young aspirants, and used her influence to get the works of others published. Allart's epistolary network, though probably less extensive than Sand's, was nevertheless important. One of her most regular correspondents, the critic Charles-Augustin Sainte-Beuve, greatly valued her insights into literature, history, and the notable persons she had known. Although book reviewing flourished in nineteenth-century French publishing, reviews by women were relatively rare, and especially reviews by women of books written by women. Still, Girardin was occasionally a book reviewer in her column, *Courrier de Paris*, and d'Agoult managed to review one of Sand's books for *La Presse*, though anonymously; she also published extensively on contemporary German literature. Yet another way that women writers participated in literary culture was through journal editing. Sand cofounded and edited *La Revue indépendante* with Pierre Leroux and Louis Viardot for a number of years, but an earlier scheme she had concocted with Allart for establishing a literary journal was never realized. In a variety of ways, then, Sand, d'Agoult, Girardin, and Allart created a place for themselves in a literary culture that frequently tried to exclude them.[14]

Overcoming Sexism and the Bluestocking Stereotype

George Sand tells a story in her autobiography about an encounter with a male author, the comte Auguste-Hilarion de Kératry, from whom Sand, as an aspiring writer in 1831, sought advice. According to the autobiography, Kératry was highly prejudiced against women writers and counseled Sand to give up her artistic aspirations: "'Take my word

for it,' he said gravely, . . . 'don't make books, make babies!'" Sand
claims that she found this hugely amusing, and that she replied,
"'Honestly, sir, . . . take your own advice, if you think it so good.'"
Sand makes light of this incident, implying that it in no way discouraged or angered her; indeed, she pokes fun at Kératry for his pomposity and his erroneous judgment of her potential as a writer. But the
name Kératry became a code for literary sexism, as in the assertion that
Balzac criticized Sand as an equal and could not be accused of "holding
the Kératry theory that women are inferior." Or when Sand indicates
that reviewers of *Indiana* assumed that G. Sand must be a man because
"the style and judgments were too virile not to be those of a man. They
were all a little 'Kératry.'"[15] Although Sand studiously avoided presenting herself as pitiable victim or vengeful harpy, the story and repetition of the name Kératry were clearly intended to show that Sand had
proved him wrong. Sand's success as a writer proved not that she was
exceptional but that those who believed women to be inferior to men
were mistaken.

Girardin, d'Agoult, and Allart also encountered the barrier of
prejudice to their becoming writers, but they were less public and direct
about the issue, at least as it involved them personally. Girardin left no
personal account of overcoming sexism at the outset of her career, but,
as we have seen, a third-hand report asserts that her mother counseled
her to be "a woman in [her] role and a man in [her] grammar" in order
to avoid being labeled a bluestocking.[16] Certainly Girardin played up
her femininity as a girl-poet, but several of the poems she wrote as an
unmarried and then as a newly married woman ponder the incompatibility of female authorship and romantic love, suggesting that she
might have internalized the stereotype of the unlovable because unfeminine bluestocking. Later in her life, when she tried her hand at
journalism and drama, both decidedly masculine genres, Girardin was
more explicit about challenging the belief of female intellectual and
creative inferiority.

D'Agoult acknowledges the prevalence of this belief in her autobiography when she claims that she was able to study and to cultivate her
mind while she was in Switzerland because noted intellectual women
had preceded her there and set an example of female intelligence: "In
view of Coppet, in the homeland of Madame de Staël and of Madame
Necker de Saussure, no one was surprised that a woman would wish to
understand the laws that governed her own mind." D'Agoult found

this receptivity to women's intellectual pursuits much in contrast to the low opinion of female rationality she claims to have encountered in France. In Switzerland, she maintains, "no one denied to the feminine sex, as they did at home, the ability and consequently the right and the duty to seek to understand the reason of things."[17] Like Sand, d'Agoult challenges the belief that women are intellectually inferior to men and that women who study are ridiculous. She invokes the examples of de Staël, Necker de Saussure, and herself as proof that women can be intellectually brilliant and indisputably feminine, and she relativizes the French denigration of studious women with the counterexample of Swiss egalitarianism.

Allart, who grew up with female writers and accomplished *salonnières*, makes no mention of any social or individual bias against women's ability to think, study, or write in her published autobiography. However, in private correspondence Allart occasionally showed herself vulnerable to accusations of bluestocking tendencies, for she once asked Sainte-Beuve in a letter: "Do you find me too pedantic?"[18] More frequently, but only to a female correspondent, she vented her frustration at a literary culture that excluded women from a host of perquisites and honors bestowed on men, a sentiment that d'Agoult apparently shared. Writing to d'Agoult in 1851 Allart notes: "You yourself said that men have everything for themselves—the academies, the newspapers; they praise and promote one another; and we [women] don't even have the vote!" A few years later, while praising d'Agoult's writing in the reissue of her book *Essai sur la liberté* in 1853, Allart asserts that in general women write better than men precisely because they are excluded from professorships and other positions that demand regular production of books. Women, according to Allart, are freer than men to write naturally and with inspiration. And again, several years later, Allart refers to a conversation that she and d'Agoult had in 1845 regarding the many benefits enjoyed by men when she states that she has just read Renan's *Vie de Jésus*. She then launches into a severe critique of his writing that she attributes to his privileged position as a man of letters: "This ambush [*ce guet-apens*], this chatter of a professor who is common, vulgar, pretentious, ignorant, pedantic. Do you remember that we said at Herblay that the advantage of women [of letters] is that they were neither doctors nor professors like this big Renan, this big Littré."[19] In these passages Allart tries to make the best of the female condition by protesting that women's exclusion from academic positions actually improves their writing. But clearly she also finds this discrimination irksome and unjust, and her purpose as a writer was, among other things, to combat sexism and improve the condition of women.

Sand adopted a variety of strategies for deflecting the label of bluestocking, including numerous disclaimers about her ambition and her "pretension" as a woman to embark on a literary career. She asserts in her autobiography that she wrote *Indiana* "without a purpose, without a hope, and without any outline, resolutely putting out of my mind all that had been proposed to me as precept or example." She maintains, with hindsight, that she writes by instinct, but that her instinct adheres to a theory of constructing ideal passions in realistic settings and through realistic characters. "In sum, the idealization of a sentiment yields the subject, leaving to the art of the storyteller the care of placing that subject within a situation and realistic framework that is drawn sensitively enough to make the subject stand out." Sand downplays her ambition and her artistic pretensions by asserting that she wrote *Indiana* out of pure emotion, that the novel was a work of feminine instinct. Yet she wishes to be taken seriously as an artist, and she expounds her theory of fiction as something that her instinct unconsciously "gave rise to."[20]

In these assertions that she was not ambitious, that she did not begin writing with preconceived theories, Sand was implicitly challenging the bluestocking stereotype. Her fear of the bluestocking label was even more evident at the beginning of her writing career, when, for example, while waiting for the publication of *Indiana*, she wrote to a friend in 1832, "Never call me a woman author [*une femme auteur*]!" And in 1834 Sand wrote in another letter, "I know that I am tainted with the label of woman of letters [*femme de lettres*]."[21] One of Sand's strategies to avoid the appellations of woman author or woman of letters was to describe herself as an artist, to emphasize the creative rather than rational components of fiction-writing. Many of Sand's novels and stories are about artists, both men and women. These characters are never writers but rather stage and opera performers, singers, musicians, painters, and mosaicists. Sand was deeply concerned with art, and these stories reveal much about the creative process, about what, in theory, constitutes art, and about the complicated relationship between art and human existence. In her fiction dealing with art and artists, both men and women confront conflicts between commitment to art and to persons. However, contrary to the bluestocking stereotype, Sand's fictional fe-

male artists put love and family relations above art when human welfare is at stake. For example, the two eponymous heroines in *Lucrezia
Floriani* (1846) and in *Consuelo* (1842–43; 1844) give up the stage where
they have triumphed as supreme artists and turn instead to tending en-
feebled or messianic lovers, aging relatives, and young children.[22]

While Sand tried to extricate herself from the taint of the term "woman of letters," she did tar other women with the bluestocking brush, including Hortense Allart. When the two first met in December 1832 Allart
had been a published author for ten years, and Sand had just become one
five months earlier. Despite Allart's generosity in passing along to Sand a
letter in praise of Sand's novels from Chateaubriand, Sand wrote dispar-
agingly of Allart in a letter to a friend, asserting that Allart conformed to
many of the bluestocking stereotypes: "I also see Mme. Allart, a woman
of letters who has an inflated style and who has written books that are
high-minded but boring and poorly constructed. She is not worth her
books; she is as pedantic as a schoolmaster—peremptory, political, man-
like—a devil of a woman author. She pretends to admire me, I think in
order not to appear to be jealous, which would be in bad taste. . . . I do not
like her at all."[23] Although Sand's first and second novels were highly
successful, she was at this time, relative to Allart, a novice. What better
way to dismiss a senior rival than to assert that she was a mere bluestocking? Moreover, though fundamentally generous and a sincere admirer of Sand's work, Allart might have reinforced Sand's accusations of
pedantry and pretension when three months later she presumed to in-
struct Sand on how better to serve in her novels the cause of social reform
and the improvement of women's condition. Sand replied humbly
enough, acknowledging the merits of some of Allart's criticism of her fiction and requesting Allart's continued patronage. But Sand's exaggerated
representations of her own inferiority to Allart ("You are much above me
in all regards, notably for productivity, reason, intelligence, and knowledge. I have only feelings [*des sensations*], no will at all"), her repetition of
feminine stereotypes applied to herself—"I am excessively woman by ignorance, insignificant ideas, and total lack of logic"—raise the possibility
that she might be invoking these stereotypes at Allart's expense.[24] Sand
reinforced prejudices against women writers in this early, private exchange regarding Allart, but not long thereafter Sand's private and public
pronouncements on Allart manifested feelings of friendship, affection,
and admiration and represented her as an individual rather than a type.

Sand's buying into the bluestocking stereotype for anyone but herself was not entirely unredeemed. For one thing, despite her stunning success Sand was constantly accused of bluestocking behavior—disrespect for marriage, immorality, failure as a mother. She learned to slough off such criticism, avoided reading it as much as possible, and in one case even comforted a repentant critic (who later wound up in an insane asylum). Second, Sand occasionally used her stature and influence to help other women writers. She was inundated with manuscripts from unpublished authors, male and female, seeking her patronage. Given the varied quality of work she received, it is not surprising that she acknowledged to her publisher, François Buloz, "On the pavements of Paris there are fifty bluestockings who get published and who in no way are worth it." But this comment accompanied Sand's recommendation that Buloz publish a manuscript by a Madame Jal, an unknown and unpublished female author whom she had chosen to help. In this case, then, Sand used the stereotype to support her cause of getting an individual woman writer's work published.[25]

Most, though certainly not all, of Sand's bluestocking references occurred in private correspondence rather than public texts. Girardin, on the other hand, addressed the subject of women writers in several published works.[26] Notably in the *Courrier de Paris* she engaged her reader in jokes and games, playing upon and simultaneously undercutting the popular stereotypes and prejudices regarding intellectual women. In several instances Girardin used her dual identities—as the male, aristocratic vicomte de Launay and "author" of the *Courrier de Paris*, and as the female, middle-class Madame de Girardin, poet, *salonnière*, and, as everyone knew, the real journalist behind Launay—to confound assumptions about women writers. In an entry of 1837 Girardin wrote in the usual amusing fashion about how common it was for elegant young society women to purchase all manner of luxurious furnishings, including designer bookcases, and then not to buy books. Instead, the author claims that women waited for months to borrow a popular book from the public reading room, when they could easily have afforded to buy for themselves any book they wanted. It is a charming tale of feminine frivolity in which bibelots replace books on the shelves, but Girardin appears to switch sides at the end of this piece. Having lamented the hard times literature is experiencing and the lack of reading on the part of leisured young ladies, the author ends by suggesting that the few women who do read are guilty also of something worse—writing. "Young women no longer read, but what is worse, alas, is that those exceptional ones who still do read a little [also] WRITE!!"[27] Girardin is saying the same thing that caricaturists and critics said or implied—that reading was bad for women because it inspired them to write, and that writing was inappropriate for ladies. Yet who is the real butt of the joke, since the reader knows that the author is, in fact, a woman who is extremely successful as a writer and whose work the reader is presumably enjoying?

Girardin plays other games with the reader regarding her literary aspirations and abilities. The next entry of *Courrier de Paris* was two months in coming, a long delay for the normally biweekly columns. The author begins with an explanation: "Launay" had been inspired by a fellow journalist with *La Presse*, Théophile Gautier, to work on some serious poetry, so "he" had taken a holiday from journalism to become a poet. "Launay" writes that if Gautier, a journalist, could become a poet, then "he" could, too. "All the columnists of *La Presse* are poets, Dumas, Méry, Théophile Gautier; we must absolutely write verse also."[28] Of course, unlike the other male journalists, Girardin had in fact started out as a poet. Girardin was again playing on her readers' knowledge of her pseudonymous and her actual identities, amusing them with her humble suggestion that, like the other male writers, "Launay" aspired to loftier literary heights than journalism; in fact, Girardin was already famous as the poet Delphine Gay.

Girardin sometimes played the joke on herself rather than on the reader. For example, shortly afterward, she explicitly abandoned lighthearted banter to offer some serious literary criticism and political commentary, and then excused herself to the reader, claiming that she really was not qualified for such analyses.[29] Was she disqualifying herself as the dilettantish male aristocrat, or as the woman writer behind the pseudonym? In any case her caveats did not prevent her from engaging in the critical analysis she desired; Girardin created the style and tone of her column from the beginning, and she asserted her independence to alter them at will.

Throughout her writing of the *Courrier de Paris* (which lasted, with some interruptions, from 1836 to 1848), Girardin periodically referred to bluestockings in the same manner as did the caricaturists and the satirists, describing them as badly dressed, unfeminine, and pretentious. But she also undercut these stereotypes of women writers, or placed them in a feminist context. In one instance Girardin trivialized the concerns of bluestockings, but she did so by juxtaposing them with the serious problems women generally confronted because of unjust and inequitable laws of marriage and gender relations. Claiming that her self-appointed job was to describe all of the inanities of the day and make jokes out of them, in 1841 she offered this example of ridiculous behavior:

When we see strict legislators occupying themselves energetically with the sorrow that some bluestockings of genius might feel when their recalcitrant husbands wish to prevent them from writing and publishing their works, instead of worrying about the condition of so many poor mothers who, thanks to our tyrannical laws, cannot even save their dowry, the fruits of their labor, or the bread of their children from the hands of a cheating, gambling, or unfaithful husband, we permit ourselves to say: this is a laughable caprice. And, to be sure, we have the right to say so.[30]

Is Girardin mocking bluestockings, or poor women in general? Or is she mocking herself and her column? She says she is merely recording contemporary history, typical practices. But this is by no means the only occasion when a feminist pronouncement is offered, or when a feminist interpretation is possible.

The issue of women writers and women's rights appears again in the *Courrier de Paris* for 23 March 1844, which opens with the question of why a French Academy for women should not be established to accompany or complement the Academy for men.[31] Girardin satirically argues against an Academy for women because it would be contrary to French customs, which discriminate against women in a variety of ways: "Why should women have a[n academic] chair in a country in which they cannot have a throne? Why do you want to grant them the pen, when you have refused them the scepter? Why, when they are nothing by their birth, should women be something by their genius? Why accord them a privilege when they are denied all rights?" She goes on to say that a female Academy would impede the progress women have made in dealing with their degraded social and legal status. That is, according to Girardin, women publicly resign themselves to subordination, the better to prevail over men on the basis of their superior intelligence, and to prevent the constant "cold war" between the sexes from breaking out into overt hostilities. Girardin maintains that this tense situation exists because women are generally more intelligent than men, and men envy them for that reason: "French men envy French women, and they are right."[32] This is a theme that Girardin presented and developed on several occasions.

For example, Girardin once asserted that intelligent women writers will always be deeply resented by aspiring male writers:

Any woman of ideas who has authored by herself important works, vigorously written, intelligently crafted, whose name is an example, whose talent is a fortune, has for natural enemies all those Molières of little theaters, stubborn workers, with black mustaches, loud voices, nervous arms, enflamed eyes, fed on succulent dishes, watered by good wines, who self-importantly lock themselves up together by the half-dozen to write collectively a little vaudeville that is booed. In vain would this woman treat such men like brothers, in vain would she lower herself to smoke their cigars and drink punch from their glasses; these strong men will never forgive this weak woman for her superiority and her genius, because this superiority and this genius satirize their impotence and their misery.[33]

It is quite possible that Girardin is writing from experience, or from the experience of other successful woman writers, perhaps even that of her own mother.

Girardin asserts that although women in general are more intelligent than men, the exceptional and true man of ideas is always superior to the woman of ideas because he combines masculine (forceful) and feminine (discriminating) types of genius, whereas a woman of ideas has only feminine genius. Girardin then poses the question, that given this analysis, how does one excuse women who write tragedies, presumably because tragedy is a masculine genre: "We reply that if [women] write feminine tragedies, they are within their rights, that a woman, without ridiculous presumption, can well celebrate in a drama or in a poem the heroic action that another woman had the courage to accomplish." Girardin goes on to suggest that Cleopatra is an appropriate subject for a woman writer of tragedy. After this digression on tragedy and women writers, Girardin draws out her larger argument and concludes that bluestockings who claim the right to a female academy threaten to undermine the facade of resignation women have struggled for years to construct and under which they exercise their significant influence. She claims that women "have sweetly accepted the modest role imposed on them, to disguise their presumption to the important role they wish to play; they have hidden their actual superiority under a willful, exaggerated, insupportable futility. . . . Thus have French women succeeded at destroying the effects of Salic law. This result was glorious, but in the last few years, *bluestockings* have almost lost everything."[34]

What is interesting is that in the midst of so much froth Girardin takes the trouble to justify her own literary endeavors, for only a year earlier her first tragedy, *Judith* (1843), had been performed at the Théâtre-Français to generally poor reviews, and she was undoubtedly contemplating her next effort, another tragedy, *Cléopatre*, which would open in 1847. Critics were fairly harsh on Girardin in their reviews of *Judith*, suggesting both that she had overreached herself with this enterprise and that tragedy was simply not a genre that women could successfully work in. One anonymous reviewer asserted, "There are some endeavors in the arts of the imagination and of the mind that are forbidden [to women]. In spite of so much effort by feminine genius, there are virile works that remain virile works. ... Of all the works that the most intelligent women must leave to a man's brain, tragedy is, indubitably, the supreme work."[35] With the *Courrier de Paris*, Girardin was clearly responding to such criticism, defending and promoting herself to some extent at the expense of other, less prominent women writers—the bluestockings.

Finally, Girardin went far beyond reiterating and challenging the bluestocking characteristics when she created a counterstereotype for male writers. In October of 1839 Girardin submitted to the Théâtre-Français a play entitled *L'Ecole des journalistes* that was a biting satire on male journalists, portraying them as gourmands and heavy drinkers with no talent who worked together to bring down governments and destroy honest reputations willy-nilly and without compunction. The plot line is complicated, but the primary focus is the Guilbert family and their involvement with a newspaper entitled *La Vérité* ("the truth"). Monsieur Guilbert is a banker who has secretly put up the money for the newspaper—secretly because he wishes to avoid the impression that *La Vérité* is associated with his son-in-law, Dercourt, who is also the prime minister. Dercourt is married to Valentine, Guilbert's daughter. An old artist named Morin, who was famous under Napoleon but whose reputation has been destroyed by bad reviews in the newspapers, appeals to Valentine through the intercession of Edgar, Valentine's future brother-in-law. Valentine agrees to obtain a commission through her husband. At this point *La Vérité* prints a hugely damaging story about the Guilbert family, suggesting that Madame Guilbert was Dercourt's lover and that she had arranged the marriage of Dercourt to Valentine. Martel, the editor of *La Vérité* and the author of the story, publishes it at the behest of his domineering mistress because she felt insulted by Monsieur Guilbert's accusation that Martel was leading an immoral life. Madame Guilbert and her daughter Valentine Dercourt are reconciled when Madame Guilbert confesses that she did, indeed, once love Dercourt but that she happily gave him up when she saw that he really loved Valentine. In the meantime Dercourt's government falls, and the artist Morin commits suicide because he has now lost his commission and with it his last opportunity to restore his reputation. Morin's model and his attendant, the entire Guilbert family, and even the newspaper editor Martel collectively curse journalism for causing such needless political, personal, and financial damage. The play ends with Edgar, the future brother-in-law of Valentine, volunteering to take over *La Vérité* and clean up journalism.[36]

The first part of *L'Ecole des journalistes* is pure satire, portraying male journalists in all their glorious weakness and viciousness. With this opening of the play Girardin offered a counterstereotype to the bluestocking—the male journalist who eats and drinks luxuriously and to excess, who is lazy, stupid, and immoral, and who carelessly maligns decent and honest folk merely to meet a deadline and with the connivance of his unholy brotherhood. Girardin thus pillories the very group that frequently articulated and perpetuated the bluestocking myth—male newspaper editors and writers and all those associated with them. Nonetheless, Girardin views journalists as capable of redemption. She asserts in a preface to the play that she appeals to male journalists who basically have good characters but who do bad things in the context of a profession, an entire society, and a government that are corrupt, materialistic, and degraded.[37]

L'Ecole des journalistes, though accepted by the Théâtre-Français, was censored by the government, ostensibly because it resembled too closely living persons and actual, recent occurrences. Notably, Dercourt bears a striking resemblance to Adolphe Thiers, who was believed to have been the lover of Madame Dosne, who then arranged for him to marry her daughter. It is possible that this play was a form of revenge on the only other political salon that rivaled Girardin's at that time, the salon of Adolphe Thiers and his mother-in-law, Madame Dosne. However, *L'Ecole des journalistes* is also a social satire generally and an ultimately generous and kind counterattack to those who commonly maligned women writers. Although Girardin never had the satisfaction of seeing this play performed publicly, she did arrange a large private staging of it, and she published it in 1840 for an intrigued and curious public. Journalists responded with generally good grace, and the brouhaha died down after a few months.[38]

The responses of Sand and especially of Girardin to negative representations of women writers as bluestockings reflected the considerable power they exerted as successful female authors. They could easily distance themselves from "bluestockings," reiterating about other women writers the stereotypes of shabby, talentless, foolish failed authors. While this suggests a classist and unfeminist position toward women less fortunate than themselves, Sand and Girardin also represented an alternative model of the woman artist to the much maligned bluestocking, female author, or woman of letters. Key to this model was continued success, for the only way to combat the stereotypes was to write well and to earn critical acclaim and financial remuneration. Women writers had to succeed on men's terms. By being exceptional they held out the possibility for other exceptions. In other words, an exceptional woman who gracefully combines femininity with intelligence is more than an exception to the "rule" of the bluestocking; she proves that the "rule" itself is wrong.

Women Writers among Themselves

Combating prejudices and stereotypes about women and about women writers was an ongoing element in the lives of Sand, d'Agoult, Allart, and Girardin. Literary culture was clearly male-dominated in several regards: with the exception of a handful of women's newspapers, all publishing was controlled by male editors; academicians, professors, librarians, and recipients of literary awards were all men; an ethos of competitiveness and masculine honor prevailed; male writers often shared a common background of education and membership in professional and social associations; and men simply outnumbered women. But women's presence in and influence on literary culture were manifested in salons, in fictionalized characters by both male and female authors, in the daily exchange of gossip and patronage, and in the published texts and the persons of female authors themselves. Overlooked in almost all studies of French literary culture during this period are the networks of relationships linking women writers themselves.[39] These relationships could be supportive and amicable, or jealous and hostile, and often reflected a combination of feelings. But the existence of other women writers was essential to the self-creations of Sand, d'Agoult, Allart, and Girardin, whether conscious or not. Each author established and developed her authorial identity in full knowledge of and often in deliberate contrast to at least one of the other three. Other women writers were involved in this process, but not as closely or as consistently. Despite their many differences, these four women writers were uniquely united by class, personal experiences, family and social networks, and ideology, and they formed a subculture within the masculine literary culture, as well as within the "dominant" culture itself.

It is important to acknowledge in these relationships among women writers the overwhelming significance of George Sand. Published and private texts by Allart, d'Agoult, and Girardin reflect her dominating presence in the culture of the July Monarchy and in their personal lives as writers. In her private correspondence Allart refers to Sand as *la Reine*, the Queen, from a comment by Béranger of 1834 that Sand was "the Queen of our new literary generation," a female counterpart to "King" Chateaubriand.[40] When d'Agoult acknowledges the importance of Sand to her own personal development, she also mentions that in the mid-1830s Sand "exerted a mobilizing [*agitatrice*] power on the [general] imagination similar to that of monsieur de Lamennais." She goes on to describe the universal appeal of Sand's exotic, mysterious novels and the popular mythology that surrounded her: "People recounted thousands of byronic stories about this young woman."[41] And in the *Courrier de Paris*, Girardin placed Sand in an august (if quirky) pantheon of famous figures, calling her France's equivalent to great intellectual and social revolutionaries from England and Germany—Byron and Luther.[42] Despite the public satires of Sand's cross-dressing and the feminist implications of her fiction, her success and influence were significant in legitimizing the existence of women writers in general, in representing the possibility of the female artist and perhaps the female genius.[43] Inspiring as were Sand's engaging novels, her unconventional life, and her extraordinary stature as a writer, she was not imitated by Allart, d'Agoult, or Girardin. To the contrary, Sand was so inimitable that d'Agoult very consciously created herself as a writer in contrast to Sand, and even Allart and Girardin, who preceded Sand as successful authors, set themselves apart from such a dominant figure by writing in genres other than fiction and by cultivating an unambiguous femininity. Sand was a foil, as well as a model, to the three other authors, following her instant stardom in 1832. However, because of her early fame as a poet within elite society, Girardin was a focal point for relations among the four women writers until the 1830s.

Among the four authors, Allart and Girardin knew one another earliest, at least in their teens if not earlier, but were least associated as adults. Allart's mother, Marie Françoise, née Gay, was the sister of Girardin's father, Sigismond Gay. There is little evidence to indicate to what extent the two cousins spent time together as children, but a letter from Sophie Gay to a friend reveals that Hortense Allart was with the Gay family in September 1818 when Allart was seventeen and Girardin fourteen. As adults they seem to have avoided one another in the Parisian literary circles; indeed, one biographer of Allart suggests that Sophie Gay and Delphine Gay had shut their door to Allart because she was an unwed mother. The only reference to Girardin in Allart's letters is a dismissal of her as being in "the enemy camp." In a passage acknowledging their differing political allegiances, Allart writes to Sainte-Beuve: "But speak to me no more of Bertin [associated with the conservative Molé government], of Marie [d'Agoult], of that woman whom you call my cousin and who is no longer [Girardin]—all persons of the enemy camp whose tasteless gibes and flagrant attacks seek to dishonor the greatest and noblest hope of our time [Adolphe Thiers]." Not only does Allart accuse Girardin of being in "the enemy camp" in terms of politics, she also states that Girardin is no cousin to her, indicating a profound feeling of alienation from the other woman that would seem to go beyond political differences.[44]

When Allart gave birth to her first illegitimate child in 1826, Sophie and Delphine Gay were dependent upon the largesse of a royal court and a social circle that upheld a conventional moral code and devout Catholic piety.[45] Whether out of personal conviction, a sense of family honor, or opportunistic pragmatism, the Gay couple might well have felt it appropriate to disassociate themselves from Allart, who was now disgraced (at least in the eyes of moralists). At the same time that Sophie and Delphine may have cut their ties with Allart (probably with no harm to themselves), they astutely cultivated relations with Marie de Flavigny, a rising star in Saint-Germain society, with her beauty, fortune, intelligence, and talent for the piano. According to d'Agoult, the Gay women requested through an intermediary an invitation to her mother's salon, expressing their desire to hear d'Agoult play the piano and to be introduced to her. The invitation was extended, and in 1826 d'Agoult and Girardin met for the first time, under circumstances that d'Agoult recalled vividly.

Delphine Gay was at this time a notable figure in elite salons, and d'Agoult asserts that she was much excited at the prospect of meeting the famous female poet: "A poet appearing before me in the guise of a woman, a beautiful young woman, a charming poet who wished to make my acquaintance, who might even give me her friendship—it was enough to make me lose my composure and be unable to sleep at night." The day of Marie de Flavigny's piano performance arrived, and Delphine Gay appeared at the Flavigny house dressed in white, calm and serious in demeanor. D'Agoult played her piece with emotion and received enthusiastic applause. At this point Sophie Gay proclaimed in a loud voice, "Delphine has understood you." Delphine Gay, who must have been accustomed to her mother's bumptious behavior, simply approached Marie de Flavigny and clasped her hand.[46]

D'Agoult used this incident as a starting point for a protracted description and analysis of Girardin. She compliments her on her beauty, sincerity, and naturalness of manner at this time in her life, and she asserts that she, Girardin, and another, titled woman of their circle were known as the "three blondes" of Saint-Germain society. But d'Agoult maintains that after she married Emile de Girardin, Delphine de Girardin adopted the aggressive and indelicate manner of her mother, initiating and sustaining lively, even vehement, conversation in her salon while Emile—silent, withdrawn, and dignified—assumed Delphine's former role in relation to Sophie. Although acknowledging Girardin's literary career as poet, fiction writer, and journalist, d'Agoult offers no opinions on her writing and does not even mention Girardin's plays. D'Agoult's commentary is strictly focused on Girardin's character, which she says improved shortly before her death, when physical suffering brought back Girardin's original seriousness, calm, and natural, if more mature, beauty. D'Agoult manifests great respect for Girardin as a person, and later in the narrative she almost expresses gratitude to Girardin for inviting her to the Girardin salon and thereby reintegrating d'Agoult into Parisian society after her "exile" with Liszt. She also describes Girardin's transformation from "the poetic and reserved young girl" to the "biting," "inexhaustible" vicomte de Launay, "the bold and paradoxical journalist [feuilletoniste]."[47]

D'Agoult draws a connection between Girardin's mature personality and her chosen literary genre, journalism, and the result is by no means flattering, suggesting the reproduction of Sophie Gay's worst features—impulsiveness, loudness, lack of restraint, artifice, vehemence, even vindictiveness. By implication d'Agoult sets up an alternative set of characteristics for a woman of letters and a *salonnière* that, not surprisingly, she herself cultivated and valued and that pervade her memoirs—reserve, forethought, rationality, high-mindedness, naturalness, and moderation. Additionally, d'Agoult avoids entanglement with a delicate subject—her relationship with Girardin's husband. For at the same time that Girardin introduced d'Agoult to major literary and political figures in her salon, she also introduced her to Emile de Girardin, who was much enamored with d'Agoult in 1840–41 and who published d'Agoult's first articles at that time. If Girardin was concerned about this quite brief infatuation, she does not appear to have let on publicly, for she occasionally socialized with d'Agoult during this period, introduced d'Agoult to Victor Hugo (which thrilled d'Agoult), and said that d'Agoult had a "magnificent literary future."[48] Neither d'Agoult nor Girardin was above private expressions of jealousy, rivalry, or petty insult. But publicly they seem to have maintained cordial, if not intimate, relations. Moreover, d'Agoult's public description of Girardin (even though her memoirs were never published in her lifetime) is a means of drawing attention to their separate identities, and especially to d'Agoult's supposed superiority to Girardin.[49] With her stories about Girardin's development from reserved girl poet to rather aggressive journalist and indefatigable *salonnière*, d'Agoult also narrates her own evolution from society lady to lofty philosopher and elegant *salonnière*.

Although Girardin commented occasionally on literature in the *Courrier de Paris*, neither d'Agoult nor her works are mentioned, and the same goes for Allart. Of course, Girardin was highly selective in her literary commentary, and reviewing was far from a major focus of her column. Girardin is more forthcoming on literary women generally than about individual female authors, which is undoubtedly related to her position as a "male" journalist who disdains those prostitutes of the mind, so to speak. The only female author she addresses at any length is George Sand, and given that Girardin considered herself a reporter of the "talk of the day," that is not surprising. Girardin's public commentary attests to the significant presence of Sand in literary culture, and, of course, perpetuates it. It also suggests both Girardin's respect for her only real rival among women writers and her difference from Sand as an author and as an individual.

Girardin addresses Sand in the *Courrier de Paris* in 1837 in a manner that is at once satirical (almost slanderous) and admiring. She begins by noting that Sand's relationship with Félicité de Lamennais, the rebellious Catholic priest, has caused a stir, because, in her opinion, it prefigures another novel, one based on this latest friend. Girardin inventories several of Sand's previous novels to prove that in each novel Sand has created a male character who represents a particular social type and who reflects Sand's personal acquaintances: "The story of her affections is complete in the catalogue of her works." Girardin thus insinuates that Sand transposes her various male lovers and friends into central characters of her fiction, and that with Lamennais, a man of the cloth, Sand's novels and their characters have become more moral and religious. Girardin offers further proof of this interpretation by quoting at length a passage from Sand's *Lettres à Marcie*, a series of letters that appeared at this time in Lamennais's journal, *Le Monde*. Girardin presents this particular passage as Sand's effort to redirect a young girl with saint-simonienne tendencies (i.e., a penchant for free love, independence, and feminism) toward acceptance of the existing condition of women and spiritual resignation to a better life after death. Complimenting Sand on the beauty and morality of this passage, Girardin ends her provocative "review" with another compliment to Sand, and to herself: "To have the right to speak thus of George Sand, it is necessary to prove that one knows how to admire her."[50]

Sand, who was usually thick-skinned about reviews of her novels, was prickly about veiled allusions to her private life, though these, too, she often ignored or dismissed. However, Girardin's somewhat malicious account of Sand's relationships with men was closely followed in *La Presse* by a series entitled *Lettres à une veuve* that Sand felt would be misinterpreted by the public as referring to a love affair between herself and the author of the *Lettres*, Sand's protégé Eugène Pelletan. In a private letter to Pelletan, Sand chastised him for this indiscretion and warned him that the next time "Mme de Girardin" listed Sand's "conquests" Pelletan's name, or least an obvious reference to him, would be included, and that would be more embarrassing to Pelletan than to her. Sand even went so far as to threaten to wage literary warfare to drive home the point: "Watch out—the desire for amusement may take hold of me as well, contrary to my usual practice of literary dignity, and, in spite of the great success of *La Presse*, in spite of the great name of Madame de Girardin, I could bring the laughers to my side, and between the two camps you might be splattered with mud despite my efforts." Sand did not follow through on this threat, and Pelletan respectfully withdrew further *Lettres à une veuve* from publication in *La Presse*, though he was chagrined that Sand might have doubted the honorableness of his friendship.[51] Sand seems to have forgotten Girardin's insinuations about her lovers and her fictional characters after she settled her concerns with Pelletan.

Sand and Girardin were clearly well aware of each other's existence and fame. In her remarks about Sand's lovers and her fiction Girardin cast aspersions on Sand's talent as an author, implying that her works were merely autobiographical. She passed judgment on Sand's morality, ultimately approving it with her compliments on the *Lettres à Marcie*. Girardin, who wrote comparatively little fiction and no full-blown novel, despite encouragement from Balzac, avoided romantic liaisons, and she highlights these differences between Sand and herself in this text. While she might have been small-minded or malicious, Girardin was also articulating Sand, and by implication herself, as individual writers with distinctive talents and styles. Publicly, Girardin wrote only one other comment on Sand, a laudatory one, in her *Courrier de Paris*. Privately, Sand and Girardin appear to have had little interaction until 1852, when Girardin extended her hospitality to Sand's daughter Solange and her husband, for which Sand was extremely grateful. Sand then entered into a regular correspondence with the Girardin couple, and she socialized with them as well, despite her protestations that she was a "bear" in the midst of their glittering society. Sand expressed admiration for Girardin's play *Lady Tartuffe* in 1853, and she was particularly touched when Girardin offered her sincere sympathy at the death of Sand's granddaughter early in 1855, even as Girardin was suffering from cancer. Sand was a regular visitor to Girardin during her illness, smoking quietly at Girardin's bedside until one month before her death on 29 June 1855. Afterward Sand praised Girardin profusely in a eulogy printed in *La Presse*, claiming that since other, male eulogists had vaunted Girardin's merits as a writer, she would focus on Girardin's warm heart and acute sensitivity. Sand asserts that with Girardin's death society was losing "the healthy and vivifying warmth of her soul. She possessed in great measure true intelligence, an imagination ever ready to embellish the objects of her thought, a lively feeling for things and persons, virile good faith, honest gaiety." According to Sand, Girardin had two missions in life that corresponded to her two great talents: one, to bequeath fine works of literature to her era, and, at the same time, to dispense instruction and edification from her superior mind and her eloquent and persuasive speech to the elite of her era's educated society.[52] While acknowledging Girardin's accomplished writings, Sand emphasized in her eulogy, as she had done in private letters, her appreciation for Girardin as a conversationalist who enlivened literary society through her mind and ideas, but by means of speech and social interaction rather than through the written word. Sand casts Girardin as quite her own opposite.

Although Girardin was well acquainted at different times with Sand, d'Agoult, and Allart, the latter three formed an intriguing triangle of relationships that lasted from the 1830s through the rest of their lives. Sand and d'Agoult experienced an intense friendship for about four years before they quarreled, and thereafter Allart managed to remain close friends with them both, often mediating between the two. Despite Sand's initial dislike for Allart and occasional tiffs over what Sand termed Allart's tale-bearing and perfidy, Sand and Allart developed an enduring friendship, as did Allart and d'Agoult. Sand and Allart were attracted to d'Agoult for her courage in abandoning her family and social position for love. D'Agoult was for Allart and Sand the living embodiment of their idealized, fictional women who placed love above conventional morality. D'Agoult, for her part, found Allart and especially Sand to be models of intellectual commitment and achievement, in addition to sharing a similar affective or moral code. Allart's good nature, generosity, and ready acknowledgment of the superior abilities of her two friends allowed her to overcome feelings of rivalry and profound political disagreements to remain friends with both d'Agoult and Sand—a feat no other person accomplished so successfully.

Sand and d'Agoult first met through Franz Liszt via Alfred de Musset late in 1834. They hardly saw one another before d'Agoult and Liszt left for Switzerland, but Sand's flattering advances to d'Agoult were irresistible. Sand claims to have loved d'Agoult before she even met her, both because Liszt, whom Sand considered a "brother," loved d'Agoult and because d'Agoult was willing to defy conventional morality out of pure, romantic love. "You are as good as an angel," Sand exclaimed in a letter to d'Agoult. She also wrote, "I admire and esteem you," before she went on in the same letter to explain her substantial differences with d'Agoult on ideas about class and social relations. Although Sand hardly knew d'Agoult, disagreed with her ideologically, and had probably seen little or nothing of her writing beyond personal letters, from the beginning she offered what she had withheld from many other aspiring female authors—her encouragement and patronage in the form of publishing contacts and favorable reviews.[53]

D'Agoult recorded more ambivalent feelings regarding her new friend in her diary from 1837 when she was a guest, along with Liszt, at Sand's home of Nohant. In these entries d'Agoult is reminded of Sand's first letters to her, two years earlier, letters that d'Agoult had found charming, graceful, and utterly appealing, but mildly disturbing in their exaggerated praise of d'Agoult. D'Agoult writes: "But it seemed to me that she poeticized me too much, and that, when she would see me in 'real life,' she could no longer love me." D'Agoult further describes her insecurities in Sand's presence, her confusion about what specific behavior would please Sand, and the fear that her own self-consciousness might make her unlovable to Sand. "I passionately wanted her friendship," d'Agoult writes, but she despaired over obtaining it. D'Agoult recognized that her own aloofness and apprehension were not qualities that Sand, in her childlike openness and daring, would admire. But at the same time that d'Agoult was uncomfortable with a situation in which Sand could penetrate her weaknesses, she also had the opportunity to discover Sand's foibles, which was a relief and a source of renewed self-confidence. "It was not useless to me to see, next to George the great poet, George the uncontrollable child, George the woman weak in her own audacity, inconsistent in her feelings and her opinions, illogical in her life that is always driven by chance and rarely directed by reason and experience." D'Agoult considered these characteristics to be flaws, imperfections in the great Sand, and she took comfort from their existence because she saw herself as possessing contrasting qualities. Moreover, d'Agoult was jealous of Sand's and Liszt's friendship; she was fearful that Sand might be Liszt's preferred companion, until she saw that she herself could offer Liszt rationality, direction, consistency, and restraint—which, in d'Agoult's view, Sand could not.[54]

With hindsight d'Agoult draws out even further the differences between herself and Sand when she represents Sand in her memoirs. She constructs Sand as vaguely dangerous in her attractiveness—

excessively Catholic and fantastic, in contrast to her own skepticism and reason. D'Agoult writes of her initial response to Sand: "Strange phenomenon! I experienced with her, as I did for Lamennais, something that both drew me and repelled me, a great admiration for this genius, but also a kind of terror. She, like Lamennais, was too Catholic even in rebellion, a being too exclusively of imagination, a makeup too extraordinary." D'Agoult emphasizes Sand's strangeness in terms of her writings, and especially of her person, including her ambiguous sexual identity: "Was this a man, a woman, an angel, a devil? Did she come, like Lélia, from Heaven or Hell?" Moreover, d'Agoult invokes testimony from another witness as to the contrast between Sand and herself, and she asserts that Sand's cross-dressing brought out a fundamentally masculine being "with a certain youthful, virile grace." When Sand was dressed in dark man's clothes, "neither the development of her bust nor the spread of her thighs betrayed her feminine sex." Elsewhere in the autobiographical narrative d'Agoult had established her own appearance as decidedly and openly feminine, in addition to being tall, fair, and slim. Her description of Sand dwells on Sand's "masculinity," her conscious mystery and indecipherability, as well as her being short, dark, and broad. D'Agoult makes clear that Sand was rebellious, almost bizarre, and certainly untrustworthy, but that she was also a compelling personality and a highly influential writer who had helped launch her on her own writing career. "Nor did she wholly open herself to me. I never was completely in her confidence, but she greatly encouraged me to write."[55] D'Agoult found Sand a troubling individual whom she by no means wished to emulate— beyond adopting the profession of letters. Indeed, d'Agoult makes every effort to distinguish her own identity from that of Sand, and even to hint at good reasons why their friendship could not last.

The dissolution of the friendship between Sand and d'Agoult has fascinated scholars, and efforts to understand it have revealed that mutual friends, Charlotte Marliani and Félicité de Lamennais, precipitated the break, though evidence suggests that the relationship had been fraying prior to that, given the very different temperaments and immediate concerns of the two protagonists.[56] Sand did not write to d'Agoult from Majorca, where she was staying with Frédéric Chopin and her children, and she claimed that letters from d'Agoult had been lost in the mail; D'Agoult expressed her bewilderment at Sand's failure to reply. Moreover, Marliani indicated to Sand that d'Agoult was writing decidedly unfriendly things about her in letters to others. Notably, d'Agoult mocked Sand's numerous love affairs and their detrimental effects on the quality of her writing.[57] Sand requested that Lamennais intervene, read the incriminating letters from d'Agoult, and determine whether she should formally break with her friend. On Lamennais's advice, Sand wrote a letter to d'Agoult in 1839 declaring that they were no longer friends and including this intriguing analysis of d'Agoult's character:

I know you well. I know that in your intelligence is a feeling and a need for greatness against which a petty worry constantly revolts. You would like to behave in a masculine and chivalric manner, but you cannot give up being a beautiful and intelligent woman immolating and degrading all others. For this reason you have no trouble lauding me as a good guy [un bon garçon], while in my guise as a woman you cannot find enough bitterness [le fiel] to dirty me [me barbouiller]. In short you have two sources of pride—one small and one great. Try to allow the great one to prevail. You can do so, because God endowed you richly, and you will have to account to Him for the beauty, the intelligence and the seductions that He bestowed on you.[58]

Sand tells d'Agoult that she is at war with herself, that her "masculine" qualities of intelligence, loftiness, and honor are undermined by "feminine" characteristics of pettiness, vanity, and vindictiveness. Sand claims that d'Agoult simply cannot abide a female friend whom she must see as a competitor to be reviled in order for d'Agoult to prevail. Sand is optimistic that d'Agoult's fine mind and great heart will ultimately prevail over this inner conflict, but she does not intend to wait around for that to happen while being the butt of more verbal abuse. D'Agoult, with Liszt's encouragement, tried to achieve a reconciliation with Sand, and she succeeded to the extent that the two agreed to maintain smooth relations in public, though they were too mutually mistrustful to resume the intimacy they had once enjoyed.[59]

The point of summarizing this famous quarrel is not to determine causes or ascribe responsibility. Rather, it is to demonstrate the importance of the relationship, brief as it was, in the lives of d'Agoult and Sand, and ultimately for French literary culture in the July Monarchy. For four years d'Agoult functioned for Sand as the living realization of Sand's ideal of love that she had created in fictional characters and had tried, unsuccessfully, to enact in her own life. D'Agoult was probably correct in her assessment that she must inevitably disappoint Sand in failing to fulfill that ideal. Despite her eventual realization that d'Agoult was not the ideal friend she had in mind, Sand indicated that the

two spent some very jolly times together, and she frequently acknowledged, both privately and publicly, that d'Agoult had a fine mind.
Moreover, several features of d'Agoult's character appeared in fictional
characters by both Sand and Balzac, and contemporaries immediately
identified those characters as having been modeled on d'Agoult. In
Sand's *Horace* (1841) the character of the vicomtesse de Chailly is blond,
beautiful, elegant, and a slave to social opinion; she seduces the vulnerable young student Horace, only to throw him off when he no longer
pleases her. Similarly, Balzac, who spent several weeks closeted with
Sand at Nohant in 1839, created the character of Béatrix, in the book of
the same name, who is blond, beautiful, elegant, and in competition
with another female character who writes books under a male pseudonym (modeled after George Sand, as far as contemporaries were concerned) for the affections of a youth whom Béatrix ultimately seduces
and renders unhappy for the rest of her life. D'Agoult's letters reveal
that she acknowledged these unflattering portraits with good grace, but
for good or ill, her relationship with Sand had catapulted her into literary culture—which, in fact, is precisely where she wanted to be, though
on her own terms. The break with Sand actually freed her from anxiety
about pleasing the famous author and allowed d'Agoult to cultivate her
own authorial voice and establish her independent and individual literary identity. A consistent supporter of this project was Hortense Allart, whom d'Agoult met in Italy at the same time that her relationships
with Sand and Liszt were deteriorating, and who proved to be a less
threatening and more faithful friend than either Sand or Liszt.

From 1839, when Allart and d'Agoult were both expectant mothers
of illegitimate children in Italy, up to and including 1845, when
d'Agoult spent four months at Allart's house at Herblay, the quality of
the two women's friendship is difficult to discern, largely because
d'Agoult's letters to Allart from that period have not survived. Allart
wrote frequently to d'Agoult about the condition of women and how to
improve it, her meetings with saint-simoniennes, and her desire to
mend the fractured relationship between Sand and d'Agoult. Additionally, Allart did not hide her jealousy of d'Agoult for attracting her
lover, Bulwer, and her would-be lover, Sainte-Beuve (there is no evidence that these men, or any other man, became d'Agoult's lover). But
Allart was irrepressibly good-natured about these matters.[60] Allart confessed to Sainte-Beuve that d'Agoult treated her as a "light" relationship, and she claimed that this did not bother her, nor diminish her ad-

miration for d'Agoult, who, by 1845, had published several learned articles. But Allart's respect for d'Agoult increased with her visit to Herblay, during which time she showed the manuscript of *Nélida*, her first
novel, to Allart. Allart wrote to Sainte-Beuve after d'Agoult's departure: "Since her visit to Herblay, since I read her novel, . . . I find her to
be a *superior woman*, as Corinne would say, a lofty imagination, a proud
and aloof nature."[61] D'Agoult returned the favor a year later when the
novel was published in *Revue des deux mondes* and she was basking in
praise from her friends. Cautioning that *Nélida* could not be definitively
deemed a triumph until it came out in book form, d'Agoult acknowledged her friend's contribution to the preliminary success of the serial-
ized version: "The whole thing benefited from your suggestions (I kid
you not), and I am not at all unhappy."[62]

The two women's stay together at Herblay marks the beginning of a
long period of correspondence and interaction between Allart and
d'Agoult that is filled with exchanges on writing and literary criticism,
ideas about women and politics, as well as personal matters. Although
the majority of available letters are still from Allart, it is nonetheless
clear that both women benefited personally and professionally from
this friendship. They shared information and tested ideas as part of the
writing process. They argued about politics and the meaning of history,
discussed the sources of women's oppression and the means to liberation, and sympathized with one another on maternal cares. Allart was
profuse in her praise for d'Agoult's various publications: with the appearance of the first volume of the *Histoire de la Révolution de 1848*, Allart exclaimed to her friend: "Never before, it seems to me, have you
shown so much intelligence, so much erudition . . . as in this book."
And regarding the reissue of d'Agoult's *Essai sur la liberté*, Allart asserted, "Your *Liberty* is full of philosophy, you have addressed the subject in its breadth."[63] D'Agoult and Allart strongly supported one another in their individual writing projects, and as women writers generally. They made a point of emphasizing their identities as intellectuals
and of admiring one another as scholars and authors. In the case of
d'Agoult and Allart, the main difference their writings established
between them was d'Agoult's superiority over Allart, and, secondarily,
d'Agoult's political liberalism in contrast to Allart's elitism. In contrast
to other relationships between the four women writers, where differentiation was important, this interaction reinforced similarity, at least
in terms of genre of writing and literary values. That is, d'Agoult and

Allart both wrote history, philosophical essays, and literary criticism, and they both strove for erudition, rationality, and critical analysis. Supporting one another in these endeavors and in the cultivation of those qualities was a primary function of their friendship.

Throughout the long friendship with d'Agoult, Allart frequently referred to her visits, discussions, and correspondence with Sand, whom she had known since 1832. In contrast to Sand's instant dislike of Allart for her bluestocking characteristics, Allart was unrestrained in her admiration for Sand, writing to Sainte-Beuve of her, "If I were a man I would be madly in love with her."[64] In the 1830s Sand and Allart socialized frequently in Paris, but in the 1840s, with both women spending more time at their country homes, much of their contact seems to have been through letters. Allart, not surprisingly, regularly paid homage to *la Reine*, and Sand clearly respected Allart's critical insights, erudition, and political ideas, even though they differed markedly from her own. After their early disagreements Sand was very affectionate toward Allart, even when Allart criticized her for degrading art by imitating life in *Lucrezia Floriani* (1847). Allart, and many others, discerned an imitation of Chopin in the character of Prince Karol, who was a frail, demanding, selfish, but compelling lover to the self-sacrificing former stage actress who is the title character. Sand replied by saying, as she says elsewhere, that her characters are entirely artistic creations, and if they imitate life, they imitate various human features that Sand has encountered in diverse individuals. Sand suggested that Allart, who as an artist herself should know better, had been maliciously influenced by others, including d'Agoult, into thinking that Karol was Chopin. Nonetheless, Sand is very intent on explaining herself to Allart, often asserting how seriously she takes Allart's comments. She writes, "My dear Hortense, I am more sensitive to your reproaches than to your praise . . . because in the reproach I find the sadness and honesty of a sincere interest."[65]

Allart believed that Sand was a truly great author, offering a long analysis of her works to Sainte-Beuve: "Aren't some of her works . . . masterpieces of morality and feeling? With this manner of genius that attains all the pinnacles, opens up [the world's] immensity, and leads us there with her?"[66] While Allart never hesitated to criticize particular works by Sand, she regularly championed her talent, along with the different abilities of d'Agoult, to Sainte-Beuve. Although Sand probably had less need of Allart's friendship and support than did d'Agoult, she appreciated it, and she esteemed Allart, enough to maintain the relationship for all their lives. Indeed, Sand was generous in her public praise for Allart, writing highly favorable reviews of Allart's *Novum Organum* (1857), a philosophical study of sainthood, and of her fictionalized autobiography, *Les Enchantements de Prudence* (1872).[67]

Sand, more than the other three authors, was in a unique position to promote or to denigrate fellow writers, and notably women writers. Her autobiography, written between 1847 and 1854, included generally positive descriptions of both d'Agoult and Allart that could only have benefited the two. Sand refers to d'Agoult during the time that the two women, Liszt, and Sand's children shared lodgings in Paris in 1837: "Although improvised in a hotel, her salon was a gathering of the elite, over whom she presided with exquisite grace and where she found her own high level among all those eminent specialists by the breadth of her mind and the variety of her faculties, both poetic and earnest." Sand's appreciation for d'Agoult's elegance and her fine mind are consistent in both her private and public statements. Similarly, Sand credits Allart with a feminine appearance and maternal devotion, along with scholarly excellence and outstanding intellect, presenting Allart as "a writer of lofty sentiment and poetic form, an erudite woman 'all pretty and pink,' as Delatouche used to say—a courageous, independent spirit, a brilliant, serious woman who brought as much serenity to her life in seclusion as she brought grace and brilliance to society, a strong and tender mother, with a woman's compassion and a man's firmness."[68] Sand's acknowledgments of her fellow women writers in her autobiography, read by so many, were informed by a gendered consciousness that pervaded her society and culture—Allart had a "*woman's* compassion and a *man's* firmness." Nonetheless, she drew attention to Allart and d'Agoult as individuals with characters and talents unique to themselves, and her positive presentation of both figures suggests a beneficent encouragement of their careers as writers. Allart, for one, was flattered by Sand's attention, writing to d'Agoult in 1854: "Yesterday I received a long letter from Nohant. She is contemplating what she will say *about me* in her Mémoires. Ste-B[euve] is in them—will we all be in them? You, of course. For myself, I do not presume to such an honor."[69]

In private the relationships among Sand, d'Agoult, Allart, and Girardin seethe with rivalries as the women seek to disengage themselves from the epithet of "bluestocking," with its connotations of unnatural masculinity, lack of talent, and literary and commercial failure. Moreover, each wishes to distinguish herself from the others and obtain recognition from the male literary establishment for her particular artistry, erudition, and intellect. In the relatively closed world of Parisian letters these rivalries extended to personal relations, and jealousy over sexual and emotional attachments with other women—but especially with men who, after all, usually wielded more power and influence. But these relations among women writers were also constructive, supportive, and affectionate. Despite their differences, Sand, d'Agoult, Allart, and Girardin shared some common goals—notably succeeding as writers in an environment generally hostile to women. Their individual triumphs did not necessarily come at the expense of each other; indeed, they were more likely to improve the chances of other women writers' success. Of course, the existence of several women writers was not the sole cause of the increase in their total numbers. But this account of the four female authors and their interactions casts a new light on a literary scene that hitherto has appeared as militantly masculine, with individual women trying in isolation to become exceptions.[70]

Cassandra, Diotima, Aspasia, and Cleopatra

All four women writers were linked in their common experience of writing and of being "bluestockings," in knowing many of the same literary and political men of the July Monarchy, and in supporting and competing with one another for literary recognition. Whatever quarrels and differences they had (and they were many), by and large they appreciated the character and qualities each possessed, with the exception of Girardin and Allart. In their personal correspondence with one another, and in public writings by one about another, they defined themselves as women who successfully combined femininity and intelligence, unlike the bluestocking.

In yet another move to dispel the bluestocking stereotype, the four authors referred to themselves with names drawn from antiquity—amazon, Cassandra, Aspasia, Diotima, Clio, Cleopatra. Taking the classical learning that was conventionally a male purview, they used this component of literary culture to combat the other—the bluestocking. In general this association with classical female figures was not an attempt to create a new stereotype of women writers, but quite the opposite—its intention was to reaffirm the individual identities of each woman writer. Antique identities were by no means the only names that women writers devised for themselves. During the period of their close friendship Sand was most often Piffoël to d'Agoult's Arabella or Mirabella, with Piffoël referring to Sand's big nose and masculine manners in contrast to Arabella/d'Agoult's svelte, aristocratic, and feminine beauty (d'Agoult was also known as the princess). Both Allart and d'Agoult referred to Sand as Lélia, naming her after one of her own most controversial characters, who sought love from many men but was dissatisfied with them all because she was really seeking a higher, spiritual love. Allart called Sand the Queen, which Sand returned in kind, and d'Agoult professed to Allart that she was a Beatrice without a Dante (after the break with Liszt).[71] But the antique names are used less playfully than the others, and they have far greater implications for the women writers' views of themselves as intellectuals, women, and even political figures.

D'Agoult and Allart were the most adept players of this naming game, for their literary careers were defined primarily in terms of history and philosophy. In their correspondence d'Agoult addressed Allart as Sappho and Clio, or as "proud amazon," while Allart frequently referred to d'Agoult as Diotima. D'Agoult thus honors her friend by associating her with the brilliant poet of Greece in the fifth century B.C.E., the muse of history, and the warrior women who helped define Athenian history and myth. This homage is returned by Allart, identifying d'Agoult with one of only two women to speak in the writings of Plato—Diotima, a woman wise in love and knowledge who was a teacher of Socrates. Each ancient figure was distinctive and reflects certain characteristics or ideals of Allart's and d'Agoult's. The reference to Sappho may or may not have involved the sexual orientation of either Sappho or Allart, but it is likely that d'Agoult thought to compliment Allart's writing style and her commitment to women's issues by invoking Sappho as a great writer and a spokeswoman for a female sensibility. And Clio would come easily to d'Agoult as a means of praising Allart, since Allart was a historian—author of the *Histoire de la République de Florence* (1837 and 1843). The amazon was a figure dear to Allart's heart for her example of female independence and sexual freedom. Her admiration for amazons was obvious in her *Histoire de la République d'Athènes* (1866), and in her autobiography Allart proposed amazons as the model for women to emulate, but bearing a pen rather than a spear: "A woman would do well to imitate [the race of amazons] replacing the trade of warrior with a career in letters." Finally, Diotima was bound to appeal to d'Agoult as a figure of comparison, since she was both an accomplished lover and a brilliant thinker, whose wisdom Socrates conveys to his interlocutors in Plato's *Symposium*. Indeed, d'Agoult becomes Diotima in her work, *Dante et Goethe* (1866), assuming the function of Socrates in dialogues analyzing the figure of the female ideal, spirituality, and the politics in the masterworks *The Divine Comedy* and *Faust*.[72] Each of these classical female figures connoted a behavior, accomplishment, or ideal of Allart's and of d'Agoult's, and all are united in representing intelligence in the form of a woman.

Even Sand, despite very ambivalent feelings about the merits of learning dead languages, named herself and Allart after classical figures in a letter to Allart of 1840. The context of this letter is unclear, as it is a direct response to an unrecovered letter from Allart, but Sand is clear that she and Allart are very different; the implication is that they have very different social ideologies and personal manners. "You are still *Aspasia*, and I am still Cassandra," Sand writes.[73] Sand disagreed sharply with Allart's social and political elitism, and the letter also suggests that Sand was chastising Allart for malicious gossip about her. Sand might be referring to the "Athenian queen" in terms of holding court and passing judgments on people. The metonym might be Aspasia, the courtesan who has risen to the side of the aristocratic ruler Pericles, mocking the incomprehensible utterances of the prophet Cassandra. Whether the "prophesies" are Sand's political views that the working masses will eventually inherit the earth, which she had just articulated in her novel *Le Compagnon du tour de France* (1840), and which Allart rejected, or some personal behavior that Allart misinterpreted or maligned, is unknown. Although Sand names Allart as Aspasia in a possibly derogatory fashion, Allart would probably have taken the reference as a compliment, and certainly the two antique identities do represent something about Allart and Sand that each would recognize as faithful to aspects of their character. That is, Allart did aspire to be an Aspasia, to rule a country through the combined powers of her sexual charms and intellectual abilities, acting upon a powerful man. For Allart was forthright in her autobiography that she wanted to be Bulwer's mistress as a means of "participating" in the British Parliament. And Sand might well have seen herself as a Cassandra, particularly after her conversion to socialism in 1835–36, writing novels that displayed the goodness and wisdom of ordinary working people who were unjustly denied access to power and resources. In short, Sand warned the rich and mighty that their self-importance and power might be challenged.[74]

From Sappho and Diotima to Aspasia and Cassandra is a movement away from women who were strictly writers and intellectuals to women with direct political impact. That is true also of Cleopatra, a figure chosen by Delphine de Girardin as the focus of her play of 1847 by the same name. For Girardin the tragedy of Cleopatra was "feminine" in nature, and hence suitable for the subject of a work by a woman writer—herself. But in addition to the tragedy of the fateful love between Marc-Antony and Cleopatra that destroys them both, Girardin's *Cléopatre* is also about a woman of great intelligence and erudition. In scene one of act two Cleopatra is surrounded by intellectuals with whom she discusses education and the restocking of the library of Alexandria. When one of them falls to his knees at Cleopatra's commitment to restore the library by military force, if necessary, Cleopatra replies with a speech that honors men of learning because they have made Egypt the great state that it is:

> What makes a man great in our country are ideas,
> And the forehead of a thinker, like that of a king,
> Must never bow down, not even before me!

The man of letters answers with this homage to Cleopatra: "This reproach honors you and proves your genius." Then, in the next scene, Cleopatra reads the poetry of Sappho.[75] Although the drama of the play is the relationship between Marc-Antony and Cleopatra and the machinations of their respective retinues to preserve the integrity of Rome and Egypt, Cleopatra's learning and statesmanship are as integral to her character as is her capacity for passionate love. Indeed, there would be no tragedy if Cleopatra were not so brilliant and powerful. Girardin, like Allart, d'Agoult, and Sand, claims a heritage of, and identification with, female figures of antiquity who were educated, intelligent, heroic, powerful—and feminine.

These four women writers both internalized and combated the bluestocking stereotype of intellectual women. Their very existences were challenges to this attempt to deny individuality to women, especially to women who competed with men in the profession of letters. By naming this prejudice that they encountered, networking with other women writers for both support and self-definition, and appropriating classical learning to redefine themselves as heroic figures instead of monstrosities, women writers undermined the negative imagery of female authors. They also wrote themselves into existence; that is, writing and getting their works published were essential to imposing their separate authorial identities on literary culture, and to asserting, by implication, the potential for all women to combine intelligence and creative talent with femininity. Writing, for these four women in the July Monarchy, was inherently transgressive and feminist. Moreover, writing made these women public figures. But Sand, d'Agoult, Allart, and Girardin were still more than writers and public figures; they became, in different ways and to varying degrees, political figures as well.

5 ☞ Women Writers as Republicans in July Monarchy Political Culture

On 12 May 1839, Auguste Blanqui and his radical republican coconspirators tried to start a popular uprising against the government of Louis-Philippe d'Orleans. This effort failed, and Blanqui and others were tried and imprisoned. However, the year 1839 was a time of political instability generally and economic crisis nationwide, and Delphine Gay de Girardin, as the male dandy, aristocrat, and journalist vicomte de Launay, offered an analysis of the beleaguered French state in the form of a family romance.[1] Girardin presents France as a female in distress, abandoned by almost all of her family. Her noble parents, presumably the aristocrats or royalty of the Old Regime, are disgusted with France's disobedience. She has married against her parents' wishes—married a constitutional monarch who came to power with a revolution—and the elders are pleased to see the feckless young girl suffer. Her brothers are no better. They, too, despise France's husband, but they are rebels; they also had counseled their sister to rebel, by not marrying at all, by staying forever under the influence of her brothers. "Your brothers . . . are wild and incurably envious; they are really *beastly brothers* [*frères farouches*]; they deplore not only your marriage, but all marriages; they are on principle enemies of engagements; they have pledged to break all chains, they will tolerate none, under the pretext of liberty."[2]

The revolutionary brothers try to persuade France to give up her husband and allow the brothers to kill him. Unhappy France refuses, and her brothers, like her parents, abandon her. No help will come from her sisters, accomplices in the July Monarchy who think only of their pleasures and who care nothing about what happens to France. Nor can she expect assistance from her friends, those advisors—politicians?— who encouraged the marriage out of self-interest and who deliberately create tension between France and her husband because they want still more power—even beyond the riches and influence they have gained. France's only support comes from a most mundane quarter—the bourgeois National Guard! Stolidly they fight and die, defending France from insurrection when nobles, revolutionaries, collaborators, and politicians care nothing for her welfare. "They make fun of [the National Guard] because they are cotton nightcap manufacturers and grocers; but the[se] anonymous heroes go to die for you." The national guardsmen, in their simplicity, are the only patriots left to serve France: "Their politics is your glory, their ambition is your joy; they know nothing about making fine speeches and grand projects for your future; but they have kept intact in their hearts the noble sentiment that constitutes the greatness of your history, this sublime instinct that the ambitious have lost, this sacred fire that egoism has snuffed; they have kept the tradition of love, and they will save you, because they love you and because they love only you!"[3]

The suggestion that the National Guard is France's salvation is hardly what a reader expects from the vicomte de Launay—or from Girardin. As Launay, Girardin gloried in poking fun at the foibles and gaffes of bourgeois women and men, and the National Guard was, as she indicates, a supremely bourgeois institution. But Girardin always considered herself a patriot (*la muse de la patrie*, as she once called herself), and in this family romance of France besieged and abandoned, she provides a stinging critique of various political positions or parties that failed to uphold the integrity of the French state.[4] Legitimists, republicans, Orleanists of the center and left—all receive a tongue-lashing in this satirical metaphor of 1839. And Girardin was definitely not a Bonapartist. Indeed, she implies that just about everyone with political power and acting upon ideology is suspect, for the patriots in her story are distinguished by their political exclusion, or at least by not being elected or appointed officials, and by abstention from party affiliation.

Does this mean that Girardin was apolitical? Not at all. Girardin, along with Sand, d'Agoult, and Allart, was intensely interested in politics, frequently wrote about politics, and, on occasion, actively engaged in politics. The four women writers could hardly avoid some minimal awareness of political events, inasmuch as they had lived through five different regimes by the time they were in their early fifties. But they were more than passive spectators to the parade of empires, monarchies, and the one republic that they witnessed. When the Revolution of

1830 ushered in the constitutional monarchy of Louis-Philippe d'Orleans, Sand, d'Agoult, Girardin, and Allart were all in their late twenties. As mature adults throughout the nearly eighteen years of Louis-Philippe's reign, the four authors' scorn for the regime steadily increased, and eventually they all came to believe that the most desirable alternative was a republic, although for different purposes. How and why did the four women writers become republicans? What did republicanism mean to them? How did they function as political, republican women in the context of July Monarchy political culture? And how did they view republicanism from the particular perspective of women? These are the questions that this chapter addresses. Although it is artificial to separate the four women's republicanism from their notions of reforming the condition of women, the latter is such an extensive program that it merits a separate chapter, which follows this one.

It should be clear by now that Sand, d'Agoult, Girardin, and Allart had all violated the norms regarding middle-class feminine behavior through sexual transgression and professional writing careers, and that in their writing they sought in different ways to legitimate themselves as intellectual women and to construct a positive alternative to the negative image of the bluestocking. As successful authors who had proven by example that women had the capacity for sustained intellectual endeavor and literary production, they had implicitly challenged one of the major arguments or phantasms for barring women from politics—their supposed irrationality and inability to understand, much less usefully contribute to, public affairs.[5] This and the next two chapters analyze the politics of the four women writers and their feminist refashioning of republicanism. They argue that, similar to their textual and performed model of the woman of ideas, who is both feminine and intelligent, they constructed a model of the political woman who was rational and humane, political and social, independent and cooperative. These four women writers sought not to compete directly with men, nor to usurp (at least in the short term) men's exclusive access to political rights; they aspired to support and even guide men through the force of their ideas and as independent thinkers and individuals. But first, each had to develop her own political identity that centered around her particular understanding of republicanism.

Republicanism in the July Monarchy

When Sand, d'Agoult, Allart, and Girardin came to political consciousness, republicanism was both a multifaceted idea and a dynamic, often
divided movement. It represented many things, both glorious and
frightening, to many people, such as civil liberties, political reform, social transformation, civic equality, revolutionary action, and moral regeneration. Although the four women writers and their contemporaries
frequently invoked *republicanism* as a code word for abstract ideals or
vague bogeys, a few fundamental principles composed an idea of republicanism in the 1830s and 1840s upon which most could agree; these
included constitutional guarantees of civil rights and liberties, equality
before the law and freedom of the press and religion; parliamentary
government with popularly accountable ministers; extended suffrage;
meritocracy; and opposition to aristocracy and monarchy. However,
republicans disagreed on several other issues—namely, whether suffrage should be extended to all adult males; the extent of state intervention in the economy and in the provision of public services; the distribution of power within a republican government; and the suitability
of or necessity for revolution, as opposed to reform, as a means of
achieving political or social change.[6] Sand, d'Agoult, Allart, and Girardin supported the common principles of republicanism, but, like
many other republicans, they differed on matters of sovereignty—the
extent of democracy—and on the valuation of republican ideals such as
freedom and equality. Moreover, republicanism also represented for
them the means of improving the civil status of all women, as we will
see in Chapter 6.

Immediately following the Revolution of 1830, which established
the July Monarchy, republicanism flourished in the form of a variety of
clubs and newspapers. Optimistic about continued social and political
reform toward democracy, groups like the *Société des amis du peuple* and
Aide-toi le ciel t'aidera upheld such principles as parliamentary rule, the
suppression of the peerage, and freedom of the press. As a minority
relatively inexperienced in daily political maneuvering and function-
ing, republicans at this time exhibited a fresh and rambunctious character that Louis Blanc described as masculine: "The republican party,
moreover, was by no means docile or tractable. If it had all the virtues
of a strong, a manly cast, it had also serious vices,—an exuberance of
zeal, hair-brained courage, a blind confidence in the efficacy of *coups de*

main, a secret leaning to distrust of superior men, intolerance, and in-discipline."[7] Popular uprisings in 1834, however, prompted the gov-ernment of Louis-Philippe to crack down on republicans and especially to censor their publications. Despite these obstacles republican move-ments persisted but fissured into moderate and radical factions. By 1840 one of the larger groups that espoused universal male suffrage and political reform centered around its newspaper, *Le National*, edited by Armand Marrast. A rival republican newspaper, *La Réforme*, was founded in 1843 to advocate social change, including the right to work and production cooperatives, as well as political reform, and its con-tributors included republicans Godefroy Cavaignac and Alexandre Le-dru-Rollin as well as socialists Louis Blanc and Pierre Leroux. Still other, more radical and socialist groups and newspapers, though criti-cal of the "moderate" positions of *Le National* and *La Réforme*, nonethe-less contributed to the spread of republican ideas throughout France, an important backdrop for the establishment of republican government in 1848.[8]

Republicanism under the July Monarchy was an ideal, or a bundle of ideals, that included the revolutionary trinity of liberty, equality, and fraternity from the first French republic. Sand, d'Agoult, Allart, and Gi-rardin were familiar with at least some of the many histories of the French Revolution published during the Restoration and the July Mon-archy that interpreted the past in light of contemporary struggles over political forms and stabilization. Histories by Adolphe Thiers and Jules Michelet that lauded bourgeois rule or celebrated popular solidarity, respectively, as the characteristic features of the French Revolution en-hanced the appeal of republicanism generally but also lent support to differing republican visions. For some the republic should consist of a representative body that governed primarily to ensure personal free-doms and security, uphold the state, and promote the best interests of its constituents. For others the republic was directly accountable to the electorate and should equalize society through progressive income taxes, free public education, and state-funded health care.[9] In short, the republic was primarily either political or social.

Sand, d'Agoult, Allart, and Girardin were all familiar with social-ism, notably the works of Charles Fourier, Claude-Henri Saint-Simon, Pierre Leroux, and their followers. Socialism in general offered a coop-erative or communitarian alternative to competitive individualism, and therefore a solution to the social and economic disparities that precipitated numerous popular demonstrations and rebellions in France and other countries during early industrialization. Socialism, like republicanism, assumed numerous and various forms that comprehended self-sufficient communities, producers' cooperatives, humanitarian religion, a revolutionary vanguard as both ends and means of eradicating poverty, even a transformed social organization.[10] Different aspects or versions of socialism appealed to the four women because, like many of their contemporaries, they were acutely aware of widespread impoverishment and underemployment among the working classes, and they blamed the government of Louis-Philippe for failing to address these problems. Both republicanism and socialism promised to rectify the situation, though often in different ways. Moreover, socialism, more so than republicanism at this time, confronted the question of the position of women in a transformed polity. Most socialists were republicans, but by no means were all republicans socialists. Still, the ideas of both contributed to the vibrancy and tumult of political culture during the July Monarchy, and to the political identities of Sand, d'Agoult, Allart, and Girardin. An account of each woman's republican awakening and development reveals more about political opportunities, and constraints, under the July Monarchy.

Politicizing Women

Chapter 1 indicated various ways that Sand, d'Agoult, Allart, and Girardin experienced politics as children, and constructed their childhoods in political terms. Politics continued to affect them as adults, and as adults they consciously developed the political ideas that then informed their remembered girl selves. Each woman came to republicanism in a different way and at different times, through the changes affecting all of France, the reading of historical, philosophical, and political texts, personal relationships, and public performances. Sand and d'Agoult became committed republicans during the July Monarchy almost simultaneously with traumatic changes in their personal lives. Republicanism helped to fill a spiritual void following their rejection of conventional elite values and practices. Allart and Girardin came to republicanism more by default than by conviction—through adherence to certain historical lessons and philosophical principles, in the case of Allart; as a result of disenchantment with constitutional monarchy and the aesthetic appeal of republicanism, for Girardin. All four experi-

enced the July Monarchy much as did the majority of the French people: immediate surprise and uncertainty, followed by hope and optimism, and then disappointment and accommodation, but increasingly
disgust and contempt. Yet their individual trajectories toward republicanism begin a new story of feminine performance in the masculine
world of politics.

Sand, who claimed to have inherited republicanism from her father's egalitarian idealism and her mother's popular origins, started
writing of herself as republican only in 1830. In that revolutionary year
she declared her independence both from her troubled marriage and
from the moderate liberalism she had shared with her husband,
Casimir. To her mother, Sand wrote: "For myself, dear mama, freedom
to think and act is a primary good."[11] Sympathetic to the masses who
sacrificed themselves for political change (and dubious rewards) in
1830, Sand was shaken by the failed insurrection of 1832, and she deplored the bloodshed and reaction that revolution unleashed. Sand
castigated men for their violence, which caused women great suffering:
"I am furious with all men. They have a hope, a duty, and a pledge to
conflict, while I have only sorrow." She continues, "I have a horror of
monarchy, horror of the republic, horror of all man[kind?]."[12] At this
time, when political action seemed so socially destructive, Sand found
in saint-simonism some appealing, nonviolent principles of social reorganization, such as the celebration of heterosexual love and the redistribution of private property. However, she stopped short of embracing
the entire doctrine, mistrusting the search for a sacred mother, deploring the emancipation of women through free love, and, later, deeming
"le Père" Enfantin a charlatan.[13] Then, in 1835 the lawyer Michel de
Bourges rekindled Sand's enthusiasm for republicanism and even for
revolution.[14]

Sand and Michel de Bourges, whom she refers to as Everard, became lovers at the same time that Everard participated in one of the
great public spectacles of the July Monarchy, the "monster trial" of 164
defendants from the uprising in Lyon of 1834.[15] Although the parade of
prominent republicans who argued for the defense displayed great
disunity among themselves, ranging from moderately liberal to radically socialist, Sand's commitment to republican politics, solidified in
large measure by Everard's eloquence, was unswayed. She was
"converted to republican sympathy and progressive ideas," and it was
Everard who inspired "the ability to feel the vivid emotions that politics

had never before awakened in me."[16] Sand describes her conversion to republicanism at this time in one of her *Lettres d'un voyageur*, in which she assumes the voice of a male narrator and disciple of Everard, and exclaims, "Hail republic, dawn of justice and of equality, divine utopia." Sand establishes a contrast between Everard as active republican leader, and her(him)self as devoted republican follower: "In a revolution your goal will be the freedom of the human race; as for me, I will have none other but to get myself killed, in order to put an end to myself and to have, for the first time in my life, served some purpose, if only to raise the barricade by the height of one corpse." Sand represents herself as a mere political apprentice—"I know nothing and I am sure of nothing"—in contrast to Everard's assured mastery. In a new republic, Sand proposes a division of labor between herself, an artist, and Everard, a politician: "I am by nature poetic and not legislative, warlike if need be, but never parliamentary. . . . Will it not be permitted for minstrels to sing romances to women, while you make laws for men?"[17] The ambiguous sexual identity of the narrator—"I am a poet, that is a weak man [*une femmelette*]"—allows Sand to acknowledge the masculine gendering of republicanism in general, and especially of its activists. At the same time she can avoid the difficult problem of where women fit into a movement dominated by virile men of action, since she presents herself as male, even if "weak."[18] However, as a woman, she eventually finds a place for herself as poet and publicist, aided by her discovery of a socialist philosophy that she grafts onto republican activism.

In 1837, as her relationship with Michel de Bourges fell apart, Sand became acquainted with Pierre Leroux and his work. Leroux's emphasis on love, community, and spirituality resonated with Sand, who saw political change as a means to a broader moral regeneration of society. Although she resisted labels, she nonetheless declared herself in both the socialist and republican camps, or rather, she sought to combine the political action of republicanism with the social and moral ideals of socialism. From 1840 several of Sand's novels—*Le Compagnon du tour de France* (1840), *Horace* (1841), *Le Meunier d'Angibault* (1844), *Le Péché de Monsieur Antoine* (1845)—addressed political issues, including revolution, artisan communities, class relations, and property distribution. Sand encouraged and even sponsored several authors of working-class origin, helping them in a variety of ways to get their works published. In collaboration with others, she started a literary review and a provincial newspaper specifically intended to publish working-class, opposition, republican, and socialist writing. Additionally, she wrote for *La Réforme*, the largest national republican newspaper in the 1840s, and, through these literary and political productions, she maintained contact with republican and socialist men such as Alexandre Ledru-Rollin, Louis Blanc, Alphonse de Lamartine, and Pierre Leroux.[19]

Like Sand, d'Agoult presented herself autobiographically as the natural inheritor of her paternal family's principles, which she constructed as republican, for she rejected their royalist politics. And like Sand her conscious adoption of republicanism occurred over several years and in response to various influences during the July Monarchy. In her autobiographical writing d'Agoult describes the Revolution of 1830 in considerable detail, calling it the "first revolution about which [she] could understand something." At that time she was pregnant and staying with her mother in Paris while her husband was away selling some property. From their house in the faubourg Saint-Germain she heard the sounds of gunfire, and she expressed sympathy for its victims, to the astonishment of her friends: "Poor folk! I cried, thinking of the men of the people who were undoubtedly being fired upon. My friends looked at me stupefied."[20]

She describes the uncertainty she and her circle experienced, her brother's frantic visits to his superiors in the Ministry of Foreign Affairs, and finally the ascension of Louis-Philippe to the throne. She received the condolences of friends on her lowered status, since the regime to which her family's fortunes were tied had fallen. D'Agoult herself expressed no regret for the passing of the Bourbon dynasty, though she agreed with other family members that the Orleans lacked legitimacy and prestige as a royal family. "We didn't take them seriously," she asserts after Louis-Philippe was declared king of the French by a joint session of the Chamber of Deputies and Chamber of Peers.[21] Although d'Agoult never associated with the Orleans court, the revolution did liberate her from the dour prudishness and conservative tastes of Saint-Germain society. Along with a few other young *salonnières*, d'Agoult began reading romantic literature and introducing new persons and new ideas into her salon. For d'Agoult romanticism was the defining feature of the 1830s, and in this context she met Liszt, and through him, the two other republicans who, according to d'Agoult, most influenced her thinking and her conduct when she and Liszt had their affair—Félicité de Lamennais and George Sand.[22]

D'Agoult describes her relationship with Liszt as revolutionary:

"The years we spent together . . . brought about a complete revolution, not only in my personal relationships [*ma vie de relation*], but also in the intimate depths of my being."[23] D'Agoult remembers Liszt as a rebel in many ways, including politically: "He despised the bourgeois royalty and the government of moderation [*le juste milieu*]; in all his prayers he called for the reign of justice, meaning . . . the republic."[24] During a long visit to Sand's house at Nohant in 1837, d'Agoult met Sand's republican friends, and she recollected with pleasure the intellectual excitement of her stay, including "speeches on the abolition of the death penalty, on all the ideas called humanitarian at that time, on the republic."[25]

With Liszt, Lamennais, and Sand, d'Agoult started her career as a republican, but she also read widely, and talked with many others in the process of articulating for herself a political and spiritual philosophy. During her stay in "Protestant and republican" Geneva, d'Agoult met several men who aided her in the examination of the philosophers Kant, Schelling, Fichte, Hegel, and Spinoza, and the historians Thierry, Guizot, Thiers, and Mignet.[26] After she left Liszt to return to Paris and start a new life as an independent woman, d'Agoult's career as a writer and her interest in politics were both stimulated by Emile de Girardin, whom she met through his wife, Delphine Gay de Girardin. Emile de Girardin was much taken with d'Agoult; in addition to falling in love with her, he encouraged her to write, and he discussed politics with her. In a letter to Liszt d'Agoult wrote of Emile de Girardin: "He thinks I have great abilities and he pushes me to work. . . . You know my growing taste for politics. He develops it by speaking to me in a most interesting manner of the men of today and of his own ideas about progress and the science of administration."[27] D'Agoult continued her political education, reading works by or about Pierre Leroux, Charles Fourier, the saint-simonians, and Robert Owen, attending lectures by Adam Mickiewicz and Jules Michelet at the Collège de France, listening to speeches in the Chamber of Deputies, and talking with a host of republicans and liberals, including Emile de Girardin, Henry Bulwer, George Herweg, baron de Viel-Castel, Hortense Allart, and Eugène Pelletan.[28] When d'Agoult listened to Lamartine's speech against the Paris fortifications proposed in 1840, her excitement led her to ignore time and sex and connect herself with the first French Revolution: "He moved me, and I really felt what must have been the passions of the Constituent [Assembly] and the Convention."[29]

The authors she read and persons she knew were an important part of d'Agoult's sense of herself as a political figure. As a writer she prided herself on being rational, logical, even classical, in a sense, following her early enthusiasm for romanticism. Similarly, she considered her political ideas to be the product of extensive deliberation and to be grounded in reason, even though she embraced them with ardor and commitment. D'Agoult was at pains to distinguish herself from her early mentor, Sand, whom she presented as frighteningly bizarre and overly reliant on fantasy.[30] D'Agoult wished to avoid extremes and emotionalism, as she suggests in this statement about her republicanism: "I was passionate about the republican idea, but I could never be fanatical. I had neither revolutionary traditions nor language."[31]

When the Revolution of 1830 occurred Allart was on a kind of vacation in the countryside, biding her time until her English lover could rejoin her. She mentions concern for the welfare of her former lover, René de Chateaubriand, who had served the Bourbon monarchy, and sadness over the death of a friend in the fighting in Paris. But the anticipation of seeing Bulwer, who finally arrived in France in August, and the pleasures of their seaside tryst seem to have been Allart's overwhelming concerns. Still, Allart's analysis of the Orleans regime and its origins, much enhanced by the hindsight of some thirty to forty years, is highly critical. She maintains that the "democracy" ushered in by revolution "opened careers to the lower classes, or rather to those ambitious men who lead them astray," and that freedom of the press (which ended in 1835, though Allart does not mention this) aroused "a host of misguided ideas called *opinion*. Yes, the opinion of the ignorant." Moreover, according to Allart, this situation fostered a backlash by extreme groups, and she mentions specifically legitimists, republicans, and Bonapartists.[32] Since Allart roundly criticizes almost all of the political possibilities in France during the July Monarchy, what were her political views? Did she adhere to any political ideology?

Allart was a lifelong champion of liberty, and she favored the republican form of government as a good, though not the only, means of securing personal and political freedom. Her first published work, an imagined account of the noble conspiracy against the Guises in 1563, singled out one of the leaders, Barri de La Renaudie, as having a strong and daring character. As an indication of praise, she suggests that he would have been even better had he been born outside of an absolutist state: "He was worthy of being a republican, and, had he been raised in a free state, he might well have been capable of only great acts."[33] Allart's political ideal was the great man (or great woman), an individual of genius completely devoted to statecraft who ruled in the best interests of the people and for the greater glory of the state. Models to her of such ideals in history included Pericles, Piero Soderini (a commoner who rose to become *gonfalonieri* for life in the Renaissance Florentine republic), Elizabeth I, Richelieu, Lord Chatham (William Pitt the Older), and Madame de Staël. Among contemporaries Allart admired François Guizot and, to a lesser extent, Adolphe Thiers as the only statesmen who came close to approximating the greatness of those in the past. In general, tyrants, emperors, and even monarchs did not fulfill Allart's ideal of the great leader, because they acquired power either by force or through inheritance, instead of through personal merit and ability. Thus a republic or a constitutional monarchy were the forms of government best suited for producing the politics or statecraft that Allart admired. Moreover, Allart wrote two major works on great republics of the past—Florence and Athens—and she was wont to agree with Thiers that "a republic is the government that divides the French the least."[34]

Allart was friendly, sometimes intimate, with men and women of a wide range of political leanings—the monarchist Chateaubriand, Restoration satirist Pierre-Jean Béranger, Bonapartist Laure Renault de Saint-Jean d'Angély, liberal Italians Gino Capponi and Niccolo Tommaseo, the Whig Henry Bulwer, the center-left Orleanist Thiers, socialist feminist Pauline Roland, and republicans Sand and d'Agoult. At different times in her youth and young womanhood she circulated in Bonapartist and then Risorgimento social circles, and as an adult she joined a saint-simonienne group and socialized with Sand, d'Agoult, and their friends. Allart's eclectic political ideas and social relationships put her almost in a class by herself. Allart was far more the political theorist and historian than the party adherent. For Allart the study of politics and history was a good in itself, a necessary prerequisite for or accompaniment to a statesman, and a task that Allart, as a woman, usually pursued on her own and in isolation.

Girardin's politicization had a more aesthetic character than did Sand's, d'Agoult's, or Allart's. A pensioner and poet of the Bourbon monarchy, Delphine Gay nonetheless attended the literary revolution that presaged the political revolution of 1830, courtesy of tickets provided by the romantic revolutionary Victor Hugo. At the riotous opening of Victor Hugo's antimonarchical play *Hernani* on 20 February 1830, Gay became the heroine of rebellious and poetic youth at the same time that *Hernani* became their rallying cry. Théophile Gautier, one of the aspiring romantic poets in the audience that night, claims that when Delphine Gay took her seat and leaned over the balustrade to view the crowded theater, he and other youth broke out spontaneously into applause at Gay's stunning beauty: "Her beauty—*bellazza folgorante*—stopped the tumult cold and earned her a triple salvo of applause."[35] Girardin subsequently invited Gautier and others from that rowdy group to her salon years later, after her marriage, and Victor Hugo numbered among her intimates until her death.

As a young, unmarried woman Girardin enjoyed some of her greatest poetic triumphs in the salons of the old aristocracy and commemorating the public ceremonies of the Restoration. Small wonder, then, that in a poem of 1830 Gay regrets the passing of the old dynasty, but at the same time she encourages the French to look forward, to youth and to the future, and to leave the past behind. Similarly, she eulogized Charles X and the monarchical glory he represented on the occasion of his death in exile in 1836, but she also acknowledged the regime's errors and, implicitly, its anachronistic character. As the vicomte de Launay, Girardin contrasted the elegant, chivalrous, poetic court of the Bourbons with its pale, prosaic, Orleanist imitation: "The *ship of state*," she wrote, "is no longer a superb vessel with spreading sails that the capricious winds move along at a whim; it is rather a heavy steam boat, loaded with coal and potatoes, leaving at a designated time and arriving on schedule to its assigned port."[36] Girardin seemed to regret more the passing of a style of life than the end of Old Regime monarchy, for even as she expresses affection for Charles X she also indicates that the old king failed to understand the people and politics of postrevolutionary France.

Girardin's political pragmatism and aesthetic sensibility were best described by her lifelong friend Alphonse de Lamartine, who claims for Girardin a republicanism very like his own.[37] Lamartine, as an aristocrat and a male, was bred for politics, and he considered his political flexibility an asset; he was a constitutional monarchist during the revolution, supporter of republican liberty under Napoleon, liberal legitimist under the Restoration, loyal opposition under the July Monarchy, and a republican in 1848. In his eulogy to Girardin, Lamartine indicates that had Girardin followed her instincts alone, she would have been a legitimist, because the Restoration was the period of her youthful beauty and she had enjoyed the favor of Charles X. But she knew that after 1830 there was no turning back, even though she, like many of her contemporaries, disdained the July Monarchy for being so prosaic, materialistic, and soulless. According to Lamartine, Girardin welcomed the Second Republic at the very least out of necessity, as a better alternative to bourgeois monarchy. But even more, he says, she embraced the republic as "the poetry of events." Because of Girardin's fundamental belief in the beautiful, "nothing could be more beautiful in her eyes than a government of *Pericles* in France. . . . This government of Pericles upheld by a unanimous nation, advised by the talents of all different opinions reconciled out of love for the common homeland [*la patrie commune*], and presided over by one of the best citizens [Lamartine himself!] . . . made her smile."[38] Despite the self-centeredness of this representation of Girardin's republicanism, Lamartine was not entirely off the mark. Girardin's own writing and the remarks of those who knew her suggest a strong aesthetic element to her political commentary and to her republicanism. Indeed, this notion might be applied to all four female authors, who depended a great deal on literary production as a mode of political expression.

The revolutions of 1830, 1832, and 1848 aroused both sympathy and fear among the four women writers, as they did among many persons of the comfortable classes. With the possible exception of Sand, none favored revolution as a means of political and social change; the 1830 event contributed significantly to their interest in politics, however, and eventually to their writing about politics. Excluded from political rights, and more or less accepting that as women they could and should not vote, Sand, d'Agoult, Allart, and Girardin were perhaps inclined to regard republicanism more as an ideal and in the abstract than in terms of power plays and institutions. Still, their ideas about republicanism, though distinctive for each woman, also matched the concerns and language of their time.

Women Writers' Republicanisms

One of the chief issues concerning republicanism for these authors was that of sovereignty. On what social basis should the republic be constructed, and who should govern? Sand, d'Agoult, Allart, and Girardin shared the belief that suffrage should be extended, and that leaders should obtain their positions through merit rather than inheritance or wealth. But they differed among themselves, as did their contempo-

raries, on the virtues of democracy, the role of leaders, the balance between freedom and equality, and the function of republican government itself. Sand was the most radical, viewing the republic as a political instrument for achieving drastic social change through universal
male suffrage. By contrast, d'Agoult, Allart, and Girardin might be
classified as liberal or moderate republicans who expected a republic to
ameliorate the conditions of the laboring poor, but who were wary of
democracy and primarily interested in the state's protection of civil liberties.

Sand was a democrat and a firm believer in the equality of all humans regardless of class background. The working-class origins of her
mother made her identify with the concerns and interests of the laboring poor. Moreover, she strongly believed that equality was a divine
creation: "It seems impossible to me . . . that humanity was authorized
and condemned by its Creator to be divided into masters and slaves."
She believed that once, long ago in the past, a golden age of equality
reigned, destroyed by human weakness and leading to the relatively
recent history of gross inequality and exploitation. But people fought to
restore God's intended condition of equality, and a stunning example
of this struggle was the French Revolution. Despite the best efforts of
the Jacobins and especially of Robespierre, "the only man of the people,
the only friend of truth, the only sincere enemy of tyranny," Enlightenment and bourgeois individualism triumphed. But Sand was confident in the power of the people to continue the struggle and eventually
to overthrow their oppressors, whom she identified with the government of the July Monarchy.[39]

Much as Sand admired great leaders of the popular cause, including
her contemporaries Ledru-Rollin, Lamennais, and Lamartine, she increasingly supported the idea that the people themselves were the dynamic force behind their own liberation and that of society generally.[40]
"The future of the world is with the people, especially with the working
class," Sand wrote in a letter of 1840, and several of her novels elaborated on this theme.[41] Sand's Le Compagnon du tour de France (1840) contains a dialogue between the artisan Pierre Huguenin and the professional (bourgeois) agitator Achille Lefort. Achille questions the capability of the people to change society without the leadership of educated, bourgeois men: "Is it necessary to cross our arms and wait for the
people to liberate themselves? Do you think they can succeed without
advice, without guides, without order [sans règle]?" Pierre replies that

yes, the people will come up with their own rules, guides, and advice, and he suggests that even the most brilliant, well-intentioned man would do well to heed the people he presumes to lead. He should say to them, "I realize that the most simple-minded among you has the right, as much as do I and those like me, to well-being, to freedom, and to education; that the weakest among you has the right to curb my power if I abuse it, and the most obscure [of you] to reject my opinion if it is immoral; that I must prove my virtue and charity to be, in my own eyes and in yours, a great intellectual, a great leader, or a great poet."[42]

This critique of bourgeois leadership that Sand started in *Le Compagnon du tour de France* she continued and developed in the newspaper *L'Eclaireur de l'Indre*, which she founded in 1843 expressly for the purpose of promoting political (and especially republican) understanding among the provincial masses. According to Sand the political achievement of the French Revolution was simply to replace aristocratic tyranny with bourgeois exploitation. To be sure she credited the eighteenth-century republicans with creating the Declaration of the Rights of Man and Citizen, "immortal monument of political science," that articulated the rights belonging to all men. But Sand believed that these earlier republicans ultimately failed because they ignored the duties that must accompany rights in a well-ordered state, duties of the rich and strong toward the poor and weak: "The great error that presided over the formulation of the rights of man derives not only . . . from a misguided and false distinction between rights and duties, but from the complete absence of the notion of solidarity among men." Sand accused the authors of the Declaration of promoting their own bourgeois class at the expense of the laboring masses because they lacked a sense of human community: "They succeeded in legitimating the right of the third estate to exercise power, but in terms of establishing human rights in society they wrote on sand. They raised their own order to the level of privileged caste, but they never established the rights of all because they did not know them."[43]

As far as Sand was concerned republicanism in her own time shared the strengths and weaknesses of the first French republic. It was political in the sense of addressing issues of power; that is, republicanism was a movement that sought to overthrow an abusive regime and replace it with a just government. But she contended that no republic would last, and hence France would have no just government, until republicans adopted socialist ideas of community and equality. And that would happen only when bourgeois republican leaders heeded the voice of the popular classes: "The people understand the source of the problem, for they ask that politics include a social religion, and they ask that socialism adopt a political organization."[44] According to Sand politics meant action and power, while socialism consisted of ideas and spirituality, and only when the two combined would her ideal polity exist. Thus she urged republicans to become socialists, and vice versa. But much as Sand appreciated republicanism as politics, her real preference was for the ideals of socialism. When the Second Republic finally was established in 1848, she declared that *"socialism is the goal, and the republic is the means."*[45]

Sand was utterly convinced that only a republic could succeed in bringing about socialism because a republic was inherently democratic and would inaugurate universal male suffrage. The voice and will of the people would eventually transform the republic from a vehicle for socialism into socialism itself. And since the republic was more of a means to an end than an end in itself, and since socialism was more of a secular religion or philosophy than a political system, Sand never bothered herself with considering just what a republic would look like. In 1848 she did address certain institutional and policy issues; for example, she opposed the institution of the presidency, and she supported the continuation of taxation, though she advocated a graduated income tax. But even in early April 1848, prior to the critical elections to the Chamber of Deputies, Sand articulated the confusion and internal conflicts that all republicans confronted: "The problem is that we are as uncertain about our choice of ideas and institutions as we are about whom we charge to represent us. . . . Well may we recommend to others to choose true republicans, but do we even know what is a true Republic?"[46] Sand trusted that over time and with education the collective intelligence of the working class, represented first by accountable bourgeois leaders but increasingly by their own members, would create the institutions of a stable, social republic. She was, of course, disappointed that the necessary time for this development did not materialize in 1848. As a republican Sand believed that political organization and action were necessary to establish a republic and to allow the (male) masses to participate through democratic suffrage. But for her the real point of the republic was to cultivate that popular voice, and attend to the needs and aspirations of working persons, that would necessarily lead to a transition to socialism created by and for the people.

Unlike Sand, who might have rewritten the republican slogan as "equality, fraternity, and liberty," d'Agoult, Allart, and Girardin placed the greatest emphasis on liberty, fearing or even shunning equality and fraternity. Although they wished to see a republic alleviate poverty through social services and some modest economic intervention, they did not share Sand's hope for social reorganization along communitarian lines. For d'Agoult, Allart, and Girardin, the most important function of a republic was to ensure meritocratic leadership through the guarantee of civil rights and liberties. This liberal republic would be governed by educated, disinterested, progressive persons (mostly men) who would serve the interests of the state and of the masses better than the masses could do themselves. Marie d'Agoult was the most pointed in her disagreements with Sand over the meaning of republicanism.

In an anonymous review of Sand's *Le Compagnon du tour de France,* d'Agoult challenged her former friend's position on democracy and equality. It is clear in this review that d'Agoult did not share Sand's confidence that the people were ready for democracy, much less that they, or some of their number, could take the lead in promoting it. D'Agoult describes the "man of the people" in unflattering terms: "Such as he is made by his burdensome labor, his crude pleasures, his native caution, and the imperfect glimmer of an education lacking in morality." Additionally, d'Agoult disagreed with Sand's representation of equality in the form of the marriage between the artisan Pierre and the aristocrat Yseult. D'Agoult proclaimed that men should "raise" themselves to the level of the elite by ambition and hard work in professions such as law, the military, and politics. She condemned Sand's cross-class marriage as promoting a social equality of the lowest common denominator: "It is a misunderstanding of equality to lower those who are above to the level of those below."[47]

D'Agoult favored democracy as a principle because democracy promised the greatest amount of human freedom, and since she viewed history as the progress of freedom, then it must also be tending toward democracy. Democracy, d'Agoult claimed, "strides alone today along the paths of freedom, that everywhere and always men have conquered by the sweat of their brow."[48] Attaining freedom and democracy is a struggle because existing states, notably the constitutional monarchy of Louis-Philippe, fail to provide the jobs, social services, and education necessary so that all citizens can enjoy freedom, which d'Agoult defines as "the complete development of the life" within each individual.[49] D'Agoult is liberal, if not egalitarian, in the sense that she views the degraded condition of the popular classes to be the result of their poverty, and not an inherent failing. She condemns equally those, like Girardin, who represent the popular classes as lazy and envious, wanting merely to enjoy the benefits of wealth without working, and those, namely Sand, who maintain that "the people alone possess all virtue, all of the genius of modern times." D'Agoult indicates that at the same time that injustice deprives the masses of the basic necessities of life, it provides too much for the elite, who are also alienated from their human potential by excessive ease and luxury. Justice clearly requires some redistribution of goods, though d'Agoult denies that equality means uniformity; she believes that a natural, divine hierarchy of individual talent will assert itself when manmade inequalities are removed. D'Agoult's formula for the ideal society is "justice that will distribute to each [person] science, work and public wealth, not in equal portions, but in sufficient portions, measured according to need."[50]

However, the burden of ameliorating the vicious condition of the masses, of granting them the freedom of self-knowledge and self-development through decent jobs, a living wage, healthful living conditions, edible food, and above all education, lies with an enlightened state rather than with the people themselves. For d'Agoult asserts that as long as the majority of people live in abjection, they are incapable of virtue. She thinks that the people are fundamentally good, but in an unreflective, childish way. "Happier than we, the people, in their energetic simplicity, have flights and enthusiasms denied to us. They abandon themselves entirely to what they admire; they love or they hate truly *with all their heart*."[51] The undefined "we," which presumably includes d'Agoult and like-minded reformers, must take the lead in implementing measures that will improve the condition of the poor and thereby maximize their freedom. In *Nélida*, for instance, the aristocratic heroine, Nélida, vows to use the money and estate left to her by her husband to help the republican cause of education and social change.[52] The democracy that d'Agoult envisions is primarily concerned with equality of opportunity in society, and she does not mention universal suffrage for women or men before 1848.

In her writings of the 1830s Allart represents democracy and popular movements in favorable terms. But over time her enthusiasm for both waned as a result of her reading of history and philosophy and her observation of contemporary events around the world. In her first major historical study, of the Florentine Republic, Allart uses the term *democracy* to describe the struggles of ordinary people to overthrow despotism and to gain representation in politics. She admires the energy, organization, and purpose of the men of the middle class who successfully toppled the noble, tyrannical Ghibeline rulers in 1251: "We see here a people armed, organized in militia, and under the authorities of elders drawn from their ranks, famous revolution and era that will provide the motivation to this entire history of a people filled with a sense of power and freedom."[53] But agitation became a pattern in the history of Florence from Dante to Machiavelli, and eventually that republic, associated with great economic, artistic, and political achievements, disappeared. For Allart the big mistake of the Florentine democrats was eliminating aristocrats from the government, thus limiting their potential for greatness and permanence: "Florence drew its glory from democracy, [but] lacked greater ambition and strength by the absence of an aristocracy and a senate."[54] Allart believed that the populace was gifted, public-spirited, and acted on the best motivation—to increase freedom. However she also believed that only an aristocracy could provide the statecraft to establish a large and enduring state. According to Allart republican Florence exemplified both the strengths and weaknesses of popular movements and uprisings; it was a "small and eternal model of what virtue, genius, and freedom could accomplish."[55]

Even before she had published the second version (which included the second volume), Allart's support for popular initiative in politics diminished in proportion as her enthusiasm for individual leadership increased. In a letter of 1844 to Charles-Augustin Sainte-Beuve, Allart wrote, "As for me, my studies of politics distance me further each day from democracy, and I believe that freedom depends on laws of exception [*la liberté s'appuie sur des lois d'exception*]."[56] And at the time she wrote her memoirs, in the 1860s, she expressed almost complete discouragement about democracy: "According to the teachings of God himself, men of talent and of enlightened society must lead the world; but the word *democracy* opens this career to the lower classes, or rather to those ambitious men who fool them."[57] Allart especially condemned democracy in what she considered to be great states, including France.[58] Moreover, she condemned democracy on aesthetic grounds as well, or rather, on the basis of her understanding of contemporary politics generally and the contemporary meaning of democracy. Allart claimed that democrats were grossly materialistic, that they wished to abolish metaphysics, the appreciation of art, and all human thought and sentiment that was removed from gainful enterprise.[59] For Allart the leveling effects of democracy were apparent in the democratic republic of the United States, a state that she regarded as horribly pedestrian and incapable of producing greatness of any sort. She agreed with her reading of Michel Chevalier, who described the people of the United States as "having their feet in the air and their head on the ground" owing to the perversity of universal (male) suffrage.[60]

Allart's notion of the best state was less a democracy than a meritocracy. She was an elitist who believed that the extension of rights and liberties to a broader swath of society was good, not to empower the masses, but rather so that superior individuals could rise to the top and become leaders and statesmen. Her political history celebrated the progress of equality and freedom in the West, but she concluded also that "an abyss will forever separate the crowd [from] public talents and great characters."[61] The lesson that Allart drew from her study of republics in history was that their success depended not only on democratic freedom but also upon the popular classes retaining an elite of talent: "At least an aristocracy remains for us in France, something lacking in Athens and Florence, and that will save all. It is an aristocracy of election: the people, by its choice, recognize well enough the talents that must guide it."[62] Allart's elitism is even evident in her appreciation for socialism. As long as socialism was administered for the benefit of the people, and not by the people, Allart would call herself a socialist: "I believed that socialism was the welfare of the people, and I was a bit of a socialist, but if socialism is the genius of the people, I am no longer a socialist."[63] Although Allart rarely identified herself as a republican, especially in public, she nonetheless concluded that a republic was the form of government best suited to the cultivation of human genius (which was, for her, the greatest good) through the guarantee of civil and political freedom and representative institutions.

Like Allart and d'Agoult, Girardin was ambivalent about the working classes and about their interpretation of republicanism. She sympathized with the poor, and she shared their dissatisfaction with the July Monarchy. However, she feared that ordinary, working-class people were susceptible to the emotion of envy, and that equally envious and unscrupulous politicians could exploit that. In one of her *Cour-*

rier de Paris entries Girardin asserted that republicans wanted to kill the rich and appropriate their wealth: "Republicans want to overthrow monarchies and disrupt France ... only in order to possess beautiful things themselves and to acquire them by the quickest means possible, by political means, that is to say, without working [for them]."[64] Girardin is not entirely clear on who is a republican. At one point she refers to leaders, politicians who were liberal in 1829 and who have already gained riches from the changes under the July Monarchy; the hypocrisy lies in their demand for equality and popular sovereignty while they enjoy the life of luxury. At another point Girardin says that it is the poor who are most envious of the rich, and hence susceptible to the republican promise of easy money, and yet she also invokes with approval poor but honest republicans from the provinces, uncorrupted by exposure to the wealth of the capital.[65] This is hardly serious political theorizing, and probably represents Girardin's effort to make light of the Blanquist uprising of 1839 and the widespread fear of imminent revolution in the midst of political instability and probable war.

Girardin's persona of the vicomte de Launay was playful and skeptical, if not cynical, and she applied those qualities to the analysis of politics as well as to society and culture. During the political crisis of 1839, when the July Monarchy confronted an attempted popular insurrection and a successful ministerial coup, Girardin portrayed the conflict in France as consisting of a stupid struggle between poor and rich, have-nots and haves. She caricatures the democrats as wanting to deprive the rich of their pleasures in order to bring them down to the same level as working people. The flaw with that system, however, is that when rich people cease to buy horses and carriages, fine clothes, and jewels, workers lose their livelihoods. Paradoxically, according to Girardin, the democrats will achieve the opposite of their goal; that is, the social leveling they propose will in fact consolidate the wealth of the rich, since they will be unable to spend their money, and it will impoverish the working poor, whose labor will not be needed.[66] But Girardin is evenhanded in her satire, and she presents the rich as similarly foolish in their selfish insouciance, willfully ignoring the real social problems in their country by their misguided belief that "political persecution, reversal of fortune, fire, even sickness" can happen to anyone but oneself.[67] Equally selfish and misguided, poor democrats and rich conservatives are together bringing France to ruin, in Girardin's representation. And she has little faith in political leaders to prevent this decline, for she sees them as utterly self-serving, pettily vying for portfolios and high-status positions while the country deteriorates.[68]

Not quite a decade later, in 1847, when Girardin anticipated another revolution, she offered a more serious analysis of the situation and recommended a more liberal position. She asserts that ministers want only power for power's sake, and that they are indifferent to "the greatness of the country, the well-being of the people, and the progress of civilization." They dole out favors solely for the purpose of securing deputies' votes, whether or not the administration of France is well served. So debased are the deputies and ministers of France that worker-poets surpass them in learning, a sure indication to Girardin that these leaders had better change their ways if they presume to continue to lead an increasingly literate people: "It is a very serious political question and in spite of your huge disdain, you had better find another way of governing this people and this country where the masons, the barrel-makers, and the carpenters are already more literary than you." Girardin reiterates that she is no advocate of "the beautiful dream of the envious they call equality," but she claims that popular discontent is grounded in real abuses that the government should address. "If we do not believe that all those on top should step down, we do believe that many among those on the bottom should rise; if we do not believe in leveling by envy, we do believe in equality through education."[69]

Girardin did not declare herself a republican until after the fact of the Second Republic in 1848. But she was explicit about her growing disenchantment with constitutional monarchy. "There are no more statesmen," she says in 1847; there are only men tending to their own business. "People so satisfied with their lot feel no need for progress; we can hope for nothing from their sordid ambition."[70] The appearance of Lamartine's *L'Histoire des Girondins* in 1847 suggested to Girardin that the only possible future for a France mired in political corruption and incompetence was revolution. Girardin "does not love revolutions," but she indicates in her review of the book that Lamartine "speaks of revolutionary ideas like a man who has discovered the secret of applying them without crimes, without violence, without tempests." Clearly Girardin would prefer political reform to revolution, and she says nothing in this review about republicanism, though significantly she devotes much attention to Lamartine's treatment of Marie-Antoinette and Madame Roland. Girardin finds "this book full

of instruction and prophecy," and she welcomes the republic that follows less than one year after the publication of *L'Histoire.*[71]

During the July Monarchy the four women either embraced republicanism or saw it as the only viable political alternative to a highly unsatisfactory regime. Sand was unique among them in her faith in the
working class and confidence in democracy. She was optimistic that
republicanism as a political movement would eventually establish a
democratic republican government and that the popular electorate
would in turn create a social republic. By contrast d'Agoult, Allart, and
Girardin championed a republic that encouraged individual ability and
effort through guarantees of personal freedom to maximize individual
potential. They believed that the state had an obligation to all its citizens, but they differed on the extent of those obligations, with d'Agoult
favoring an extensive welfare plan, and Allart and Girardin concerned
mostly with meritocratic opportunity. These three considered the masses wholly unprepared for democracy, and they relied on an educated,
progressive elite to make the political and social reforms necessary for
liberty and stability.

All four women writers developed distinctive understandings of
republicanism that mirrored many of the ideas and complications of
male republicans in their time. Yet as women they could not participate
in republican politics in the same manner that men did, and even their
writing reflected alternative modes of political engagement. Sand and
d'Agoult were explicit about their commitment to republicanism, but
they developed different styles of promoting the cause. While Sand la-
bored to disseminate political awareness to the masses and bring them
into the political process, d'Agoult cultivated her republicanism in the
elite setting of the salon, and she sought to appeal primarily to bourgeois, male republicans through her writing. Allart, too, wrote for the
educated, and she aspired to political theorizing of a high order that
transcended both time and geographical boundaries but could also be
applied to contemporary practices. Nonetheless, her ideas about leadership qualifications led her almost invariably to republicanism as the
government best suited for the formation of capable leaders. Of the four
female authors, Girardin was best integrated into the political system of
the July Monarchy, through her salon and her journalism. An astute ob-
server of political practice, she engaged in politics as a satirist and a
prophet, precisely reflecting the growing mood of discontent in 1847.

Although politics generally and republican politics especially were gendered masculine, each woman writer devised for herself a distinctive means of contributing to politics through writing and sociability.

Styles and Forms of Political Engagement

Sand's style of engagement was to communicate her political ideas to a large audience through newspapers and novels. It was a style that suited her abilities and her sex, in contrast to the action, bravery, and heroics of the men's republican clubs. But even in a movement that required masculine strength to combat a repressive regime there was a place for other qualities. Emmanuel Arago wrote to Sand in 1835 that the cause of social and political change needed brains as well as brawn, both to construct a new society and to tear down the existing structure. "Only arms are necessary to overthrow, but it takes a mind to rebuild. We never lack for arms, be assured, but we do lack for minds. Give us yours; work, work, it is your duty, you have a great and sacred mission." Arago envisioned Sand leading the people "out of the desert," raising society from its misguided and degrading worship of the doctrinaire school.[72] Sand accepted this sacred mission, though with perhaps more modesty than the Moses references imply. Well aware of the limitations of her education, a condition Sand shared with all women and with the working class, she nonetheless asserted their right to pursue knowledge publicly. In 1844 Sand charges that those brought to power through the revolutionary actions of the popular classes have not deigned to share with their supporters the benefit of their education: "We accuse everyone of failing to ensure that the ideas [of liberty, fraternity, and equality] made headway among us, and that those who say they possess [these ideas] have done so little to popularize them."[73] Sand proposes to accomplish what men of action and authority have neglected to do—to disseminate broadly the ideas of equality, justice, and community upon which a new society could be based, but only with the informed participation of all.

Even after she called herself republican and socialist, Sand mistrusted doctrines and systems and advocated a politics of quest, or philosophizing, as she said. She considered the republican newspaper *Le National* to be insufficiently concerned with philosophizing—or trying to figure out, with the input of the people, just what form a new republican government and society should assume. Thus Sand's goal in starting the republican journal *La Revue Indépendante* in 1841 was to fill that gap. She wrote to her friend Charles Duvernet that the republicans of *Le National* were adept at criticizing the existing political and social organization and calling for revolutionary action, but that Sand's journal would focus on ideas about the new institutions and the new laws that would replace the old ones: "We [in contrast to the republicans of *Le National*] say to ourselves, let us make a revolution, but let us consider what we will have thereafter."[74] Sand's representation of politics, and she clearly means revolutionary, or at least reformist, politics, is similar to Louis Blanc's representation of republicans as combative, brave, and definitely masculine. Sand writes that these agitators, for she sees them as primarily occupied with rallying the populace to act, are short-sighted in their goals. "A generous but blind faith pervades them [*les enivre*]. Men of action, their simple and strong slogan is thus: 'let us act forever, we will see [what happens] afterward.'" Sand calls this ardor for action "heroic but dangerous," because she claims that these political men ignore "the real needs of humanity, the need of a social doctrine and a political religion for the future."[75]

By contrast Sand believed that socialists were so intent upon abstract ideas like justice and truth that they ignored the social struggle taking place. According to Sand, socialists rightfully claimed that neither the bourgeoisie nor the working class was yet prepared to implement a society along the lines of liberty, equality, and fraternity. She agreed with them, therefore, that what needed to be done, even more than overthrowing the existing government, was "to change thinking, to win hearts, to transform beliefs." It was a difficult task, to be sure, one made more difficult by the fact that socialists were internally divided, socially marginalized, and sometimes discouraged to the point of immobility.[76] Yet that was the task to which Sand committed herself, engaging all in a quest to solve social and political problems, in a dialogue or conversation about complex issues that was ongoing in pursuit of consensus. In a letter of 1841 Sand invites her correspondent to join the quest:

Debate, examine, question, clarify, express all the principles, proclaim your doctrine and your science and your faith on all of these points. If you possess the truth, we will bow on our knees before you. If you do not, but you search for truth in good faith, we will esteem you and contradict you only with the respect that is due to brothers.[77]

Sand's sense that no single doctrine provides all the answers, and that people must experiment in order to achieve social justice, is evident in her novel *Le Péché de Monsieur Antoine* (1845).

In this story a reclusive old aristocrat, the marquis de Boisguilbaut, has adopted socialist ideals similar to those of the young student Emile Cardonnet, idealistic son of a very materialistic industrialist. After many years of solitary study, of reading Saint-Simon, Fourier, the writings of communists, and all the great works of philosophy from the past, Boisguilbaut is convinced of one principle: "the equality of rights and the inevitable necessity of the equality of pleasures." Boisguilbaut shares Emile's belief about combining liberalism and socialism toward a better society. Emile says that his father's ideal, "Each will be compensated according to his ability," is incomplete, and he adds the formula "to each according to his needs" in order for justice and happiness to reign. Boisguilbaut then bequeaths his large fortune and estate to Emile and his fiancée, Gilberte, for the express purpose of implementing these principles: "I wanted for the future that his vast property be destined for the foundation of a *commune*." Boisguilbaut even provides a tentative outline for establishing the community, but he readily admits that it might require revision: "I have tried to sketch a plan and provide the bases [for the commune]. But this plan may be defective and its foundations fragile." He counsels Emile and Gilberte to apply "social science" to their community, and he warns them that it will take a lot of work and a lot of time—"Perhaps it will not be you, my children, but rather your children who will see the final maturation of my project." Boisguilbaut is completely satisfied that Emile is worthy to take on this immense task of putting their communitarian ideals into practice, because when he asks Emile exactly what he would do with such a property, Emile replies, "I would try! [*J'essayerias!*]"[78]

For Sand, idealism and willingness to work and experiment were more important than systems or ideology for social transformation. It was her mission to cultivate among the people the kind of philosophizing that she attributes to the aristocrat Boisguilbaut and the bourgeois Emile in order to create a public-spirited citizenry. At the same time that Sand aspired to educate the popular classes to think for themselves and to contribute to the establishment of a better government and society, she identified herself with the students and not the masters. Early in 1848 she assumed the identity of a Berrichon peasant, Blaise Bonnin, to recount to her compatriots the history of France and the meaning of republicanism, and to begin the process of an inclusive, popular, political education that the new republic would continue: "From this moment [the government] will educate us, it will send us printed materials, it will encourage us to gather together and teach one another. . . . Finally, little by little, we will learn what it means to be citizens."[79]

D'Agoult, unlike Sand, counted herself among the elite and not the people. Her salon was her first mode of entry into politics, and her writing was almost equally elite-oriented—articles and essays that were clearly intended to engage the ideas of great thinkers of the present and past. D'Agoult established herself first as a literary and artistic authority, publishing art reviews and fiction and cultivating a literary salon in Paris with luminaries such as Sainte-Beuve, Alfred de Vigny, and Eugène Sue. But her friendships with Lamennais, Emile de Girardin, and Lamartine brought a more political tone to her salon.[80] Encouraged by her publisher, she wrote a series of essays on German literary and political figures, and so she turned to more philosophical and political writing. According to d'Agoult her writing brought her into contact with republican men—indeed, brought republican men to her. She asserts that her *Essai sur la liberté*, first published in 1847, was not very successful in terms of the number of readers, but that a few of its readers embraced it, and its author, with enthusiasm. The *Essai*, d'Agoult writes, "had attracted to her many youthful spirits, republicans, humanitarians, all those around the *Revue Indépendante*, all those who more or less openly preached the republic."[81] Similarly, she writes that the publication of a later work also drew republican men to her salon: "The *Histoire de la Révolution de 1848*, in the process of publication, brought to [her salon] eminent men in the republican party."[82] At the same time that d'Agoult acknowledged that she made her first contacts with republicans through Liszt and Sand, she wanted to show that republican men sought her out because they admired her ideas, the products of her brain and her pen. She believed that she had original and well-conceived views to contribute to republicanism, an idea her growing circle of republican friends confirmed.

If she could have, d'Agoult might have liked to disseminate her ideas from a university lectern as a professor, or from the podium of a legislative chamber as a politician. In her book *Dante et Goethe* of 1866, d'Agoult creates the figure of Diotima, who resembles herself, and who explains to a rapt audience of four young people the similarities be-

tween the two great writers of Italy and Germany. In the course of the
lessons, thinly disguised as dialogues, Diotima confesses to be embar-
rassed at the idea that she, a woman, is presuming to teach like a professor. An adoring pupil asserts the absurdity of excluding capable
women from the professoriat: "Why does it seem ridiculous to the
French that women should teach what they know? Why would it be un-
seemly for them to say in a university hall, with a little more polish and
continuity, what is thought to be very natural and very agreeable for
them to say in salons, where supposedly they reign and govern opinion
in all things?" Diotima then considers how ridiculous Madame de Staël
would have appeared, with her turban and bare arms, declaiming from
the tribune of the Assembly as she did in her salon. But on second
thought, she says that Staël "would have been truly in her place there,
beautiful like Mirabeau, like him conveying conviction in her gaze, in
her gesture, in her virile voice." The conversation continues, and one
character marvels that "this prejudice against the direct involvement of
women in teaching and politics" exists only in France, in contrast to the
United States, where men support women's equality of rights and duties (!), and to Italy, where women hold university chairs. Diotima as-
sures her listeners that female intellectuals in Italy were no less beautiful and feminine for their brilliance of mind and then returns to her lesson on Dante.[83]

D'Agoult creates a model of the intellectual and political woman
with Diotima, who expounds calmly, rationally, and persuasively
while retaining a modest but attractive femininity. Diotima is d'A-
goult's ideal of herself, a woman of brilliance and beauty toward whom
men (especially young men) of intelligence and republican politics are
drawn. D'Agoult cannot be a professor or politician in nineteenth-
century France, but she can profess her ideas from the center of a republican salon. Without sacrificing her femininity d'Agoult cultivates a
republican leadership elite through her salon conversation and her
learned books.

Allart is Aspasia to d'Agoult's Diotima. She was the mistress of several political men, and their involvement in politics was part of their
appeal to her. During British parliamentary elections following the
1832 Reform Act, Allart asserted that her lover Bulwer worried that he
might not be elected and that Allart would leave him. Allart claims to
quote Bulwer as saying, "If I am not elected you will no longer love me;
you love Parliament." Allart goes on to admit that "with my tastes,

must not the man who would please me be the one who would choose to be in Parliament?"[84] In fiction Allart celebrated the role of female companion to a political man with her character Marpé. One evening in Paris, Marpé and her lover Remi have "a happy conversation" as they stroll through the park at the lower end of the Champs-Elysées: "We spoke a long time about his career and about politics. . . . Should he, under these circumstances, go along with a particular party?" Marpé prides herself on her political knowledge and claims that Remi could have such a conversation with no other woman because he would have to explain everything to her. "I was more in his confidence than anyone," she boasts.[85] Allart's ideal of political engagement, at least for herself in nineteenth-century France, was the woman who was mistress, confidante, and advisor to a political man. For this role a woman needed intelligence and learning (among other things), and Allart aspired through her own scholarship to prove that women were just as capable as men of intellectual and political endeavors. She dedicated her history of the Republic of Florence to "reformed women" and to the cause of the "improvement of women's condition." Asserting that the mind has no sex, she continues: "As soon as woman has intelligence, she addresses all that human intelligence addresses, and never does one inquire about the sex of truth." Allart hopes that all women will become more enlightened, but she maintains that only some have the exceptional ability to join equally exceptional men in a new "moral aristocracy" of merit.[86]

Until the world recognized the "equality of exceptionalism" among women and men, Allart had to settle for involvement in politics through male lovers. But writing was still another means of contributing to politics, if not actively participating in it, and it proved far more reliable than men. Throughout the years of active heterosexuality Allart never stopped reading and writing, but she suggests, perhaps facetiously, that in middle age she enjoyed politics almost as much as she had earlier enjoyed sex with politicians. "[Politics] is now my only pleasure [jouissance]!"[87] she wrote to Sainte-Beuve in 1846, following a favorable remark on Thiers's political performance that year. It is possible that Allart was joking to Sainte-Beuve that, absent his physical embraces, she was forced to seek her pleasure elsewhere, and she also indicates in the same letter that being well into middle age she no longer desires the sexual passions of youth. In any case Allart enjoyed politics. She avidly followed the contemporary political scene in

France, analyzing events and individuals in terms of how they measured up to her own theories about freedom, political organization, and statecraft.

Allart's style of political engagement was to amass historical data, examine and test different philosophies, and compile this material into books intended to further the science of statecraft. She spent several years researching and writing *Histoire de la République de Florence* (1836 and 1843), *Essai sur l'histoire politique* (1857), and *Histoire de la République d'Athènes* (1866). Although her books do not appear to have sold very well, and some were not even reviewed, Allart never lost faith in the merits of her ideas.[88] She was living out, at least in part, what she considered to be the practice of the ideal statesman who studied the science of politics and applied that knowledge to statecraft. It is therefore not surprising that Allart greatly admired Adolphe Thiers as a historian and as a politician, and that she considered him, along with François Guizot, the leading light of contemporary French politics.

Allart regularly praised the political adroitness of Thiers.[89] Indeed, she castigated her cousin Delphine Gay de Girardin for publicly ill using Thiers, referring perhaps to Girardin's satire of Thiers in the privately performed *L'Ecole des journalistes* of 1839. In 1841 Allart commanded Sainte-Beuve to refrain from discussing "that woman whom you call my cousin and who is no longer, [for she is part] of the enemy camp, whose tasteless gibes and flagrant attacks seek to diminish [*flétrir*] the greatest and most noble hope of our time."[90] Allart was not above criticizing Thiers, but perhaps Girardin's dislike of him inclined her to defend him all the more forcefully. Allart related Thiers's strengths and weaknesses as a politician to his analysis of history, notably his history of the French Revolution. She faulted him for what she considered errors of interpretation—namely, failing to appreciate the greatness and accomplishments of the early phase of the French Revolution.[91] Moreover, she suggested that Madame de Staël wrote a better history of the same events, by more accurately identifying Napoleon's violation of freedoms, in contrast to Thiers, who justified his breaking of the representative body. Allart infers from this historical interpretation grounds for mistrusting Thiers as a minister in the government, because he might well curtail civil liberties. Ultimately, however, she still hoped that he would rise to the occasion in the future, for he was a strong and capable leader; in 1848 she supported the idea of a republican government under his presidency (see Chapter 7).[92] Allart herself could not practice politics as Thiers could, but she was the consummate scholar, for whom research and writing were good in themselves, and which, for the most part, only exceptional women and men could appreciate.

On the surface Allart's political courtesanship and detailed scholarship made her quite the opposite of Girardin, the brilliant *salonnière* and witty satirist. But while Allart re-created an elite of philosopher kings (and queens) mostly out of thinkers and statesmen from the past, Girardin cultivated a new elite of writers and politicians in her salon. Girardin effected an aesthetic and social transformation in her salon, promoting an elegance that was neither royalist nor bourgeois and a society judged by innate worth rather than by birth or wealth.[93] Girardin named this standard *individual* or *natural rank*, by which she meant more than talent or character but a collection of qualities that defined a person no matter what that individual's social position or occupation. Indeed, individual rank and social rank often conflict, and Girardin admired those who overcame low social origin by virtue of their merit—such as the great tragedienne Rachel, honored by all France.[94] During the July Monarchy few outspoken republicans met Girardin's standards of style and achievement (notable exceptions were Sand and d'Agoult), but she entertained major figures from the left and center opposition parties, whose increasing dissatisfaction with the government of Louis-Philippe Girardin shared and expressed in her feuilleton.

At the same time that Girardin the *salonnière* cultivated a stylish opposition politics in her home, the vicomte de Launay often parodied the political process in general and passed judgment on political groups and individuals. In 1840 Girardin deemed Parliament to be a carnival far more entertaining than the social whirl that preceded Lent. The dance of the parliamentarians is one of exchanging votes for favors, she writes in her column, with a particularly stunning coup coming from the deputy who knows that a particular person with daughters to marry will sell his vote in exchange for husbands, even if it means voting against his own party. "I know the House as well as my house [*Je connais la Chambre comme ma chambre*]," the successful vote-getter explains, and paraphrasing Louis XI, he says, "In our century, *to pay is to reign*."[95] In the same year she parodied political speeches, attaching fabricated words to individual deputies. For example, Girardin includes a "summary" of a speech by Odilon Barrot: "I have nothing to say; all the same, I will speak for three hours"; and from Guizot: "I will not tolerate that someone today speak of the crown as I did two years ago," and "The king, sirs, is not at all interested in what happens in his realm."[96] Though grounded in July Monarchy events and personalities, Girardin's rendering of pomposity, hypocrisy, and banality among politicians still amuses. Her satires made light of politicians and politics, but they also drew attention to abuses and incompetence. From the private boudoir or the garden where she penned the *Courrier de Paris*, Girardin engaged in politics as a satirist and commentator, aided by visits to the Chamber debates and by personal contacts among politicians. She asserted clear positions on certain politicians and policies alongside her pronouncements on fashion, balls, and social customs.

A figure that Girardin loved to attack was Adolphe Thiers, more for personal than for political reasons, but on occasion because she truly objected to his policies. Girardin disliked Thiers because he did not fit in with her more literary friends, and because he quarreled with Emile de Girardin over the political uses of *La Presse*, French intervention in Spain, and Emile de Girardin's eligibility for the office of deputy. Moreover, Thiers's salon, hosted by his mother-in-law (and rumored mistress) Madame Dosne, rivaled Girardin's, particularly in its capacity to attract prominent political figures, inasmuch as Thiers was almost always in the ministry and on occasion the prime minister.[97] Although the vendetta between the Girardins and the Thiers/Dosne couple provided juicy gossip for Parisian society, peaking with Girardin's play *L'Ecole des journalistes*, which included characters closely resembling Thiers, Madame Dosne, and the young Madame Thiers, Girardin's commentary on Thiers the politician had some merit. Girardin was not the only one who viewed him as a man without principle or conviction, a hypocrite who used his eloquence to bring down governments and to advance misguided policies, only later to deny responsibility for creating instability and uncertainty—and all in the interest of his personal desire for power rather than for the good of France.[98] When Thiers made a speech deploring France's diplomatic impotence in the Mediterranean, Girardin reminded readers that the situation was of Thiers's own making.[99] She was particularly incensed at his proposal to fortify Paris in 1840, after his aggressive colonial policy in the Middle East had nearly caused a war between France and Europe. Like many liberals and leftists, Girardin opposed this measure as a first step toward civil war, strengthening the government against internal, popular opposition rather than protecting France from invasion. She presented the fortifications proposal as an attempt to muzzle free speech and thought: "We view with terror a project intended to stifle a nascent reign of intelligence in Paris."[100] In the end, the Chamber voted in favor of the fortifications, but France backed down in the Middle East, Thiers's ministry fell, and he was replaced by Guizot, who held on to power for almost the entire decade of the 1840s, until 1848.[101]

Girardin was kinder in her column to Guizot, who was a regular guest at her salon, though he did not entirely escape caricature and criticism. She even excused him for having to compromise his principles and honesty in the interest of maintaining a majority, evoking sympathy for his position rather than condemnation.[102] However, her real hero throughout the July Monarchy was Alphonse de Lamartine, the man she might have fallen in love with on her visit to Italy in 1825, and who, in any case, remained a close friend for life. Invariably, Lamartine brought poetry, reason, and sound political judgment to the Chamber of Deputies, according to Girardin's accounts of his speeches. Girardin quotes Lamartine as saying that to fortify Paris "is to fortify the guillotine," and she admonished the peers to take heed, since "poets are prophets."[103] And Girardin devoted almost an entire column to Lamartine's history of the Girondins that appeared in 1847, calling it a revolution in itself for the debates it engendered and the conflicts it both reflected and prophesied. Much as she feared revolution Girardin supported Lamartine in his opposition to the July Monarchy and, eventually, in his leadership of the Second Republic in 1848.

The different styles of political engagement of Sand, d'Agoult, Allart, and Girardin suggest that the legal exclusion of women from politics was by no means complete. Women could neither vote nor run for office, but they could read and write; they still had access to political ideas. Moreover, these four authors generated their own political ideas and succeeded in getting them published. They maintained their middle-class status and the aura of the exceptional woman, and did not try to compete with men entirely in male terms. That is, Sand left to men the active roles of clubs, public speaking, and, on occasion, street fighting, while she assumed the role of writer and publicist. Sand aspired to convert through the word rather than the deed, though this gender division of labor was not so neat as it appeared inasmuch as part of Sand's mission was to empower workers and women to challenge the exclusive leadership of middle-class men. D'Agoult claimed an intellectual authority that was feminine in its trappings; she wanted to be a professor whose feminine beauty was enhanced by academic robes.

Over time and in other circumstances women might become accustomed to effective public speaking and acceptance by audiences, but d'Agoult herself would be the model of attractive femininity combined with assured intelligence. Allart saw nothing demeaning in the role of mistress and advisor to a political man, and it was only a step away from her ideal of an elite of exceptional women and men thinking and ruling together. But short of sustaining such a relationship and position, she settled for an intellectual authority more isolated, scholarly, and textual than d'Agoult's. Finally, Girardin fashioned herself as political satirist, closely linked to politicians and government through her salon and personal relationships, but also positioning herself as an outsider to prod, expose, and ridicule, so that others might effect political change.

Republicanism, Women, and Gender

Sand very clearly discerned the masculine and bourgeois quality of republicanism. She admitted that bourgeois men were better educated than poor men and than all women: "We do not recognize in the opposite sex an innate superiority, but we are forced to acknowledge the result of the incomplete education we have received and that does not allow us to attribute to ourselves any type of teaching."[104] But Sand presumed to rectify this situation through her own literary and political efforts. She would further the quest for new political institutions that would guarantee liberty, equality, and fraternity, and she would propagandize republican and socialist efforts to that end. At the same time that she believed that the people needed guidance and enlightenment in order to become agents of their own liberation and contributors to social transformation, she also admonished male leaders to overcome their "brutal instinct of masculine priority that society consecrates and sanctifies" and heed the questions and efforts of "thirty million proletarians, women, and children, the ignorant and oppressed of all kinds."[105] Sand's commitment to republicanism was steadfast, and she did indeed offer her "brains" to support the "brawn" of republican men in the campaign to win popular support to the cause. However, she also drew attention to injustices against women and to how republicanism must address women and the family as part of its promised moral regeneration, the embodiment of the revolutionary principles of liberty, equality, and fraternity.

D'Agoult asserts her commitment to republicanism as deriving from her liberalism. From her perspective that the best state promoted the greatest freedom, she concluded that the republic was the superior form of government. People speak of "republican virtues," she notes, but never of "monarchical virtues." The reason was that people living in a monarchy had no freedom to be virtuous. "A republic is composed of *citizens*; monarchy requires *subjects*. The institution that creates public freedom is the only one that admits of public virtue."[106] Public freedom for d'Agoult did not necessarily, or immediately, entail women ascending the podium as political leaders. However, she did conceive of a role for women as educators and promoters of liberty, and even as heroines of French greatness—"France converted by Clotilde, saved by Joan of Arc, illustrated by Héloïse, Sévigné, Lafayette, Dacier, Duchatelet, Roland, de Staël."[107] But the spread of liberty and the accessibility of greatness to all required changes in women's conditions that d'Agoult would champion as part of her republican ideal of liberty.

In her autobiography Allart's assertion about the best form of government, led by an elite of the educated and the intelligent, most closely resembles the republican ideal of Plato, including the participation of exceptional women: "The world must be led by an intellectual aristocracy of men and of *women*."[108] Allart's understanding of "aristocracy" was distinctive; she meant a meritocracy, a select group distinguished by intelligence and knowledge in which sexual difference was irrelevant.[109] Devotion to politics as a science was a criterion for membership in the "aristocracy" of ability, and women, as well as men, could be able students of politics. Thus Allart considered certain historical female figures—Aspasia, Elizabeth I, Madame de Staël, to name only a few—and some contemporary women—George Sand, Marie d'Agoult, and herself—as part of the elite who should govern in behalf of the masses. For her a republic was the most likely form in which this ideal could be realized—elitist and at the same time preserving liberty. But like male members of this elite, women needed freedom and education in order to exercise statecraft and contribute to national greatness, and Allart's republic, like Sand's and d'Agoult's, would significantly improve the civil status of women.

Girardin was far less outspoken in her efforts to feminize republicanism than were Sand, d'Agoult, and Allart—that is, until the revolution of 1848 and the Second Republic. Nonetheless all four to some extent reshaped republicanism by performing and articulating a model of republican womanhood. Simply by being republican women, creating republican identities as, respectively, seeker and popularizer, rationalist and professor, courtesan and scholar, *salonnière* and satirist, Sand, d'Agoult, Allart, and Girardin opened up possibilities for a less rigidly gendered republicanism. But they went even further than that. They made improvements in women's civil status a significant component of their republicanism. For them republicanism was not only about the protection of liberties and electoral reform. Their republican goal of social transformation necessarily entailed the reform of women and the family, and on those subjects Sand, d'Agoult, and Allart especially spoke with the authority of experience as well as of principle.

6 ⌒ Republican Women and Republican Families

In her (unfinished) memoirs, Marie d'Agoult reconstructs a favorite house she bought in Paris in 1851 near the Champs Élysées. She describes in detail its setting, design, and her own decoration of the interior. D'Agoult appears to have been particularly fond of a small octagonally shaped salon whose doors were ornamented with medallions representing great Italian creative artists—"Dante, Giotto, Guido d'Arezzo, Leonardo, Raphael, etc." She writes, "Above the portrait of Michelangelo I put the adage of Sallust: *Pulchrum est bene facere reipublicae* ["It is beautiful to do well by the republic"], as if to give myself the illusion that we lived, like these Florentines, in the heart of a proud and beautiful republic."[1] The passage from Sallust, historian and supporter of the late Roman Republic, was certainly an appropriate maxim for d'Agoult, who spent much of her life furthering the republican cause in France.

The rest of the passage that these lines introduce is also highly significant in terms of d'Agoult's self-conception as a republican woman. The larger passage reads: "It is beautiful to do well by the republic, and not at all worthless to speak well on its behalf, for renown can be attained through military or peaceful means."[2] Sallust is making a distinction between serving the republic as a statesman or soldier, and as a writer, since he in fact was forced to leave public office and then became a historian. Similarly, d'Agoult, barred by her sex from a military or legislative career, believed that her contributions to republicanism as a writer were by no means unworthy. Indeed, in the preface to the first volume of her autobiography d'Agoult asserts that women can influence public life just as much as men. The implication here is that women's mode of influence is conversation and especially writing. According to d'Agoult, an exceptional woman, "by conquering the imagination, exciting the mind, and stimulating the brain to reexamine received opinions, will make an impact on her century by other means than, but perhaps just as effectively as, a legislative assembly or an army captain."[3] D'Agoult, like Sallust, served the republic as a historian and writer, but unlike Sallust, she did not have the option or opportunity of becoming a statesman or soldier. D'Agoult, along with other female supporters of republicanism in the nineteenth century, articulated for herself a political and public identity despite republicanism's exclusion of women from political rights and even from public life.

For d'Agoult, Sand, Allart, and Girardin, the construction of republican womanhood was inseparable from the construction, or reconstruction, of the republican home or family. D'Agoult created her "proud and beautiful republic" in the home and among selected family members, as a model and inspiration to all French republicans both before and especially after the short-lived Second Republic (1848–52). Just as the four authors wrote of their own families as supportive of and cultivating republican daughters, they wrote of families in general, and the families they formed as adults in particular, as alternatives to the patriarchal model originating in the first French Republic and enshrined in the Napoleonic legal code.

This chapter analyzes how, in their writing and in their self-representations, d'Agoult, Sand, Allart, and Girardin created themselves as republican women and offered alternative family configurations and relationships to the separate spheres construct and patriarchal family of republicanism. It begins by charting their ruptures with male republicans and their independence as republican women. It then addresses their ideas about gender relations, marriage, women's civil status, female education, and divorce, analyzing their arguments for improvements in women's condition as a distinctive feminist contribution to republicanism, one that was between republican motherhood and feminist equality. Scholars have chided these four women writers for failing to support their less privileged sisters in their quest for gender equality. But neither did they simply reinforce or even revise republican motherhood, the notion that women best served the republic as wives and mothers who imparted republican ideals and virtues to their children in the family setting. Instead, they articulated a republicanism that entailed a transformation of the couple and the family into egalitarian, rather than patriarchal, relations, such that women like themselves might serve the republic as rational and public actors, and not only as emotional and private moralizers. This is evident in the personal conduct of the four authors "living" as republican women, representing in themselves educated, independent, and professional women, and establishing households and lifestyles that eliminated the boundary between public and private that underlay republicanism's exclusion of women.

Republican Motherhood, Socialism, and Feminism

One of the most significant accomplishments of the first French Republic (1792–1804) was the construction of the concept now known as republican motherhood, which successfully excluded women from political rights in France for more than 150 years. A key text in the formulation of this notion is the speech by André Amar to the meeting of the National Convention on 9 Brumaire 1793 justifying the abolition of women's political clubs. Amar enumerated the capabilities required to govern as including "extensive knowledge, unlimited attention and devotion, a strict immovability, and self-abnegation," and he asserted that women in general are incapable "of these cares and of the qualities they call for." He goes on to say that "the private functions for which women are destined by their very nature are related to the general order of society; this social order results from the differences between man and woman. Each sex is called to the kind of occupation which is fitting for it." Amar contended that man is suited for "everything that calls for force, intelligence, capability, . . . he alone seems to be equipped for profound and serious thinking which calls for great intellectual effort and long studies which it is not granted to women to pursue." Female characteristics, according to Amar, suit women for educating children and imbuing them with republican virtue: "Such are their functions, after household cares." "We believe, therefore, that a woman should not leave her family to meddle in affairs of government," and "we believe, therefore, . . . that it is not possible for women to exercise political rights."[4]

Amar, like many others, argued that women and men were naturally different, and that women's inherent nurturing abilities and limited rationality disqualified them for participation in politics, Although such assertions about female incapacity for politics were contested, both within and outside the legislative chamber, they nonetheless carried the day, resulting in the short term in the prohibition against public political activity by women in 1793. In the long term these ideas were embedded in the Civil Code of 1804, which subjected married women to their husbands' authority within the family, as well as in practices that restricted the public activity of women generally. Provisions of the Civil Code included clauses such as the following: a double standard on the prosecution and punishment of adultery; married women must reside where their husbands choose; wives owe obedience to their husbands; and the requirement of a husband's permission for a wife to do such things as transfer property, sue in court, or make a will.[5] In 1816 divorce was prohibited. Additionally, the state slighted female education in contrast to what it provided for males, women were barred from serving on juries and from access to professions, and women were prohibited from voting or running for public office.[6] Most lawmakers expected women to devote themselves primarily to domestic pursuits and to confine their political involvement to the rearing of good (male) citizens within the home.

Scholars offer various interpretations of the meaning and implications of this republican exclusion of women from political rights. Some emphasize the fundamentally masculine character of republicanism that eradicated the feminine from its so-called universal principle of equality. They argue that male republicans contrived to deprive women of independence, autonomy, and the status of individuals, then to assert that only (male) individuals were eligible for political rights. The implication here is that by equating the universal with the masculine, republican men put feminists in the weak position of challenging a general principle from a particular perspective. Feminist arguments for political equality were stymied from the outset because by speaking on behalf of a subset of humanity they reinforced the difference that they were trying to overcome.[7] Other scholars maintain that republicanism and the meanings of republican concepts (such as the individual, equality, citizenship, suffrage) were and continue to be mutable and contestable. In this view the basis for the exclusion of women from politics was somewhat arbitrary and highly phantasmagoric, and feminists could readily combat it by addressing the many component parts of the case against women—for example, their supposedly deficient rational capacity.[8] The latter interpretation of the masculine gendering of republicanism is the most useful for understanding Sand, d'Agoult, Allart, and Girardin because rather than claiming political equality for women and men, they exposed the flaws in several assumptions about women and the family that undergirded the exclusion of women from politics—namely that women's primary or sole occupation was motherhood, and that they were dependent upon men.

Republican motherhood originated in men's efforts to articulate a civic function for women while at the same time preserving for themselves the field of political activity. For some women, as well as men, this valuation of motherhood and of women's nurturing abilities was a positive basis for female citizenship and even involvement in politics. In the late eighteenth century British author Mary Wollstonecraft maintained that women who as intelligent mothers educated their children to be rational and virtuous were contributing just as much to republican (or at least progressive) government as men were through politics. During the same period in North America, Judith Sargent Murray, Benjamin Rush, and others justified rigorous education and the promotion of self-reliance for women precisely to enable them to carry out their civic duty as mother-educators in a new republic. Thus supporters of a political role for women endowed the mother and the home with serious political purpose. Implicit or explicit in these elaborations of republican motherhood was the assumption that women would marry and raise families, and that their sexual and political activities would be confined to the home. Nonetheless, the republican mother could also be an important figure for reform, even radical change, both within the family and by extension to the larger society, a possibility not lost on a wide range of French thinkers, writers, and activists in the first half of the nineteenth century.[9]

The July Monarchy was rife with feminist publications and movements that sought a variety of reforms and transformations in women's condition. Some women of the same social class as Sand, d'Agoult, Allart, and Girardin advocated legal changes to improve women's civil status and position within marriage and the family. These Christian or moral feminists argued that such reforms would make women better mothers and homemakers. Another group of middle-class feminists associated with the journal *Gazette des femmes* espoused additional reforms, including the suppression of articles of the Civil Code that subordinated women in marriage, the legalization of divorce, access to professions for women, and the extension of suffrage to women who met the existing property qualifications.[10] Although the four women writers agreed with many of these proposed changes, and even wrote for some of these groups' publications, they differed in their approach. For one thing, much as they valued motherhood, along with women's other family relationships, they also conceived of women as independent beings, not solely defined by maternity and often living apart from men. Additionally, with the exception of Allart, they sought first to change women and popular attitudes toward women before considering the issue of equal political rights. Moreover, their feminist ideas were closely linked with larger political and social transformations that they believed only republicanism could accomplish.

Socialist feminists, too, made their case for female liberation within the context of republican and socialist transformation. But Sand, d'Agoult, and Girardin were wary of these women, and Allart's elitism was incompatible with their egalitarianism. Adherents of saint-simonism, such as Prosper Enfantin, and the utopian socialist Charles Fourier, denounced the marriage law that required obedience of women and allowed for men's tyranny, the prohibition against divorce, and the common practice of basing marriages on economic and social considerations rather than love. Female saint-simonians such as Suzanne Voilquin, Désirée Veret, and Claire Démar went even further than male socialists in their proposals for transformed gender and family relations, and their mode of achieving them. Saint-simonienne feminists started their own newspaper in 1832, written and run by women, and for a time they lived almost as a female community, sharing work and family responsibilities. They envisioned a society that was cooperative and egalitarian, rather than individualistic and hierarchical, one in which women as well as men enjoyed respect, freedom, and autonomy. A very few feminists, such as Démar and Pauline Roland, claimed the right for women to experiment with sexual relations and to bear children outside of marriage. However, such sexual radicalism was by no means common to all socialist feminists, and many viewed it as accommodating male sexual license. Indeed, the majority of socialist women rejected sexual freedom as part of a feminist agenda, though for varying reasons, including the difficulty unwed mothers would face surviving and providing for a family on a female worker's wages. Instead, they celebrated maternity as representing the best qualities of women and hence the basis for women's leading role in the moral regeneration of society.[11]

Again, Sand, d'Agoult, Allart, and Girardin shared many of socialist feminists' ideas, but all except Allart repudiated the movement as a whole. Sand, d'Agoult, and Girardin considered sexual liberation to be nothing more than promiscuity, and they reiterated in some of their writings the popular misconception that socialist feminists were all free-love advocates. This may seem hypocritical on the part of Sand and d'Agoult, but despite their liaisons and flirtations they clung to a romantic ideal of perfect, enduring, heterosexual love. Moreover, Sand, d'Agoult, and Girardin were reared in the upper class; their social and, to some extent, economic standing benefited from a certain amount of respectability. Allart, who sacrificed even a modicum of respectability by bearing and raising two children out of wedlock, was thus freer than the others to proclaim publicly her support for the sexual freedom of both women and men. However, Allart believed that only exceptional women should exercise this freedom, since only they had the strength of mind to balance passion with reason. Sand, d'Agoult, Girardin, and, to a lesser extent, Allart deliberately distanced themselves from both bourgeois and socialist feminists, but they also adopted a very different position from that of republican men regarding women. Republican men, like some socialist feminists, viewed motherhood as regenerative, but strictly within the confines of the patriarchal family and the domestic sphere. Moreover, republican motherhood was effectively the only civic function republican men accorded to women, and both the women writers and socialist feminists found this too limiting.

While some scholars lump Sand and d'Agoult indiscriminately with male republicans in condemning feminist socialists, it is important to acknowledge that Sand and d'Agoult, along with Allart and Girardin, also set themselves apart from even the republican men they most admired, largely over substantive issues such as divorce but also over patriarchal behavior.

Declaring Independence from Republican Men

We have seen how Sand credited Michel de Bourges, under the name of Everard, with awakening her to the passions of politics generally and revolutionary republicanism in particular (to say nothing of sexual pleasure). In her 1835 story of this conversion Sand presents herself as a boy, a poet and therefore a "weak man" following the lead of the virile Everard, and utterly committed to the founding of a new republic. This youthful poet is an indeterminate creature, neither masculine nor feminine, or rather, combining characteristics of both.[12] Yet in the autobiography, written more than a decade after her infatuation with Michel de

Bourges had cooled and two or three years after her experience of the Revolution of 1848, Sand totally recasts the boyish apprentice trope. She presents herself as a woman and as disabusing Everard of precisely the illusion of her masculine identity; she has Everard saying, "I saw you in my mind's eye as a young boy, a child poet, whom I made my son." Sand indicates in this section of the autobiography that she seriously questioned Everard's apocalyptic and dictatorial republicanism. Indeed, she invokes the image of the traveler (*le voyageur*) again to tell Everard that she is leaving and rejecting his presumed authority over her, though she is grateful for his introducing her to a democratic political ideal. In re-created (or fabricated) dialogue, Sand first acknowledges the benefits she gained from Everard's tutelage: "You made me foresee an ideal of fraternity which warmed my glacial heart. In that, you were truly Christian, and you converted me through my feelings."[13]

Sand goes on to say that while Everard posed as one with a clear solution to the social and political ills of the day, he really was still seeking it; Sand claimed for herself the right to search on her own for an appropriate political philosophy or ideology: "Let me go now to meditate on the things you are seeking here, on the principles which may perhaps be formulated and applied to the needs of the hearts and minds of mankind. . . . You are no wiser than I, although you're a better person." Sand says that she resents and rejects Everard's attempt to control her and others through his eloquence and false promises: "Your mind needs to dominate those who listen to the enraptured beliefs that reason has not yet ripened. It is at that point that reality seizes me and distances me from you."[14] Significantly, Sand upbraids Everard for behaving as if he were her father and she his son. Unlike Sand's own (created) father, who liberated Sand's thoughts, feelings, and desires, Everard was trying to control Sand, according to Sand's autobiographical version. Moreover, Sand claims for herself *as a woman* the ability to reason out for herself a political framework for the correction of social problems.

Sand then presumes to re-create Everard's response to her accusations of his tyranny, and Everard's words are explicit about his belief in natural sexual differences and their implications for politics. Everard expresses disappointment in discovering that Sand is not what he had imagined her to be—a boy, his son. "I see well . . . that you have the ambition and the imperiousness of undeveloped minds, of beings of pure feeling and imagination—of women, in short." Everard goes on to say that pure feeling is not adequate for politics, and he asserts a Robes-pierrist position that action and especially duty often must take prece-dence over feelings in politics. He accuses Sand of misguided idealism in a belief that feelings and actions can be harmonious in politics. The nub of their disagreement, in Sand's representation, is over the issue of individual freedom. In this rendition Everard elevates some abstract commitment—duty—to a cause or a state above human liberty, and Sand, apparently, espouses freedom above duty. Everard's chastise-ment of Sand's position uses language highly suggestive of his or Sand's awareness of the struggle of women in the midst of a masculinist republicanism: "Your dream is of an individual freedom that does not fit in with the concept of duty in general. You worked hard to win this freedom for yourself. . . . You tell yourself that your body belongs to you and that the same is true for your soul."[15]

Everard accuses Sand of abandoning a worthy cause—the cause of truth as he defines it—in order to contemplate freely and in solitude other possibilities, that, from his perspective, can only be chimeras. Significantly, Sand links her femaleness with individual freedom and independence, strikingly in contrast to Everard's male, tyrannical authoritarianism. Sand leaves it to the reader to decide who is right, and she asserts that she included this long dialogue in the autobiogra-phy as an example of a conflict that was very common among republi-cans at the time. Sand is by no means launching a frontal, feminist at-tack against the republican exclusion of women from politics. How-ever, her allusive play and probing of gender in relation to republican politics suggests a tempered, skeptical approach to masculinist republi-canism and its adherents.[16] Indeed, she challenges the authority of men to define the meaning of republicanism and to bend women to their political will. She asserts the strength of female intellect and independ-ence that might imply a public, if not political, role for women in re-publicanism.

Resisting male republican tyranny was also a defining experience for d'Agoult. Sand and Liszt were instrumental in drawing d'Agoult to republicanism, and at different times and in different ways she broke relations with both of them to chart her own independent way as a woman writer and republican. However, d'Agoult makes much of her triumphant victory in a battle of wills with Lamennais, Liszt's mentor and a republican, when he tried to talk her out of abandoning her fam-ily and fleeing with Liszt.

D'Agoult had heard about Lamennais from Liszt, who in fact had spent several months at La Chênaie, Lamennais's Breton home, before deciding on the plan of flight with d'Agoult. Just days after Liszt persuaded d'Agoult to run away with him, Lamennais, whom she had never met, showed up on her doorstep. D'Agoult describes in dramatic terms Lamennais's efforts to dissuade her from carrying out the plan. She suggests that Lamennais, having failed to change Liszt's mind, considered d'Agoult, a woman, easy prey to his exhortations. But d'Agoult portrays herself as clever and steadfast in her resistance to Lamennais's indisputable eloquence.

She talks back mentally to Lamennais when he cautions her about the perils that await the revolutionary, saying to herself that Lamennais did the same thing that he warns her against:

In presenting to me with eloquence the unhappiness of he who is led by the spirit of revolt, the reproval of honest folk that creates little by little a void around him, the doubts and regrets that assail him in his solitude . . . , the necessities of an implacable order that sooner or later triumph over the most courageous, and wreak revenge on the audacious person who thought he could escape their control, the abbé Lamennais evoked a mute protest from me drawn from his own example. "But he," I said to myself softly, "isn't this just what he did?"[17]

D'Agoult suggests that if Lamennais could withstand condemnation for his revolt against the Catholic Church and the French government, then she, too, can brave disapproval for rebelling against social convention. Much as she admires Lamennais, d'Agoult claims that she will not submit to his authority, and that she asks that she be accorded the same respect that Lamennais has for himself as a man of conscience and a rebel. Clasping his hands in her own, she says, "Let me follow my destiny. I know and I feel that it is terrible, but it is too late to wish for any other." D'Agoult is very proud of herself when Lamennais leaves in defeat, muttering that he has "never before encountered such a resistant will in a woman."[18]

That was only the beginning of d'Agoult's resistance to Lamennais. Acknowledging his many merits, including his friendship with her after she left Liszt and returned to Paris and his encouragement of her writing, d'Agoult also delineates their sharp disagreements over feminist issues—notably her argument in favor of divorce and her critical perspective on maternity, which she published in 1847 in her *Essai sur la liberté*. She writes, "My *Essay on Liberty* made him furious. The chapter on divorce seemed monstrous to him, and he deemed materialistic a chapter in which I portrayed the suffering of childbirth and the joys of delivery." D'Agoult asserts that Lamennais is too old to be a good republican, and too blinkered by priestly intolerance: "Although he was carried away with the ardors of the revolutionary movement, and he rebelled against Rome, something of the priesthood, its prejudices, its narrow-mindedness, its bitterness remained with the abbé Lamennais."[19] The implication, of course, is that d'Agoult is a better republican than Lamennais, and that she is more than justified in resisting his authority. She asserts that he was never able to dominate her, though he tried: "He did not exercise the absolute influence [over me] that he sought."[20] Resisting the patriarchal domination of male republicans was an important part of d'Agoult's republicanism. In her autobiography, as well as in her other texts, d'Agoult, like Sand, exercised her reason to articulate for herself a republican vision that prominently included various improvements in the social condition of women and in their civil rights.

In contrast to Sand and d'Agoult, Allart tells no similar stories of rebellion against male republican authority, although she frequently disagreed with male politicians and male writers on politics, republican or otherwise. Allart mentions challenging Chateaubriand about politics. Similarly, at the time that her lover Bulwer was involved in the Reform Act of 1832 as a member of the Whig government, Allart argued vehemently against the measure.[21] So confident was Allart in her political opinions from a young age that she never had to declare her independence from male political tutelage. Moreover, Allart considered women to be equally as capable as men in intelligence and political thought, as her writings on Madame de Staël, as early as 1824 and continuing throughout her life, indicate. "The model in politics seems to me always to be Madame de Staël who [pledged] to the Republic in the present and while waiting."[22] Allart, unlike Sand, d'Agoult, and Girardin, attended meetings of socialist feminists in 1836–37 and appears to have continued a friendship, if only by correspondence, with Pauline Roland, whose death in 1852 grieved her.[23] Allart thus had clearly defined political and feminist views long before she married in 1843, and marriage itself reinforced her abhorrence of political despotism. In a letter critiquing Adolphe Thiers's history of Napoleon, she writes: "Since my marriage, I especially hate tyranny."[24]

Girardin made a different kind of move of independence in her *Courrier de Paris* in 1841. Suggesting that her last column had elicited some reader complaints, Girardin affirms, as she claims to have done before, that "*La Presse* and *Le Courrier de Paris* are completely distinct and independent of one another. *La Presse* is in no way responsible for what *Le Courrier de Paris* says, just as *Le Courrier de Paris* is in no way responsible for what *La Presse* publishes." She goes on to say that the newspaper is constrained "by political considerations [and] questions of propriety" but that her column is not: "It is absolute in its opinions as are all indifferent minds." In politics, for example, Girardin asserts that "*La Presse*, ... despite the revolting injustice of the Chamber of Deputies, recommends a great respect for this third power of the state; it speaks of this venerable body with nothing less than the most correct propriety." By contrast, Girardin maintains that her own column refuses the docile reverence of the newspaper: "*Le Courrier de Paris* ... sees no reason ever to pardon cowardice or injustice."[25] Girardin, as usual, makes a joke out of this contrast between the newspaper and her column, asserting that her specialty is "silliness," which excuses her column's deviations from *La Presse*'s serious purpose. Under the guise of humor and self-deprecation Girardin nonetheless asserts her right and ability to write whatever she pleases, and even to flout the newspaper's, and her husband's, more staid political positions.

Girardin always supported her husband, Emile, especially in his many moments of political difficulty. But that did not stop her from disagreeing with him, as she did, for example, when she sided with Lamartine against Emile de Girardin's belief that political reform could occur within the existing structure of the July Monarchy and under conservative leadership.[26] And although Girardin was also loyal to Lamartine, she resisted his optimism about revolution as a means of political change, advocating consideration of alternatives. In her review of Lamartine's *L'Histoire des Girondins*, Girardin wrote:

We do not love revolutions. M. de Lamartine seems to say that if the [French R]evolution was cruel and imperfect, that is because, unfortunately, it was made by men. ... It is all very well to say that revolutionary processes are flawed, but tell us how it is that in a century as enlightened as ours, in a country where industry discovers marvels, only one means has been discovered for giving money to the poor—cutting off the heads of the rich. The method is expeditious, but, frankly, it is not very innovative [*ingénieux*]. It seems to us that with some real effort a better way could be found.[27]

Girardin clearly had her own political ideas and did not hesitate to express them. Several years later, after Emile de Girardin had accommodated himself to the emperor Napoleon III, he wrote to Victor Hugo in exile and suggested that his wife was more intransigent than he about Louis-Napoleon's coup: "Madame de Girardin is as red as you are. She is indignant, and like you she calls him *that bandit*."[28]

Independence, both material and intellectual, was essential to Sand, d'Agoult, Allart, and Girardin. It was part of their public identity as writers, and it allowed them to function as republicans but not as republican mothers. Republican motherhood as male republicans understood it usually presumed male authority over women both within and outside of the family, and that was a condition the four women writers aspired to change. Being female set them outside of the constraints (and the privileges) of party politics, and it allowed them to engage or not to engage in politics at will. But the four were more than token female republicans, or exceptional women justifying only their own existence. Their various writings explicitly criticized the circumstances of women in France, notably the laws that gave men inordinate power within marriage and the family, the abysmal education afforded to most females, and the absence of divorce. Their call for reforms in the condition of women was part of their vision of a better society and political organization under a future republic that would avoid the mistakes of the first French Republic.

The Problem of Male Authority

George Sand's *Indiana* is a story about a young sensitive woman unhappily married to an old boorish husband. The heroine, Indiana, leaves her husband one night and, in the bedroom of a man she thinks she loves, she offers to flee with him, sacrificing her reputation, her conscience, and her security as a married woman for love. The would-be lover, terrified by the strength and seriousness of Indiana's passion, rejects her offer, and the spurned woman returns to her husband, Colonel Delmare. Delmare is enraged at her absence and demands that Indiana account for her behavior. The fragile and usually meek Indiana defies Delmare and in dramatic fashion explains the limits of his authority as a husband over a wife who is also a human being:

I know that I am the slave and you the master. The laws of this country have made you my master. You can tie me up, pin my hands behind my back, control my actions. You have all the rights of the one who is stronger, and society confirms those rights—but you have no rights over my will, monsieur, and you cannot command it.[29]

Sand here identified a fundamental problem with the law and theories of the patriarchal family—the conflict between the subordination of women in the family and women's individual identities. Indiana knows that Delmare has the legal authority, sanctioned by society, to restrain her physically, but her spirit remains unbowed. The characters and plot line of *Indiana* compel the reader to view the unequal gender distribution of power in marriage as unjust, destructive to both men and women, and inhibiting happiness. Delmare abuses his authority to tyrannize Indiana, even humiliating her (and himself) with a violent attack on her person; Indiana adopts a weapon of the weak, making a show of obedience to Delmare but provoking him with her mechanical, superficial passivity. Delmare and Indiana bring out the worst in each other, but both are locked into these unfortunate actions because of the inequality (and indissolubility) of marriage.

Allart's account of her own marriage in her autobiography reproduced the gender relations and issues of Sand's novel. Unlike Indiana, and Sand herself, who were very young when they entered into arranged marriages, Allart was a mature woman (forty-one years old) who chose Napoléon de Méritens de Malvezie as much as he chose her. However, after only a few months of living in Méritens's home, Allart complained in letters to her friend Charles-Augustin Sainte-Beuve that only after being married did she truly understand how the legal inequality of spouses encouraged men to abuse their power. "I believed that the oppressive and bad aspects of the marriage law had nothing to do with a man's love and promises, but the most generous [man], if he is violent and jealous, gets support from the law in his fit [*son transport*] and says to the wife: I want." She goes on to celebrate d'Agoult and Sand for rebelling against marital tyranny in both their actions and their writing: "You other men, you will never know what it is. There is [in marriage] the oppression of force [*de la force*] and definitely of strength [*du bras*]. So, praise be to Marie, to Lélia, to all those women who refused to submit to the yoke!" As she was planning her escape from her husband's house, Allart wrote: "It is a bad law that subordinates a free being."[30]

Years later, in her autobiography, Allart explained how her husband had abused his authority over her by simultaneously flaunting his sexual liaison with a neighbor and asserting his conjugal rights by barging through Allart's barred bedroom door. His threatened punishments for her unwillingness to satisfy his desires were bad enough, but what incensed Allart was his taunting of her powerlessness: "He repeatedly invoked this oppressive law that put me in his power." "My husband, with his furious scenes, initiated me to the horror of a law that subordinates weakness to strength." Although Méritens does not appear to have carried out his threats of physical abuse as Delmare did in *Indiana*, the possibility was not lost on Allart. She invokes the memory of a woman she apparently knew from Herblay who died at the age of twenty-two from a blow from her husband, and she writes, "I imagined under what worse yoke so many women had suffered, even perished! I awakened to a new dawn of awareness regarding the frightful condition of women." Allart, like Indiana, viewed marriage under the existent laws as analogous to the relationship of master and slave. She was happy only after she had fled Méritens and returned to her own home: "The happiest of beings is the liberated slave." Generalizing her experience to that of all women, Allart wrote: "What does woman want? What does she ask for? She wants not to be bound over to man like a black slave from Saint-Domingue."[31]

In contrast to Sand, d'Agoult, and Allart, who suffered in different ways from the laws and practices regarding marriage, Girardin appears to have avoided such frustrations and disappointments. Her marriage with Emile was a true partnership, for Emile and Delphine joined forces to overcome their respective sources of social marginalization and to become highly influential as a couple in society.[32] Girardin describes this relationship in a poem from 1839:

> A man grew up in the midst of a sordid struggle.
> He possessed nothing but the love of a woman;
> But both of them well-armed, holding each another by the hand,
> They followed in life a perilous road.
> . . .
> He was without parents, had no name and no support,
> He was alone and proud . . . she ran to him.[33]

The Girardin marriage was a union of equals. Girardin enjoyed considerable independence to write when, how, and what she wished, and to entertain in her salon and in her bedroom whomever and whenever she wished, often in Emile's absence. Her friend Théophile Gautier reveals that she habitually wrote during the day, wearing a comfortable white peignoir and with her hair loose, alone in a small salon within the confines of a Chinese screen, or, during the summer, outdoors in a small tent set up in the garden. In the evenings Girardin, dressed in black velvet, held her salon, directing brilliant conversation among the celebrated elite of literary Paris. Emile would on occasion attend his wife's salon, but he spoke rarely and left early, as he worked at night on the newspaper.[34] Emile seems to have encouraged Delphine's independence, writing, and sociability, for her contacts and tact were extremely useful to him, procuring him outstanding writers for *La Presse* and keeping him in touch with leading political figures. Moreover, he held progressive views on women and the family, proposing in 1854 an end to patriarchal families and legal inequalities between men, women, and children.[35] Thus, Girardin did not experience marriage as tyranny but rather as the egalitarian partnership that Sand, d'Agoult, and, to a lesser extent, Allart, sought and valued but were unable to attain.

Nonetheless, Girardin was by no means uncritical of marriage as it was practiced in her time. In her collaborative story *La Croix de Berny*, the character Irène de Chateaudun condemns the double standard of masculine and feminine behavior in the aristocracy that permitted husbands to squander their wives' fortunes on mistresses. Irène threatens to abandon marriage altogether to avoid handing over her fortune to an irresponsible husband: "No, no, I will not give the millions that providence threw my way, to be distributed as encouragement to all the miserable courtesans of Paris. . . . If I must absolutely give my fortune to women, I will take it to a convent where I will lock myself up for the rest of my days. But, indeed, I would rather become the wife of some poor, obscure student."[36] Irène, of course, eventually meets and marries a man who is an aristocrat but not a playboy. However, they both die after only one week of wedded bliss, he at the hands of Irène's former suitors seeking revenge on the man who thwarted their desires, and she out of grief. Although four different authors wrote this story, with three of them "pursuing" Irène/Girardin, it is Girardin's voice that condemns the double standard of masculine and feminine behavior and the legal authority of men over all property in marriage.

The condemnation of marriage as an abuse of male power over women was a common complaint among middle-class women writers and socialist feminists alike.[37] Many authors echoed Sand's and Allart's suggestion that women could not be fully realized human beings in the condition of subordination to which marriage law condemned them. Allart essentially rested her argument against existing marriage law on the basis of its injustice to women as rational, capable individuals. But Sand offered yet another critique in her autobiography, invoking the language of feminine difference that so commonly justified women's subordination in the family. Sensitive, no doubt, to public condemnation of her separation from her husband as motivated primarily by her unbridled lust for other men, and her disregard for hallowed and orderly institutions—a reputation based as much on her fiction as on her actions—Sand explained her decision to seek a marital separation from Casimir Dudevant on the grounds of better fulfilling her responsibilities as a mother.

Sand suggests that she willingly endured Dudevant's overbearing authority and his denigration of her own capabilities for several years of their marriage.[38] Indeed, the autobiography makes no mention of the repeated verbal and physical abuse to which Dudevant subjected her, especially in his many drunken rages.[39] Rather than delineating Dudevant's abusive behavior and Sand's own victimization, Sand emphasizes the breakdown of her family as a result of the flaws in marriage law itself. She charts Dudevant's increasing authority over their home of Nohant and over their children, writing that in 1835, "For all intents and purposes, neither my children nor my house belonged to me."[40] Here was a mother dispossessed of the two things that most defined motherhood—a home and children. Sand avoids any mention of her own love affairs and glosses over the fact that she voluntarily left her children with Dudevant while she spent several months in Italy with the young poet Alfred de Musset. She claims instead that the legal separation from Dudevant was necessary in order for her to fulfill her responsibilities as a mother.

As long as it had only been a personal problem, from which my children's moral development did not suffer, I thought I could sacrifice and allow myself the inner satisfaction of leaving in peace a man whom I had not been born to make happy according to his tastes. For thirteen years he had enjoyed the comfort that belonged to me and that I had deprived myself of in order to satisfy him. . . .

He was no longer able, nor duty bound, to have given me a sense of security. . . . I had to separate my future from his or sacrifice more than I had already, that is to say, my dignity in the eyes of my children, or my life—by which I set no great store, but which I owed to them as well.[41]

Sand argues here that for thirteen years she had fulfilled her wifely duties to Dudevant, putting up with a man whose habits and values were antithetical to her own, and allowing him to mismanage the household and effectively dispossess her of the home that she had inherited and brought to the marriage. She claims that she could have withstood more of this highly unsatisfactory situation had only her personal exasperation and frustrations been involved. But she asserts that Dudevant's lack of respect for his wife was threatening her children's respect for their mother. Moreover, his almost undisguised infidelities (Sand maintained that Dudevant would always make concubines out of his female servants) and his physical and mental abuse of wife and children were harmful to the children's health and moral well-being.

By raising the issue of children's moral condition Sand challenged a major justification for male authority in the family—the father's function to instill morality owing to his superior reason and control over passions. Sand implied that she, by separating from her husband, was preserving her children's morals against Dudevant's corrupting influence. She claimed for herself a high purpose behind the serious act of breaking up a family and argued that the laws themselves forced some women into this terrible dilemma of choosing either to preserve family unity or promote children's welfare.

A timid or generous wife must choose between respecting her husband or protecting her children. One of these duties will stand in opposition to the other. Will they then praise her—if maternal love does not win out—for having sacrificed her children's future to the demands of public morality, family sanctity? That sophism would be hard to sustain.[42]

In contrast to those theorists who assumed that family unity and the morality of children were inseparable and assured by paternal authority, Sand revealed how the moral welfare of children might have to be achieved at the expense of family unity, and hence of paternal authority.

D'Agoult developed this position to construct what she considered properly constituted authority in the family for the purpose of rearing and educating children. From the moment a child was born, she maintained, its education began, and for d'Agoult, either mother or father . might assume that responsibility after the baby was weaned. However, she thought that being a good teacher would be more difficult for men than for women because most men thought that they had "divine right" authority over their children. D'Agoult wrote: "I know that I offend all received ideas in asserting this fundamental truth: that parents, no more than teachers, have . . . any *rights* over children."[43] D'Agoult proposed an alternative model to authoritarianism in the rearing and teaching of children: "Parents and teachers must view themselves not as masters but as initiators, not as infallible legislators but as time-bound interpreters of an immutable law."[44] D'Agoult's perspective on education was Rousseauean; she believed that children must be guided toward self-knowledge that would make them free and autonomous beings. However, she made no gender distinctions, either in terms of teachers and parents, or pupils and children; males and females shared similar obligations as educators, and males and females had the same right to an education for self-knowledge.

On the grounds then of individual (especially female) self-fulfillment, maternal responsibilities for children's welfare, and the proper education of children, women writers attacked the principle of male authority in the family. By and large they accepted marriage and the nuclear family as viable institutions, albeit pending major transformations, as did other middle-class female and male reformers, and in contrast to some socialists who maintained that marriage and the family must be abolished and new types of relations constructed. Clearly the legal equality of spouses in marriage, equal responsibility for children, and an end to complete male control of property would redress the imbalance of power in the family. But equality in marriage also required changes in women's civil status generally, and especially improvements in female education.

The Civil Status of Women

Marie d'Agoult placed the reform of authority in the family in the larger context of the history of human progress and rationality. Asserting in the *Essai sur la liberté* of 1847 that "the laws of Europe are unanimous in conferring authority on the husband and subordinating the wife to him," d'Agoult then declared that these "laws that retain the female sex in bondage or inferiority are . . . vestiges of barbarism."[45] These unconsidered, manmade laws went against the "natural" law of human society to progress toward greater freedom and equality, according to d'Agoult: "To the extent that civilization improves, that habits ameliorate and that moral force substitutes stability for the convulsions of brute force, inequality tends to decrease; . . . one can hope that man will finally realize . . . how the grandeur of woman is inseparable from his own grandeur."[46] Buoyed by her view that human history is one of increasing freedom for an increasing number of people, d'Agoult was optimistic that the "barbaric" laws inhibiting women's freedom would soon be obliterated. However, she felt that she needed to convince her audience of the fallacy of women's inferiority, on which such laws were based.

D'Agoult explained that men's assertion of female inferiority had occurred for so long and in so many societies that it had assumed the unquestioned ring of truth. Women, she allowed, were not as naturally inclined as men toward abstract reasoning, but she denied that this gender difference was sufficient grounds for denying women access to what she called moral freedom. "If the realms of abstraction are less familiar to her than to man, her reason is equally sound, her grasp of detail is stronger; in practical matters she exhibits a wisdom, a capacity for observation that borders on genius." As far as d'Agoult was concerned, the differences between women and men were not great enough to justify women's legal subjection. Moreover, she believed that such laws actually fostered feminine inferiority, with dire social consequences. Because the legal responsibilities of husbands toward their wives assumed the shape of paternity, rather than fraternity or conjugality, women showed "all the vices of the slave and all the deficiencies of a child."[47] Happy, companionate marriages were thus impossible, and men as well as women suffered from lack of equal, supportive partners. According to d'Agoult, and Sand as well, the assumed and encoded inferiority of women was a source of dissension and amorality, if not immorality, in the family. It also was a deterrent to marriage for intelligent young women, as Sand suggested when she assumed the role of a male friend counseling a young woman of marriageable age: "Many men today make a career out of affirming . . . that the male creature is of an essence superior to that of the female. This preoccupation seems rather sad to me, and, if I were a woman, I would resign myself with difficulty to becoming the companion or just the friend of a man who styled himself as my god."[48]

D'Agoult supported family stability and motherhood for women, as did conservative and liberal theorists of the family. But whereas conservatives thought that male authority and female subordination were the means to achieve such ends, d'Agoult disagreed. Addressing herself to her imagined critics, she wrote: "Like you, perhaps more than you, I want competent mothers, assiduous and thrifty homemakers—in short, *strong women* capable of policing the small state that they rule."[49] The legal equality of women and men in marriage and the family, according to d'Agoult, would be the source of fulfilling marriages, stable families, and, ultimately, social harmony and political freedom. But for Sand, d'Agoult, and Allart, equality in marriage entailed improvements in the education of females in France, and their greater involvement in the marriage process.

Sand wrote that women needed an education similar to what men received so that they could contain their misguided impulses themselves, rather than being reined in by male authority. "In the life of women nothing replaces this first instruction, this *armed Minerva* that, according to Diderot, leaps suddenly from the brain of the young [male] graduate to combat his first impressions, his first mistakes."[50] Not that women were inherently more impulsive than men, for Sand dismissed as implausible that God could have created human beings with similar passions and desires and not instilled in males and females the same capacity for self-control.[51] According to Sand men had deprived women of education, of the means to achieve virtue and moral strength, in order to appropriate unjustly to themselves the position of family authority: "To prevent woman from procuring . . . moral ascendancy over the family and in the house, man had to find a way to destroy in her the feeling of moral strength, in order to rule over her solely by brute force; it was necessary to stifle her intelligence or leave her uneducated."[52] To rectify this situation d'Agoult believed the state must attend to the education of females, that issue "most neglected" by legislators. D'Agoult, like others, argued that better education would form better mothers, but she also argued that women needed education for their own self-fulfillment and to free themselves from the tutelage of men. "The time has come for all those authorities in the life of a woman (father, husband, confessor, lover) who pass from one to the other their despotic scepter, to be replaced by the only legitimate authority—that of reason."[53]

Female education, or the cultivation of women's reason, was, for women writers, a good in itself; it would allow women to be autonomous, fulfilled human beings. But it also contributed to the good of society. Allart contended that laws must allow women the same educational and occupational opportunities as men in order to increase the number of intelligent individuals heading families and capable professionals providing services and goods—even beyond the occupations deemed appropriately "feminine" by the bourgeois authors of the *Gazette des Femmes*.[54]

Justice creates rights. If a woman succeeded in trade, ruled her family; if she were queen and warrior, could one contest her right to engage in trade, rule her family, be queen and warrior? We call for a better education for women, tailored to the intelligence they promise.[55]

For Allart the principle of equality that she admired in France must extend to women as well as men, but it would make a difference mainly among those few beings of exceptional talent. She and d'Agoult both hastened to reassure their readers that female education would not result in a horde of women seeking to rule families, run businesses, and govern nations. "Aspasias are as rare as Pericleses," d'Agoult asserted.[56] And Allart, dismissive of the masses, contended that most women were fit only for motherhood and child-rearing, just as most men were fit only for manual labor and craftsmanship, but that equality would permit those exceptional women to flourish and contribute their genius to society; in that way all classes would benefit.[57]

According to Sand, d'Agoult, and Allart, female education would improve women as human beings, wives, and mothers, and it would add to the general pool of social talent. It would also entitle women to a more active role in the choosing of marriage partners, in contrast to the practice of arranged marriages that dominated in the upper classes during the July Monarchy. In her autobiography d'Agoult asserted that marriage was nothing more than a mercenary contract between two families, supported by the church in order to increase the Catholic population. Features of society that d'Agoult hated generally— materialism, lack of idealism, cynicism—were vividly embodied in marriage as she understood it. Under these circumstances, how could marriages be happy and families pure? D'Agoult summarized her views as follows:

Thus are consummated these sad marriages with neither love nor virtue, these cynical exchanges that the French nobility calls *marriages of convenience*, these indissoluble unions in which no sympathy, either of the soul, the mind, or the senses is consulted.[58]

Sand reiterated d'Agoult's contention that the principle of "family interests" justifying arranged marriages among elites was unsound and hypocritical, and that young girls did not know enough to make informed decisions about marriage.[59] Sand and d'Agoult maintained that arranged marriages should be abolished, and that girls should be taught to be more self-reliant and self-confident about their own instincts and reasoning. But even intelligent young women and men of all classes could err in choosing their spouses. And in those cases Sand, d'Agoult, and Allart believed that divorce should be permitted.

Dissolving Families

In an early novel, *Gertrude* (1827), Allart created a strong-willed female character who falls in love with a man and defies her family by marrying him. She foreshadowed the heroine's disappointment in marriage with the omniscient narrator's observation that even an intelligent and independent young woman can make mistakes about her future:

Must we condemn her for this disastrous marriage? Could she defend herself simultaneously against nature and society? What! Could Gertrude at eighteen years old have known that she should wait? Could she have known the future? Could she have anticipated the development in herself of powers she did not yet know existed?[60]

Gertrude and her husband, Alphonse, prove to be incompatible; Alphonse takes several mistresses, and Gertrude improves her mind through reading. Eventually Gertrude meets a man whom she truly loves, and while Rodrigue initially upholds the stricture of both church and state against divorce, Gertrude is ecstatic when she finally persuades him that male rationality can be mistaken. Rodrigue, admitting that he has experienced passion for the first time through his love for Gertrude, concedes that legalizing divorce would be humane and reasonable: "To understand humankind and morality is to ensure happiness by institutions that are responsive to the mind and will of nature."[61] Ultimately Gertrude's husband dies, and the issue of divorce becomes moot. But Allart's story made a strong case for the legalization of divorce, particularly in behalf of women and the realization of their potential as intelligent human beings.

Divorce was a hotly contested issue throughout the nineteenth century, and it remained so even after its legalization in 1884. Prohibited by a law of 1816, divorce became a topic of discussion following the Revolution of 1830 when the Chamber of Deputies voted to reintroduce it, but the proposal was vetoed by the Chamber of Peers.[62] Saint-simonians and saint-simoniennes advocated divorce in their writings of the early 1830s, and some even tried to implement free and dissolvable unions, only to be censured with arrest, imprisonment, or public ridicule.[63] Some liberal men argued in favor of divorce on the grounds that it would stabilize the family, and by and large, Sand, d'Agoult, and Allart agreed. However, as Allart emphasized in her novel, divorce was necessary also to accommodate the changes in human character that occur with growth and maturity, especially for women.

For d'Agoult the ban on divorce perpetuated bad marriages and that, in turn, held back society from positive development. "Marriage contains the seed of all of society. As long as this seed cannot develop naturally, no real progress will be accomplished; liberty will be only a meaningless word; the education of the human species will be corrupted at its source."[64] Divorce was necessary, especially for women, because they so often entered into marriage at a young age when they hardly knew themselves, much less the powerless condition they were assuming by becoming a wife. Moreover, divorce might actually help preserve the family, according to Sand, since the more judicious the process of family dissolution, the more husbands and wives would consider carefully the consequences of their actions. "The more the paths of deliverance are eased, the more the castaways of a marriage will bend every effort to save the vessel before abandoning it."[65]

Legalization of divorce would certainly alleviate problems of loveless and abusive marriages, and might benefit family unity, but the three authors did not spend much time publicly agitating for this reform. Indeed, although Sand and d'Agoult consistently supported the principle of divorce, they indicated that the time was not yet right for its introduction, when in 1848 the July Monarchy ended and a new republic was being created. D'Agoult asserted in *Esquisses morales*, first published as a whole in 1849, that females' debased condition and lack of education rendered most women unfit for divorce: "Given her current inferiority, her limited knowledge and malleable character, the possibility of changing husbands would be for woman [today] only a means of changing masters."[66] Sand took a position that many liberal and socialist men also adopted when the issue was raised in 1848—that the political circumstances of revolution were not favorable to the successful legalization of divorce:

You cannot settle the destiny and ritual practices of the family at a time when society is in a state of complete moral disorder, if not anarchy. . . . If the possibility of divorce were to be rejected, it would consecrate a condition contrary to actual public morality. If adopted, it would occur in such a way and under such circumstances as to disserve the cause of morality, thus further dissolving the concept of family as a sacred pact.[67]

None of these women writers mentioned the problem that socialist feminists identified—that divorce might disadvantage women as long as they were kept in legal and economic dependence on men.[68] For women writers the foundation of marriage and the condition of women had to be radically transformed in order to preserve the sanctity of the family and to make divorce an effective support of family unity. Conservative male legislators argued that divorce would destroy the family and undermine male authority. But if marriage and the family were predicated on something other than male authority, that position fell apart.

Love in Marriage and the Family

Rather than authority being the basis of the family, d'Agoult proposed that heterosexual love was a firmer foundation: "The man and the woman who love each other with true passion have in them the hearth of the ideal life."[69] Whereas conservatives (and the socialist Pierre-Joseph Proudhon) considered passion something that men should repress, particularly in their wives and daughters since it might lead them into disobedience, d'Agoult, Sand, and Allart celebrated passion as a natural or divine sentiment that men's laws should not thwart. But true love in marriage could occur only between equals, and the corollary to d'Agoult's position on love was improvement in the status of women. She wrote that the human race could look forward to experiencing moral love for the first time when women finally were men's equals intellectually: "When woman will be . . . truly . . . the other half of man, the feeling of love . . . will become . . . the supreme harmony of human life."[70]

Even before she became a novelist Sand considered love to be the only legitimate foundation of a marriage. As a young, frustrated wife and mother reflecting on her husband's frequent absences to go hunting, Sand concluded: "Marriage is the ultimate goal of love. If love is no longer, or never was, a part of it, what remains is sacrifice."[71] All romantics idealized love, considering it divinely inspired and so a means of spiritual oneness with God. But by asserting that love was the only legitimate foundation of marriage and the family, the three women writers suggested that the loss of love necessarily legitimated the dissolution of the family. In Sand's novel *Jacques* (1834) the main character, Jacques, and his younger wife, Fernande, cease to love one another, and Fernande falls in love with a man closer to her own age, Octave. Jacques does not blame or punish Fernande; he believes that "no human creature can command love, and no one is guilty for feeling it or for losing it." Since divorce was not an option, Jacques commits suicide so that Fernande and Octave will be free to fulfill their love, and he will have fulfilled his promise never to restrain Fernande's liberty or force her to lie.[72] D'Agoult also invoked the sanctity of love to justify the end of her marriage, though she ended it in flight rather than in death. She purports to reproduce Liszt's arguments impelling her decision to abandon her family and flee with him as sanctioned by a law of love that was higher than men's laws on the indissolubility of marriage. After Liszt told her that "there is no [other God] but love," the two broke all their other ties to seal the bond of love that united them. "The unknown God, *the stronger God*, took possession of us and of our destiny."[73]

Love could legitimize both heterosexual union and female independence, as Allart asserted in the introduction of her autobiography. She wrote that she wished to present readers with the happy story of a woman who "freely follow[ed] her heart, and place[d] love and independence above all else in her destiny."[74] Allart wanted women to be able to choose their lives according to their desires, and not to be punished by society for doing so. A modified, peaceable amazon was the model she invoked for women. According to Allart the amazon was free to satisfy her passion, bear children, and lead a public life, without male authority and without nuclear families: "A woman would do well to imitate [the race of amazons] replacing the trade of warrior with a career in letters."[75]

Allart went so far as to promote single motherhood in her private correspondence, and in her fiction, notably in the story of "Marpé." "Single women, especially single mothers, know how to survive, to breathe, to live proudly and happily," she wrote in a letter to Sainte-Beuve.[76] In "Marpé" Allart publicly supported a principle that she expressed privately in a letter to Marie d'Agoult—the right of a woman to give birth, whether married or not.[77] The main character, Marpé (not unlike Allart), gets pregnant and chooses to deliver her baby away from the father.

I had wanted to marry; the choice, the talents, the honor, the gracefulness [of Remi] were worthy of a lifelong attachment. But I could not decide, and my son was born like those children on the banks of the Hellespont that a woman warrior delivered in silence. Oh, Julie! When you were a mother far from Saint-Preux, did you think that you found Saint-Preux in motherhood? My compensating maternity gave my child the voluptuousness of my only love. It is Remi himself, it is my son, my heart deceives itself.[78]

The story of Marpé and Remi continues, and Marpé still loves him. But ultimately, the story ends with Marpé's independence. "Thus ended successfully this voyage undertaken with audacity, conducted with prudence. Oh you women of strong souls, if you read these lines they will perhaps reassure you, and reconcile you with yourselves. My love has only terrestrial beauty, but here below, can we search for any other kind?"[79] Allart has taken to its logical extreme the principle that love is the only legitimate foundation of heterosexual relationships. Not even marriage is necessary for women who "freely follow their hearts," and their love can be transferred to their children in the absence of the adult lover.

Despite the radical implications of love as the foundation of marriage, Sand and d'Agoult denied that they advocated the free love associated with saint-simonians, and even Allart suggested that only the exceptional, supremely intelligent and strong woman could successfully conduct her life by giving free rein to her passions. Sand, for example, in an unfinished epistolary novel, advised a young girl against free love and in favor of fidelity to one love: "As for these dangerous attempts that some saint-simoniennes have made to taste of pleasure in freedom, think of them as you like, but do not try it yourself, it is not for you. You would not know how to love in half measure, and if one day you do love, you will love forever."[80] In all of their writings the three authors pointedly differentiated between lust and love, between sensual satisfaction and spiritual communion. Allart claimed that she told the father of her first child, "I think that being loved by you raises me to the greatest height of morality I am capable of attaining."[81] In the context of narrating the process of her separation from Dudevant, Sand explicated at some length the divine aspects of love that should be involved in heterosexual intercourse. "There must be three [to procreate]: a man, a woman, and God in both. If the thought of God is unfamiliar to their ecstasy, they will indeed make a child, but they will not make a human being. The true human being will only emanate from true love."[82] Sand celebrated the spirituality of love, the ideal union of love with physical pleasure, and she again emphasized the context of individual identity and human fulfillment.

In different ways and in different genres, Sand, d'Agoult, Allart, and, to a lesser extent, Girardin voiced their objections to laws, practices, and attitudes that degraded women and hindered their freedom and self-realization. They were not alone in calling for the reform of laws regarding marriage, better education for women, and the legalization of divorce. For the most part they believed that such reforms would make marriage a better institution and the nuclear family a stronger and healthier unit. Sand, d'Agoult, and Girardin believed in marriage, and Sand and d'Agoult thought that mothers and fathers should share more or less equally in the rearing of children. Allart was less convinced of this, and more than the others she praised independent women and unwed mothers. Indeed, she chastised Sand for failing to criticize marriage enough: "I render her a serious accusation, that of not being sufficiently wounding of marriage and of not warning the human species adequately in her books. She often ends her novels with a marriage. Nothing should end that way any longer."[83] But all four authors created female characters and communities that did not conform to the republican ideal of motherhood.

Imagining Republican Women

Despite Sand's aversion for what she considered to be the promiscuity of saint-simonian feminists, she created in her novel *Horace* (1841) a very sympathetic character, Eugénie, who is a working-class seamstress and a saint-simonienne. Eugénie is an unabashed feminist; not only does she demand equality for the female sex but also, as she says to the skeptical Horace, a provincial bourgeois studying in Paris: "I demand it and I practice it, even though it is difficult to win in today's society." Eugénie lives with Théophile, a law student of aristocratic origins and progressive ideas. They are both republicans, and the two form a couple that provides stability for the other tormented characters in the novel and that represents Sand's ideal of gender relations. Eugénie does not believe in the institution of marriage, and she explains why: "You know that I am of the saint-simonian religion in certain aspects, and that I see in marriage only a free and voluntary engagement, to which the mayor, witnesses and the sacristan give a character no more sacred than do love and conscience. . . . I will never speak of legal marriage. But there is a truly religious marriage that is contracted before heaven." Eugénie and Théophile practice this "truly religious marriage." Théophile shares Eugénie's beliefs about marriage, and as the narrator he elaborates on the need for equality between two persons in order for true love to exist:

To he who understands the sanctity of reciprocal engagements, the equality of the sexes before God, the injustices of the social order and of vulgar opinion in this matter, love can reveal itself in all of its grandeur and beauty; but to he who is imbued with the common error of the inferiority of woman, of the difference of her duties from ours with regard to fidelity, to he who seeks only emotion and not an ideal, love will not reveal itself. And because of this, this feeling that God has for us is known by only a small number.[84]

The loving and faithful relationship between Eugénie and Théophile contrasts sharply with Horace's manic and abusive behavior toward his mistress, Marthe. In the end Marthe, who becomes a successful actress, enters into a "truly religious marriage" with Paul Arsène, a working man and a republican revolutionary. In both cases the women work for wages, as do the men, and the partners share a commitment to republicanism or socialism. Respect for women is an important feature of the male characters Théophile and Paul, and it is a lesson that is lost on Horace, who also proves to be an unreliable revolutionary and republican. *Horace* is an explicitly political novel that caused Sand to break with her long-time publisher Buloz, who wanted her to tone down the revolutionary republican advocacy.[85] Although the female characters do not actually participate in the street fighting of 1830 and 1832 that Sand describes, they are in other respects the equals of the republican men they love. For Sand republicanism is as much about egalitarian gender relations as it is about political revolution, and Eugénie is a model of a republican woman who is intelligent, politicized, earns her own living, and enjoys the respect of her mate.

Girardin's fiction was not as overtly political as was some of Sand's, but her short novel of 1836, *La Canne de M. de Balzac,* contains several references to gender politics and even to saint-simonism. The hero, Tancrède, makes use of a magic cane that renders him invisible in his quest for love. He tries it on a young wife who does not love her husband, but he is disappointed to find that the woman is utterly conventional, and loving in an instinctive way. She offers little in the way of intelligence: "Her imagination was asleep." Tancrède determines that he must look for a very different kind of woman: "I will never again love widows or girls, he says to himself. It is THE EMANCIPATED WOMAN for me!" "La femme libre," or the emancipated woman, refers to the unconventional women of saint-simonism. Although the term commonly connoted sexual license, and Girardin's putting it in capital letters signals her awareness of this, she undermines this prejudice by creating a character who is virtuous and whose "emancipation" consists of using her intelligence to be a professional writer.

This character, the next woman Tancrède encounters, is a poet,

Clarisse Blandais, a poor young girl whose mother encourages her po-
etry-writing and reading as a respectable profession. And just to make
sure that readers understand the self-reference, Girardin writes that
Clarisse's mother decided on this course with the models of Marceline
Desbordes-Valmore, Elisa Mercoeur, and even Delphine Gay de Girardin in mind: "Mademoiselle G . . . , who wrote verses as my girl
does, enjoys a most agreeable position in society." Tancrède falls in love
with Clarisse, both because she is a poet and in spite of it, "He had
found her so kind, so simple, that he had forgotten that she wrote poetry. Out of vanity he remembered it. This role of the ideal that he was
preparing himself to play singularly flattered his pride and reconciled
him to his excessive beauty, an advantage from which he had suffered." Girardin plays upon the social disapproval of women writers
with the character of Clarisse. Tancrède knows that he is not supposed
to be attracted to her because she is a bluestocking, a woman of intelligence, and even THE EMANCIPATED WOMAN that he thinks he wants
as a wife. Against all expectation, however, Clarisse is virtuous, beautiful, and kind, as well as intelligent, gifted, and a professional writer.
When she reveals to Tancrède in a poem that she returns his affection,
he responds: "These lines were for him, and when he understood that
his love had inspired them, he pardoned her for having the talent to
write them."[86] It is not easy for a man to marry an equal, much less a superior, and fortunately for Tancrède, Clarisse gives up her writing profession after they are married. Girardin parodies popular ideas about
women writers in order to explode them, although the end of the story
appears to be conventional and not subversive.[87] Yet Girardin is also
suggesting that equality can be a source of happiness in marriage; Tancrède gives up his supernatural advantage of the cane that makes him
invisible, and Clarisse gives up the manifestation of her natural advantage, her career.

   Sand, d'Agoult, Allart, and Girardin routinely wrote about marriage, and often offered insightful criticisms of it and possibilities for its
change away from male domination and double standards of behavior.
On occasion three of the four authors suggested that women might be
better off without marriage at all, that women could find complete fulfillment in independence and intellectual pursuits, or in serving a
larger cause of social and gender transformation. They created female
characters who were men's equals both within and outside of marriage,
and who were capable of accomplishments other than married love,

housekeeping, and child-rearing. Such figures contributed to the three women writers' republican ideals as women, and not as mothers or wives.

In addition to the story of "Marpé," in which the main character abjures the father of her son and rears her child independently, Allart also wrote *Settimia* (1836), a novel about an independent woman working for the cause of reform. In the preface Allart suggests that the only way republicans will be able to succeed is to implement public education for girls: "Is it you, republicans, who will open schools, and preach love of country and of freedom to children? Is your small force stronger than the vulgar taste of interest? Look at girls' education!" The character of Settimia, who is a superior woman, draws out the need for female education and an end to discrimination against women. She leaves her lover, Marcel, her friend Adélaide, and all of society in order to study alone in Naples and so contribute to the emancipation of women:

Such is, my dear Adélaide, the work I aspire to do—a work of independence and impartiality. I would like to serve as an example to the small number of women who, suffering too much, seek to escape from the long minority in which men have kept them. . . . In changing the lot of women, we also change that of men. Consider what a difference for them [it would be] to find, instead of frivolous and unfaithful spouses, clever and dependable companions who understand them and support them![88]

Settimia is torn between her love for Marcel and her commitment to the cause of improving women's condition. Indeed, when Marcel urges her to marry him and help him to create a new political elite of competence, and to reform society, Settimia thinks he would do better to focus entirely on the feminist cause. Ultimately, Settimia and Marcel marry, but not before she has made very clear her capacity for independent thought and action. The story implies that the fraught relationship between Settimia and Marcel that occupies this very long book will continue after marriage as Settimia struggles to balance her desire for love and her passionate nature with her superior intelligence and her devotion to the cause of women.

Characters similar to Settimia appear in Sand's *Lélia* (the revised version of 1839) and in d'Agoult's *Nélida* (1846). Lélia finally realizes that she will not find spiritually satisfying love in the arms of men, and she becomes abbess of a convent. With the support of the sympathetic Cardinal Annibal, who recognizes Lélia's superior intelligence, extraordinary faith, and strong will, Lélia turns the convent into a school for the ecclesiastical and secular empowerment of women. Admitting that she and the other nuns are sacrificing the joys of sensuality and motherhood, she explains that they will accomplish a higher purpose, that of reforming men: in adhering to "the cult of the ideal," "we will protest against the indecency and coarseness of the century, and we will force these men, quickly tiring of their abject pleasures, to make a new place for us at their side and to bring to us as a dowry of the same purity in the past, the same faithfulness in the future that they demand of us." Additionally, Lélia pledges to disabuse female pupils of the lies that society presents to them regarding love and marriage. Women flock to the convent to hear Lélia speak on theology and faith and to tell her their problems; Lélia and Cardinal Annibal effect "a sort of revolution."[89] Lélia's Catholicism might appear to be antithetical to republicanism, but it is a faith more of her own making than of church dogma, for which she eventually pays a high price. Following the death of her patron, Annibal, the church accuses Lélia of fornication, corruption, heresy, and of aiding the carbonari, among other crimes; she is demoted and sent away and eventually dies. In this novel Lélia's greatest fulfillment comes not from heterosexual love, marriage, or maternity but from living in a community of women and from educating and empowering women.

The character of Mother Saint-Elizabeth in *Nélida* resembles Lélia in many ways. Called "a little Madame Roland" when she was a girl, Mother Saint-Elizabeth is inspired to follow her model: "One thing only struck me . . . it was the serious role that a person of my sex could play, the ascendancy she exercised over male intelligences and the sublime martyrdom that crowned her heroic struggle." She studies Madame Roland, along with other female heroes of French history, and becomes a committed republican. Tricked by her stepmother into a compromising position she enters the convent, but she is not unhappy there: she feels that she would never be able to accomplish anything if she were married and under the control of a man. Instead, Mother Saint-Elizabeth views the convent as a means of social transformation through the education of girls; she explains to Nélida, her former pupil: If "I succeeded in imbuing [these young hearts] with the principles of true equality; if I awakened in their soul a pure and enthusiastic love for the people, I would have made a revolution." Like Lélia, Mother Saint-Elizabeth is eventually forced to leave the church for her radical ideas, although she never abandons the revolutionary cause. In Nélida she finds her perfect complement, if not instrument: Nélida is a gentle, loving soul—in contrast to her own single-minded ambition—and, after the news that her husband, Kervaëns, is dead, a woman of means. Mother Saint-Elizabeth converts Nélida to the popular cause, and she tells her friend, the republican Férez, who questions Nélida's commitment: "On her own she made the strong and wise resolution to retake control of her fortune, to return to Brittany, and to devote her income to realizing, in part, plans that we hardly dared to imagine six months ago."[90] Nélida was first disillusioned over marriage, and then over love, but the implication at the end of the novel is that her endurance and intelligence will lead her to a more fulfilling occupation, implementing social and political reform through republican ideals.

In their fiction, Sand, Girardin, Allart, and d'Agoult imagined different ways for women to be married and to be women. The ideal republican marriage for them was egalitarian, and the role of women included work, study, reflection, writing, sociability, and politics, in addition to love. As Allart wrote, "Woman, no more than man, is made for love alone."[91] And when heterosexual love or marriage proved impossible or disappointing, Sand, d'Agoult, and Allart imagined women without men, living in female communities or independently, but fighting for social changes that included better education for women and recognition of women's many capabilities. To the young woman who has no husband and wonders about her future, Sand writes: "And if you do not find this support necessary to women, will your life be impossible? Aren't you so strong that you can take the path of sublime exception? I do not know if I am mistaken, but it seems to me that nothing is impossible to a person of great courage aided by critical reflection."[92]

Sand might have been speaking for all four women writers with this suggestion that women can do a great deal as unmarried, independent persons. But the four authors did, in fact, marry, and three of them had children. Although heterosexual love in marriage and as the basis of the family was a shared ideal for Sand, d'Agoult, and Allart, it was an experience denied them. The most satisfying families they experienced as adults, and that they conveyed to the public in their autobiographies, lacked male partners. The families they created were headed by women and combined public activity and private nurturing—a model contrary to most other discourses on the family. They were neither the exclusively domestic families of conservatives and liberals nor the female communities of working saint-simoniennes. Women writers' privileged position in society, combined with their success as authors, allowed them to create independent, female-headed families. And although Girardin remained married until her death, she was an example of a woman writer who successfully pursued a career, led a public, social life, and was a devoted wife.

Writing Republican Families

Throughout their autobiographies, as well as in other works, Sand, d'Agoult, and Allart suggest family relations and configurations alternative to the model of patriarchal authority.[93] They sought a new synthesis of female intellect, sociability, and motherhood in a family setting that was egalitarian and not rigidly separated from public life. They operated within the limits of the heterosexual marriage and the nuclear family, reconfiguring the power relationships and division of labor within those units. While awaiting the republican state and the legal transformation of the family, the three women writers created families of their own that, both by circumstance and by choice, realized many of their republican ideals. As unmarried mothers for much of their lives, Sand, d'Agoult, and Allart combined domestic, private functions with professional, public activity and made a virtue out of doing so. The fact that none of the three ever established enduring marital relationships with one man does not mean that they rejected the possibility. They implicitly attributed their unwed state to the failings of the existing legal system and of social practices. Sand and d'Agoult especially upheld the ideal of egalitarian marriage, with mothers and fathers sharing the responsibilities of child-rearing. But by portraying in their autobiographies the satisfactions of their own, female-headed families, they offered proof that women could succeed as intellectual professionals and heads of households. By their own examples, Sand, d'Agoult, and Allart held out the promise that women were worthy equals to men as marital partners.

After her separation from Dudevant, Sand returned to Nohant and experienced the fulfillment of the dream of her own house, in which she could truly be a writer. As the new head of her household, Sand appropriated space that she felt had not been hers before, and she relished this unprecedented freedom.

I had a large room on the ground floor, furnished with a small iron bed, a chair, and a table. After friends had left and the doors were closed, I could, without disturbing anyone's sleep, walk in the garden shielded like a citadel, work for an hour, go out and return, count the stars as they were disappearing, greet the sun when it rose, . . . believing myself finally to be in the deserted house of my dreams. . . . That was perhaps the place where, right or wrong, I most thought myself a poet.[94]

Soon thereafter Sand's children returned from boarding school and the homes of family friends, where they had stayed during the separation trial, and Sand began the arduous task of "sailing the fragile bark of family security" as an unmarried parent and working mother.[95] In her own home and in the family of her own design, Sand freely cultivated her multiple identities as writer, mother, lover, and friend, though not without difficulty. "Respect for art; obligations of honor; moral and physical care of children, which always comes before all else; details of the house; duties of friendship, charity, and kindness! How short are most days for keeping disorder from taking over the family, the house, business affairs, or the brain!"[96] Sand's experiences of marriage, love, and separation suggested to her that the legal and social conditions of her time prevented the loving and egalitarian relationship between spouses that she considered the foundation of ideal, republican family life. Sand's stories about her own families were inseparable from her ideas about gender relations and families in general. "I conclude that marriage must be made as indissoluble as possible. . . . But the indissolubility of marriage is possible only on the condition that it is voluntary, and to make it voluntary, it must be made possible. So, if to get us out of this vicious circle, you find something besides the insistence on equal rights between man and woman, you will have made a still better discovery."[97]

Allart hardly spoke of a family as such in her autobiography. She asserted that bearing, nurturing, and rearing her first illegitimate child were her conscious choices, made to conform to her love of openness and truth.[98] She made a home for herself and her seven-year-old son in a small village just outside of Paris that she described primarily in terms of its conduciveness to her writing: "Here in the country . . . I begin a new life, studious as before but also happily calm, surrounded with books."[99] Allart's country homes with her two sons were always presented in similar terms, first as promoting her individual development as a writer, and second as providing an affordable setting for rearing her children. In an intriguing passage from a letter to Sainte-

Beuve, Allart compared her satisfaction with an independent life and motherhood to the joys of a male head of household. Describing her return from Paris, after walking alone from the coach station to her home in the country on a beautiful winter night, Allart wrote: "Everything was quiet, everything gently recalled the man in his own home [*l'homme à son foyer domestique*]. And finding myself here, all alone, I feel a charm that I cannot express. I hear only the tender breathing of my sleeping child; everyone in the village is asleep except I who write to you." Allart then indicates that she would like to share this quiet life with Sainte-Beuve, and that she would love to have them read books together. She tells Sainte-Beuve that one can live very well alone with books; indeed, she writes that she lives surrounded by books written by wise men that are her "true lovers."[100] For Allart, then, a family, even with a man, would exist fundamentally for female intellectual endeavor, and she would never give up her own sense of being the "man" of the house.

D'Agoult was the most explicit about her determination to create a miniature republic out of her home and family, presenting in her autobiography a household that might serve as a model of a woman's own republicanism. She pointedly included among her portraits of great artists from the Florentine republic and the quotation from Sallust a replica of the *Mona Lisa*, "to remind [viewers] of the feminine influence in these glorious lives."[101] A feminine influence on republicanism is something that d'Agoult sought to cultivate in her own life as well by gathering in her home "prominent men of the republican party" who "formed a salon around us, a real salon, enlivened by a liberal spirit, but varied in its nuances."[102] The center of this salon was, however, Marie d'Agoult and her offspring. D'Agoult describes her house as filled with beautiful children and grandchildren, playing the piano, drawing, doing lessons—all under the leadership of the female head of the household—d'Agoult herself. "In our pleasant existence we had a penchant for work. The mother set the example; all, including the smallest child, followed suit."[103] D'Agoult goes on to describe the elevated and genial atmosphere of her house, which smoothly combined private, family life with public, political sociability: "A charming intimacy formed in my house that was like a sweet and gentle little republic."[104] In the family and home d'Agoult describes in her writing she constructed a republic that differed significantly from the fraternal brotherhood that excluded women from public activity and designated them solely to domestic obedience. While acknowledging women's identities as daughters, lovers, and mothers, d'Agoult, Sand, and Allart indicated that women also existed independently of their relations with men and other family members. Their own stories revealed that women could promote republicanism through public life as well as through the family.

Rearing Republican Children?

To some extent Sand, d'Agoult, and Allart practiced what they preached in terms of rearing their children in an atmosphere of liberty, equality, and fraternity. Because they were themselves heads of households, and they did not rely on husbands to represent them politically, they did not fit the mold of republican motherhood. Although they clearly sought to instill in their children many of their own republican ideas, they also adhered to their liberal and nurturing principles of treating children as individuals with independent personalities. Much as the three authors might have wanted their children to share their values and ideals, they also tried to accord them the autonomy and freedom that had enabled them to become writers and republicans. Additionally, they had to deal with other circumstances that interfered with the systematic implementation of their ideas about child-rearing, circumstances familiar to single mothers to this day, such as work, love, and relations with the absent father.

Although Sand believed profoundly in the benefits of having two parents, a father and a mother, involved in child-rearing, she regarded Casimir Dudevant as a poor father for several reasons, including her belief that he could not bear to be thwarted: "He had never tolerated contradiction, and what is a child but the living contradiction of all paternal plans?"[105] By contrast, Sand gave her children considerable freedom, but she looked at her own mothering practices with a critical eye. "My friends criticized the way I indulged my children, and I knew very well that it was extreme. I surely did not do it for my own amusement, for it was tearing me apart."[106] Sand understood her two children to have very different personalities, and she tried to accommodate them with appropriate schooling. She tried for a time to teach her children herself, at home, but she found it impossible both to write and to teach. Additionally, she feared that her own education was defective and that her children needed more knowledgeable teachers. Maurice hated the years he had spent at boarding school and desired nothing more than to be at home with his mother, and accordingly Sand provided him with tutors, particularly numerous and specialized when she lived with her children and Chopin in a shared apartment arrangement with the Marliani couple in Paris. However, Sand believed that Solange was happier in a more formal school environment, away from Sand herself, and with more activities and structure to focus her attention.[107]

D'Agoult also believed that parents should rear children in order to develop their own, innate abilities and according to their natural characteristics, but she was one of the critics of Sand's indulgence. She had little enough opportunity to implement her ideas on education, however, because she left her daughter Claire when the child was some four years old, and she gave up her children by Liszt as part of her mother's and brother's terms of reconciliation when she returned to France in 1840. Privately, Sand accused d'Agoult of being a bad mother, of willingly abandoning her children and having "them raised in shacks" while she lived "in velvet and ermine." It is true that the children appear relatively rarely in d'Agoult's memoirs and journals. A notable exception is a series of journal entries focused entirely on Blandine, the eldest of her children with Liszt, who lived with Liszt and d'Agoult for a few months in 1839. During this time d'Agoult was very attentive to Blandine, observing all of her physical and mental characteristics. She effectively followed her own precept of "equity in the meting out of punishments and rewards," judging on the basis of what most improved Blandine's health and behavior. Her plans for a rigorous course of study were never carried out.[108] Blandine and Cosima were reared by Liszt's mother until they were old enough to go to boarding school, and Daniel stayed with a wet nurse in Italy, under the supervision of d'Agoult's friend, the painter Henri Lehmann. After they parted, d'Agoult and Liszt disputed bitterly over the children, and only when Blandine and Cosima were in their late teens were they allowed to live with d'Agoult, to have their education finished and their manners polished.[109]

Allart wrote far less about child-rearing principles and practices than did Sand and d'Agoult, but she was very concerned about the education of her sons. She indicated once to d'Agoult that she delayed a planned move because she had found an excellent teacher of Latin and Greek for Marcus.[110] Although Marcus accompanied her on many of her trips to be with various lovers, and Henri lived with her and her hus-

band for the one year of her marriage, much of the boys' education occurred in Herblay under a local priest, even though the boys were
raised as Protestants. Allart allowed her children to behave as freely as
she had. The epitaph on Henri's grave, inscribed following his death at
the age of twenty-three, reads: "After too short a life, but a very independent and very happy [one]."[111] Starting at the age of eighteen Marcus talked with her openly about his mistress, and "the pretty pink
hat," as Allart referred to her, actually lived in Allart's house with Marcus for days at a time.[112] Given Allart's very negative views of marriage,
particularly after her own terrible experience, she probably did not encourage her sons to marry. Indeed, right after she left Méritens she
wrote to d'Agoult: "Let us prohibit marriage to our sons and daughters."[113]

Sand hoped that her children would marry for love, and d'Agoult
also gave way when Cosima's choice of a husband did not accord with
her own. Sand was most explicit about her wish that her children might
benefit from her own experience. In a letter of 1844 she begged her
friend Charlotte Marliani to refrain from mentioning marriage in front
of Solange, then fifteen years old. She said: "I want that Solange marry
as late as possible, at twenty-five years if I can persuade her to wait that
long." At that moment Solange's response to marriage was to
"pronounce herself strongly against the enslavement of women," although Sand believed that as soon as she fell in love she would
"undoubtedly be as eager as any other [female] blindly to sacrifice her
freedom. Well, at least if she must make this sacrifice, she should be of
an age of true passion." Sand believed in marriage, and she wanted
only that Solange be mature enough to marry wisely and for love. She
thought it was only too common for young women to "give themselves
over to the first comer, without knowing themselves, often for the
pleasure of calling themselves Mrs., and to have new clothes. God save
me from letting my child commit such a crime of ignorance!"[114] Just
three years later Solange married the sculptor Jean-Baptiste Clésinger,
with Sand's blessing, for Sand considered the two to be very much in
love. Clésinger, however, was an abusive husband, and the couple
separated in 1852. Maurice, by contrast, after a passionate attraction to
and perhaps love affair with Pauline Viardot, a married singer, was just
shy of forty years old when he married Lina Calamatta in 1862, apparently a successful love match.

Despite her personal experiences and her severe criticism of arranged marriages, d'Agoult sought to arrange marriages for her daughters. In the case of her oldest daughter, Claire, d'Agoult explicitly viewed her involvement in Claire's marriage as compensation for her having abandoned the girl as a child. D'Agoult designated a young aristocrat, the comte Guy de Charnacé, who appears to have been in love with Claire, as the appropriate husband. Claire complied, but the couple separated after six years of marriage. Claire eventually took a lover, and d'Agoult broke with her daughter, whose life proved so similar to her own—including the writing of essays and reviews. D'Agoult had less influence over the children she had had with Liszt than she exercised over Claire; she saw them only rarely and with Liszt's acquiescence. Cosima fell in love with and married Hans von Bülow, a musician and devotee of Liszt, in 1857. Bülow's deference to d'Agoult won her over, but she supported Cosima a decade later when she became Richard Wagner's lover, and eventually his wife, in order to escape the unstable and abusive Bülow. D'Agoult intervened again in the marriage of Blandine. She planned a voyage for herself and Blandine with Demosthène Ollivier and his son Emile, both republicans, in the hope that Blandine and Emile might fall in love. They did, and were married also in 1857, but Blandine died from complications during childbirth in 1862. The only boy, Daniel, died at the age of twenty, virtually a stranger to d'Agoult.[115]

Allart more than the others lived out her ideal of republican equality and freedom with her children, but her relative poverty may have had as much to do with that as her principles; she had little in the form of property or social standing to bequeath to her children. Henri seems to have adopted her love of learning, for she acknowledges his help with her Greek in the dedication of her *Histoire de la République d'Athènes*. And Marcus certainly followed his mother's example of "freely following his heart" by taking up mistresses at a young age and delaying marriage until 1863, when he was thirty-seven. Marcus was divorced in 1890 (following the birth of eight children), and after his death in 1901 he was buried alongside his mother and brother.[116]

The autobiographies of Sand, d'Agoult, and Allart are, not surprisingly, concerned with themselves, and not terribly much with their children. To the extent that they mention their children it is almost entirely when they were very young. The children's lives were their own, and Sand, d'Agoult, and Allart could not always control them after adolescence, whether they wanted to or not. The personal narratives of the women writers indicate that most of their children favored republicanism as a political ideology. But more important to the authors and to this study are their self-representations as mothers, especially in relation to their other identities as daughters, lovers, writers, and republicans. Motherhood was important to the three women, but it was one of many important aspects of their lives, and this was the alternative they offered to republican motherhood. And what of Girardin, who had no children? Her own words, and those of Sand, regarding her situation further reveal the complexity of women creating lives and families outside of the prescribed norm.

Girardin was devastated by her childlessness. Her poem "La Fête de Noël" is like a prayer to the Virgin Mary, offering up the author's wealth and beauty in exchange for a son of her own. Girardin's desire for children and especially for a son was no doubt sharpened by Emile de Girardin, who, as an illegitimate child, had to fight to bear his father's name; biographers indicate that he desperately wanted a legitimate son of his own.[117] Indeed, the final lines of the poem suggest that the author wanted a child as much to retain the affection of her husband as to satisfy her own maternal longings:

> Indeed, I could even
> See the ungrateful spouse whom I love
> Walk away from me
> And keep my faith in him.
> No bitter recriminations!
> My sorrow would be silent;
> I would say: I am a mother,
> Be brave, he will come back.[118]

Emile de Girardin did introduce into their home a son, whom Delphine adopted, that he had had by another woman.[119] Nonetheless, Sand maintains that in her dying days, Girardin confessed her disappointment at never having had a child, to which Sand responded that God had wanted Girardin to contribute something else to society. "What you berate yourself for as a disgrace is a logical consequence of your superiority over other women. If you had been a mother, three-quarters of your life would have been lost to your mission [in letters and society]." Girardin replies that she would gladly have sacrificed society, but Sand says with conviction: "Providence does not concern itself with us in terms of our personal satisfaction, but in terms of our more general utility, and we should be grateful for [its] placing us in conditions where we can fulfill its design."[120]

Sand was probably offering more than superficial comfort to a dying woman, although she did revere motherhood. Sand knew well the difficulties of combining motherhood with other pursuits, which contributed to her conviction that marriage must be a union of equals and that both father and mother must share the responsibilities of child-rearing. Her reading of Emile de Girardin's book on marriage and the family suggested to her that, had he been a father of a legitimate child, he might not have been much involved in child-rearing, despite his "admirable" socialist politics and reform legislation. "He admits into the composition of the family only mother and children. I said above, and I shall say again, always and everywhere, there must be both father and mother."[121]

Sand, d'Agoult, and Allart wrote themselves as women into the narrative of republicanism. And Girardin represented gender relations and marriage to be egalitarian rather than male-dominated. Unlike other feminists—for example, Olympe de Gouges in 1791 or socialist feminists in 1848—they avoided engaging directly in a theoretical debate with male republicans about whether equality for all included women.[122] Nonetheless, they rescripted republicanism to include a feminist program of reform. They shifted the ground of discussion from the political rights of the individual to the implementation of republican principles in a truly egalitarian family. They proposed a transformation of the family that eliminated the barrier between private and public life and that denied the exclusion of women from republican politics. In fiction, essays, and self-representations the four authors challenged certain assumptions about femininity—irrationality, lack of self-control, dependency—to articulate women as possessing a broad range of characteristics, competencies, and potentials that a republican regime should cultivate to its long-term benefit. Although the first French Republic was erected on the foundation of the patriarchal family, separate spheres, and rigid notions of sexual difference, these women writers constructed a new basis for a future republic with a variety of egalitarian family configurations, a home less isolated from public affairs, and a greatly expanded conception of femininity (and to some extent masculinity). They offered the figure of a republican woman to replace the more limited ideal of the republican mother.

Sand, d'Agoult, and Allart believed that improvements in the female condition and in attitudes toward women must necessarily precede political equality. Indeed, early in 1848 the three, along with Girardin, appeared to trust their fellow male republicans to implement the political and legal changes that would eventually equalize the civil status of women and men. But in the face of the disappointing outcome of the Second Republic, the three authors were fortunate enough in their education, talent, and financial condition to be able to act on their ideals about female capability and to present them to the reading public. The female-headed families of Sand, d'Agoult, and Allart, and the partnership of the Girardins, were perhaps truer to republican ideals of liberty, equality, and fraternity (broadly defined to include both sexes) than anything imagined by most male republicans. According to these family romances, republicanism begins in the family, and the women and men in families have the power to determine the gendering, or ungendering, of republicanism.

7 ☞ Writing and Rewriting the Revolution of 1848

Few could have been as ecstatic as George Sand with the establishment of the French Second Republic in 1848: "Everyone is crazy, everyone is drunk, everyone is happy to have gone to sleep in the muck and awakened in the heavens."[1] She was overjoyed that her dream of a republic was finally being realized, and she rushed to Paris to assist in its establishment. Helping her friends in the provisional government with the selection of provincial officials to replace those of the previous regime, Sand also wrote articles and propaganda pieces to persuade all French people to embrace the republic. For Sand, the republic had momentarily replaced her own family as the object of her love and concern: "Personal sorrows disappear when public life calls to us and absorbs us. The republic is the best of families, the people are the best of friends."[2] Sand exhorted her friends, including her literary friends, to do as she did— that is, set their talents to serving the republic: "Poetry, now, is in action; all other is hollow and dead. . . . Our home [*notre chez nous*] is the public square, or rather the press, the soul of the people, after all."[3] For Sand, in 1848, the boundary between private and public, literature and politics, family and state, was dissolved. She, along with d'Agoult, Allart, and Girardin, articulated and enacted a public role for women in the new French republic.

The four women were all in Paris for at least part of the year in 1848, and all witnessed firsthand the revolution or the establishment of the provisional government and the Second Republic. As writers and republicans they left extensive accounts of the events as they unfolded, including their own experiences and developing views. Their accounts are both immediate and insightful, for the four were in the thick of the political events of 1848; at the same time they were somewhat distanced from them by virtue of their sex. The experiment in republicanism occurred when the four were mature women in their forties, and it marked them all. This is evident in many of their writings about the revolution and the republic, as well as about other subjects, from 1848 until the end of their lives. Sand, d'Agoult, Allart, and Girardin were disappointed in the outcome of the republic, even as early as April 1848, and definitely by June. Nonetheless, they drew lessons from this experience that informed their subsequent writing, including feminist interpretations and alternatives to political change and republicanism in the masculine version of 1848–52. None of the four authors supported the socialist feminist claim for including women in the republic's "universal" suffrage, and Sand and d'Agoult were explicit in their denunciations of the women who advocated political equality. To the extent that Sand and Girardin overtly engaged in politics through their writing and personal contacts, they were pilloried in caricatures, as were socialist feminists. In general the four authors articulated their feminist perspectives in literary ways—in poems, plays, novels, and histories that subverted male authority, highlighted feminine concerns, and suggested possibilities for women to make many of the changes in society, the family, and in gender relations that the men of 1848 had failed to accomplish.

A Revolutionary Year—1848

The events leading up to revolution, and the political consequences of the Revolution of 1848, might be summarized as follows: Republican ideas had been gaining ground in the 1840s, while discontent with the July Monarchy was deepening and broadening. The problems of poverty and social unrest led many, like the four women writers, to espouse the expansion of political representation as a means of dealing with them, but Prime Minister François Guizot and King Louis-Philippe were intransigent. Republican and center opposition deputies had scheduled a banquet in behalf of electoral reform for 22 February 1848, and they anticipated a good turnout of students, workers, and other sympathizers. Guizot banned the banquet, and the organizers finally decided to comply at the last minute. However, working people and students showed up anyway, and the canceled banquet turned into a large demonstration against the government. When crowds filled the streets again on 23 February the king ordered the National Guard to stop them, but the National Guard joined the demonstrators. Violence broke out that night, and people started building barricades to defend themselves against anticipated attack by royal troops.

Louis-Philippe tried to appease the crowd by dismissing the hated Guizot and appointing a moderate opposition figure, Molé, to head a new government, but that did not answer. On 24 February the king abdicated in favor of his grandson, but in response to popular sentiment, republican leaders, many of whom had served in the Chamber of Deputies under the July Monarchy, formed a provisional government on the same day, and on 26 February, Alphonse de Lamartine, as foreign minister of the provisional government, officially declared the establishment of a republic. Among the many tasks of the provisional government were the quick appointment of various civil servants to establish the republic in the provinces; the reception of many delegations with different claims on the new regime, notably workers' groups demanding a solution to unemployment; and the scheduling of elections for a constituent assembly. These elections would be crucial, for they were to inaugurate universal male suffrage; they were likely to determine the character of the republic—whether liberal or socialist.

Eventually the date was set for 23 April, and the result was a predominantly liberal body that met in Paris on 4 May and redeclared the Second Republic. These representatives completed a constitution that was adopted on 4 November, but in the interim the body was responsible for quelling two popular demonstrations, one on 15 May in favor of supporting the liberation of Poland, and the other on 22 June to retain the National Workshops, the only form of assistance for unemployed workers. The latter demonstration had ended in bloodshed, and the head of the troops that put down the revolt, General Eugène Cavaignac, effectively ran the Second Republic from 24 June until the new constitution was approved and implemented. The constitution required popular election of a president, which occurred on 10 December, and the victor was Louis-Napoleon Bonaparte, nephew of the first emperor. Although the constitution limited the president to a single term, Bonaparte tried—and failed—to persuade the Assembly to amend this provision and allow him to continue in office. In 1851 Bonaparte resorted to force, arresting deputies and calling in the army to back his claim that in the interest of state security he be president for life. After a plebiscite ratified this coup d'état, Bonaparte finally ended the republic definitively on 2 December 1852 and declared himself emperor.[4]

Did Delphine de Girardin foresee revolution when she wrote her last *Courrier de Paris* of 1847, in July, asserting that "the ultra-bourge-oisie will lose the royalty of July, just as the ultra-gentlemen lost the royalty of the Restoration"? In typical fashion Girardin made a joke of the anticipated revolution—"Oh! how boring! another revolution!" Yet her comments on corruption and ambition among ministers, and their failure to address serious problems of political and social inequality, were right on target. She lightly satirized the banquets held in behalf of electoral reform: "The people, who are dying of hunger, feel reassured that their devoted friends [politicians] eat cold veal in their name." And she halfheartedly assured readers that Louis-Philippe would not make the same mistake as Charles X: "Louis-Philippe is not at all attached to M. Guizot; he will not make the least coup d'Etat to retain him. So we hope."[5] Everything that Girardin had addressed in July 1847 as causes for revolution—self-serving ministers, deputies campaigning for electoral reform but ignoring widespread poverty, and an oblivious king adamant in retaining an unpopular prime minister—indeed contributed to revolution in February 1848.

By contrast, the revolution took Sand completely by surprise. She had been staying at Nohant for much of the previous year, occupied with a series of personal crises and writing obligations. She had been quarreling with her daughter Solange and son-in-law Jean-Baptiste Clésinger almost steadily for several months over financial matters, and Solange's accusations that Sand had been a negligent and jealous mother. Partly because of these disagreements Sand ended her nine-year relationship with Frédéric Chopin (who sided with Solange), and she embarked on the major project of writing her autobiography, both for her personal satisfaction and because she needed money for her children. In a letter to Allart of 16 February, Sand indicated that she considered their particular historical moment decidedly uninspiring, and that regarding politics, she had only "a little hope mixed with a great deal of sadness."[6] Moreover, on 18 February, Sand dismissed a friend's prophecy of revolution, writing to her son Maurice in Paris that the controversy over the banquet was merely a power struggle between the prime minister and the man who wished to take his place: "I do not think the people will take sides in a quarrel of M. Thiers against M. Guizot."[7]

D'Agoult, like Sand, was deeply involved in family affairs in February 1848. Her mother had died the previous year, and she and her brother and sister-in-law were at odds over the terms of the inheritance.

Allart had started her memoirs and was finishing a long study of political history from the barbarians to the present. She was staying in Passy,
just outside Paris, and frequently visiting Chateaubriand, whose wife
had died in 1847. Girardin had enjoyed a considerable triumph with
her play *Cléopatre* in November 1847, and she published no installments
of the *Courrier de Paris* between July 1847 and May 1848. But both she
and her husband closely followed political developments through their
personal networks. Anxiety over the political situation pervaded the
social scene in Paris and threatened to ruin it on the night of 21 February. Girardin attended a ball that night at the house of the Belgian am-
bassador, where men read newspapers instead of dancing; several
guests, notably government ministers and one of the Orleans princes,
had not yet arrived, nor would they ever arrive that evening. Girardin
communicated to the assembled group her husband's estimation that a
confrontation was likely in response to the canceling of the banquet.
However, putting up a brave front, she reputedly started the dancing,
finally, at this last official ball of the July Monarchy.[8]

Girardin was probably aware of Emile's efforts to persuade Louis-
Philippe to abdicate in favor of his grandson, and her husband did, indeed, obtain the king's signature on an abdication document he had
drawn up. But the revolutionaries would have none of monarchy, and,
after the failure of this unlucky move for a regency, the provisional
government of the republic would have none of Emile de Girardin.
Nonetheless, Emile initially supported the provisional government,
using *La Presse* to call for confidence in the new regime and suggesting
that his wife hold parties and socialize as usual in order to convey publicly a sense of security and trust in the republic. This Delphine de Girardin did, for she was ambitious for her husband, and both undoubtedly anticipated during the first weeks of the provisional government
that Emile would have a place in the government in the near future. Girardin's devotion to her husband's political career precluded the possibility of close relations with the leaders of the evolving Second Republic, from whom Emile became increasingly alienated. Sand and
d'Agoult, however, were eager to assist their republican friends finally
heading a republican government.[9]

Sand's immediate concern in February was for her son, and she ordered Maurice to return to Nohant and assume responsibility for the
household and the spread of the revolution to the locality. Sand then
hastened to Paris, where she advised the minister of the interior, Alex-

andre-Auguste Ledru-Rollin, on whom to appoint for provincial positions. With the republic safely installed, Sand's letters from the first few
weeks in March are euphoric. She anticipates great things from the new
republic, and she presents herself as a knowledgeable insider to her
older, conservative cousin René Vallet de Villeneuve:

This republic will not repeat the mistakes and the misconduct of the one you
saw [the first French republic]. No party is inclined toward that. The people
were sublime in their courage and gentleness. The government [*le pouvoir*] is
generally composed of pure and honest men. I went to assure myself of this
with my own eyes, for I am closely associated with several of them, and I return tomorrow to Nohant with the certainty that they will do their best.[10]

Sand appears to have had no second thoughts at this time about engaging, as a woman, in public life. She enjoyed the negotiations involved in
getting her friends into office, and she accepted with enthusiasm the
task of writing bulletins for the Ministry of the Interior. Sand returned
to Nohant in mid-March for two weeks to oversee preparations for the
elections there, and, on the eve of traveling back to Paris to resume her
work, she wrote, "The dream of my entire life is happening."[11]

Allart was both closer to the revolutionary action of February than
was Sand and more distanced from the leadership of the Second Republic that followed it. Allart got most of her news about the street
fighting from her son Marcus, who would spend days or nights in Paris
and then report back to Allart in her rented quarters in Passy. Together
they would observe the crowds from the bridge that divided the suburb
from the city, and Allart noted the increasing strength in numbers and
influence of the people as the days passed. Her autobiographical account, written long after the fact, includes much skepticism about the
political maturity of the revolutionary crowd, but her letters from the
time are more hopeful about the viability of the republic and the potential of some of its leaders—at least until the June Days. Moreover, Allart
often tried to reassure her correspondent, Sainte-Beuve (who was politically conservative), that he should stay in France rather than emigrate, and that the revolutionary republic was not entirely a disaster.
On 21 May she applauds the notion of supporting Polish independence,
and she credits the revolution with creating "an excellent public spirit."
She continues: "We will come out of this well, I hope. The left, which
has done everything, will reassume authority, and power will remain
with the intelligence to whom God intends. Let us not restore a king too
soon. Let us at least try the Republic a little longer." Earlier, in April,

she had conveyed her impression that people in the countryside were very receptive to republican government, despite the anticipated taxes: "The provinces are annoyed and threaten to refuse the tax. However, they would not be at all hostile to a wise and moderate republic, and they would like to see it organized by the left." Allart was a great fan of the socialist Pierre Leroux (a former friend of Sainte-Beuve) and looked forward to his performance in the National Assembly, while at the same time she supported her old friend Adolphe Thiers. Allart's ideals and beliefs pulled her in different directions; she desired strong and effective leadership, maximum freedom for all, and humanitarian reform. She believed that the republic upheld her positions, though she knew also that Sand and others emphasized a democratic, egalitarian ideal in contrast to her preference, a representative republic.[12]

When Sand was back in Paris on 21 March, one of her first intentions was to start a newspaper to educate the general public about the republic. She had long been dissatisfied with the two republican newspapers, *Le National* and *La Réforme*, for a lack of socialist enthusiasm in the former and just not being sufficiently up-to-date in the latter. At her own expense, then, she put out her own paper, *La Cause du Peuple*. Sand could find no one else to help her in this endeavor, so she did all the writing herself and managed to publish three issues before the time, effort, and expense became too much for her. *La Cause du Peuple*, the official bulletins, and other pamphlets and statements that Sand wrote articulated her views on the principle of popular sovereignty, the equality of the people, and the urgent need for workers and peasants especially to become involved in the political process. At this point Sand assumed that universal suffrage meant men only, and she was eager to see working-class men declared candidates for public office. Sand called upon the people of both the countryside and the city to unite behind the republic, to see in democracy their shared interest in self-representation. She told her readers that God had "created men perfectly equal," and that this was the basis of popular sovereignty. At the same time that Sand encouraged working people to exercise their political rights responsibly, she reassured the bourgeoisie about the new republic, to rally them behind it as well. It would not, she promised, exercise a Reign of Terror, nor would it confiscate property—at least, not immediately. Sand asserted that socialism was the ultimate goal of the republic, but that property redistribution would proceed very gradually and nonviolently. It is impossible to measure the effects of Sand's publications on the republic, but clearly she viewed it as a popular, democratic, and socialist government, and her sympathies were obviously with the laboring poor who, she believed, rightfully had so much to gain.[13]

Sand's association with Ledru-Rollin and her many republican publications were a goad to Marie d'Agoult to do similar things, but in her own style, and not at all in a way to be confused with what she considered to be Sand's "masculine" involvement at the level of the streets and her excessive emotionalism regarding the popular classes. D'Agoult, by contrast, operated in the salon rather than in the streets and clubs, and among the leaders of the provisional government rather than the republican revolutionaries. She gathered men such as Lamartine and Lamennais to her salon, which, for a short time, became the center of this form of republican sociability. Additionally, she started writing her own republican articles, a series entitled *Lettres républicaines* for *Le Courrier français*, that were published from 25 May to 7 December 1848. D'Agoult, like Sand, was enraptured with the new republic, but her ideal of it differed from Sand's. D'Agoult's definition of equality, for example, did not justify the principle of popular sovereignty, but rather referred to equal opportunity: "Equality is the right . . . to arrive at the complete development of one's physical and moral being, and to rise, according to the measure of one's abilities, in the elective hierarchy of social relations." To be sure, d'Agoult accepted democracy, and she even chastised the members of the Constituent Assembly for hindering its long-term establishment by being too caught up in factionalism and intrigues at the expense of the people who had brought them to power. D'Agoult offered this advice: "A frankly democratic constitution that gives unity to power by disseminating freedom widely to the popular masses is what the country demands and what it must be given without delay." Furthermore, as a means of fostering unity and of checking the expansion of state power through the legislative body, d'Agoult advocated the institution of a presidency in the constitution, a position that Sand strongly disputed as inimical to democracy.[14]

Sand's and d'Agoult's republican publications reflect their different republican identities and styles of engagement. Sand addressed herself to the people, to a class of laboring peasants and workers, and occasionally to the bourgeoisie or the rich. She often identified herself explicitly with the people. For example, in a statement intended to persuade "the rich" to accept the republic, and to alleviate their fears, she writes: "Do you think yourselves under the regime of the terror? Have we demanded the head of the king, of the queen, of the princes and princesses?" Assuming the identity of the Berrichon peasant Blaise Bonnin, Sand explains to her fellow peasants the need to educate themselves in order to avoid being duped by the bourgeoisie, especially in the election of candidates: "A few years from now, when we will all know how to read and write without having to pay anything to learn, we will know exactly what each [candidate] does, what each says, what each is worth. . . . But today we are not yet knowledgeable enough to avoid being taken in by the bourgeoisie, some of whom might take advantage of us by making us vote for them or for their friends, against our own interests." On occasion Sand admits to being a bourgeois truly interested in the cause of the people, but in any case her appeal is to the popular classes from one who believes that their historical destiny is about to be realized.[15]

By contrast, d'Agoult's intended audience was primarily political leaders and members of the bourgeoisie. Her republican letters, for example, were each addressed to different individuals—leaders including the Prince de Joinville of the deposed Orleans family, Lamennais, Pierre-Joseph Proudhon, General Cavaignac, and Lamartine, and bourgeois intellectuals like Adam Mickiewicz, Emile Littré, Anselme Petetin, and the German author and middle-class feminist Fanny Lewald. When she does address "the workers of Paris" regarding election results, she makes no pretense of being one of them; indeed, her tone is hectoring and condescending from the beginning: "Why don't I say it to you freely, in comradely fashion, and without pulling any punches? The electoral success for which you congratulate yourselves is not, in my opinion, of a nature to give you any real power, and the tactics you used on this occasion, in spite of their apparent success, far from helping you achieve your end, have only distanced you from it, as I see it."[16] In fact, d'Agoult's audience was the same whether she addressed her letter to the Comte de Chambord or the workers of Paris. D'Agoult sees herself as an intellectual, a political analyst providing insights and even advice to an educated elite. Additionally, d'Agoult often wrote about leaders, describing their appearances, their personal characteristics, and the strengths and weaknesses they brought to politics. This suggests that she viewed leaders as essential in themselves, determining policy and conducting affairs as much by their own merits as by following the wishes of their constituents, perhaps more so. She supported the republic more from the position of an advisor to leaders and potential leaders than as popular propagandist, which was Sand's chosen stance.

Sand, as propagandist, however, generally avoided any particular party line beyond celebrating the republic, encouraging readers to engage in politics and to help solve social problems through thought, discussion, and the democratic political process. She wrote of her newspaper *La Cause du Peuple*, "We do not offer it as a body of doctrine, as a political dogma fabricated at our fireside and destined infallibly to save the world. We bring it simply as an element of discussion." Sand had always eschewed dogma both religious and secular, and she poses a question that perhaps should have been acknowledged more often: "Do we really know what is a true republic?" Sand, of course, thought the answer was no, not just because the last republic in France had failed but because undemocratic regimes had prohibited open discussion of republicanism. Her sense of democracy was collective problem-solving in which all people had their say, at least through elected representatives, and she believed that a consensus would eventually form around the best idea or solution. The problem with society in the past, according to Sand, was that political systems required people to operate in isolation; leaders and intellectuals never could establish the best societies because their vision was too limited; they failed to account for the needs and ideas of all. Sand used a family metaphor to explain this deficiency to her audience of working people.

Deprived of political rights you were in a state of minority and eternal infancy. Experts in social science behave like a father who determines a priori the educational plan for all his children without ever considering the aptitudes, needs, and aspirations of each one of them. Such an education produces only fools or insane persons, and he who would conceive of and apply it would be mad himself. Do not then be surprised that so many powerful intelligences have become ill under a regime guilty of depriving clever persons of the contributions of the simple. Simple folk are as necessary to the clever as is the free and pure voice of the child to paternal ears.[17]

For Sand politics was a quest for truth, and the democratic republic was the political form most conducive to the successful outcome of that quest. Sand believed that all should be involved in this process, but that since the working poor had been excluded the longest, she felt obliged to devote herself to helping that class articulate its concerns and suggestions to representatives and leaders with more education and experience. Sand did not entirely ignore leaders, calling her readers' attention to the republican and popular commitment of men such as Ledru-Rollin, Pierre Leroux, and Armand Barbès. But her primary concern was to alert ordinary people to the possibilities and responsibilities of democracy.

Uncertainty and a great deal of hope characterized the mood of Sand, d'Agoult, Allart, and Girardin in the early months of 1848. Sand and d'Agoult became publicists for the Second Republic, while Allart at this time wrote about the events and personalities in private correspondence, and Girardin momentarily put her writing aside in the interest of her husband's political career. All four idealistically believed that the change in regime would correct the abuses and improve the poor conditions that had beset the July Monarchy. They expected republican politicians to be honest, hard-working, and selfless in their devotion to public service. They awaited a judicious solution to the problems of poverty and unemployment that would alleviate suffering without harming the comfortable classes. Reluctant revolutionaries, they nonetheless acknowledged that the public demonstrations of the popular classes had succeeded where reform-minded, bourgeois politicians had failed. With a minimum of bloodshed workers in Paris had overthrown a repulsive regime and inaugurated a democratic republic about which many could be optimistic. But the optimism and idealism of the four women writers suffered several setbacks. No doubt they expected too much from a very hastily contrived government, forced immediately to confront grave and complex difficulties. The disappointments of Sand, d'Agoult, Allart, and Girardin with the Second Republic were with different individuals and with different conditions, but they shared a sense of being highly interested observers, unable to act, or able to do so in only limited ways, when the experiment went awry.

Analyzing the Revolution

Sand became frustrated with the Second Republic before the other three authors, and that may have been because she was in such close contact with the provisional government. Sand's first impression of the leaders of the new republic in early March was that they were well intentioned and fundamentally good, but she wondered whether they, or anyone, could effectively address the enormous task of establishing a viable republic in the midst of hardship and strife. She wrote in a letter to a friend, "the provisional government is composed of men who are excellent for the most part, all a little incomplete and insufficient for a job that requires the genius of Napoleon and the heart of Jesus. But the gathering of all these men who have soul, or talent, or determination, will answer for the situation. They want the good, they seek it, they will try for it." Sand went on to say that the merit of all of these men, above that of their individual abilities, was their commitment to acting as representatives for "the will of all, the right of the people."[18] Sand had a high opinion of the good sense and common purpose of the masses, and she believed that this constituency would help leaders to govern in the best interest of the majority and of the nation. Sand's generous optimism was not shared by her daughter Solange, who wrote of the same men on 20 March: "Here we have at the head of the government some ambitious men who quarrel among themselves and seize power for themselves. I wonder how these people, who could never agree among themselves when they were in the opposition against a common enemy, who could never see eye to eye to edit a journal [*La Réforme*], hope to act in concert to direct an entire nation."[19] Solange was correct that Ledru-Rollin, Louis Blanc, Flocon, and François Arago differed on the extent to which the republic should be liberal or socialist, yet despite these disagreements they had managed to keep *La Réforme* afloat since 1843. Nonetheless, by mid-April Sand expressed similar concerns about factionalism and self-interest among members of the provisional government.

Sixteen April was a turning point for Sand, a confused day of demonstrations by workers and by the National Guard that entailed no violence or changes in the provisional government, but from Sand's perspective it was the death knell of liberty, fraternity, and equality. She discerned four separate conspiracies within the provisional government to consolidate power and eliminate rival factions, reflecting the different tendencies toward democratic socialism, liberalism, and radical insurrection among revolutionary and republican leaders. Although nothing came of the intrigues, real or imagined, Sand felt that the power struggle among leaders was a betrayal of the people and of the republic. Acknowledging a legitimate concern that the masses were by no means politically mature and that they needed more time to understand the meaning of democratic republicanism before they would be able to vote responsibly for representatives, Sand nonetheless asserted that the real evil that threatened the republic was the weak character of its leaders. "Men are false, ambitious, vain, egotistical, and the best is not worth the devil; it is truly sad to see this up close." Mentioning a few individuals whom Sand considered honest and pure, she indicated that they were all on the second level of power, and hence unable to combat the self-interested leaders at the top: "All on the first level live with this ideal: *Me, me, me.*"[20] She reiterated this concern about power-hungry leaders a month later, after the election of a constituent assembly, writing: "The *leaders* of the true social idea are hardly more enlightened than the men they combat, and they play the game too much for their own benefit." The people, Sand claims, realize that the men at the head of the government are inadequate for their task.[21]

Part of Sand's frustration with the republican leaders, many of whom were her friends and acquaintances, probably derived from her own marginalized position. To be sure Sand occasionally boasted of securing posts for her friends, and she teased Maurice with a play on words about getting his instructions as mayor of Nohant (*le maire*) from his mother (*la mère*) writing bulletins for the Interior Ministry. "What amuses me is that all [the government circulars] are addressed to the mayors, and that you will receive by official channels instructions from your *mother* [*ta mère*]. Ah! Ah! Mister *Mayor* [*Monsieur le* maire]!"[22] But the limits of Sand's influence became apparent to her, especially with the incident of the Bulletin No. 16.

Sand wrote several bulletins put out by the Ministry of the Interior, and the one dated 15 April caused an uproar because it asserted the right of the people to revolt again in order to save the republic. She wrote that in the event that the elections of 23 April produced too many conservatives and threatened the survival of the republic: "There will be only one appropriate path for the people who erected the barricades, and that would be to demonstrate their will a second time, and to reject the decisions of a false national representation."[23] This bulletin drew further attention just over one month later, in a special committee formed to investigate the June Days, and it was cited as an official provocation to the rebellion. The ministry repudiated the bulletin, indicating that it had not passed through the appropriate channels of editing and approval. As Sand explained to a friend after the fact, she was indeed morally responsible for the content of the bulletin, but not politically responsible. Elias Regnault, the official who normally reviewed the bulletins, was out of the office the day that Sand's bulletin crossed his desk. It appears that no one had read the bulletin before printing and distributing it.

Sand, who had voluntarily accepted the conditions of writing anonymously for the ministry and allowing her work to be edited or censored by it, nonetheless felt betrayed by her "employer," because she had merely written what other men in the government had said. Sand claimed later that she "thanked God for having such an impolitic inspiration. Everyone else said it as much as I did, but only a woman was crazy enough to dare to write it. No man would have been so stupid or hot-headed as to bring down from the heights so ordinary a truth."[24] Sand may indeed have acknowledged a lack of political savvy on her part, but at the same time she prided herself on her honesty and resented those in power who dissimulated in order to stay in power. Moreover, she bitterly objected to accusations that she had conspired in any way or on any occasion, and that she had been paid for her incendiary remarks. She wrote a letter to the prefect of police denying rumors that she had harangued the crowds and incited them to action on 15 May, and she told her cousin not to believe any of the stories circulating about her. "As for my *triumphs*, they consisted in Paris of living in an attic room at 100 écus a year, dining out for 30 sous, paying my debts, and working *gratis* for the republic. Those are the honors, profits, and grandeurs that I have finagled up to this time."[25]

Sand's initial sense of the transparency of politics—reflected in her euphoric words at the beginning of the Second Republic that "our home is the public square"—changed through her experience of March through June 1848. She became skeptical about politics and understood that disagreeable and even dishonest acts were necessarily involved in it. She accepted that politics was gendered masculine, and she gladly distanced herself from the sordid enterprise. Writing to a friend in June, she asserted:

If ever you hear that I involve myself in what is today called *politics*, don't believe it. I have absolutely no taste or ability for such a vile thing. . . . One must know a host of things that one would not like to know, and a host of people with whom I would just as soon not have relations. That is the misfortune of political men. I have the happiness of not being a man and of being able to maintain candor in all contingencies.[26]

Sand seemed happy to leave the most negative aspects of politics to men, but she left open for herself the possibility of other modes of political involvement—for example, fighting against the bourgeoisie in a revolution and dying on the barricades. Power plays and the expediencies practiced by leaders had no appeal for Sand. This was an important lesson for her from 1848. Yet she expressed all these criticisms and frustrations in personal letters; she did not write them for the larger public.

Sand left Paris after the demonstration of 15 May, suspected by many of having fomented the unrest. She might well have been arrested, though she stayed until 17 May, claiming that she did not wish to appear to be escaping. Sand was disheartened with political developments, and she did, in fact, wish to escape the intrigues, in-fighting, and setbacks of republican politics. Resuming the narration of her life that the February revolution had interrupted, Sand explained to her readers the change in herself caused by the experience of political involvement: "I have witnessed a campaign in the world of action and am no longer the same as before. I have lost the youthful illusions that my privileged life of reclusive contemplation had allowed me to hold onto longer than one reasonably should." Sand presents herself, and therefore the rest of her book, as sadder than either had been before the revolution. But she is wiser as well, and rather than curse people for the many failings she observed, she identifies herself with humanity and with the capacity for optimism and renewal: "The rest of humanity is no different than I, which is to say that others get discouraged and recover with great ease."[27] Her commitment to the republic as an ideal and as a form of government was unswerving. From Nohant she continued to write articles in favor of the republic's policies and, until 11 June, even some of its leaders for a newspaper called *La Vraie République*. News of the June Days horrified her, and she was physically ill and sick at heart. But living in the countryside and returning to writing fiction and autobiography eventually lifted her spirits, and she found different ways to support republicanism.

While Sand confined much of her disillusionment and frustration to private correspondence, Girardin made public her disappointment and even her outrage at republican leaders. Publishing her first installment of the *Courrier de Paris* for 1848 during the month of May, Girardin lamented that the republican ideal—"the dream of all generous and independent spirits"—had been betrayed. She held the leaders responsible, maintaining that they had failed to understand what a republic should be, "and the proof that they do not understand [the republic] is that they have not made it beloved; they have rendered it ridiculous, shabby, and vain, instead of making it powerful, serious, and dignified." Girardin contended that in numerous ways leaders made the republic a parody of monarchy. For example, they set off cannon every time they did something, they strutted about in the fine ministerial halls with large entourages, and they used the police to violate the civil liberties of private citizens. Girardin advised readers that the only appropriate behavior for ministers of a republic, as opposed to a monarchy, is utter simplicity and constant work; they must make their positions of power as disagreeable as possible to discourage the self-serving from seeking office. "Under royalty power is almost inaccessible; it can, without too much danger, be surrounded by seductions; but a republic is another matter; a rebellion can give power to anyone who desires it; it must therefore be made austere, tedious, painful, ultimately undesirable, to discourage ambitious dreamers." According to Girardin, yet another indication that leaders betrayed the republic was that, for their own personal gain, they exploited the people who had fought on the barricades: "With the blood of the poor they have demanded the money of the rich. They throw you [the people] into the arena with rousing words like fanfares, and they hide themselves in ambush to see what happens." Girardin thought that a real republic would regenerate the soul and inspire genius. It would employ thousands in the construction of great public works, monuments to fraternity that "would surpass in grandeur and pride the most famous edifices of antiquity, raised by thousands of slaves bowed under the whips of tyrants." Public art and industry would flourish under Girardin's ideal republic for the well-being of all. "Ah! how beautiful would be the republic, how beautiful without republicans!"[28]

Girardin's critique of the republic is playful and witty, though not without some basis. She reminds readers of the promises to the people who brought them to power that republican leaders are expected to uphold, even as she emphasizes the aesthetic components of republicanism, indicating ways in which republican men and institutions should be transformed from their appearances and functions under monarchy. She jokes about how women who married fools under the previous regime in order to acquire noble titles have now, under a republic, lost the title but are stuck with the foolish husbands. Girardin even confronts the problem of her own pseudonym, as titles of nobility have been abolished. But she determines that the name vicomte de

Launay is a title "of fantasy" with "no value at all," so no one could possibly be offended by its use.[29] This, however, proves to be the last time that Girardin uses the name, and it is the end of her lighthearted, distanced criticism of the republic.

Girardin's subsequent charges against the republic are sharp and on occasion personal, because in June the republic hurt her personally. Ever since the beginning of the revolution her husband, Emile, had spent most of his time away from home in an apartment above the offices of La Presse so that his newspaper could print the very latest of rapidly changing political developments. La Presse's initial call for confidence in and support for the Second Republic had changed to criticism, and with the outbreak of street fighting on 22 June, Emile was arrested and imprisoned and La Presse suspended, along with other newspapers accused of contributing to the unrest. Girardin's entry for the Courrier de Paris of 30 June recounts her experience of Emile's arrest, expressing her distress and narrating her failed efforts to visit Emile and to learn more about why he had been arrested. There is no pretense here of an alternative identity; Girardin is presenting herself as Madame Emile de Girardin, a frantic wife concerned about the welfare of her absent husband: "I was supposed to dine at a friend's house, but I wrote to her that I was half dead and that I couldn't walk. I give all these details to explain the feverish overexcitement that the news of the arrest of M. de Girardin caused me." After ten days Emile was released, having apparently suffered no harm. But Delphine de Girardin berated the republic, calling it a nest of conspirators bent on its destruction, while men of genius (implying Emile) are prevented from establishing a pure, effective, and generous republic.[30]

Girardin's final installment of the Courrier despaired of France and interpreted the social struggle that plagued the republic as an ignoble and baseless tussle over private property. The column was heavily censored, and paragraphs that appeared to address individuals in government included long ellipses indicating extracted material. Girardin ends by acknowledging the censorship and asking the reader if France really continues to exist: "Is this really France, this country where it is no longer permitted even to try to have wit and courage?"[31] The vicomte de Launay was dead, and the Courrier de Paris was finished. But the Girardin couple campaigned against General Cavaignac, who was a candidate for the presidency and whom they held responsible for Emile's imprisonment.

In November *La Presse* published a poem by Delphine de Girardin that bitterly denounced Cavaignac for the June Days and their excessive bloodshed. In the poem Girardin positions herself as a woman, outside of politics, but, for that very reason, capable of insights not available to a man enmeshed in the political process:

> Now then, I, before God, before God I accuse him!
> I am only a woman, a madwoman, a muse!
> But my thoroughly French heart rebels at the horror,
> I feel the spirit of truth speaking in me.

Girardin claims that she "hates all [political] parties," and that had Cavaignac really saved the republic she would have excused the bloodshed. But describing the conflict in lurid terms—"Everywhere blood flowed in rivers, in waterfalls"—she proclaims that Cavaignac himself admitted to having slept through the killing, unlike the men fighting and the women waiting at home, unable to sleep out of anxiety and fear. Girardin portrays Cavaignac as a shockingly heartless and incompetent leader, and she implies little better for the Assembly that applauded his actions. She appeals to the dead and to the survivors, notably women, to consider the actions of this government on the eve of presidential elections:

> You inconsolable wives, sisters, mothers,
> With broken hearts, wounded flanks, torn guts,
> Who having nothing left of a son but cold bones—
> Have you heard this applause?[32]

Girardin was the most vociferous of the four women writers in her denunciation of June and of Cavaignac. However, Allart shared some of her indignation, although she never expressed it publicly. To Sainte-Beuve, Allart vented her frustration and disapproval. She claims to have learned of the June Days from refugees, combatants from both sides, who had left Paris and passed through Herblay. She considers the workers who fought to be "barbarians lacking both critical judgment [*sans plus de réflexion*] and religion," because they had led her to believe that they took up arms merely on the word of friends and had fired them out of anger at the Mobile Guards, who fired on them precipitately. But Allart blamed the leaders of the republic even more than she blamed the popular classes for the civil war and the deterioration of the republic. "The people are not responsible for the madness to which the Government pushes them," she asserted, and she maintained that despite the stupidity and setback of June, the French deserved a chance at freedom: "All people are made for liberty." Allart bewailed the return of July Monarchy men to positions of power following the elections and the June Days: "Republicans and their leaders are in prison, their instruments are reversed, and the people of Louis-Philippe, reestablishing the past, maintain the Republic that prevents anything from succeeding."[33] The path to a reformed and free republic had proven to be a rocky one, and Allart was sensitive to the less heroic aspects of the process. She proclaimed that "89 was a revolution; 1848 is a brawl," but she thinks that France will survive the ugly scene of June. She reassures Sainte-Beuve (and perhaps herself) that the disturbance of June is only a temporary derailment of progress toward a liberal republic, and that all will learn from this mistake: "From these convulsions we will become better educated, more determined." She expresses faith in the humanitarian ideals of Pierre Leroux, and she thinks that Ledru-Rollin could stabilize the republic if he adopted a moderate position. But after Bonaparte's election to the presidency, Allart had little hope left for republicanism, less because at that time she feared a dictatorship (like many, Allart considered Louis-Napoleon Bonaparte a mediocrity) than because his election opened the way to the return of monarchy.[34]

Several years later Allart published works that assessed the events again. Her skepticism about popular democracy was undiminished; she thought that the laboring masses had much power in their numbers, but she feared that their understanding and capacity to establish enduring governments did not match that power. Allart thought that the French revolutions by the people in 1789 and in 1848 had been justified, because they brought about progressive changes and necessary improvements in the lives of the poor. The real problem for Allart was that some revolutions, notably that of 1848, failed to produce capable leaders. A lesson of 1848 for Allart was the revelation of the legitimate power of the working class and the need to channel that strength under capable leadership: "*Association* which, in politics is nothing more than the union of parties (a contribution of M. Guizot, and which Pierre Leroux wishes to apply to workers), would render workers masters of society, masters for one day if in themselves their knowledge did not measure up to their unity and force. And this is what we have to fear, workers well enough rallied and conducting themselves well, but powerless in their victory." Allart thought that it would take centuries to educate the masses sufficiently for complete democracy, yet she also

maintained that freedom was essential for the cultivation of great leaders. Her ideal government was a representative republic, which she
thought combined freedom, equality of opportunity, and rule by the
most intelligent and the most capable.[35]

Even more than Allart, d'Agoult prided herself on dispassionately
assessing the Revolution of 1848 and the Second Republic. In the introduction to the first volume of the *Histoire de la Révolution de 1848*, published in 1850, she claims: "I brought to my research, with the most
scrupulous good faith, a sincere desire for impartiality."[36] To be sure
she was open and enthusiastic about her support for the republic, and
in the *Lettres républicaines* that she published concurrently with the un-
folding of events in 1848 she did not hide her anguish over the June
Days or her apprehension over the presidential elections of December
that she had (rightfully) feared Bonaparte would win. D'Agoult expressed the emotions of hope, and increasingly of fear, as the events
played out in 1848, but she also strived to analyze those events and to
be somewhat objective regarding popular revolutionaries and republican leaders. She could do this during the writing of the *Lettres républicaines* in 1848 and of the *Histoire de la Révolution de 1848* until 1853,
through her belief that the revolution was almost historically prede-
termined, and that republicanism was part of the inevitable progress of
history.

The Second Republic, she asserts, was "the natural consequence of
the double initiative of the eighteenth century, which simultaneously
conquered for the educated classes the freedom to think and for the
working classes the freedom to act."[37] Moreover, the February Days
were historically, morally, and even divinely justified, and she strongly
denied the work of any conspirator or putschist behind the people's inspired and, for the most part, peaceful revolt. "The people of Paris, in
taking over Hotel-de-Ville and in spontaneously declaring there the republican government, despite the majority of democratic leaders, were
acting only as executors of a decree long suspended on the legal citizenry." From her perspective the July Monarchy had forfeited its right
to rule by ignoring the legitimate claims of the people, and "Providence
withdrew from it the exercise of its power."[38]

According to d'Agoult the revolutionaries were fulfilling a historic
destiny: the progressive improvement of the "moral and material life of
the people." They did not make the same mistake as in 1792, destroying
the republic through violence. So what, d'Agoult asks, derailed the re-

public of 1848? "The mediocrity of those who tried to establish it," she answered. In short, d'Agoult blamed leaders who were well intentioned but flawed. D'Agoult drew numerous portraits of leaders in 1848, many of whom she knew personally, and she characterized, often with great insight, both their strengths and their weaknesses. No great man or great men seemed capable of taking control of a situation that was so difficult but also so promising. Of the provisional government, which d'Agoult considered to be made up of decent men, she wrote that it was "composed of heterogeneous elements, disunited from the very beginning, pulled in two different directions, hesitating between the people and the bourgeoisie, ceding without firm convictions, first to one, then to the other, not daring to look boldly ahead, nor returning behind, [the provisional government] was reduced to practicing a policy of expedients, lacking grandeur and power."[39] The gravest error of the leaders of the Second Republic was to ignore the masses, their new democratic constituency. According to d'Agoult, they mistakenly taxed the poor equally with the rich, at the same moment that they granted universal male suffrage, thus providing the people with the means of showing their dissatisfaction. "Of all the mistakes [the provisional government] made, no other created a swifter, more direct, more blatant backlash."[40]

D'Agoult sought not to blame either leaders or the people, but rather to present the facts and assess the situation. Nonetheless, she discerned that both the leaders and the people had made mistakes in 1848. Leaders were factionalized and often deluded into modeling themselves after the great men of the first French Revolution. The people were unnecessarily violent in June and were carried away by feelings of revenge in the presidential elections. Of one thing she was sure, and that was that "the national genius, *the voice of God* in the nineteenth century" consisted of "*the proletariat instituting democracy.*"[41] Successful governments were those that heeded the voice of the people and helped the people to political maturity. D'Agoult viewed 1848 as a lesson to the French and to Europe of the inevitability of democratic republicanism: "The reign of democracy will be founded. The French Revolution that has become the European revolution, that is the greatest of social revolutions since the establishment of Christianity, will be accomplished."[42]

Sand, d'Agoult, Allart, and Girardin all followed, even actively participated in, and tried to understand the establishment of the Second Republic in 1848. Their positioning as both insiders and outsiders contributed to their interpretations and modes of literary and political expression. Happy to assist her friends when the possibilities for establishing a republican government were the greatest, Sand was powerless to stop the course of the closing of possibilities brought about by leadership alliances, government moves toward self-preservation, and election results. In contrast to Sand's retreat from active involvement in national politics in May, Girardin became more outspoken in her criticism of the republican leadership when her husband failed to get a government position, and especially after his imprisonment. D'Agoult attempted a judicious apportioning of fault in the face of historical inevitability, and Allart, the most distanced from political power of the four women, checked her own theories about politics against the developments of 1848 in private and published works. For the most part they engaged in politics in 1848 in the same manner as before the revolution; that is, they wrote about politics and republicanism in various genres, while at the same time associating with political men in salons, through newspapers, and in other social settings. In the midst of upheaval, however, Sand and Girardin, but not d'Agoult or Allart, became the subjects of caricature, sometimes extremely hostile, for their political interventions.

Representing Political Women

Sand's association with the provisional government and in particular with Ledru-Rollin precipitated caricatures, both verbal and in the form of drawings, that suggested how unnatural and disorderly was the involvement of women in politics, at least to the caricatures' creators and presumably to their audience. Earlier caricatures of women writers had represented them as unfeminine and monstrous for their presumption to intellectual endeavor and literary success. Similarly, a spate of caricatures appeared in 1848 that represented females as ugly, masculinized, and behaving outrageously in order to convey their unsuitability for political activity. Several scholars have analyzed these caricatures, including those of generalized female figures, notably socialist feminists, and those of particular individuals, notably Sand, Girardin, Eugénie Niboyet, and Jeanne Deroin. They suggest that these images ridiculing political women represent an effort to stabilize a very tenuous and fluid political situation by eliminating women from public debate, and that such images attributed the failure of 1848 to women's unsuitable, disruptive participation in politics.[43] What must be added here are a few more specifics about the political activities of Sand and Girardin behind the particularized caricatures of them.

Two caricatures of Sand showed female political participation as reversing gender roles and therefore perverting or at best sexualizing masculine politics. In one image Sand follows her "boss," Ledru-Rollin up to a podium in front of an audience of feminists. The caption reads, "This handsome candidate / Will garner all the votes for the presidency . . . / of the Women's Club. / Wouldn't these women like to play this desirable role?" [*Ce Beau candidat/Réunira toutes les voix pour la Présidence . . . /du Club des femmes./Ces dames voudraient elles jouer le Beau Role—hein?*] The caption suggests that the women in the audience would like both to vote for the "handsome candidate" and to fill Sand's role as his "assistant." But the caption is also a play on words so that the final line can be read as "Wouldn't these women like to play with this good-looking Rollin?" meaning that the women gathered to hear Ledru-Rollin discuss politics are in fact more interested in the minister of the interior as a sexual object. (See Fig. 9.) The implication is that women could not possibly take politics seriously, and that Sand, though carrying Ledru-Rollin's portfolio, symbolizing her work for him on the bulletins, must be sleeping with him. Thus, Sand in particular and women in general are represented as sexualizing and degrading politics, normally a masculine activity, and Ledru-Rollin is also caricatured for employing Sand and therefore being responsible for this degradation. (See Fig. 10.)

Another caricature represents Sand as a giantess whose knitting needles and yarn have fallen from her hands, and instead, she wields a whip, while tiny male figures run out from under her skirts. The title reads "La Gigogne politique de 1848" ["The Political Old Woman Who Lived in a Shoe of 1848"]. Here Sand is likened to the fairy-tale figure, the old woman who lived in a shoe and had so many children she didn't know what do to. In this case, the children are the men whom Sand contrived to put into administrative and judicial positions in the Berry region as part of the new republic of 1848. In this caricature Sand is made monstrous by spawning revolutionary men instead of children; she has abandoned feminine pursuits (knitting) and is wreaking havoc by getting involved in politics.[44]

Both caricatures imply that Sand's modest participation in the provisional government was far greater and more damaging than it was, and it is her sexualized body, more than any political ideology, that

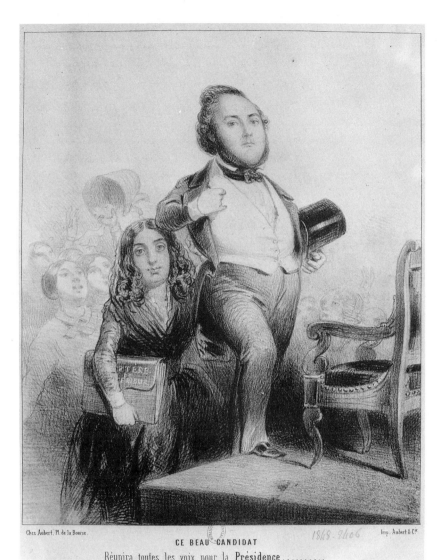

CE BEAU CANDIDAT

Réunira toutes les voix pour la **Présidence**..........
du Club des femmes.
Ces dames voudraient elles jouer le Beau Role-hein ?

FIG. 9. Anonymous, *Ce beau candidat* (1848). Paris, Bibliothèque nationale de France, Cabinet des Estampes. Photo Bibliothèque nationale de France, Paris.

FIG. 10. Anonymous, *La Gigogne politique de 1848* (1848). From *Le Monde Illustré*, 16 August 1884. Chicago, Center for Research Libraries. Photo Division of Instructional Services, Photographics, Purdue University.

Chez Aubert & C.ie Pl. de la Bourse, 25   Imp. Aubert & C.ie

UNE MUSE EN 1848.

FIG. 11. Anonymous, *Une Muse en 1848* (1848). From *Le Charivari*, 15 December 1848. Washington, D.C., Library of Congress Rare Books. Photo Library of Congress.

« Je ne suis qu'une femme, une folle, nne buse. »

— Extrait d'un grand journal —

FIG. 12. Anonymous, *Je ne suis qu'une femme, une folle, une buse* (1848). From *La Revue comique*, 1848–49. Washington, D.C., Library of Congress Rare Books. Photo Library of Congress.

causes the problem. Sand's femininity is also at the heart of two textual critiques of her political involvement, though less overtly so. A reviewer of Sand's *Lettres au Peuple* claimed that prior to 1848 Sand's political writing had merely echoed the ideas of men—namely, Pierre Leroux, Félicité de Lamennais, and Adam Mickiewicz. However, since these men were actively involved in the new republic, Sand had to rely on her own thought, which the reviewer characterized as "too incoherent and diffuse." The review then asserts that the *Lettres au Peuple* are bad writing—"forty pages of sentences without ideas"—that will not appeal to the working class to whom it is directed. Saying nothing about Sand's political ideas, this reviewer dismisses them by dismissing Sand's ability to think and write. Another commentator goes further in examining Sand's sexual ambiguity as a writer prior to 1848, and then asserting that she wrote extreme republican articles in order to revive her flagging reputation as an author. Moreover, the commentator accuses Sand of influencing the republic with radical feminism: "There are some usually well-informed persons who assure [me] that there is a red republican program that includes a ministry for the emancipation of women, whose portfolio will be confided to George Sand."[45] Both articles erroneously claimed that Sand was in the pay of the provisional government, thus denying that she might have any principles and hinting that she was not much more than a prostitute. She was sufficiently involved in politics to warrant a fairly general caricature of the nefarious effects on politics that women, by virtue of their sex, entail, but she avoided the kind of direct, personal attack against a political figure that led to far more hostile pillorying of Girardin.

Two caricatures of Girardin appeared following the publication of her poem in November denouncing the June Days and Cavaignac. One shows her writing at her desk for *La Presse*, her poet's lyre cast aside, her hair, like Medusa's, a mass of snakes, and her pen dipped in an inkwell of vitriol. Underneath the image the label reads "Une Muse en 1848," referring to the transformation of Delphine Gay, the innocuous girl poet who called herself the patriotic muse, into Madame de Girardin, a vicious, man-hating political journalist. (See Fig. 11.) The other caricature even more directly links Girardin with the November poem. It shows a creature whose body is that of a bird of prey with a woman's head. Beneath its claws are a sword and the remains of a soldier's uniform, and above the creature is a blazon with a blue stocking, pierced by a pen and bleeding, with the date 1848. The second line of her poem is parodied below the image: "I am only a woman, a madwoman, a buzzard," with the words *une buse* replacing her original *une muse*. (See Fig. 12.) Yet another caricature represented Girardin as Judith (about whom she had written a play in 1841 that was performed in 1843) approaching a sleeping soldier with sword in hand.[46]

In addition to the visual images, two different verses with the same title, "A Madame Delphine Gay de Girardin," appeared at about the same time, one in *La Revue comique* and the other in *L'Illustration*. Like the images, the verses condemned Girardin's personal attack against Cavaignac, and they also regretted the loss of the gentle, feminine girl poet Delphine Gay. Moreover, one advised her to stick to housework and leave politics to her husband:

> But today, Delphine, as a good housekeeper
> Leave to your husband, who understands them so well,
> These tedious duties of the man and the citizen.
> You, woman, guardian angel of the domestic hearth,
> Don't let your white dress be soiled
> In the bloody arena where [political] parties struggle.[47]

These caricatures of Girardin and the poems about her suggest that, like Sand, she was derided for being a woman involved in politics. But unlike Sand, Girardin had published a personal attack against a male politician just before an election. Such moves were typical of male political journalism at the time and often led to furious, slanderous exchanges.[48] Indeed, caricatures of Emile de Girardin, who had campaigned vigorously against Cavaignac in *La Presse*, also appeared in *La Revue comique*. Girardin, as a woman, complicated the practice of male journalists' defense of their honor through political invective. Moreover, she was married to one of the major participants in this cutthroat game. Girardin's entry into the ring of journalistic combat opened her to the kind of personal attacks usually reserved for male journalists, but with the added hostility resulting from her transgression onto masculine territory. Neither Sand nor Girardin appear to have responded to these caricatures, unless their withdrawal from political activity and overtly political writing could be considered a response. D'Agoult and Allart, who were more discreet in their behavior and writing, were not subject to personalized caricatures. However, 1848 brought many feminists into the political arena, editing newspapers, forming clubs, and calling for political rights for women both in the press and in speeches. For their pains they were mercilessly caricatured, and their actions forced women writers to address the issue of female suffrage and the position of women in politics.

Responses to Feminism

It would seem logical, after the stunning display of male egotism and incompetence in the Second Republic, that Sand, d'Agoult, Girardin, and Allart would support the principle of female suffrage in the expectation that female public officials and voters might avoid the mistakes of men. But that was not the case. While all four advocated sexual equality, they did not view the enfranchisement of women in 1848 as an effective means to that end.

Sand is well known for disavowing any connection with the feminists who proposed her candidacy for the constituent assembly in the April 1848 issue of *La Voix des Femmes*. Addressing herself to the editors of *La Réforme* and *La Vraie République*, Sand stated that she hoped no one would ruin a ballot by putting her name on it, and she asserted in different ways that she was not personally acquainted with "women who form clubs and edit journals." Scholars have interpreted this reply as being Sand's haughty, scornful, bitter, and perfidious denunciation of feminists and feminism.[49] After all, Sand refused to address the author of the nomination, Jeanne Deroin, and *La Voix des Femmes*, choosing to tell male editors and presumably male readers that she did not associate with feminists and that she had no part in this "ridiculous pretension" of running for the assembly. However, a different interpretation is possible when considering the document as a whole, along with other texts that Sand produced on the subject of women and politics in 1848. Sand asserts that women, like men, have the right to discuss ideas freely among themselves, but she draws the line at having her name implicated with a group without her permission: "I cannot permit that, without my consent, I be taken for a representative figure of a feminine group with which I have never had any relations good or bad." Sand also recognizes that the women's nomination of her was intended as a compliment: "I beg pardon of these women who, to be sure, have treated me with much good will, for taking precautions against their zeal."[50] Sand definitely wanted to distance herself from socialist feminists, who were calling for political equality at a time when Sand thought that educating male voters on republican principles and democratic responsibilities was of primary importance, just two weeks before the assembly elections. She put the establishment and maintenance of the republic above women's rights, but women's issues were no less important to her vision of republicanism.

"Should women participate in politics some day? Yes, some day, . . . but is this day near? No, I think not, and in order for women's condition to be transformed, society must be radically transformed," Sand wrote in an unfinished letter to the Democratic Socialist Central Committee in 1848. In one of the republican bulletins, Sand asserts that social and family reform must be priorities of the new republic, and that "the condition of women is that which has up to now least occupied the attention of legislators." Working-class women have suffered from low wages and insufficient education, and that has put them into a position of extreme degradation and dependency, Sand maintains. "It has been shown and proven by statistics, that the jobs consigned to the majority of women offer such derisory wages that it is materially impossible for them to live independently." The only alternative that society offers poor women is prostitution—or suicide. Sand counts on the republic to change the economic condition of women. Additionally, "one of the first questions that a socialist republic will have to address" is how "to render to woman the civil rights that marriage alone removes." Sand anticipated that marriage in a republic would be based on equality, and "the principle of untrammeled individual authority will disappear along with divine right." With new laws, husbands would no longer have the right to commit adultery outside of the home, to control children's education without a mother's approval, or to beat their wives. "Civil equality, equality in marriage, equality in the family, these are what you can, what you should demand," Sand counsels women, but out of respect for marriage and the sanctity of the family.[51]

Sand believed that women should begin their revolution in the family, that poor women should discuss their issues with their republican husbands, who, Sand was certain, would be moved by their wives' suffering. She acknowledged that women in public administration could improve society, but she considered feminist demands too precipitate because the majority of women were in no position to benefit from them. She thought that women needed more time to gain an education, along with moral and economic independence: "For if a large portion of men are inexperienced in the exercise of this new life we are entering, a still larger portion of women are inexperienced, and their entrance would badly complicate an already difficult situation." At this stage Sand tells feminists who demand political equality that they "are playing childish games. Your house is burning, your hearth is imperiled, and you expose yourself to public ridicule. . . . What strange whim urges you to parliamentary struggles, you who cannot bring to them even the exercise of personal independence?"[52]

In general Sand disputed feminists' tactics and timing rather than their goals, writing of socialist women involved in political clubs that "these women are right to concern themselves with the progress that the Republic promises to inject into our habits, into legislation, into the material and moral condition of women of the people, in the education of both sexes. But these women are wrong to want to throw themselves into the movement." According to Sand, the majority of women simply were not prepared for political participation; having been oppressed so completely and for so long, they needed even more time than men to cultivate independent characters and ideas. Moreover, Sand thought that feminists risked public ridicule at the expense of their cause. Sand presented herself as a mentor to feminists, someone who shared some of their experiences of injustice and discrimination and who had supported the improvement of women's condition through her writing. "Excuse me for speaking to you with such ardor, but my mature age and perhaps some services rendered to my sex by numerous writings give me the right of remonstrance." Indicating that she was "a woman who has vividly felt the injustice of laws and prejudices," Sand expressed concern that feminists' demands for political rights would set back a movement in which Sand, too, had a large stake. Sand claimed to speak for others when she warned feminists that they would lose all credibility by calling for all rights, because many would think that included free love, meaning sexual promiscuity. "Seeing that you demand the complete exercise of political rights, many think that you demand still another thing, the freedom of passion, and from then on, people reject all ideas of reform." Sand suggested that feminists, who clearly possessed talent and the ability to write and speak, should operate among themselves, outside of masculine politics. In short, Sand proposed that they do as she did, and that they then would find a more sympathetic male audience than if they intervened into male politics. "If in your writings you make the case for civil equality, you will be heeded."[53]

Similarly, d'Agoult believed that political equality should be the culmination, not the starting point, for the advancement of women. In her *Histoire de la Révolution de 1848*, published between 1850 and 1853, she, like Sand, admonished the feminists who called for female suffrage in 1848 as being too zealous and alienating potential supporters among liberal men.

Instead of . . . addressing simply and modestly the questions regarding the education of women of all classes, the careers that could be opened to women, the wages of working-class women, the authority of the mother in the family, the dignity of the wife . . . instead of progressing step by step with prudence as public opinion becomes more favorable, [feminists] acted very impoliticly; they noisily started political clubs that quickly became laughable.[54]

In her mind, women should change popular attitudes through rational persuasion and gradual social reforms before engaging in political activism. D'Agoult urges women to think more carefully about feminist demands, to build upon the ideas and practices put forward during the French Revolution by men and women like Condorcet, Olympe de Gouges, and Madame de Staël. It is worth noting that Condorcet and de Gouges advocated political rights for women; thus, d'Agoult appears to object more to women's formation of clubs than to the principle of equal rights. Another reason that d'Agoult counsels feminists to postpone their demands for female suffrage is her belief that the popular revolution will somehow automatically promote sexual equality. She asserts that the popular classes are more receptive to equality between the sexes because they have not "learned" prejudice as bourgeois men have, and they daily witness the capability of women struggling to survive. Like many socialists, d'Agoult concluded that "all progress toward democracy in France will lead to corresponding progress in the condition of women. The day that the people can express its feeling in the making of laws, equality and fraternity will no longer apply exclusively to one sex."[55]

Girardin approached the issue of female suffrage differently, seeing in the provisional government's failure to grant it further evidence of the government's general incompetence. "Proof that they do not understand the republic, is that in their fine promises for universal suffrage, they forgot women." Asserting that women do not want political rights, Girardin explains that by enfranchising male servants without enfranchising bourgeois women, republican leaders have deprived women of their authority in the home, which women deeply resent. This passage suggests that Girardin is more concerned about class domination than gender equality. Or perhaps Girardin is basically satisfied with the gender division of labor in the middle class that allows husbands public authority over the working classes, and, for women, private authority over servants. In fact, Girardin challenged male presumption to privilege and authority at the expense of women: "Oh! French men are always the same—envious tyrants over their wives whom they pretend to love. . . . The most abject cretin, if his imbecility has the honor [of] being masculine, counts more in their eyes than the most noble woman gifted with the greatest mind." And Girardin goes on to question why obscure male deputies prohibit the famous and accomplished George Sand from voting: "And the author of *Indiana, Valentine,* . . . and so many masterpieces, George Sand, . . . oh deputies too proud of your masculine obscurity! George Sand did not have the right to spell out on a ballot, with her immortal pen, a single one of your unknown names!"[56]

Girardin reiterates that women do not claim political equality—"Women by no means demand the right to vote"—but she enumerates several serious improvements that women do want—namely, to be able to earn a living wage, and not to be subject to husbands who deprive them and their children of sustenance in order to support mistresses. So how should women act politically, according to Girardin? They should exercise the best of feminine qualities behind the scenes, and in that way influence political men to act in the best interests of the republic. Excoriating men for fighting over issues of mere "cupidity and egotism," Girardin asserts that "only women can preach a crusade of generosity against these hordes of wild egotists; only women . . . can save the country with an intelligent magnanimity, can by their eloquence before combat, force men to be generous, and, by their love after [men's] sacrifice, console them for having been so." A model to Girardin of a political woman was Madame de Staël, with her elegant and engaging salon, in contrast to Madame Roland, whom Girardin despised as being motivated to support the Girondin cause out of vengeance, frustration, and hypocrisy. Girardin might have been describing herself in this admiring account of Staël as *salonnière*: She is a "queen, hospitable, . . . illuminating all with her genius, watching over, drawing out, inspiring conversation, devoted to getting the best out of her mind and the minds of her friends, openly sharing her glory with the man she loves and creating him in her own image!"[57] Girardin shared with feminists similar goals of improving women's economic and social position, but she advocated a mode of action that was suited to privileged women attached to male political leaders.

Sand, d'Agoult, and Girardin did not believe in 1848 that female suffrage could achieve the civil equality for women that they desired. In a society in which democracy for men was so precarious, few women could imagine a situation in which men and women of all classes enjoyed equal political rights. From Sand's and d'Agoult's perspective (and probably Girardin's), if men, especially bourgeois men, with all their advantages of education, economic independence, and political experience were still, in 1848, incapable of governing democratically, then women in general—in their ignorance, dependency, and exclusion from politics—could not be expected to do any better. Just as men must wait, according to d'Agoult, for the eventual, inevitable reign of liberty, women, too, must wait for equality in that ideal future.

That is not to say that women should passively endure until the coming millennium. Indeed, all four women writers indicated that exceptional women, like themselves, should actively pursue improvements in women's condition and in society in general. D'Agoult frequently invoked female figures from history as models of thinkers and activists who promoted freedom and justice without the aid of political rights: Madame de Staël, Madame de Genlis, Madame Roland, and Charlotte Corday fought for liberty in the late eighteenth century, for instance.[58] Allart, too, in 1836 cites women's past influence as an argument for their continued contributions to political and social improvements: "As in earlier times women's culture advanced civilization [and] gentled manners, so this new age of culture for women will lead society far toward justice and equality; as before coarse and warlike man was gentled by women, so the free man will be moralized by them."[59] Allart, unlike Sand, d'Agoult, and Girardin, was receptive to the idea of female suffrage, insofar as it would allow intelligent women access to political affairs, rather than out of adherence to the general principle of democracy. In 1869 Allart wrote to d'Agoult, "It is not I who would oppose votes for women, but I would like first to deprive many men of the vote."[60] For her, this was not incompatible with the notion that women, particularly exceptional women, should rule alongside exceptional men, both being "elected" in a meritocratic system. Women writers believed that women could and should exercise a beneficent influence that would have a better chance of bringing about the conditions for sexual equality than either the good intentions of republican men or the political activism of socialist feminists. In a long letter of 1850 analyzing Sand's oeuvre, Allart juxtaposes Sand's literary genius with male political inadequacy. "In a time when political men are all more or less unsuccessful, . . . isn't it a pleasure to be able to praise merit so complete, . . . and when *political genius* is wanting, to have a *poetic genius* in full force."[61] Sand, d'Agoult, Allart, and Girardin had always exercised their influence through writing, and following the Revolution of 1848 they would continue to do so. When Girardin enumerated the many failings of the Second Republic in May, she wrote: "If the republic can be saved, it will be by women."[62]

Rewriting the Republic

Just as the four women writers articulated a feminist republicanism before 1848, so their analyses and writings after the revolution reveal a gender and feminist consciousness. Sand, d'Agoult, Girardin, and Allart had hoped that the Second Republic would change the laws regarding women's family, economic, and social positions so that women and men would be civilly, if not politically, equal. As writers, *salonnières*, friends, and supporters, they had confidence in republican men to implement reforms regarding women, but the republic that they hoped for did not last. Politics itself was a major factor contributing to the downfall of the republic, and Sand especially, but perhaps also Girardin, found politics as men practiced it too distasteful and ineffectual to want to demand political rights for women. Instead, their feminist politics was to influence society by example and by writing, and to persuade men to alter their laws and opinions regarding women. In a variety of ways and genres, all four women rewrote the Revolution of 1848 and the republic in a manner to promote their ideas of a feminist republicanism and of republican women.

Sand survived the revolution committed to her ideals of social and gender equality, but firm in the belief that she, as a woman, could serve those ideals better through writing than through engaging in men's power struggles. Reflecting on the political scene she had just left in Paris days earlier, Sand wrote to the editor of a republican newspaper to which she had agreed to contribute that she would write about politics from an ideal perspective, in contrast to the passion of the male politicians she had observed on the ground floor, so to speak: "Women and children, always disinterested in political questions, are more in touch with the spirit that breathes from above on the agitations of this world."[63] In a letter of June 1848 to Hortense Allart, Sand renounced politics, writing: "I detest politics in the conventional sense; I find it to be a school of rigidity, ingratitude, suspicion, and falseness. . . . Let us leave politics and therefore men to deal with one another as best they can."[64] For Sand as an individual and as a woman, writing fiction was a better way of promoting her ideals than was engaging in politics: "Novels speak to the heart and to the imagination, and when one lives in an era of egotism and callousness, one can, in this way, strike hard to awaken consciences and hearts."[65]

Literary scholars cite Sand's novel *La Petite Fadette*, written in 1848, as an example of her putting this idea into practice. *La Petite Fadette* is the apparently simple story of an outcast girl's integration into respectable society through her relationship with an honorable young man, but it also reveals complex personal changes in both male and female characters and the positive implications of feminine power. On one level Naomi Schor sees *Fadette* as reflecting the mark of the Revolution of 1848 on Sand in its portrayal of an ideal, rather than a real, world, and in conveying a moral lesson of tolerance and the transforming power of heterosexual love based on respect rather than domination.[66] Margaret Cohen offers a more literal interpretation of the historical setting of the novel—the French Revolution and the Napoleonic Wars—to argue that *La Petite Fadette* was Sand's answer to feminists' demand for female suffrage in 1848. In the novel, according to Cohen, Sand presents the theory that women's most effective means of social change is their domestic functions, rather than political activity in the manner of men.[67] Indeed, Fadette effects a revolution in the family that she joins through marriage. The patriarch, father Barbeau, who had firmly opposed any connection between his son and Fadette, comes to appreciate Fadette's intelligence, even more than her wealth: "That girl has a great mind, and I think it would bring happiness to have it in a family." Astonishingly, after Fadette and Landry Barbeau are married, Fadette effectively replaces the patriarch as the head of the family, though rather as the fount of wisdom than as a domineering authority: "They were forced to consult with Fanchon [Fadette's adult name] who was the cleverest and wisest in the family" [*qui était la meilleure tête et le meilleur conseil de la famille*].[68]

Sand wrote another novel about a woman in the French Revolution, this one much later, in 1871, following the establishment of the Third Republic and Paris Commune. *Nanon* traces the history of the French Revolution through the eyes of a peasant girl who is a true revolutionary and republican hero. Nanon is the embodiment of republican ideals; she is intelligent, virtuous, loving, courageous, hard-working, egalitarian, principled—and she abhors violence. As a child she learns to read from an aristocratic youth, Emilien, who is in training at the local monastery, and her diligence and curiosity lead him to abandon his careless and lazy habits. Both welcome the revolution that liberates the peasants, allows them to purchase and work their own land, and establishes civil equality. During the Terror, Emilien is arrested and imprisoned under suspicion of trying to emigrate with his royalist family. Nanon, dressed as a boy, delivers him from the guillotine and hides him until the danger has passed, and he volunteers for the republican army. He returns from the wars, minus one arm, and marries Nanon, who has become a landowner with money inherited from a former monk whom she had rescued and cared for.

Nanon is the feminine, pacifist conscience of the republic. When a local, bourgeois Jacobin official, Monsieur Costejoux, defends the Terror as the only means of saving the republic, Nanon accuses him and other leaders of betraying the people and the republican cause. The Jacobins erred, Nanon maintains, in resorting to violence. To Costejoux she says, "You gave inordinate power to monsters" who aroused the hatred of the common people by abusing that power. The Jacobins could have saved the republic if they had not alienated the popular classes: "You could have made it last if you had not permitted the persecutions and everything else that troubled the consciences of simple folk." According to Nanon, Costejoux and the Jacobins, all educated and intelligent men, were taken in by a minority of self-serving vengeance-seekers, and they failed to account for the vast majority of simple, peaceable people who wanted only to enjoy their new freedoms and earn an honest living. Later, when Costejoux despairs that the republic is foundering, Nanon explains that political men need to keep faith with their ideals, even if they must wait for their full implementation: "A man of action and immediate response, he did not know how to preserve his ideal from the moment when its application was not immediate and irrevocable. It was up to me, a poor ignorant girl, to show him that all the great efforts of his party were not in vain." After all, Nanon herself was a major beneficiary of the revolution and of republican ideals; she was a rich landowner, she was married to a former aristocrat, and she taught other peasants how to read and understand so that they, too, could benefit from equality and freedom. Nanon represents the republic as Sand would want it, and as she hopes it can still become. And although Nanon often protests her feminine ignorance and subordination, even as she verbally demolishes her male, educated, and powerful interlocutors, and she iterates the belief that a wife should obey her husband and think as he does, Emilien makes clear that their republican union will be one of equals, or if anything, the wife will be superior: "It is often the husband who obeys the wife. When the wife has the better understanding . . . that is a good thing, and I think that he who marries her will be wise to consult with her on all things."[69]

In her personal relations, as with her fictional characters, Sand practiced toleration and love as alternatives to men's political factionalism. Writing to Hortense Allart in June 1848, Sand acknowledges the political differences between the two women: "Thus my dear Hortense, you fear the republic such as I would like it, and I resign myself sadly to the republic such as you wish it." But Sand will not let such differences interfere with their friendship. "I do not see and do not think as you do on anything that happens. But I know you are good, brave, honest, and disinterested. That is why I love you in spite of everything."[70] In both theory and practice Sand adhered to a politics of public service, toleration, and persuasion, in the cause of her ideal of egalitarian republicanism; the events of 1848 taught her that male politics was nothing more than power-seeking. She wrote the republic through ideal, republican women.

Similarly, d'Agoult imposed upon herself the task of writing the history of the Revolution of 1848 as a means of promoting social reform, indicating that she is particularly well-equipped for this endeavor precisely because she is a woman. In the preface to the second edition of the *Histoire de la Révolution de 1848*, d'Agoult asserts that objectivity regarding—or at least limited involvement in—the daily events of the revolution was forced upon her by her class background and her sex. "Under all regimes my sex prohibited me from harboring political ambitions; nor was feminine covetousness for power for my friends permitted to me; for if I was outside of the party that the Revolution wanted to overthrow, neither did I belong to that whose triumph it prepared."[71] This later declaration of forced objectivity is somewhat disingenuous, for d'Agoult showed a marked interest in seeing her friends—notably Lamartine—in power, and her other texts suggest approval for a political role for women, though not for their exercise of voting rights or holding office. Still, being female certainly inclined d'Agoult toward writing the revolution rather than leading it.[72]

In the *Histoire* men are the chief actors in the revolution and especially in the governments that follow, but the most vivid images of the February Days are female figures that symbolize d'Agoult's understanding of different phases of the revolution. In d'Agoult's rendition of the Revolution of 1848 the bankrupt July Monarchy was symbolized not by a king on his way into exile but by his young, intelligent daughter-in-law—the duchesse d'Orleans, mother of the presumptive heir to the Orleans throne. According to d'Agoult the duchesse d'Orleans showed courage in facing her possible death at the hands of revolutionaries while still hoping that her son would inherit the throne and that she would serve as regent with a new government. Despite rumors in royal circles that the duchesse had long aspired to that position, d'Agoult asserts that she was not an ambitious woman but a concerned mother. "The inner flame that makes a Maria-Theresa or a Catherine did not blaze from her forehead. . . . She was a noble princess, neither a heroine nor a woman of genius. She would have had to have been one or the other to stop the torrent carried by revolutions at this supreme moment."[73] D'Agoult attributed to the duchesse d'Orleans characteristics typical of the July Monarchy itself—adequate in normal times but incapable of rising to exceptional occasions. Implicit also in d'Agoult's portrayal was a criticism of the bourgeois ideal of domestic womanhood, for d'Agoult suggests that being a concerned mother is good enough ordinarily, but other models of womanhood are equally if not more important in particular historical moments.

One such moment, of course, was the revolution, and d'Agoult evokes another image—that of a prostitute—when she describes the triumphant people invading the royal residences. In the midst of a carnivalesque scene in which children and women of the popular classes dressed themselves in royal finery and made up their faces with royal makeup belonging to the recently ousted Orleans family, one figure stands out for d'Agoult:

One of the women, a pike in her hand, a red cap on her head, stood immobile in the great hallway for several hours, lips shut, eyes straight, in the pose of a statue of liberty; she is a prostitute. People pass in front of her with all signs of deep respect. Sad image of the capricious justice of fate; the prostitute is the living symbol of the degradation of the poor and of the corruption of the rich. Insulted by the rich in so-called normal times, she has the right to her moment of triumph in all our revolutionary saturnalias.[74]

D'Agoult shows much sympathy for the prostitute, whose very existence was linked with the abuse and corruption of bourgeois and aristocratic male leadership. D'Agoult sees some justice in the temporary reign of the prostitute in the middle of revolutionary change. But the prostitute hardly symbolizes the ideal republic, which was stillborn; she is certainly not the noble Eve personifying "the emancipation of human genius." Rather, the ideal image for a republican woman is herself—Marie d'Agoult.

Although the *Histoire de la Révolution de 1848* contains many acute and generous word portraits of male politicians involved in the revolution and the new republic, in the privacy of a letter to Hortense Allart, d'Agoult suggests that her own political contribution—the writing of the history of the revolution—was on par with, if not superior to, the efforts of the men of 1848 to achieve liberty, justice, and democracy. Regarding the publication of the *Histoire*, d'Agoult writes: "I will confess to you, then, but only to you, proud Amazon, that I feel some joy in showing that a woman can, on occasion, equal and even surpass men a little in battle. And this battle is great and beautiful because it no longer concerns merely such and such a form of government; it concerns freedom of conscience and the dignity of the human spirit."[75] Thus, d'Agoult exemplified the revolutionary Eve in assuming a leading role in the struggle against tyranny and for the progress of human freedom.

Three years after the disheartening Revolution of 1848, Girardin completed a play, a comedy, that is a metaphor for the revolution that she would have preferred. The play is entitled *C'est la Faute du mari*, and the plot is very straightforward. The husband of the title, comte Edgar d'Hauterive, is jealous; he suspects his wife, Laurence, of being in love with the comte's young protégé, Fernand. The climax of the play occurs when Fernand tells the comte that he is wrong about his wife, and in the end Hauterive and Laurence are reconciled. But the dialogue explaining Hauterive's mistakes contains language very similar to Girardin's account of the republicans' failure in 1848.

Fernand represents a wise youth, necessarily precocious because he lives in troubled times, and therefore capable of discerning that Hauterive, the older man, has become set in a conservative, unproductive, untenable position regarding his marriage. With Fernand's prodding the comte admits that he views his position as husband as similar to the position of a king:

> But to govern well, to govern as a master,
> One must be severe, or at least appear to be so.

Fernand indicates the problem with this analogy of marriage and government:

> You wish to govern? Then you must show your love openly
> Love is the secret of a good government.
> But, for you husbands, love terrifies you;
> For you the ideal wife is a servant![76]

Fernand goes on to say that a truly good wife, one such as Laurence, wants love, and can provide her husband with a relationship much richer than that of a housekeeper to a master, if only the husband will cease to tyrannize her. Gradually, Hauterive comes to realize that he treated his wife like a schoolgirl because he was afraid that her intelligence and beauty would seduce him and undermine his authority. Significantly, Girardin used similar language regarding political and gender relations during 1848: then, she called the political leaders "tyrants jealous of their wives, whom they appear to love."[77] However, unlike the situation in 1848, when men were incapable of generosity, the revolution in the marriage of Hauterive and Laurence is accomplished painlessly when the comte admits his mistakes and resolves to change his ways:

> Sometimes, I believe, I was only falsely strong;
> I made myself a tyrant in order to avoid being a slave;
> I will change the system.[78]

And the wife happily proclaims that she and Edgar have assumed their truly proper roles, she as a "sensible wife" and he as a "young husband." The play shows how an ideal revolution is effected and the happy results. Men must stop being jealous of their power and generously allow freedom and responsibility to others. The reward is a republican family based on equality.

Girardin presents another republican family in her last play, performed after her death, *Une Femme qui déteste son mari*. The play is set in 1794, and it is about Julie, who proves her loyalty to the Terror by publicly disavowing her husband and family as moderate republicans. Her servant describes her with approval as "a pureblooded female republican, who broke with her moderate husband, his moderate family, and their moderate children." When challenged by one of Julie's children that her mother's repudiation of them is unnatural, the servant explains, in a perversion of Rousseauean republicanism, that loyalty to the state takes precedence over everything, including nature: "One sacrifices everything to the homeland, even nature, always out of civic-mindedness." In fact, Julie's public pretense of fanatical republicanism is a cover, because she is hiding her moderate husband, de Langeais, and she profoundly misses and loves her children and her husband's family. A Jacobin official, Rosette, pressures Julie to divorce her husband so that she can marry him, and Julie is in desperate straits to maintain her cover and to prevent her husband from being discovered. But de Langeais, tired of hiding, wants to kiss his wife, and Julie chides him that he is distracting her from her purpose: "It's when I need all of my reason that you make me lose it with your absurd teasing." Just when Rosette discovers de Langeais, and he and Julie give themselves up to the scaffold, Robespierre falls from power, and the family is reunited.[79]

Like Sand's novel *Nanon*, this play condemns the Terror and makes a female character the hero, the savior of her loved ones. Women may be excluded from politics, but this very marginality allows them to see politics more clearly, to hold more firmly to ideals and purpose than men, who easily lose sight of them in the midst of action. Unlike *Nanon*, Girardin's play does not offer an alternative to the Terror, feminine advice to men on how better to save the republic, such as Nanon offered to Costejoux. Nor is *Une Femme qui déteste son mari* as explicit as *C'est la Faute du mari* in representing a revolution in gender relations as a starting point or analogy for political change. Nonetheless these texts all rewrite the Revolution of 1848, or the French Revolution, to include women in prominent roles. Allart, too, wrote the Revolution of 1848 in the final section of her *Essai sur l'histoire politique*, and her *Histoire de la République d'Athènes* even more constructs models of republican womanhood.

In the preface to the *Essai sur l'histoire politique* Allart indicates that she had finished writing the book in 1847; "however, we wanted to wait for the half-century mark to publish it and take there our own country [*et mener jusque-là notre pays*] . . . and then the events of February arrived! What a change before the end of the half-century!" So the last part of the book includes Allart's analysis of 1848 juxtaposed with the French Revolution, but that is followed by a final section entitled "Political Women." Was this inspired by the events of 1848? Possibly so, since Allart opens the chapter with these words: "Popular reformers demanded more freedom and a better condition for women. In this they will have all our gratitude." Allart then asserts that French women in particular have good reason to concern themselves with politics, because "they perished en masse on the scaffold; and on this subject, let us remember the excellent phrase of the woman, who, when Emperor Napoleon told her that he did not like women to engage in politics, replied *that in a country where they cut off their heads, it was natural enough that they should ask why.*"[80] Allart goes no further with this discussion of women's political rights in France. Instead, she devotes most of her analysis to the historical, and mythical, subjects of amazons and queens, from which she concludes that the accomplishments of exceptional women prove that women can be successful political actors.

Allart regards the story of the amazons as being above politics, a poetic, prelapsarian paradise where women lived without men and in a state of nature. Although the amazons governed their own kingdoms and lost them in battle, Allart does not draw political lessons for the present from their glorious exploits. But she does hammer home her long-standing belief in the capability, even superiority, of women leaders from her consideration of Queen Elizabeth I: "Among the sovereigns we have studied, one of the greatest, the most prudent, the most truly wise, Elizabeth, was a woman." Allart then invokes historical and scientific experts to buttress her argument: "If woman has been oppressed in private life, it is through politics that she has been raised up and has been able to show her talents." She refers to the naturalist Buffon, who observed that among birds of prey the females are bigger and more powerful than the males, so that males are called tercels [*tiercelets*] because they are only one-third the size of females; Romans called female eagles *aquilae*, to indicate that they were "female kings of the skies." Allart triumphantly concludes with an analogy of this gender condition among birds of prey and among humans: "Well then! the fact presented by Buffon, and that *always* holds true for birds of prey, presents itself *sometimes* in the human species. In the human species, in politics, we have seen some *aquilae* and a great number of *tiercelets*. We understand better now how Elizabeth was *l'aquila fulva*, and the Stuarts were *tiercelets*." And with that Allart concludes the entire study by stating that although equality is progressing there will always be a gap between the masses and the talented elites.[81] Her historical studies and contemporary observations lead her to believe in gender equality within a hierarchy of intelligence and political capability.

Allart also rewrote the Revolution of 1848, or rather the Second Republic, in the *Histoire de la République d'Athènes*, published in 1866. In this book Allart presents much more social history than in her previous works, and there is more history of women and daily life. She interprets the history of ancient Greece as a lesson in the flaws of democracy. She maintains, for example, that the monarchy of Sparta guaranteed freedom to its people better than did the republic of Athens, and that it encouraged more equitable distribution of property and more collective, community activities. She suggests that the Athenian republic in general and the ideas of Demosthenes in particular should be viewed as a warning to revolutionary France: "We must pay close attention to Demosthenes, because in modern times France since 89 has tried to speak like him and to uphold . . . the most dangerous cause of democracy."[82]

According to Allart, however, yet another major failing of Athenian republicanism was its mistreatment of women, and she addresses this in the context of the history of Aspasia, the mistress and later wife of Pericles, and of her analysis of Plato's *Republic*. Aspasia was a woman of great beauty and intelligence, and she had "an eloquence that enraptured Pericles and Socrates. Even though her house was full of courtesans, husbands brought their wives to listen and to learn from her beautiful conversation. (This seems to us very strange)." Allart further claimed as evidence of Aspasia's political acumen: "They say, and I believe, that Pericles studied politics and government with her, and Plato reports that she trained several orators." Pericles adored Aspasia, and separated from his wife in order to be with her and eventually to marry her. But publicly Aspasia was accused of various forms of debauchery and impiety, and Allart castigates a popular prudery that she considers harmful to freedom. Sarcastically she writes: "Let us then admire these democratic governments more intolerant even than Louis XIV! How the people enjoyed making these denunciations." Much as Allart admires Aspasia, she is troubled that Aspasia encouraged Pericles in the waging of devastating wars, and, when Elpinice, alone, takes Pericles to task for causing so many deaths in the war against Samos, Allart asks, "Why didn't the beautiful Aspasia have the lofty ideas of Elpinice?"[83]

Allart builds a strong case against Athenian democracy, based on its laws that discriminated against women, its ceaseless wars, and a crude populism that pandered to the worst emotions of the crowd. But she also invokes other authorities to buttress her case, including Aristophanes, whose plays satirized democracy, and Hobbes and Bayle, who also discerned flaws in Athenian republicanism. Just when it seems that

Allart finds no redeeming qualities in democracy or even republicanism, she turns to Plato, of whom she writes: "Plato nonetheless accepted democracy for lack of anything better." Allart greatly admired
Plato, though he, too, comes in for criticism, for she thinks that in his
Republic laws restrict human freedom excessively, and his plans for arranged marriages are "impossible." However, Plato admits women
into his leadership hierarchy on an equal basis with men, and Allart
applauds that. In the *Republic*, "women, at least, are treated with justice.
They are permitted the same occupations as men." Women, like men,
can practice medicine, play music, do gymnastics and military exercises, and be philosophers. Allart presents Plato's plan for educating
men to become philosopher kings, and appears to quote from the dialogue in the *Republic*.

"Here are stupendous political men that you have constructed like a skill-
ful sculptor."
"Say also political women, my dear Glaucon, for do not think that I was
speaking of men rather than women, every time women are gifted with appropriate abilities."[84]

Allart interprets Plato's *Republic* as presenting an ideal state very similar to her own, in which democracy will be tempered by leaders consisting of the ablest women and men.

Conclusion

For Sand, d'Agoult, Allart, and Girardin, a major lesson of 1848 was
that when men—even liberal, idealistic, well-intentioned, republican
men who were their friends—achieved power, they behaved no differently than did politicians under monarchy. Although these writers accepted a degree of gender differentiation in political practice—that is,
voting rights and eligibility for elective office for men only—they criticized and contested the masculinization of politics that linked the July
Monarchy and the Second Republic, despite the promised changes of
the Revolution of 1848. Implicit or explicit in this criticism was the fact
that republican politicians ignored women and did not practice politics
as Sand, d'Agoult, Girardin, and Allart recommended.

The accounts of 1848 by the four authors indicate that part of their
disappointment in the Second Republic was the lack of improvement in
gender relations and the status of women under the new regime. None
of the women expected that these changes would be the republic's first

priority, but they were convinced that only a new government committed to much broader social transformation could eventually address
these issues. When they realized that the Second Republic was failing in
social reform, it then became clear that gender relations and the status
of women were not going to change either. These feminist issues were
obviously important to the women personally, but the four women
writers believed that education and civil rights for women were essential to equality and prosperity for all social classes. For them, the Revolution of 1848 should have been a feminist revolution as much as a social and democratic revolution, although not in the same terms as envisioned by socialist feminists.

Sand, d'Agoult, Allart, and Girardin thus returned to writing, confirmed in their belief that it represented a better means of promoting
equality and freedom than either male republican politics or socialist
feminism. In the literary world they were recognized as women and as
writers, whereas the political realm did not as yet offer them the respect
and efficacy that writing did. It is possible that the spectacle of power
corrupting their male friends caused these women to eschew political
authority and instead to exercise influence. Certainly it warned them
that the politics of even liberal men were not in the interest of society,
much less in the interest of women and families. The failure of 1848
suggested that neither men nor women were ready for social democracy, and in pursuit of that propitious moment, Sand, d'Agoult, Girardin, and Allart continued to do what they did best, write as republican women, and in behalf of an ideal of republican womanhood.

8 ⌒ Conclusion

Sand, d'Agoult, Allart, and Girardin accepted the coup d'état of 1851 and the establishment of an authoritarian empire in 1852 with a mixture of disgust and resignation. They never lost their faith in the ideal of a republic, although the experiences of 1848 brought home to them the practical difficulties of creating and maintaining a republican government in France. Factionalism and extremism among republican leaders, the division between city and province, a general penchant for violence, and inexperience and ignorance among the electorate were among the causes that the four women writers blamed for the republic's demise. In their view, improvements in social conditions and in the status of women would have to wait until these other problems were addressed and a stable republic put in place by peaceful means. In the meantime the four authors pondered republicanism in light of the lessons of 1848 and continued their work as writers and republican women, disseminating these ideas through a variety of literary productions.

Following 1848 the Girardins would never know quite the same social, literary, and political ascendancy they had enjoyed during the July Monarchy. To be sure Emile continued to publish his newspaper (he eventually sold *La Presse* in 1856); both Emile and Delphine socialized with literary and artistic elites, and their political hopes (and Emile's aspirations to political office) did not wane. But Delphine de Girardin's socializing was more restrained and exclusive than before. Although the Girardins, and especially Delphine, supported the republic, they were distanced, if not alienated, from some of its leading figures. All of Delphine de Girardin's literary energy focused on the theater, and she brought out her comedy, *C'est la Faute du mari*, in 1851 to a positive reception. Girardin wrote four additional plays, three of which were performed before her death and enjoyed moderate to considerable success.

She did not attempt to write another tragedy, perhaps because she sensed a tragic element in everyday existence under dictatorship. Count Alton-Shée quoted her with approval on this matter: "Madame de Girardin is indeed correct to say that in continuing to live bowed under such a yoke, each of us, even the most honest, little by little takes part in the infamy." She died in Paris of stomach cancer on 29 June 1855, much mourned by literary friends and acquaintances. She was fifty-one years old.[1]

Sand completed the writing of her autobiography in 1854; while she was doing so, she also wrote *La Petite Fadette* and *Les Maîtres sonneurs*, and she took a lover, Alexandre Manceau, who remained her companion until his death in 1865. She wrote several other novels and plays, and much of the time she spent in Paris was devoted to the theater, as well as to meeting with literary friends, notably Gustave Flaubert. In 1867 Sand resettled permanently at Nohant to live with her son, Maurice; his wife, Lina; and their two children, Aurore and Gabrielle. Sand was profoundly satisfied in her family life, but she never lost her enthusiasm for literature and her interest in politics. The war with Prussia of 1870 devastated her, but she was pleased with the establishment of the Third Republic following Napoleon III's capture, and she advocated a moderate leadership and policies as the best means of stabilizing the republic and winning over to it the majority of the French people. To her communard friend Edmond Plauchut, she wrote: "You should know, you [radicals], that advanced republicans constitute a proportion of one percent on the entire surface of the country, and that you will only save the republic in showing a great deal of patience and in trying to rein in the extremists." Thus she deplored the Paris Commune of 1871 for its violent radicalism, which threatened to topple the fragile republic through civil war and by inciting a reactionary backlash. As in 1848, Sand turned to writing as a means of assuaging the pain she felt over the failures of republicanism, and to present an alternative vision of a peaceful, persuasive, principled republicanism in the form of a female character. Sand was hard at work on *Nanon* by September 1871. On 8 June 1876 Sand died and was buried at her home in Nohant.[2]

With the publication of the *Histoire de la Révolution de 1848* (1850–53), Marie d'Agoult came into her own as a serious writer. She followed this with a historical study of the seventeenth-century Dutch republic, a series of historical plays, her memoirs, an analysis of contemporary Italy, and a work of literary criticism. D'Agoult traveled a great deal in the 1850s and 1860s, both for research purposes and to visit her children. Moreover, she never reestablished a permanent home for herself in Paris following the demolition of the Maison Rose as part of Baron Haussmann's rebuilding project. D'Agoult was initially satisfied that her daughters had married well, but two of those unions were dissolved, and one ended with the death of Blandine in childbirth. The author suffered a nervous breakdown in 1868–69, from which she recovered just in time to witness the Franco-Prussian War. The war pained her deeply, especially given her French-German heritage; however, she supported the French side. D'Agoult considered Thiers's leadership the most promising for maintaining the Third Republic, and she left Paris during the Commune to visit Cosima and her family in Germany. D'Agoult took pleasure in her work and the acknowledgment of its value by reviewers, friends, and experts. Additionally, she prided herself on her unflagging support for republicanism as a *salonnière* and an author. D'Agoult wrote to Allart in 1854, after she had finished her history of 1848 and started the history of the Dutch Republic: "This history of Holland will later show my friends that I never ceased for one day to love liberty and to serve obscurely but with constancy the just cause. The republic is still in my eyes the most beautiful form of government." She died in Paris on 6 March 1876.[3]

Hortense Allart devoted the remainder of her life to scholarship and reflection, and to the welfare of her sons, especially seeking a suitable climate for the delicate Henri and a good position for Marcus. Among the many works she published following the Revolution of 1848 were *Essai sur l'histoire politique depuis les invasions barbares jusqu'en 1848* (1857), *Novum Organum, ou sainteté philosophique* (1857), and *Histoire de la République d'Athènes* (1866). Additionally, Allart served as something of a consultant to Sainte-Beuve, and though he published many of her insights, memories, and letters written to her by others that she loaned him, he never acknowledged her contributions by name. Allart condemned the Franco-Prussian War of 1870 as an imperialist conflict, and the popular insurrection in 1871 as mob violence. Her autobiography, or "fragments of memoirs" as she preferred to call it, entitled *Les Enchantements de Prudence*, caused a considerable stir following its publication in 1872 and reissue in 1873, with prominent critics excoriating Allart for revealing Chateaubriand as a lovesick fool in his later years. Nonetheless, the scandal surrounding the memoirs led them to be reprinted three times, and Allart was able to republish many of her earlier works under the guise of sequels—*Nouveaux Enchantements* (1873) and *Derniers Enchantements* (1874). In a eulogy composed for and to d'Agoult, Allart ended with an acknowledgment of their shared belief in republicanism and the liberation of (superior) women: "Democracy? All right, I accept it if you concede to me a restricted suffrage that will consist of similar characters; that of Sparta. These are terms on which we can agree, and then, heroic women will obtain the honors due to elite natures." She died at her country home in Montlhery of a ruptured aneurysm on 28 February 1879.[4]

As these summaries suggest, the four authors hardly ceased their literary, social, familial, and political activity following 1848. However, this study has centered upon their self-creations as writers and as republicans, which were accomplished by mid-century, if not completed. I have analyzed how Sand, d'Agoult, Allart, and Girardin embarked on literary careers in defiance of social, cultural, and material obstacles to writing by women. Additionally, I have demonstrated how they wrote themselves into republicanism and rewrote republicanism to encompass egalitarian gender and family relations. They represented their own childhood families as embodying republican values and principles, with the significant exception of the patriarchal family. In their varied self-narratives these women writers created fathers or female authority figures who approved of their decisions to become authors and so legitimated a host of life choices they made that were contrary to the tenets of republican motherhood. As adults the four authors confronted the challenge of articulating female sexual desire and love in terms that were more or less acceptable to a reading public more used to male than female romantic fantasies, and that at the same time justified their own, often transgressive, experiences. On a broader scale they redefined feminine identity more generally when they engaged with the stereotype of the unfeminine, unnatural bluestocking to assert a more appealing image of the woman who combined "feminine" characteristics of maternity, elegance, beauty, and sensitivity with "masculine" attributes of intelligence, independence, application, and authority. Writing was the primary, but by no means the sole, mode for Sand, d'Agoult, Allart, and Girardin to engage in politics. Each developed her own, distinctive version of republicanism within an already diverse spectrum, and each devised different methods and personae of political expression. Uniting the four, however, was a conviction that republicanism would effect the civil equality of women and men through changes in marriage and family law, and female education. The implication of this position was the transformation of the ideal for female citizenship, in the guise of republican motherhood, to a new ideal of republican womanhood. As republicans the four women writers welcomed the Revolution of 1848 and the Second Republic, but their hopes turned to disappointment. Their writings from this period and its aftermath were, in a sense, rewritings of 1848 in which female figures successfully promoted gender, social, and political reform by peaceful means.

The self-narratives and literary productions of Sand, d'Agoult, Allart, and Girardin manifest and connect a wide range of phenomena characteristic of postrevolutionary France, and especially of the July Monarchy. Romanticism, socialism, feminism, liberalism, and republicanism all influenced the thought and behavior of the four female authors, and they, in turn, helped shape or recast these discourses. Additionally, they marked significant transitions in constructions of femininity—the *salonnière* in an era of increasing democracy and bourgeois ascendancy; the female genius versus the bluestocking during a booming but intensely competitive period in the publishing industry. Underlying the women writers' different performances of femininity was the domestic ideal that they rejected and aspired to reform—the dependent, subordinate wife and mother removed from public affairs. Their innovation was to unite different threads of influential social, cultural, and political developments into the idea of republican womanhood, a construct that they performed in their own lives and that they held up as a model to other women. For Sand, d'Agoult, Allart, and Girardin, a republican woman combined motherhood and intellectual pursuits, love and sociability, household management and political engagement. A republican woman was a reformer who sought improvements in women's condition, family relations, the social distribution of wealth, and government structure and accountability.

Were Sand, d'Agoult, Allart, and Girardin feminists? In my opinion, yes. They sought to open possibilities for female endeavor, not just for themselves but for all women through changes in the law, social practice, and cultural assumptions. They "feminized" republicanism by offering alternative family romances to the patriarchal fraternity of most republican men. In their texts, republican marriages and families were egalitarian, with women and men sharing responsibilities like child-rearing and the drawing up of political programs. There were no separate spheres in the authors' literary and self-representations, no boundary between private and public, and little distinction between feminine and masculine abilities. Provisionally, they accepted certain parameters of sexual difference that underlay republican notions of male and female citizenship—namely, that women, because of their debased condition, were not yet ready to assume full political equality with men, and that men should represent women politically while simultaneously changing the laws and the state policies to equalize opportunities. But they lived as republican women to prove that a future of gender equality under republicanism was possible.

In categorizing Sand, d'Agoult, Allart, and Girardin as feminists I am positing a definition of the term that is broader than that of scholars who emphasize the claim for political equality and organizational solidarity among women as key, even the sole, components of feminism.[5] By contrast, my work with the four women writers leads me to include as part of feminism the undermining of restrictions on feminine identities, and the positive legitimation of a wide range of activities for women as human beings. Sand, d'Agoult, Allart, and Girardin were remarkable individuals who defied convention and led lives that fascinate us in their transgressiveness, originality, and accessibility through the authors' written and published texts, and, notably in the case of Sand, through the public myths that surrounded them. But this exceptional quality does not separate them from the historical conditions they shared with other women of their time and engaged with in different ways to create new possibilities for feminine identity and behavior. These historical figures appeal to us not only because they are exceptional, but even more so because they worked *with* as well as *against* the language, ideas, and practices that might have limited them on the basis of their sex. They appropriated a political idea—republicanism— and transformed it into a feminist politics through the configurations of their own lives.

REFERENCE MATTER

☞ Notes

Chapter 1: Introduction

1. Marie d'Agoult, *Esquisses morales: Pensées, réflexions et maximes*, 3d ed. (Paris: J. Techener, 1859), 308.

2. Kathleen Canning, "Feminist History after the Linguistic Turn: Historicizing Discourse and Experience," *Signs* 19 (winter 1994): 368–404; Lloyd Kramer, *Lafayette in Two Worlds: Public Cultures and Personal Identities in an Age of Revolutions* (Chapel Hill and London: University of North Carolina Press, 1996); Jo Burr Margadant, "Introduction: Constructing Selves in Historical Perspective," in *The New Biography: Performing Femininity in Nineteenth-Century France* (forthcoming); Carolyn Steedman, *Childhood, Culture and Class in Britain: Margaret McMillan, 1860–1931* (London and New Brunswick, NJ: Rutgers University Press, 1990); Kali A. K. Israel, "Writing inside the Kaleidoscope: Re-Representing Victorian Women Public Figures," *Gender & History* 2 (spring 1990): 40–48; Janis Bergman-Carton, *The Woman of Ideas in French Art, 1830–1848* (New Haven and London: Yale University Press, 1993); William M. Reddy, *The Invisible Code: Honor and Sentiment in Postrevolutionary France, 1814–1848* (Berkeley: University of California Press, 1997).

3. Christine Planté, *La Petite Soeur de Balzac* (Paris: Seuil, 1989); Roger Bellet, ed., *Femmes de lettres au XIXe siècle: Autour de Louise Colet* (Lyon: Presses universitaires de Lyon, 1982); Maïté Albistur and Daniel Armogathe, *Histoire du féminisme français du moyen âge à nos jours* (Paris: des femmes, 1977), 263–94; Laure Adler, *A l'Aube du féminisme: Les Premières journalistes (1830–1850)* (Paris: Payot, 1979); Béatrice Slama, "Femmes écrivains," in *Misérable et glorieuse: La Femme du XIXe siècle*, ed. Jean-Paul Aron (Bruxelles: Editions Complexe, 1984), 213–48; Léon Abensour, *Le Féminisme sous le règne de Louis-Philippe et en 1848*, 2d ed. (Paris: Plon, 1913), 167–81.

4. Claude Nicolet, *L'Idée républicaine en France (1789–1924): Essai d'histoire critique* (Paris: Gallimard, 1982), 133–37; Pamela M. Pilbeam, *Republicanism in Nineteenth-Century France, 1814–1871* (New York: St. Martin's Press, 1995), esp. chs. 5–7; Ronald Aminzade, *Ballots and Barricades: Class Formation and Republican Politics in France, 1830–1871* (Princeton, NJ: Princeton University Press, 1993), ch. 2; Gabriel Perreux, *Au Temps des sociétés secrètes: La Propagande républicaine au début de la Monarchie de Juillet (1830–1835)* (Paris: Rieder, 1931).

5. Claire Goldberg Moses, *French Feminism in the Nineteenth Century* (Alba-

ny: State University of New York Press, 1984); Abensour, *Le Féminisme sous le règne de Louis-Philippe*.

6. Cited in Léon Séché, *Hortense Allart de Méritens* (Paris: Société du Mercure de France, 1908), 135.

7. Marie d'Agoult, *Mémoires, souvenirs et journaux de la Comtesse d'Agoult*, ed. Charles F. Dupêchez (Paris: Mercure de France, 1990), 2:28. D'Agoult's words, written sometime in the late 1860s or early 1870s, reproduce part of a biographical sketch written by Jules Janin and published in 1835 and again in 1843. Janin opened his sketch of Sand with the questions, "Who is he, or who is she? Man or woman, angel or demon . . . ?" "Galerie contemporaine: George Sand," *La Mode* 24 (September 1835): 177; and Jules Janin, "Mme George Sand," in *Les Femmes célèbres contemporaines françaises* (Paris: Le Bailly, 1843), 439.

8. Bergman-Carton, *The Woman of Ideas in French Art*; Kirsten Powell and Elizabeth C. Childs, *Femmes d'esprit: Women in Daumier's Caricature* (Hanover: University Press of New England, 1990); Naomi Schor, *George Sand and Idealism* (New York: Columbia University Press, 1993); Planté, *La Petite Soeur de Balzac*.

9. Some examples of the literary, and the women-through-famous-men approaches are the following: Léon Séché, *Delphine Gay* (Paris: Mercure de France, 1910); Séché, *Hortense Allart de Méritens*; Henri Malo, *La Gloire du Vicomte de Launay: Delphine Gay de Girardin* (Paris: Emile-Paul frères, 1925); Henri Malo, *Une Muse et sa mère: Delphine Gay de Girardin* (Paris: Emile-Paul frères, 1924); Georges d'Heilly, *Madame E. de Girardin (Delphine Gay)* (Paris: Bachelin-Deflorenne, 1869); Wladimir Karénine, *George Sand: Sa Vie et ses oeuvres, 1804–1876*, 4 vols., 2d ed. (Paris: Plon, 1926); André Maurois, *Lélia: The Life of George Sand*, trans. Gerard Hopkins (New York: Harper & Row, 1953); Juliette Decreus, *Henry Bulwer-Lytton et Hortense Allart* (Paris: M. J. Minard, 1961); André Billy, *Hortense et ses amants* (Paris: Flammarion, 1961); Lorin A. Uffenbeck, *The Life and Writings of Hortense Allart (1801–1879)*, Ph.D. dissertation, University of Wisconsin-Madison, 1957. A spate of works appeared in the 1970s taking different positions on whether or not Sand was a feminist: Renée Winegarten, *The Double Life of George Sand: Woman and Writer. A Critical Biography* (New York: Basic Books, 1978); Ruth Jordan, *George Sand: A Biographical Portrait* (New York: Taplinger Publishing Company, 1976); Curtis Cate, *George Sand* (Boston: Houghton Mifflin, 1975); Joseph Barry, *Infamous Woman: The Life of George Sand* (Garden City, NY: Doubleday, 1977); Tamara Hovey, *A Mind of Her Own: A Life of the Writer George Sand* (New York: Harper & Row, 1977). A comprehensive biography of d'Agoult is Jacques Vier, *La Comtesse d'Agoult et son temps*, 6 vols. (Paris: Armand Colin, 1955–63). Works addressing d'Agoult as feminist and as mother, respectively, are: Dominique Desanti, *Daniel, ou le visage secret d'une comtesse romantique, Marie d'Agoult* (Paris: Stock, 1980); Charles Dupêchez, *Marie d'Agoult, 1805–1876* (Paris: Perrin, 1989). No recent biographies of Girardin and Allart exist, but works in progress by different scholars should soon rectify that situation.

10. Nancy K. Miller, *Subject to Change: Reading Feminist Writing* (New York: Columbia University Press, 1988); Personal Narratives Group, *Interpreting Women's Lives: Feminist Theory and Personal Narratives* (Bloomington: Indiana

University Press, 1989); Susan Stanford Friedman, "Women's Autobiographical Selves: Theory and Practice," in *The Private Self: Theory and Practice of Women's Autobiographical Writing*, ed. Shari Benstock (Chapel Hill: University of North Carolina Press, 1988), 34–62; Nancy K. Miller, "Writing Fictions: Women's Autobiography in France," in *Life/Lines: Theorizing Women's Autobiography*, ed. Bella Brodzki and Celeste Schenck (Ithaca: Cornell University Press, 1988), 45–61; Naomi Schor, "Reading Double: Sand's Difference," in *The Poetics of Gender*, ed. Nancy K. Miller (New York: Columbia University Press, 1986), 248–69; Leslie Rabine, "Feminist Writers in French Romanticism," *Studies in Romanticism* 16 (fall 1977): 491–507.

11. Moses, *French Feminism in the Nineteenth Century*; Michèle Riot-Sarcey, *La Démocratie à l'épreuve des femmes: Trois figures critiques du pouvoir, 1830–1848* (Paris: Albin Michel, 1994); Edith Thomas, *Les Femmes de 1848* (Paris: Presses universitaires de France, 1948). Several scholars are ambiguous about the feminism of women writers, namely: Albistur and Armogathe, *Histoire du féminisme français*; Abensour, *Le Féminisme sous le règne de Louis-Philippe*; Marguerite Thibert, *Le Féminisme dans le socialisme français de 1830 à 1850* (Paris: Marcel Giard, 1926).

12. Roger Magraw, *France 1814–1914: The Bourgeois Century* (New York and Oxford: Oxford University Press, 1986); Philippe Vigier, *La Monarchie de Juillet* (Paris: Presses universitaires de France, 1962); A. Jardin and A. J. Tudesq, *La France des Notables: L'Évolution générale, 1815–1848* (Paris: Seuil, 1973); Maurice Agulhon, *The Republican Experiment, 1848–1852*, trans. Janet Lloyd (Cambridge and Paris: Cambridge University Press, 1983); Roger Price, *The French Second Republic: A Social History* (Ithaca, NY: Cornell University Press, 1972). A notable exception is Anne Martin-Fugier, *La Vie élégante, ou la formation du Tout-Paris, 1815–1848* (Paris: Fayard, 1990). See also Reddy, *The Invisible Code*.

13. James Smith Allen, *Popular French Romanticism: Authors, Readers and Books in the Nineteenth Century* (Syracuse: Syracuse University Press, 1981); Martyn Lyons, *Le Triomph du livre: Une Histoire sociologique de la lecture dans la France du XIXe siècle* (Paris: Editions du Cercle de la Librairie, 1987); William M. Reddy, "Condottieri of the Pen: Journalists and the Public Sphere in Postrevolutionary France (1815–1850)," *American Historical Review* 99 (December 1994): 1546–70; Priscilla Parkhurst Clark, *Literary France: The Making of a Culture* (Berkeley: University of California Press, 1987); Bergman-Carton, *The Woman of Ideas in French Art*.

14. Pilbeam, *Republicanism in Nineteenth-Century France*; Nicolet, *L'Idée républicaine en France*; Aminzade, *Ballots and Barricades*; Philip Nord, "Republican Politics and the Bourgeois Interior in Mid-Nineteenth-Century France," in *Home and Its Dislocations in Nineteenth-Century France*, ed. Suzanne Nash (Albany: State University of New York Press, 1993), 193–214.

15. Lynn Hunt, *The Family Romance of the French Revolution* (Berkeley: University of California Press, 1992), 203; Lynn Hunt, "Reading the French Revolution: A Reply," *French Historical Studies* 19 (fall 1995): 289–98.

16. Carole Pateman, *The Sexual Contract* (Stanford, CA: Stanford University Press, 1988); Joan Wallach Scott, *Only Paradoxes to Offer: French Feminists and the*

Rights of Man (Cambridge, MA, and London: Harvard University Press, 1996). See also Joan B. Landes, *Women in the Public Sphere in the Age of the French Revolution* (Ithaca, NY, and London: Cornell University Press, 1988); and Siân Reynolds, "Marianne's Citizens? Women, the Republic and Universal Suffrage in France," in *Women, State and Revolution: Essays on Power and Gender in Europe since 1789*, ed. Siân Reynolds (Amherst: University of Massachusetts Press, 1987), 102–22.

17. Geneviève Fraisse, *Reason's Muse: Sexual Difference and the Birth of Democracy*, trans. Jane Marie Todd (Chicago and London: University of Chicago Press, 1994).

18. Moses, *French Feminism in the Nineteenth Century*; Claire Goldberg Moses and Leslie Wahl Rabine, *Feminism, Socialism and French Romanticism* (Bloomington and Indianapolis: Indiana University Press, 1993); Riot-Sarcey, *La Démocratie à l'épreuve des femmes*; Abensour, *Le Féminisme sous le règne de Louis-Philippe*; Thibert, *Le Féminisme dans le socialisme français*; Thomas, *Les Femmes de 1848*.

Chapter 2: Growing up Female in Postrevolutionary France

1. George Sand, *Story of My Life: The Autobiography of George Sand*, ed. Thelma Jurgrau (Albany: State University of New York Press, 1991), 557. This is an unabridged translation of George Sand, *Histoire de ma vie*, in *Oeuvres autobiographiques*, vol. 1 and part of vol. 2, ed. Georges Lubin (Paris: Gallimard, 1970–71 [orig. 1854–55]).

2. Mme P. de Saman [Hortense Allart], *Les Enchantements de Prudence*, 3d ed. (Paris: Michel Lévy frères, 1873), 4–5.

3. Ibid., 5.

4. Sand, *Story of My Life*, 587.

5. Ibid.

6. Alan B. Spitzer, *The French Generation of 1820* (Princeton, NJ: Princeton University Press, 1987). Even though Spitzer includes Allart and Girardin in his list of 183 members of the generation of 1820, he excludes women from his analysis because they were excluded from the schools, institutions, organizations, and editorial boards that helped unite men born between 1792 and 1803 into a recognizable group with shared experiences, ideologies, ideas, and social networks. A study of French autobiographies groups Sand with Alfred de Musset and Edgar Quinet as constituting a generation that the author calls "the founders," laying the foundation of a new sense of the self following the destruction of the Old Regime and the upheaval of the revolutionary era. Denis Bertholet, *Les Français par eux-mêmes, 1815–1885* (Paris: Olivier Orban, 1991), 113–22.

7. D'Agoult, *Mémoires, souvenirs et journaux*, 1:64.

8. Personal Narratives Group, *Interpreting Women's Lives*; Friedman, "Women's Autobiographical Selves"; Miller, "Writing Fictions"; Carolyn G. Heilbrun, *Writing a Woman's Life* (New York: Ballantine Books, 1988); Sidonie Smith, *A Po-*

etics of Women's Autobiography: Marginality and the Fictions of Self-Representation (Bloomington and Indianapolis: Indiana University Press, 1987).

9. Sand, *Story of My Life*. Biographies of Sand are numerous. Probably the most comprehensive is Karénine, *George Sand*, written with the intention of correcting errors and omissions in earlier biographies and representing Sand's life and works as informed by excesses of feeling that were both Sand's strength and weakness. Perhaps the most popular biography is Maurois, *Lélia*, which implies that Sand's fame rests solely on the famous men whom she attracted as lovers. A list of Sand biographies is included in a footnote to Chapter 1 and in the bibliography. Two works by literary scholars that offer a psychoanalytic interpretation of Sand's childhood, particularly her relationship with her father, are: Kathryn J. Crecelius, *Family Romances: George Sand's Early Novels* (Bloomington and Indianapolis: Indiana University Press, 1987), 5–9; Schor, *George Sand and Idealism*, ch. 5.

10. Marie d'Agoult, *Mes Souvenirs, 1806–1833* (Paris: Calmann Lévy, 1877). D'Agoult's autobiographical writings have recently been collected and edited by Charles F. Dupêchez as *Mémoires, souvenirs et journaux de la Comtesse d'Agoult (Daniel Stern)* (Paris: Mercure de France, 1990), 2 vols. A comprehensive biography of d'Agoult is Vier, *La Comtesse d'Agoult et son temps*. A feminist biography is Desanti, *Daniel, ou le visage secret d'une comtesse romantique*; and a recent biography that defends d'Agoult from the accusation that she was a bad mother is Dupêchez, *Marie d'Agoult*.

11. D'Heilly, *Madame E. de Girardin (Delphine Gay)*; Séché, *Delphine Gay*; Malo, *Une Muse et sa mère*; Alphonse de Lamartine, "Madame de Girardin," in *Portraits et salons romantiques* (Paris: Le Goupy, 1927), 153–87.

12. Saman, *Les Enchantements de Prudence*; Séché, *Hortense Allart de Méritens*; Uffenbeck, *The Life and Writings of Hortense Allart*. The only recent published biography of Allart is Billy, *Hortense et ses amants*, which, as the title suggests, presents her as an amiable floozy whose merit lies primarily in the love affairs she had with famous men.

13. Margaret H. Darrow, *Revolution in the House: Family, Class, and Inheritance in Southern France, 1775–1825* (Princeton: Princeton University Press, 1989); Lynn Hunt, "The Unstable Boundaries of the French Revolution," in *A History of Private Life*, ed. Philippe Ariès and Georges Duby, vol. 4, *From the Fires of the Revolution to the Great War*, ed. Michelle Perrot (Cambridge, MA, and London: Belknap Press of Harvard University Press, 1990), 29–36; Elisabeth G. Sledziewski, "The French Revolution as the Turning Point," in *A History of Women*, ed. Georges Duby and Michelle Perrot, vol. 4, *Emerging Feminism from Revolution to World War*, ed. Geneviève Fraisse and Michelle Perrot (Cambridge, MA, and London: Belknap Press of Harvard University Press, 1993), 36–38; Suzanne Desan, "Rewriting Family and Nation: Women's Political Pamphlets in the Early Revolution," paper presented at the 23d annual meeting of the Western Society for French History, Las Vegas, Nevada, 1995; Isabelle Bricard, *Saintes ou pouliches: L'Éducation des jeunes filles au XIXe siècle* (Paris: Albin Michel, 1985), 16–17.

14. Sand, *Story of My Life*, 294, 399.

15. D'Agoult, *Mémoires, souvenirs et journaux*, 1:45–46, 157.

16. Saman, *Les Enchantements de Prudence*, 6–8.

17. Malo, *Une Muse et sa mère*, 36–37.

18. Margaret H. Darrow, "French Noblewomen and the New Domesticity, 1750–1850," *Feminist Studies* 5 (spring 1979): 41–65; Roderick Phillips, *Family Breakdown in Late Eighteenth-Century France: Divorces in Rouen, 1792–1803* (Oxford: Clarendon Press, 1980); Hunt, "The Unstable Boundaries of the French Revolution"; Bricard, *Saintes ou pouliches*, 16–17.

19. Sand, *Story of My Life*, 484.

20. D'Agoult, *Mémoires, souvenirs et journaux*, 1:59.

21. Ibid., 35.

22. Ibid., 122, 123.

23. Sand, *Story of My Life*, 169.

24. Ibid., 468–69, 418.

25. D'Agoult, *Mémoires, souvenirs et journaux*, 1:165. Personally, I found Marie-Elisabeth far more intriguing than d'Agoult allows, and Alexandre far duller than d'Agoult's representation. For example, d'Agoult discusses religion in several different contexts, including indifference to it on the side of both her father and mother. Yet she also mentions in passing that Marie-Elisabeth converted to Catholicism sometime after d'Agoult was grown. Given that the old Mrs. Bethmann "hated Catholics," this conversion suggests that Marie-Elisabeth may have been less conformist and passive than d'Agoult insists. As for Alexandre, objectively he seems almost doltish in his knee-jerk ultraroyalism and passion for hunting; the enlightened rationalism, egalitarianism, and republicanism that d'Agoult attributes to him are extremely difficult to discern.

26. According to Leslie Rabine, women writers in the nineteenth century in England and France commonly ignored or denigrated mothers in their fiction. Rabine offers only one example of this from France—Sand's novel *Valentine*. D'Agoult in the autobiography appears to fit this generalization, though the case is difficult to sustain for the other three women writers and might require interrogation in terms of fictional versus autobiographical representations. Leslie Wahl Rabine, "Feminist Texts and Feminine Subjects," in *Feminism, Socialism, and French Romanticism*, ed. Moses and Rabine, 85, 125.

27. Saman, *Les Enchantements de Prudence*, 7–9.

28. Ibid., v, 8, 6, 8, 3.

29. Madame Emile de Girardin, "Préface" to *Contes d'une vieille fille à ses neveux*, in *Oeuvres complètes de Madame Emile de Girardin, née Delphine Gay* (Paris: Henri Plon, 1861), 2:267.

30. Séché quotes letters from Sophie Gay that suggest a female-dominated household. One letter in particular, inviting Madame Gay's friend Sophie Gail to visit the family, mentions Sigismond as obtaining good tea for the guest to drink, but the sense of the letter is that Gail will be surrounded by female companionship in the form of Sophie Gay's as yet unmarried daughters and Del-

phine's cousin Hortense Allart. "Isaure prepares for you some delicious coffee, Delphine wants to be your music copier, and Hortense your secretary." Séché, *Delphine Gay*, 14–29, 24–25.

31. Malo, *Une muse et sa mère*, 65–88; Lamartine, "Madame de Girardin," 162–64; Séché, *Delphine Gay*, 14–29.

32. Girardin, "A ma mère," in *Oeuvres complètes*, 1:n.p.

33. Sand, *Story of My Life*, 582, 467.

34. D'Agoult, *Mémoires, souvenirs et journaux*, 1:115–16.

35. Ibid., 157–59. Auguste Bussman Ehrmann committed suicide in 1832. D'Agoult notes in her autobiography that she is drawn to persons "whose lives or deaths were tragic," and she lists several family members and acquaintances who took their own lives. Ibid., 106, 159–60, 376 n. 4. D'Agoult herself suffered from depression and attempted to take her own life in 1832. Dupêchez, *Marie d'Agoult*, 53–54.

36. Saman, *Les Enchantements de Prudence*, 8; Uffenbeck, *The Life and Writings of Hortense Allart*, 11; Letter from Hortense Allart to Marie d'Agoult, 31 July 1839; letter from Hortense Allart to Marie d'Agoult, 10 August 1839. Bibliothèque Nationale, Manuscrits, Fonds Daniel Ollivier, N.A.F. 25185, 88, 90.

37. Séché, *Delphine Gay*, 14, 101–5; Malo, *La Gloire du Vicomte de Launay*, 120, 162; d'Heilly, *Madame E. de Girardin (Delphine Gay)*, 9.

38. Sand, *Story of My Life*, 581.

39. D'Agoult, *Mémoires, souvenirs et journaux*, 1:78.

40. Ibid., 113–15.

41. Sand does not discuss puberty or menstruation in her autobiography. However, in a letter from 1840 she mentions to a male friend who is also a doctor that her daughter Solange has started menstruating at the age of twelve, and Sand fears that this is too early and that Solange's growth will be stunted. Letter of Sand to Gustave Papet, 28 August 1840, in George Sand, *Correspondance*, ed. Georges Lubin (Paris: Garnier, 1969), 5:112. See also Marilyn Yalom, "Towards a History of Female Adolescence: The Contribution of George Sand," in *George Sand: Collected Essays*, ed. Janis Glasgow (Troy, NY: Whitston Publishing Company, 1985), 204–15.

42. D'Agoult, *Mémoires, souvenirs et journaux*, 1:112, 140–41.

43. Philippe Ariès, *Centuries of Childhood: A Social History of Family Life*, trans. Robert Baldick (New York: Vintage Books, 1962).

44. Maurice Crubellier, *L'Enfance et la jeunesse dans la société française, 1800–1950* (Paris: Armand Colin, 1979); Yvonne Knibiehler, Marcel Bernos, Elisabeth Ravoux-Rallo, and Eliane Richard, *De la Pucelle à la minette: Les Jeunes filles de l'âge classique à nos jours* (Paris: Temps actuels, 1983); Michelle Perrot, "Roles and Characters," in Perrot, *From the Fires of Revolution to the Great War*, 204–27; Bricard, *Saintes ou pouliches*; Bertholet, *Les Français par eux-mêmes*; Yalom, "Towards a History of Female Adolescence."

45. Françoise Mayeur, *L'Education des filles en France au XIXe siècle* (Paris: Hachette, 1979); Perrot, "Roles and Characters," 205–6, 216, 309; Bricard, *Saintes ou pouliches*. Excerpts on female education by vicomte de Bonald, Napoleon,

and Louis Aimé-Martin are in Susan Groag Bell and Karen M. Offen, eds., *Women, the Family, and Freedom: The Debate in Documents* (Stanford, CA: Stanford University Press, 1983), 1:89–91, 94–96, 166–68.

46. Sand, *Story of My Life*, 534, 540, 597, 549.

47. Ibid., 539.

48. D'Agoult, *Mémoires, souvenirs et journaux*, 1:59, 86.

49. Ibid., 59, 102–4. Sand also was exposed to the Gaultier method by the mother of the girlfriend who gave her lessons in Paris. "She used Father Gaultier's method for all these subjects, which was then in vogue, and which I believe was excellent." Sand, *Story of My Life*, 547. See also Crubellier, *L'Enfance et la jeunesse*, 80.

50. D'Agoult, *Mémoires, souvenirs et journaux*, 1:134–36; Sand, *Story of My Life*, 637.

51. D'Agoult, *Mémoires, souvenirs et journaux*, 1:145–46.

52. Sand, *Story of My Life*, 649–52.

53. D'Agoult, *Mémoirs, souvenirs et journaux*, 1:153. Sand writes of the lessons in dancing, etiquette, and deportment at the convent: "Those studies for which my grandmama sacrificed the pleasure of seeing me were more or less worthless." Sand, *Story of My Life*, 694.

54. Sand, *Story of My Life*, 640–41.

55. Ibid., 734.

56. D'Agoult, *Mémoires, souvenirs et journaux*, 1:148–49.

57. Ibid., 161.

58. Saman, *Les Enchantements de Prudence*, 8.

59. Ibid., 8–9; letter of 10 November 1845 in Hortense Allart de Méritens, *Lettres inédites à Sainte-Beuve (1841–1848)*, ed. Léon Séché, 2d ed. (Paris: Société du Mercure de France, 1908), 154–55.

60. Saman, *Les Enchantements de Prudence*, 9.

61. Malo, *Une Muse et sa mère*, 161–62; Séché, *Delphine Gay*, 27–29, 38–39.

62. D'Heilly, *Madame E. de Girardin (Delphine Gay)*, 13.

63. D'Agoult, *Mémoires, souvenirs et journaux*, 1:154–55.

64. In 1842 the literary critic G. de Molènes generally condemned women who aspired to be poets, but he asserted that the intimate novel (*roman intime*) was suited for feminine talents, and that certain women were capable of writing poetry without losing their femininity. Still, he concluded that he preferred intelligent women who did not write, and that true feminine poetry lay in the feminine appearances of women, their muselike capacity to inspire poetry in men, rather than in women writing poetry. G. de Molènes, "Simples Essais d'histoire littéraire. I: Les femmes poètes," *Revue des deux mondes* 31, no. 3 (1842): 48–76. The following year a review of Girardin's journalism asserted that Girardin should have stuck with poetry instead of abusing her talent on politics and literary criticism in her newspaper column. F. de Lagenevais, "Simples essais d'histoire littéraire. III: Le Feuilleton.—Lettres parisiennes," *Revue des deux mondes* ser. 2, no. 4 (1843): 133–50. Even within the genre of poetry, Antoine de Latour maintained that simple love poems expressing feminine sentiments were "better" than more ambitious forms, especially, in Girardin's

case, political elegies and epics. "Les Femmes poètes au XIXe siècle. II: Madame Emile de Girardin," *Revue de Paris* 25 (1835): 191–202. A critic of George Sand contends that women are naturally good storytellers, and Sand is among the best, but that her efforts to address political, philosophical, spiritual, or artistic issues in her fiction are failures, or at best, flawed. Lerminier, "Poètes et romanciers contemporains. Seconde phase. I: Mme Sand," *Revue des deux mondes*, nouv. sér. 6, no. 14 (1844): 84–117. Girardin herself indicated that tragedy was considered a masculine genre. Girardin, *Lettres parisiennes*, 23 March 1844, in *Oeuvres complètes*, 5:243. Roger Bellet, "Masculin et féminin dans les pseudonymes des femmes de lettres au XIXe siècle," in *Femmes de lettres au XIXe siècle*, 249–81. On history as a male genre and fiction as female, see Mary Rice, "Masculin/Féminin: Daniel Stern's *Histoire de la Révolution de 1848*," *L'Esprit créateur*, 29 (fall 1989): 84–91.

65. *Victor Hugo raconté par un temoin de sa vie*, 2:56, cited in Séché, *Delphine Gay*, 37.

66. Malo, *Une Muse et sa mère*, 161–62;

67. D'Heilly suggests that Sophie cultivated even more Delphine's literary education after Sigismond's death. D'Heilly, *Madame E. de Girardin (Delphine Gay)*, 13.

68. Girardin, "A ma mère," in *Oeuvres complètes*, 1:n.p.

69. Ibid.

70. Malo, *Une muse et sa mère*, 182–83.

71. Christine Planté discerns a tendency among nineteenth-century French women writers to deny any motivation to create art with their writing; rather, she claims that women writers often wrote as therapy, for didactic purposes, or to earn money. Planté, *La Petite Soeur de Balzac*, 175.

72. Saman, *Les Enchantements de Prudence*, 12.

73. Ibid., 11.

74. Sand, *Story of My Life*, 426.

75. Ibid., 476–77.

76. D'Agoult, *Memoirs, souvenirs et journaux*, 1:81.

77. Ibid., 116.

78. Geneviève Fraisse, "A Philosophical History of Sexual Difference," in Fraisse and Perrot, *Emerging Feminism from Revolution to World War*, 48–79; Michelle Perrot, "The Family Triumphant"; Bell and Offen, *Women, the Family, and Freedom*, 1:112–15, 169–70. For the family in relation to property and inheritance as a result of the French Revolution, see Darrow, *Revolution in the House*. Yet another discourse on the family involved the regulation and moralization of working-class and poor families; see Rachel G. Fuchs, *Poor and Pregnant in Paris: Strategies for Survival in the Nineteenth Century* (New Brunswick, NJ: Rutgers University Press, 1992), ch. 2; Katherine A. Lynch, *Family, Class, and Ideology in Early Industrial France: Social Policy and the Working-Class Family, 1825–1848* (Madison: University of Wisconsin Press, 1988), ch. 2; Jacques Donzelot, *The Policing of Families*, trans. Robert Hurley (New York: Pantheon, 1979).

79. *Code Napoleon; or, the French Civil Code. Literally Translated from the Original and Official Edition, published at Paris, in 1804* (Reprint, Baton Rouge, LA:

Claitor's Book Store, 1960), esp. 59–61, 103, 107; Max Rheinstein, "The Code and the Family," in *The Code Napoleon and the Common-Law World*, ed. Bernard Schwartz (New York: New York University Press, 1956), 139–61.

80. Sand, *Story of My Life*, 346.

81. Ibid., 317.

82. Ibid., 177.

83. D'Agoult, *Mémoires, souvenirs et journaux*, 1:39.

84. Marie d'Agoult, *Histoire de la Révolution de 1848*, 3 vols., 2d ed. (Paris: Charpentier, 1868), 1:ix.

85. D'Agoult, *Mes Souvenirs*, 59.

86. Saman, *Les Enchantements de Prudence*, 2, 9, 22–23, 14, 6.

87. Ibid., 4–5, 13–15. In an early novel, reprinted much later, Allart creates a character, Elizabeth, whose youthful dreams of public and perhaps political involvement resemble Allart's own: "Born in England and left as a young orphan in the care of a tutor who raised me to love my country and freedom, I associated with this love a love of ancient peoples whose history enchanted my youth, and initially I dreamed only of great actions and public virtues." *Jérôme, ou le jeune prélat* (1829), in Hortense Allart, *Les Nouveaux Enchantements* (Paris: Michel Lévy frères, 1873), 243.

88. Lamartine, "Madame de Girardin," 163, 173; Séché, *Delphine Gay*, 32–36, 42.

89. Girardin, "A ma mère," in *Oeuvres complètes* 1:n.p.

90. D'Heilly, *Madame E. de Girardin (Delphine Gay)*, 10–12; Séché, *Delphine Gay*, 44; Girardin, "La Quête au profit des Grecs," in *Oeuvres complètes*, 1: 399–403.

Chapter 3: The Erotics of Writing

1. Saman, *Les Enchantements de Prudence*, 1.

2. Michel Foucault, *An Introduction*, vol. 1 of *The History of Sexuality*, trans. Robert Hurley (New York: Vintage Books, 1980), 58–65. See also Biddy Martin, "Lesbian Identity and Autobiographical Difference[s]," in Brodzki and Schenck, *Life/Lines*, 77–103.

3. Perrot, "The Family Triumphant," and "Roles and Characters," and Alain Corbin, "Intimate Relations," in Perrot, *From the Fires of the Revolution to the Great War*, 123–24, 180–81, 590–93; Foucault, *History of Sexuality*, 36–40; Antony Copley, *Sexual Moralities in France, 1780–1980: New Ideas on the Family, Divorce and Homosexuality* (London and New York: Routledge, 1992), 79–89.

4. Peter Gay, *Education of the Senses*, vol. 1 of *The Bourgeois Experience from Victoria to Freud* (New York and Oxford: Oxford University Press, 1984), 144–68. See also Thomas Laqueur, *Making Sex: Body and Gender from the Greeks to Freud* (Cambridge, MA: Harvard University Press, 1990), 198–207.

5. Jacqueline Guiot-Lauret, "Amour et taboux linguistiques dans quelques romans et nouvelles des années 1833–1836," in *Aimer en France 1760–1860*, ed. Paul Viallaneix and Jean Ehrand (Clermont-Ferrand: Association des Publica-

tions de la Faculté des Lettres et Sciences Humaines de Clermont-Ferrand, 1980), 1:205–15; Bertholet, *Les Français par eux-mêmes*, 123–29.

6. Margaret Waller, *The Male Malady: Fictions of Impotence in the French Romantic Novel* (New Brunswick, NJ: Rutgers University Press, 1993). Waller analyzes Chateaubriand's *René* (1802), Constant's *Adolphe* (1816), as well as de Staël's *Corinne* (1807) and Sand's *Lélia* (1833). Other works by male romantics that address male passion are Senancour's *Oberman* (1804), Sainte-Beuve's *Volupté* (1832), and Musset's *La Confession d'un enfant du siècle* (1836). See also Guiot-Lauret, "Amour et tabous linguistiques"; D. G. Charlton, "Prose Fiction," in *The French Romantics*, ed. D. G. Charlton (Cambridge: Cambridge University Press, 1984), 1:163–203.

7. Peter Gay, *The Tender Passion*, vol. 2 of *The Bourgeois Experience from Victoria to Freud*, 56.

8. D'Agoult, *Mémoires, souvenirs et journaux*, 1:189, 191, 196, 197.

9. Dupêchez, *Marie d'Agoult*, 53–54.

10. D'Agoult, *Mémoires, souvenirs et journaux*, 1:292. In a farewell letter to her husband, d'Agoult accuses him of nothing worse than incompatibility, and she writes, "Your name will never cross my lips but that it will be pronounced with the respect and esteem that are due your character." Letter of 26 May 1835, Bibliothèque Nationale, Manuscrits, Fonds Daniel Ollivier, N.A.F. 25181, 134.

11. Marie d'Agoult, *Valentia. Hervé. Julien. La Boite aux lettres: Ninon au couvent* (Paris: Calmann Lévy, 1883), 24. For an analysis of this passage, see Rabine, "Feminist Writers in French Romanticism," 499–500.

12. For a more extended analysis of d'Agoult's views on marriage, see Chapter 6.

13. D'Agoult, *Mémoires, souvenirs et journaux*, 1:294–95.

14. Vier, *La Comtesse d'Agoult et son temps*, 1:107–38.

15. D'Agoult, *Mémoires, souvenirs et journaux*, 1:299–300.

16. Ibid., 308.

17. Vier claims that d'Agoult and Liszt did not consummate their relationship until they left France for Switzerland. Vier, *La Comtesse d'Agoult et son temps*, 1:168–69. However, Dupêchez's interpretation of the d'Agoult/Liszt correspondence suggests that they had sexual relations in 1834. Moreover, the birth of Blandine Liszt on 18 December 1835 places her conception around March 1835—three months before the flight to Switzerland. Dupêchez, *Marie d'Agoult*, 64–69.

18. D'Agoult, *Mémoires, souvenirs et journaux*, 1:317.

19. Marie d'Agoult, *Nélida* (Paris: Calmann-Lévy, 1987 [orig. 1846]), 146.

20. D'Agoult, *Mémoires, souvenirs et journaux*, 1:318.

21. D'Agoult, *Nélida*, 144.

22. Saman, *Les Enchantements de Prudence*, 30.

23. Ibid., 44.

24. Ibid., 20, 22–23, 34, 46.

25. Ibid., 64.

26. Ibid., 79, 87, 99.

27. Ibid., 120, 166.

28. Ibid., 183, 184, 191, 196, 216. See also Decreus, *Henry Bulwer-Lytton et Hortense Allart*.

29. Hortense Allart, *Settimia* (Bruxelles: Ad. Wahlen et Cie., 1836), 1:vi.

30. Letter of 2 March 1844 in Allart, *Lettres inédites à Sainte-Beuve*, 86.

31. Sainte-Beuve, "A Hortense," cited in Léon Séché, "Les Correspondants d'Hortense Allart de Méritens: Sainte-Beuve—Madame d'Agoult: Documents inédits," *La Revue de Paris* 14, no. 5 (September–October 1907): 294.

32. D'Agoult, *Mémoires, souvenirs et journaux*, 1:241.

33. Lamartine, "Madame de Girardin," 157–58.

34. "Introduction," in Girardin, *Oeuvres complètes*, 1:iii.

35. D'Heilly, *Madame E. de Girardin (Delphine Gay)*, 34–37; Séché, *Delphine Gay*, 46–47, 66–67; Martin-Fugier, *La Vie élégante*, 277–79.

36. Girardin, "Le Départ," in *Oeuvres complètes*, 1:311. Séché maintains that Girardin was in love with Lamartine; Lamartine's protestations in his biographical sketch of Girardin that "it was poetry, but not at all love, as some have later interpreted my attachment to her as passion," could be interpreted as either dispelling or confirming that notion. Séché, *Delphine Gay*, 67; Lamartine, "Madame de Girardin," 161–62.

37. See, for example, "Le Bonheur d'être belle" (1822), "Le Malheur d'être laide" (1826), "La Folle des Champs-Elysées" (1826), "Il m'aimait!" (1828), "Le Rêve d'une jeune fille" (1828), "L'Une ou l'autre" (1828). All of these poems are found in Girardin, *Oeuvres complètes*, vol. 1.

38. Girardin, "Le Rêve d'une jeune fille," in ibid., 1:305.

39. Girardin, "A ma mère," in ibid., 1:n.p.

40. Girardin, "Corinne aimée," in ibid., 1:313.

41. Ibid., 316.

42. Girardin, "A ma mère," in ibid., 1:n.p.

43. Pierre Pellissier, *Emile de Girardin, Prince de la presse* (Paris: Denoel, 1985), 11–52.

44. Girardin, "Aux jeunes filles," in *Oeuvres complètes*, 1:349.

45. Girardin, "Désenchantement," in ibid., 1:341.

46. Cited in Malo, *La Gloire du Vicomte de Launay*, 4.

47. Ibid., 5.

48. D'Heilly, *Madame E. de Girardin (Delphine Gay)*, 83.

49. Malo, *La Gloire du Vicomte de Launay*, 4–5, 15–18.

50. Martin-Fugier, *La Vie élégante*, 281–84.

51. Letter from d'Agoult to Liszt, 17 January 1841, in Franz Liszt, *Correspondance de Liszt et de la Comtesse d'Agoult, 1840–1864* (Paris: Bernard Grasset, 1934), 2:108.

52. Girardin, "Le Vote du 13 avril 1839," in *Oeuvres complètes*, 1:431. See also Malo, *Le Gloire du vicomte de Launay*, 55–56.

53. Marie d'Agoult frequently passes judgment on Sand's love affairs in her correspondence with Liszt. Tocqueville mentions Sand's affair with Mérimée in *The Recollections of Alexis de Tocqueville*, trans. Alexander Teixeira de Mattos (Lon-

don: Harvill Press, 1948), 157. See also Karénine, *George Sand*, 1:1–69, 335; Maurois, *Lélia*. Georges Lubin mentions controversies over Sand's sexuality in footnotes dispersed throughout her *Correspondance*. On the possibilities and limitations of homosexual love during the July Monarchy, see Victoria Thompson, "Creating Boundaries: Homosexuality and the Changing Social Order in France, 1830–1870," in *Homosexuality in Modern France*, ed. Jeffrey Merrick and Bryant T. Ragan, Jr. (New York and Oxford: Oxford University Press, 1996), 102–27.

54. Sand, *Story of My Life*, 77.

55. Ibid., 830–31, 832–33.

56. Ibid., 838, 841, 878.

57. Letter from Sand to Michel de Bourges, 22 October 1835, in Sand, *Correspondance*, 3:77. I agree with Bernadette Chovelon that the father may be Grandsagne, or it may well be Casimir Dudevant. Bernadette Chovelon, *George Sand et Solange, mère et fille* (N.p.: Christian Pirot, 1994), 13–14.

58. Sand, *Story of My Life*, 880–81.

59. Letter from Sand to Michel de Bourges, 15 October 1836, in Sand, *Correspondance*, 3:563–64.

60. "I begin to have almost absolute ideas about relations between the sexes and they are completely in line with Christ [*conformes à l'évangile*], and so completely contrary to practice and customs. I will explain them to you at length, but I can summarize them in two words: conjugal fidelity is the only possibility for maintaining love and fidelity, but it is practicable only on condition that the two sexes will be equally committed [*engagés*] and that the same blame will strike the man who seeks the wife of another, as to the wife of one man who cedes to another." Sand, letter to Abbé Georges Rochet, ca. 12 June 1837, ibid., 4:125.

61. George Sand, *Indiana*, trans. Eleanor Hochman (New York: Penguin Books, 1993), 76. Lélia says of her contest over her passion, "Truly, I had at first some happiness in seeing content and tranquil the man whom I could enflame and let loose with one word. When he was peacefully seated at my side, holding my hand between his and speaking of heaven and of angels, I fixed his pure forehead and calm breast with a long and penetrating gaze. I told myself that in letting flash a gleam from my eye, in pressing his hands more strongly with my fingers, I could simultaneously set fire to his brain and make his heart race. I enjoyed feeling this feminine temptation and resisting it. I loved the voluptuous suffering that resulted for me from his secret struggle." Her lover complains, "Why just a moment ago were you leaning toward me with a burning look, with lips parted, with an exciting and cruel indolence?" George Sand, *Lélia*, rev. ed. (Paris: Garnier, 1960), 200; Guiot-Lauret, "Amour et taboux linguistiques." On Sand's representations of sexuality in fiction, see Lucy MacCallum-Schwartz, "Sensibilité et sensualité: Rapports sexuels dans les premiers romans de George Sand (1831–1843)," in *George Sand*, ed. Simone Vierne (Paris: CDU et Sedes Réunis, 1983), 171–77.

62. Friedman, "Women's Autobiographical Selves," 34–62.

63. Sand, letter to Jules Boucoiran, 4 March 1831, in *Correspondance* 1:817.

64. D'Agoult, *Mémoires, souvenirs et journaux*, 1:334. See also Liszt, *Correspondance de Liszt et de la Comtesse d'Agoult*, vol. 1.

65. Vier, *La Comtesse d'Agoult et son temps*, 1:200.

66. Sand, letter to d'Agoult, 15 December 1835(?), *Correspondance* 3:290.

67. Sand, *Correspondance*, 4:560–843; S. Rocheblave, "Une Amitié romanesque: George Sand et Madame d'Agoult," *Revue de Paris* 6 (November–December 1894): 792–836.

68. D'Agoult, *Mémoires, souvenirs et journaux*, 2:28.

69. Ibid., 28–29.

70. Ibid., 30. For more extended coverage of the relationship between d'Agoult and Sand, see Vier, *La Comtesse d'Agoult et son temps*, 1:206–67; Dupêchez, *Marie d'Agoult*, 83–88, 90–99.

71. Letter from d'Agoult to Liszt, 26 February 1840, *Correspondance de Liszt et de la Comtesse d'Agoult*, 1:398.

72. Letter from d'Agoult to Liszt, 16 December 1840, and continuation, ibid., 2:79.

73. Letter from d'Agoult to Liszt, 10 January 1842, in ibid., 192–93. Vier, *La Comtesse d'Agoult et son temps*, 2:96–101. D'Agoult, *Mémoires, souvenirs et journaux*, 2:31–33.

74. D'Agoult, *Mémoires, souvenirs et journaux*, 2:35.

75. Ibid., 30.

76. Letter from d'Agoult to Sainte-Beuve, April 1846, cited in Séché, "Les Correspondants d'Hortense Allart de Méritens," 307.

77. D'Agoult, *Mémoires, souvenirs et journaux*, 1:30.

78. Ibid.

79. Saman, *Les Enchantements de Prudence*, 11.

80. Ibid., 12.

81. Uffenbeck, *The Life and Writings of Hortense Allart*, 257.

82. Saman, *Les Enchantements de Prudence*, 233, 253.

83. Ibid., 287.

84. Uffenbeck, *The Life and Writings of Hortense Allart*, 290–91.

85. Saman, *Les Enchantements de Prudence*, 317.

86. Ibid., 314.

87. Sand, *Story of My Life*, 882–87.

88. Ibid., 936.

89. Sand, *Correspondance*, 1:796, 801, 817–18, 821.

90. Sand, *Story of My Life*, 903.

91. Ibid., 892–93, 904–5.

92. Ibid., 916–21, 1057–63.

93. Ibid., 922.

94. Mme Emile de Girardin, Théophile Gautier, Jules Sandeau, and Méry, *La Croix de Berny*, new ed. (Paris: Calmann Lévy, 1882); Claude Senninger, "*La Croix de Berny*: Grand Steeple-chase non académique," *Bulletin de la Société Théophile Gautier* 6 (1984): 51–66; Malo, *La Gloire du Vicomte de Launay*, 86–87.

95. Girardin et al., *La Croix de Berny*, 131–32.

96. Planté, *La Petite Soeur de Balzac*, 32–35; Carla Hesse, "Reading Signa-

tures: Female Authorship and Revolutionary Law in France, 1750–1850," *Eighteenth-Century Studies* 22 (spring 1989): 469–87; Bellet, "Masculin et feminin," 249–81. See also, Annie Prassoloff, "Le Statut juridique de la femme auteur," *Romantisme* 77 (1992): 9–14.

97. Sand, *Story of My Life*, 907.

98. D'Agoult, *Mémoires, souvenirs et journaux*, 2:32.

99. Sand, *Story of My Life*, 908.

100. Ibid.

101. A novel of 1829 was published anonymously; four were under the name of Hortense Allart de Thérase; all the rest were Allart until 1850, the first publication after her marriage; Uffenbeck, *The Life and Writings of Hortense Allart*, 70, 484–85. Uffenbeck notes that Allart used the indication "Mme Allart de Thérase, rentière," on a passport to Naples when she was pregnant with Marcus. Hortense Allart, *Nouvelles Lettres à Sainte-Beuve (1832–1864)*, ed. Lorin A. Uffenbeck (Geneva: Droz, 1965), 25. Perhaps this was intended to avoid questions about her unmarried and pregnant condition, though she made no attempt to hide her son's existence and she gave him her name of Allart. Moreover, she had already received positive reviews for works published under the name of Allart, so she had no need to alter her identity in order to be taken seriously as a writer.

102. Saman, *Les Enchantements de Prudence*, 312.

103. In a letter to Sainte-Beuve, Allart explained her husband's illustrious names, and she assumed them as her own through marriage: "I am Méritens de Malvezie de Marcignac l'Asclaves, de Saman et l'Esbatx. I date from Charlemagne and we were part of the Crusades." Letter of 28 May 1843 in Allart, *Lettres inédites à Sainte-Beuve*, 80. The first edition of Allart's autobiography was entitled *Les Enchantements de Mme Prudence de Saman l'Esbatx* (Sceaux, 1872), but subsequent editions gave the author as "Mme P. de Saman" and the title as *Les Enchantements de Prudence*. Uffenbeck, *The Life and Writings of Hortense Allart*, 334.

104. Indeed, after the critic Jules Barbey d'Aurevilly excoriated the author of *Les Enchantements de Prudence* for tarnishing the name of the great René de Chateaubriand with tales of his submissive love for the young Allart, Allart's son Marcus went to the offices of the newspaper that published Barbey's review to challenge the man to a duel and avenge the insult to his mother. In the absence of Barbey, Marcus Allart beat up the editor of *Le Constitutionnel*. Séché, *Hortense Allart de Méritens*, 25–27.

105. Bellet, "Masculin et féminin," 276.

106. Ibid., 260–66; Reddy, "Condottieri of the Pen," 1546–70.

107. Sand, *Story of My Life*, 931–32.

Chapter 4: Cassandra, Diotima, Aspasia, and Cleopatra

1. Claude Bellanger et al., *Histoire générale de la presse française*, vol. 2: *De 1815 à 1871* (Paris: Presses universitaires de France, 1969), 109–43; Lyons, *Le Triomphe du livre*; Allen, *Popular French Romanticism*; Petra Ten-Doesschate Chu and

Gabriel Weisberg, eds., *The Popularization of Images: Visual Culture under the July Monarchy* (Princeton: Princeton University Press, 1994).

2. Planté, *La Petite Soeur de Balzac*, 43–44. See also Bellet, *Femmes de lettres au XIXe siècle*; Adler, *A l'Aube du féminisme*.

3. Bergman-Carton, *The Woman of Ideas in French Art*; Reddy, "Condottieri of the Pen": Albistur and Armogathe, *Histoire du féminisme français*, 263–90.

4. Bergman-Carton, *The Woman of Ideas in French Art*; Powell and Childs, *Femmes d'esprit*; Planté, *La Petite Soeur de Balzac*; Jules Janin, "Le Bas-bleu," in *Les Français peints par eux-mêmes: Encyclopédie morale du dix-neuvième siècle* (Paris: L. Curmer, 1842), 5:201–31; C. Feuillide, "Les Bas-bleus: Fragment," *L'Europe littéraire* 69 (9 August 1833): 4; Frédéric Soulié, *Physiologie du bas-bleu* (Paris: Aubert, 1841).

5. These prints are reproduced and insightfully analyzed by Janis Bergman-Carton, "Conduct Unbecoming: Daumier and 'Les Bas-Bleus,'" in Powell and Childs, *Femmes d'esprits*, 67–85.

6. Planté, *La Petite Soeur de Balzac*, 65–66; Albistur and Armogathe, *Histoire du féminisme française*, 254, 263–86; Ann MacCall Saint-Saëns, "Du bas-bleuisme et des correspondantes: Marie d'Agoult, Hortense Allart et la surenchère épistolaire," *Romantisme* 90 (1995): 77–88; Moses, *French Feminism in the Nineteenth Century*, 36.

7. Letter to Charles Duvernet, 6 July 1832; and to Laure Decerfz, 3, 6, and 7 July 1832, in Sand, *Correspondance*, 2:115, 118–20.

8. Letter to Sainte-Beuve, 25 August 1833, in ibid., 406–7; Sand, *Story of My Life*, 878; Cte. Théobald Walsh, *George Sand* (Paris: Hivert, 1837), esp. 77–170; Anonymous, "Galerie de Portraits: Lélia," *Revue critique* 4 (March 1840), 2–3; Annarosa Poli, "George Sand devant la critique, 1831–1833," in Vierne, *George Sand*, 95–100.

9. Letter to Casimir Dudevant, 15 January 1831, indicates that Sand was planning on attending Madame Recamier's salon, where Delphine Gay would read her poetry; letter to Laure Decerfz, 1 April 1833, says that Sand is seeing "Mme Allart, a woman of letters"; letter from Allart to Sand, 26 July 1833; letter from Sand to Allart, July 1833; letters to Sainte-Beuve of 15? January and 20? January 1842, explaining Sand's disagreement with Buloz over *Horace*, in Sand, *Correspondance*, 1:780, 2:291, 359, 390, 5:569–73; Lyons, *Le Triomph du livre*, 58; Isabelle Hoog Naginski, *George Sand: Writing for Her Life* (New Brunswick, NJ, and London: Rutgers University Press, 1991); Schor, *George Sand and Idealism*.

10. D'Heilly, *Madame E. de Girardin (Delphine Gay)*; Martin-Fugier, *La Vie élégante*, esp. ch. 9; Malo, *La Gloire du Vicomte du Launay*; Séché, *Delphine Gay*; Girardin, *Oeuvres complètes*; Bellet, *Femmes de lettres au XIXe siècle*; Allen, *Popular French Romanticism*, 97, 99, 139–45; Lyons, *Le Triomphe du livre*, 50–51, 58, 73.

11. Uffenbeck, *The Life and Writings of Hortense Allart*; Allart, *Nouvelles Lettres à Sainte-Beuve*; Saman, *Les Enchantements de Prudence*. Henry Bulwer called Allart's books "unsellable and unreadable," though he also loved and admired her; Decreus, *Henry Bulwer-Lytton et Hortense Allart*, 43.

12. D'Agoult, *Mémoires, souvenirs et journaux*; Vier, *La Comtesse d'Agoult et son temps*.

13. Sand's letters to would-be authors who sent her manuscripts indicate very clearly the competitiveness of the literary profession. Sand, *Correspondance*. See also Honoré de Balzac, *Illusions perdues* (Paris: Librairie Générale Française / Le Livre de poche, 1972 [orig. 1843]); Reddy, "Condottieri of the Pen."

14. Martin-Fugier, *La Vie élégante*; Allart, *Nouvelles Lettres à Sainte-Beuve*; D'Agoult, *Mémoires, souvenirs et journaux*; Sand, *Correspondance*; Clark, *Literary France*.

15. Sand, *Story of My Life*, 915, 923, 931–32. Sand's letters from 1831 represent Kératry more favorably, but one of them also dismisses him and suggests that such an exchange as reproduced in the autobiography might indeed have occurred. Moreover, the letters from this period also mention the difficulty Sand experienced in submitting a manuscript to a journal editor who "detested women." Letter to Charles Duvernet, 19 January 1831; letter to Casimir Dudevant, January 1831; letter to François Duris-Dufresne, 4 February 1831; letter to Jules Boucoiran, 4 March 1831; in Sand, *Correspondance*, 1:784, 790, 794, 819.

16. *Victor Hugo raconté par un temoin de sa vie*, 2:56, cited in Séché, *Delphine Gay*, 37.

17. D'Agoult, *Mémoires, souvenirs et journaux*, 2:18. For other manifestations of d'Agoult's internalizing the bluestocking terminology, see Saint-Saëns, "Du Bas-bleuisme."

18. Letter of 28 September 1841, in Allart, *Lettres inédites à Sainte-Beuve*, 24.

19. Letters from Allart to d'Agoult, 22 April 1851, 22 November 1853, and 20 July 1863, Bibliothèque Nationale, Manuscrits, Fonds Daniel Ollivier, N.A.F. 25185, 219, 277, 366.

20. Sand, *Story of My Life*, 916–22, 899.

21. Letter to Charles Meure, 27 January 1832; letter to Alfred Tattet, 22 March 1834; in Sand, *Correspondance*, 2:16, 546.

22. Sand's stories and novels about art are collected in George Sand, *Vies d'artistes* (Paris[?]: Presses de la Cité, 1992). Far too long to be included in this (already lengthy) collection is George Sand, *Consuelo, La Comtesse de Rudolstadt*, 3 vols. (Grenoble: Les Editions de l'Aurore, 1991). In *Les Maîtres sonneurs* (1853) a male bagpiper devotes himself so completely to his art that he sacrifices all family and human attachments, and eventually his life. In *Vies d'artistes*.

23. Letter to Laure Decerfz, 1 April 1833, in Sand, *Correspondance*, 2:291.

24. Fragments of a letter from Allart, 26 July 1833; letter to Allart, July 1833, in Sand, *Correspondance*, 2:359, 389–90. See also Uffenbeck, *The Life and Writings of Hortense Allart*, ch. 6; Mary Anne Garnett, "La Reine noire et la reine blanche: George Sand et Hortense Allart," in *George Sand Today: Proceedings of the 8th International George Sand Conference—Tours 1989*, ed. David A. Powell (Lanham, MD: University Press of America, 1992), 255–68.

25. The second and third volumes of Sand's *Correspondance* are filled with references to malicious reviews, Sand's shrugging them off, and letters to importunate writers. Excerpts from the vicious review by Charles Lassailly and Sand's forgiving response, occurring in 1840, are in *Correspondance*, 5:19–20. Letter of 4 June 1836, in Sand, *Correspondance*, 3:418.

26. Leyla Ezdinli, "*La Canne de M. de Balzac*: Parody at the Intersection of Politics and Literature," *Esprit créateur* 33 (fall 1993): 95–103. See ch. 6.

27. Girardin, *Lettres parisiennes*, 16 December 1837, in *Oeuvres complètes*, 4:226.

28. *Lettres parisiennes*, 17 February 1838, in ibid., 242.

29. *Lettres parisiennes*, 30 November 1838; 12 January 1839; in ibid., 261–66, 284–87.

30. *Lettres parisiennes*, 26 April 1841, in ibid., 5:140–41.

31. Such an Académie des femmes had, indeed, been founded in 1843 by Jules de Castellane, a man of some wealth who was sympathetic to saint-simonism. Daumier caricatured this female academy, portraying ugly, spinsterish bluestockings being awarded laurels by a pretentious, fatuous man. Bergman-Carton, *The Woman of Ideas in French Art*, 81–82. Jules Janin refers mockingly to a female academy in a publication of 1842. Janin, "Le Bas-Bleu," 226.

32. Girardin, *Lettres parisiennes*, 23 March 1844, in *Oeuvres complètes*, 5:240–42.

33. *Lettres parisiennes*, 21 June 1839, in ibid., 4:357–58.

34. *Lettres parisiennes*, 23 March 1844, in ibid., 5:243, 248–49.

35. D'Heilly, *Madame E. de Girardin (Delphine Gay)*, 69–71; Malo, *La Gloire du Vicomte de Launay*, 79–84; Anonymous, "Feuilleton du Journal des Debats. Théâtre-français: *Judith*, tragédie en trois actes," *Journal des débats politiques et littéraires* (1 May 1843), 1–2. Malo asserts that the author of this review was Jules Janin, who attended Girardin's private performance of *Judith* before it was staged publicly. Since the private performance was better received than the public one, he got out of his difficulty by blaming himself and the others in the private audience who were so seduced by Girardin's own, inspired reading of the play that they failed to discern the weaknesses of the tragedy, which became apparent on stage. Malo, *La Gloire du Vicomte de Launay*, 80–81.

36. Girardin, *L'Ecole des Journalistes*, in *Oeuvres complètes*, 6:9–88.

37. Girardin, "Préface de *L'Ecole des journalistes*," in ibid., 6:3–7.

38. D'Heilly, *Madame E. de Girardin (Delphine Gay)*, 66–69; Malo, *La Gloire du Vicomte de Launay*, 57–65.

39. Clark, *Literary France*; Planté, *La Petite Soeur de Balzac*; Lyons, *Le Triomphe du livre*; Allen, *Popular French Romanticism*; Bellet, *Femmes de lettres au XIXe siècle*; Bergman-Carton, *The Woman of Ideas in French Art*; Slama, "Femmes écrivains," 213–48. Notable exceptions are Saint-Saëns, "Du bas-bleuisme"; Garnett, "La Reine noire et la reine blanche"; Jacques Vier, *La Comtesse d'Agoult et Hortense Allart de Méritens sous le Second Empire* (Paris: Archives des lettres modernes no. 33, 1960).

40. Cited in Séché, *Hortense Allart de Méritens*, 135. Letter of 18 April 1844, Allart, *Nouvelles lettres a Sainte-Beuve*, 18 (also footnote 10, p. 20). See also letter of 28? December 1840, from Sand to Allart, in which Sand acknowledges Allart's compliment and returns it: "Dear Cousin, (for if I am queen according to you, you are no less queen according to me)," Sand, *Correspondance*, 5:190.

41. D'Agoult, *Mémoires, souvenirs et journaux*, 2:28.

42. Girardin, *Lettres parisiennes*, 24 May 1837, in *Oeuvres complètes*, 4:100–101.

43. On the mythology surrounding Sand, see Isabelle de Courtivron, "Weak Men and Fatal Women: The Sand Image," in *Homosexualities and French Literature: Cultural Contexts/Critical Texts*, ed. George Stambolian and Elaine Marks (Ithaca, NY, and London: Cornell University Press, 1979), 210–27; Schor, *George Sand and Idealism*. Sand's stature as a writer and as an advocate for women was viewed so positively by feminists that they proposed Sand as a candidate for the Chamber of Deputies in 1848; Riot-Sarcey, *La Démocratie à l'épreuve des femmes*, 202–6; Moses, *French Feminism in the Nineteenth Century*, 140–41. See Chapter 7, above.

44. Séché, *Delphine Gay*, 24–25; Decreus, *Henry Bulwer-Lytton et Hortense Allart*, 64; Letter of 7 October 1841, in Allart, *Lettres inédites à Sainte-Beuve*, 25–26.

45. Darrow, "French Noblewomen and the New Domesticity." Allart refers to the prudery of the Restoration, embodied by the aloof and rigid Duchesse d'Angouleme (Madame la Dauphine) when she complains to d'Agoult of her sister Sophie's initial refusal to see Allart after the birth of her second illegitimate child: "My sister no longer writes to me since I had my child; have you seen anything so ridiculous in the nineteenth century since the time of the court of Mme la Dauphin[e]?" Letter of 31 July 1839, Bibliothèque Nationale, Manuscrits, Fonds Daniel Ollivier, N.A.F. 25185, 88. D'Agoult describes the Restoration court and Saint-Germain society as very traditional, hierarchical, formal, and routine. D'Agoult, *Mémoires, souvenirs et journaux*, 1:204–34. For a summary of religious revival under the Restoration, see Roger Magraw, *France 1815–1914*, 29–31.

46. D'Agoult, *Mémoires, souvenirs et journaux*, 1:240–41.

47. Ibid., 241–43; 2:30–31.

48. Letters from d'Agoult to Liszt, 17 January 1841; 21 May 1841; 13 June 1841; in Liszt, *Correspondance de Liszt et de la Comtesse d'Agoult*, 2:108, 154–55, 142. D'Agoult's letters to Liszt relate her many meetings with Emile de Girardin; ibid., 14–108.

49. D'Agoult makes a similar move of criticizing a woman writer for being the opposite of d'Agoult in her analysis of Bettina von Arnim. Among other things, d'Agoult accuses Arnim of "immoderate ambition," of being too romantic, of eccentricity; she writes of her, "another salient feature of Bettina's mind, ... is the distaste, one could even say the hatred, of all that is scientific, rational, logical. ... Personal feeling [*Le sentiment intime*] is all for her." D'Agoult's critique of Arnim's emotionalism implicitly favors her own presumption to rationalism, moderation, philosophy, and so on. Marie d'Agoult, "Ecrivains modernes de l'Allemagne: Mme d'Arnim," *Revue des deux mondes* 6 (1844): 265–97.

50. Girardin, *Lettres parisiennes*, 8 March 1837, in *Oeuvres complètes*, 4:68–70. It is worth noting here that just about one week before Girardin's letter was published Sand had a falling out with Lamennais precisely over the *Lettres à Marcie*. Their ostensible disagreement was over the issue of divorce; Sand advocated the legalization of divorce in the *Lettres* and Lamennais, who opposed it, refused to print Sand's writing in its entirety. In a larger sense the two disagreed fundamentally over the position of women in society and how to ap-

proach it. Girardin's representation of Sand's position as resignation was over-simplified, if not downright erroneous. Sand stopped writing the *Lettres* for Lamennais's journal. Letter from Sand to Lamennais, 28 February 1837, in Sand, *Correspondance*, 3:711–14. D'Agoult also writes of this quarrel in her letters to Liszt and in her memoirs. See Chapter 6.

51. Letter of mid-June 1837, in Sand, *Correspondance*, 4:128–29.

52. Sand, *Correspondance*, vols. 11–13. Sand, cited in *Esprit de Mme. de Girardin* (Paris: Hetzel, 1863), 345–51. See also Lamartine, "Madame de Girardin," 184; Séché, *Delphine Gay*, 310–17; Malo, *La Gloire du Vicomte de Launay*, 272–74.

53. Letter to Marie d'Agoult, early January and 26? February 1836, in Sand, *Correspondance*, 3:222–30, 290–91.

54. D'Agoult, *Mémoires, souvenirs et journaux*, 2:125 ,131–32.

55. Ibid., 2:28–29.

56. Vier, *La Comtesse d'Agoult et son temps*, 1:258–67, 302–9; Rocheblave, "Une Amitié romanesque"; André Maurois, "George Sand et Marie d'Agoult: Mort d'une amitié," *Revue de Paris* 58 (July–December 1951): 3–15; Marie d'Agoult and George Sand, *Marie d'Agoult George Sand: Correspondance*, ed. Charles F. Dupêchez (Paris: Bartillat, 1995).

57. Cited in Maurois, "George Sand et Marie d'Agoult," 3–4; also cited in Sand, *Correspondance*, 4:562–63, 721, 758–59.

58. Letter of 26 November 1839, in Sand *Correspondance*, 4:803.

59. Liszt, *Correspondance de Liszt et de la Comtesse d'Agoult*, 1:280–361.

60. Parts of the correspondence between Allart and d'Agoult are located in the Bibliothèque Nationale, Manuscrits, Fonds Daniel Ollivier, N.A.F. 25181 and 25185. See also Liszt, *Correspondance de Liszt and de la Comtesse d'Agoult*, vol. 1; Allart, *Lettres inédites à Sainte-Beuve*.

61. Letter from Hortense Allart to Sainte-Beuve, early August 1845, in Séché, "Les Correspondants d'Hortense Allart de Méritens," 312.

62. Letter of 2 March 1846, cited in ibid., 306.

63. Letters from Allart to d'Agoult, 28 April 1850; 22 November 1853; in Bibliothèque Nationale, Manuscrits, Fonds Daniel Ollivier, N.A.F. 25185, 194, 277. See also Vier, *La Comtesse d'Agoult et Hortense Allart de Méritens*; Saint-Saëns, "Le Bas-bleuisme."

64. Letter of 19 February 1833, Allart, *Nouvelles Lettres à Sainte-Beuve*, 7.

65. Letter of 22 June 1847, in Sand, *Correspondance*, 7:756–57.

66. Letter of 13 February 1850, in Allart, *Nouvelles Lettres à Sainte-Beuve*, 91.

67. George Sand, "Variétés: Madame Hortense Allart," *Le Courrier de Paris* 255 (23 December 1857): 3–4. Sand's review of *Les Enchantements* was reprinted as a preface to a later edition of the book—Saman, *Les Enchantements de Prudence*, iii–xix.

68. Sand, *Story of My Life*, 1073, 1103.

69. Letter from Allart to d'Agoult, 16 November 1854, cited in Sand, *Correspondance*, 12:627. Allart had written earlier to d'Agoult, on 7 June 1851: "You will be interested to know that the Queen wrote to me some time ago. She called both you and me *femmes artistes*. I had thought the only female artists were she and you. She calls 'Marpé' a sad and strong story, and says she did not know I

was a woman such as that, etc." Bibliothèque Nationale, Manuscrits, Fonds Daniel Ollivier, N.A.F. 25185, 221.

70. Fraisse, *Reason's Muse*. Other scholarly works demonstrate solidarity among women, many of whom wrote, but these were working-class and lower-middle-class persons who sought change primarily through social movements and political organization rather than through writing. Moses, *French Feminism in the Nineteenth Century*; Riot-Sarcey, *La Démocratie à l'épreuve des femmes*; Moses and Rabine, *Feminism, Socialism and French Romanticism*.

71. Sand, *Correspondance*, vols. 3 and 4; Bibliothèque Nationale, Manuscrits, Fonds Daniel Ollivier, N.A.F. 25181 and 25185.

72. Bibliothèque Nationale, Manuscrits, Fonds Daniel Ollivier, N.A.F. 25181 and 25185; Letter of 13 March 1846, in Allart, *Lettres inédites à Sainte-Beuve*, 192; Hortense Allart, *Histoire de la République d'Athènes* (Paris: n.p., 1866) 15–16, 457–58; Saman, *Les Enchantements de Prudence*, 269; Marie d'Agoult, *Dante et Goethe: Dialogues* (Paris: Didier, 1866); Saint-Saëns, "Le Bas-bleuisme"; Mary Anne Garnett, "Marie d'Agoult and the 'Anxiety of Authorship,'" in *Continental, Latin-American and Francophone Women Writers*, ed. Ginette Adamson and Eunice Myers (Lanham, MD: University Press of America, 1990), 2:123–30. For works on women in ancient history and literature, see Elaine Fantham et al., *Women in the Classical World: Image and Text* (New York and Oxford: Oxford University Press, 1994), 128–35; Bonnie S. Anderson and Judith P. Zinsser, *A History of Their Own: Women in Europe from Prehistory to the Present*, 2 vols. (New York: Harper & Row, 1988), 1:54–55, 64–66. For works on the historical constructions of ancient female figures, see Joan DeJean, *Fictions of Sappho, 1546–1937* (Chicago and London: University of Chicago Press, 1989); Madeleine M. Henry, *Prisoner of History: Aspasia of Miletus and Her Biographical Tradition* (New York and Oxford: Oxford University Press, 1995), 40. In contrast to Allart's positive representation of the amazon as a model for women of letters, male literary critics used the figure of the amazon to disparage women writers with violent hostility. For example, "We no longer believe in amazons. . . . Their memory . . . evokes only an ironic smile. Nonetheless, I maintain that . . . [an amazon] seems to me a being less chimerical and less monstrous than a woman [writer]"; Molènes, "Simples essais d'histoire littéraire," 49. See also Janin, "Le Bas-bleu," 231.

73. Letter from Sand to Allart, 28? December 1840, *Correspondance*, 5:191.

74. For Allart's scholarly treatment of Aspasia, see Allart, *Histoire de la République d'Athènes*, 190–91, 223–24. Allart refers to her desire both to be with Bulwer and to be near political power in Saman, *Les Enchantements de Prudence*, 183–84. From the beginning Sand's novels challenged the status quo, particularly regarding women's condition and later regarding the working classes. In the introduction to the 1832 edition of *Indiana*, for example, Sand denies any conscious, revolutionary social critique in the novel, but she also writes: "If [the author] sometimes allows the characters to complain of the injustices they endure, or to voice their hopes for a better life, let the blame be laid on society for its inequities and on fate for its caprices!" Sand, *Indiana*, 19. In a letter of 1837, when Sand was writing *Mauprat*, she vows to raise women from their debased

condition: "Female slavery must also have its Spartacus. I will be it, or I will die trying." Letter from Sand to Frédéric Girerd, late April or early May 1837, in Sand, *Correspondance,* 4:18–19. In 1841 Sand quarreled with her publisher François Buloz over the political implications of Sand's novel *Horace.* Buloz apparently wanted Sand to alter the text, claiming that it was too inflammatory against the government. Sand angrily refused, broke with Buloz, and found a different publisher. Letter from Sand to Buloz of 15 September 1841, in Sand, *Correspondance,* 5:418–23. See Chapter 7.

75. Delphine Gay de Girardin, *Cléopatre,* in *Oeuvres complètes,* 6:150, 154.

Chapter 5: Women Writers as Republicans in July Monarchy Political Culture

1. The notion of the family romance for analyzing French history is elaborated in Hunt, *The Family Romance of the French Revolution.*

2. Girardin, *Lettres parisiennes,* 17 May 1839, in *Oeuvres complètes,* 4:346.

3. Ibid., 349–50.

4. Girardin, "La vision" [1825], in ibid., 1:391–97. The phrase occurs in the last line of the poem, "The French, weeping for me as for a cherished sister, / One day will call me, 'Muse de la patrie'!" Declarations of patriotism appear in several other poems as well.

5. Fraisse, *Reason's Muse,* see Chapter 6, above.

6. Nicolet, *L'Idée républicaine en France,* 133–37; Pilbeam, *Republicanism in Nineteenth-Century France,* 106–15; Aminzade, *Ballots and Barricades,* 37–39.

7. Louis Blanc, *The History of Ten Years, 1830–1840,* 2 vols. (London: Chapman and Hall, 1845), 1:429.

8. Pilbeam, *Republicanism in Nineteenth-Century France,* chs. 5–6; Aminzade, *Ballots and Barricades,* ch. 2; Nicolet, *L'Idée républicaine en France,* 133–38; Perreux, *Au Temps des sociétés secrètes.* See also Vigier, *La Monarchie de Juillet;* Jardin and Tudesq, *La France des notables;* Magraw, *France 1815–1914,* ch. 2.

9. Ceri Crossley, *French Historians and Romanticism: Thierry, Guizot, the Saint-Simonians, Quinet, Michelet* (London and New York: Routledge, 1993), 30–31, 40–43, 53–54, 74–77; Aminzade, *Ballots and Barricades,* 39–45; Pilbeam, *Republicanism in Nineteenth-Century France,* chs. 2, 5–6; Pierre Rosanvallon, *Le Moment Guizot* (Paris: Gallimard, 1985).

10. Paul Bénichou, *Le Temps des prophètes: Doctrines de l'âge romantique* (Paris: Gallimard, 1977).

11. Letter from Sand to Madame Maurice Dupin, 31 May 1831, in Sand, *Correspondance,* 1:886.

12. Letter from Sand to Laure Decerfz, 13 June 1832, in ibid., 2:103–4.

13. Letter from Sand to Marie Talon, 10 November 1834; letter from Sand to Adolphe Guéroult, 6 May 1835; letter from Sand to René de Villeneuve, 29 January 1846, in ibid., 2:739–42, 878–81; 7:256–57.

14. Michelle Perrot, "Présentation," in George Sand, *Politique et polémiques (1843–1850)* (Paris: Imprimerie nationale, 1997), 7–16.

15. Robert J. Bezucha, *The Lyon Uprising of 1834: Social and Political Conflict in the Early July Monarchy* (Cambridge: Harvard University Press, 1974), ch. 8.

16. Sand, *Story of My Life*, 1031–32.

17. George Sand, *Lettres d'un voyageur*, new ed. (Paris: Calmann-Lévy, 1927), 167, 182, 183, 165.

18. On the fluidity of sexual and gender boundaries during the July Monarchy, see Thompson, "Creating Boundaries," 102–27. On the ambiguity of androgyny and the influence of Sand's cross-dressed image in French literature during the July Monarchy, see Courtivron, "Weak Men and Fatal Women," 210–27.

19. Sand, *Correspondance*, vols. 2–7; Perrot, "Présentation," 18–22.

20. D'Agoult, *Mémoires, souvenirs et journaux*, 1:249–52.

21. Ibid., 256–58.

22. Ibid., 1:260–62, 282, 303–4; 2:28; Vier, *La Comtesse d'Agoult et son temps*, 1:102–27.

23. D'Agoult, *Mémoires, souvenirs et journaux*, 2:11.

24. Ibid., 1:304.

25. Ibid., 2:30.

26. Ibid., 17–18.

27. Letter from d'Agoult to Liszt, 29 November 1840, in Liszt, *Correspondance de Liszt et de la Comtesse d'Agoult*, 2:56–57.

28. D'Agoult, *Mémoires, souvenirs et journaux*, 2:36; Liszt, *Correspondance de Liszt et de la Comtesse d'Agoult*, 2:57, 99, 100, 114, 252, 320.

29. Letter from d'Agoult to Liszt of 21 January 1841, in Liszt, *Correspondance de Liszt et de la Comtesse d'Agoult*, 2:114.

30. D'Agoult, *Mémoires, souvenirs et journaux*, 2:29. See also Vier, *La Comtesse d'Agoult et son temps*, 1:266–67.

31. D'Agoult, *Mémoires, souvenirs et journaux*, 2:36.

32. Saman, *Les Enchantements de Prudence*, 189–94.

33. Hortense Allart, *Conjuration d'Amboise* (Paris: A. Marc, 1822), 98.

34. Hortense Allart, *Second petit livre: Etudes diverses* (Paris: Renault, 1850), 47.

35. Théophile Gautier, "Introduction: Madame Emile de Girardin," in Girardin, *Oeuvres complètes*, 1:iii.

36. Girardin, *Lettres parisiennes*, 23 November 1836, in ibid., 4:22.

37. Alphonse de Lamartine, *Mèmoires politiques*, vol. 37 of *Oeuvres complètes de Lamartine* (Paris: chez l'auteur, 1863), 1:6–7, 11–14.

38. Lamartine, "Madame de Girardin," 181. See also Martin-Fugier, *La Vie élégante*, ch. IX.

39. Letter of Sand to Luc Desage, 1837 (date uncertain) in Sand, *Correspondance*, 4:10–16.

40. Sand, "Pétition pour l'organisation du travail," and "La Politique et le socialisme," in *Politique et polémiques*, 160–62, 184.

41. Letter from Sand to Agricole Perdiguier, 20 August 1840, in Sand, *Correspondance*, 5:103.

42. George Sand, *Le Compagnon du tour de France* (Grenoble: Presses universitaires de Grenoble, 1988 [orig. 1840]), 276–77.

43. Sand, "La Politique et le socialisme," in *Politique et polémiques*, 172–73.

44. Ibid., 183.

45. Sand, "L'Application de l'égalité, c'est la fraternité," in ibid., 322. Italics in original.

46. Sand, "Introduction pour *La Cause de Peuple*," in ibid., 303.

47. "Variétés," *La Presse*, 9 January 1841, 3; Vier, *La Comtesse d'Agoult et son temps*, 2:99–101. See also letter from d'Agoult to Allart, April 1849: "I do not at all have the same faith as Madame Sand. Her letters and her other political works express nothing but vague aspirations toward some imagined ideal of *equality*, and a sort of adoration of the divinity of the people about which I can understand nothing." Bibliothèque Nationale, Manuscrits, Fonds Daniel Ollivier N.A.F. 25181, 143.

48. D'Agoult, *Esquisses morales*, 244.

49. Marie d'Agoult, *Essai sur la liberté* (Paris: Aymot, 1847), 144, 222–23.

50. D'Agoult, *Esquisses morales*, 253–69.

51. Ibid., 255, 263, 271.

52. D'Agoult, *Nélida*, 251. See Chapter 6. In a letter to Charles-Augustin Sainte-Beuve of April 1846, d'Agoult explains her intention regarding the character of Nélida: "She will love again, but not a man (for no man is worth being loved as she knows how to love); she will love *all those who suffer*, she will act, free and strong from thenceforth; she will lend a hand to the oppressed." Séché, "Les Correspondants d'Hortense Allart," 307.

53. Hortense Allart, *Histoire de la République de Florence*, part 1 (Paris: Moutardier, 1837), 32.

54. Hortense Allart, *Histoire de la République de Florence* (Paris: Garnier frères, 1843), 1:xi.

55. Ibid., 2:545.

56. Letter from Allart to Sainte-Beuve of 18 April 1844, in Allart, *Nouvelles Lettres à Sainte-Beuve*, 18.

57. Saman, *Les Enchantements de Prudence*, 193.

58. Ibid., 256.

59. Letter from Allart to Sainte-Beuve of 18 June 1846, in Allart, *Lettres inédites à Sainte-Beuve*, 208–9.

60. Letter from Allart to d'Agoult, 26 April 1852; 22 December 1851; in Bibliothèque Nationale, N.A.F. 25185, 240, 244. Allart, *Second petit livre*, 36.

61. Hortense Allart, *Essai sur l'histoire politique depuis l'invasion des barbares jusqu'en 1848*, 2 vols. (Paris: Just Rouvier, 1857), 2:354.

62. Allart, *Second petit livre*, 33.

63. Letter from Allart to d'Agoult, 24 March 1849, in Bibliothèque Nationale, N.A.F. 25185, 172.

64. Girardin, *Lettres parisiennes*, 13 September 1839, in *Oeuvres complètes*, 4:394.

65. Ibid., 393–97.

66. *Lettres parisiennes*, 6 March 1839, in ibid., 320–25.

67. *Lettres parisiennes*, 22 March 1839, in ibid., 329.

68. *Lettres parisiennes*, 27 April 1839, in ibid., 334.

69. *Lettres parisiennes*, 11 July 1847, in ibid., 5:456, 459–60.

70. Ibid., 460.

71. *Lettres parisiennes*, 4 April 1847, in ibid., 437–44.

72. Letter from Emmanuel Arago to Sand, 22 October 1835, in Sand, *Correspondance*, 3:67–68.

73. Sand, "Réponse à diverses objections," in *Politique et polémiques*, 191.

74. Letter to Charles Duvernet, 27 December 1841, in Sand, *Correspondance*, 5:535–47.

75. Sand, "La Politique et le socialisme," in *Politique et polémiques*, 167.

76. Ibid., 167–69.

77. Letter to Charles Duvernet, 27 December 1841, in Sand, *Correspondance*, 5:542.

78. George Sand, *Le Péché de Monsieur Antoine* (Meylan: Les Editions de l'Aurore, 1982 [orig. 1845]), 149, 187, 372–73.

79. George Sand, "*Histoire de la France* écrite sous la dictée de Blaise Bonnin," in *Politique et polémiques*, 263.

80. Vier, *La Comtesse d'Agoult et son temps*, 2:15–66.

81. D'Agoult, *Mémoires, souvenirs et journaux*, 2:36; Vier, *La Comtesse d'Agoult et son temps*, 2:169–89, 238, 244.

82. D'Agoult, *Mémoires, souvenirs et journaux*, 2:41.

83. D'Agoult, *Dante et Goethe*, 152–56; Garnett, "Marie d'Agoult and the 'Anxiety of Authorship,'" 123–30.

84. Saman, *Les Enchantements de Prudence*, 225.

85. Ibid., 294. "Marpé" also appears in Hortense Allart, *Troisième petit livre: Etudes diverses* (Paris: Renault, 1851), 79.

86. Allart, *Histoire de la République de Florence*, v–vi.

87. Letter from Allart to Sainte-Beuve, 2 March 1846—"Voilà mes seules jouissances désormais: la politique!" Allart, *Nouvelles Lettres à Sainte-Beuve*, 33.

88. Henry Bulwer wrote in his diary in 1832 that Allart's "books are neither sellable nor readable." Decreus, *Henry Bulwer-Lytton et Hortense Allart*, 43. Additionally, Allart was unable to find a publisher for her history of Athens, and she published it herself.

89. Letter from Allart to d'Agoult, 4 April 1839, Bibliothèque Nationale, N.A.F. 25185, 82—"I admire and adore M. Thiers; I think he dodges perfectly the tricks that Pasquier plays on him."

90. Letter from Allart to Sainte-Beuve of 7 October 1841, in Allart, *Lettres inédites à Sainte-Beuve*, 25–26.

91. Letter from Allart to Sainte-Beuve of 19 September 1845, in ibid., 116–17.

92. Letter from Allart to Sainte-Beuve of 6 April 1845, in Allart, *Nouvelles Lettres à Sainte-Beuve*, 20–21. For Allart's continued ambivalence regarding Thiers, see Vier, *Le Second Empire*, 9–10; Allart, *Essai sur l'histoire politique*, 1:282. Letter from Allart to Sainte-Beuve of 15 February 1848, in Allart, *Lettres inédites à Sainte-Beuve*, 293.

93. Martin-Fugier, *La Vie élégante*, ch. IX.

94. Girardin, *Lettres parisiennes*, 28 March 1840, in *Oeuvres complètes*, 4:478–79.

95. *Lettres parisiennes*, 7 March 1840, in ibid., 465–66.

96. *Lettres parisiennes*, 5 December 1840, in ibid., 5:73–77.

97. Malo, *La Gloire du Vicomte de Launay*, 53–57.

98. Girardin, *Lettres parisiennes*, 30 May 1839; 31 July 1840; in *Oeuvres complètes*, 4:353–54; 5:57.

99. *Lettres parisiennes*, 28 November 1840, in ibid., 5:70. For contrasting journalistic treatment of Thiers's foreign policy debacle, see Reddy, *The Invisible Code*, 27–30.

100. Girardin, *Lettres parisiennes*, 24 January 1841, in *Oeuvres complètes*, 5:94.

101. Vigier, *La Monarchie de Juillet*, 90–92, 118; Jardin and Tudesq, *La France des notables*, 188–90.

102. Girardin, *Lettres parisiennes*, 11 May 1837; 10 February 1841; in *Oeuvres complètes*, 4:95; 5:107.

103. *Lettres parisiennes*, 24 January 1841; 10 February 1841; in ibid., 5:94, 106.

104. Sand, "Réponse à diverses objections," 191.

105. Sand, *Horace*, 377; Sand, "Réponse à diverses objections," 190.

106. D'Agoult, *Esquisses morales*, 110.

107. D'Agoult, *Essai sur la liberté*, 245, 200.

108. Saman, *Les Enchantements de Prudence*, 251. In a letter to Marie d'Agoult of 1847 (no other date), Allart wrote: "Plato will save us, he who said *political man* and *political woman*." The underlining is in the original. Bibliothèque Nationale, Manuscrits, Fonds Daniel Ollivier, N.A.F. 25185, 163.

109. Hortense Allart, *La Femme et la démocratie de nos temps* (Paris: Delaunay, 1836). Allart's meritocracy is reminiscent of Napoleon, but I hesitate to label her a Bonapartist since she objected strenuously to misogyny, militarism, and imperialism.

Chapter 6: Republican Women and Republican Families

1. D'Agoult, *Mémoires, souvenirs et journaux*, 2: 40.

2. I am very grateful to Nicholas Rauh for identifying the larger passage in Sallust, and for his translation and interpretation. The passage in Latin is "Pulchrum est bene facere rei publicae etiam bene dicere haud absurdum est; vel pace vel bello clarum fieri licet." Sallust, *Bellum Catilinae*, 3.1. English translation by J. C. Rolfe (Cambridge, MA, and London: Harvard University Press / W. Heinemann, 1965), 7.

3. D'Agoult, *Mémoires, souvenirs et journaux*, 1:30.

4. "The National Convention Outlaws Clubs and Popular Societies of Women," in *Women in Revolutionary Paris, 1789–1795*, ed. Darline Gay Levy, Harriet Branson Applewhite, and Mary Durham Johnson (Urbana: University of Illinois Press, 1979), 215–17.

5. *Code Napoleon*, esp. 59–61, 103–7; Rheinstein, "The Code and the Family," 139–61.

6. Moses, *French Feminism in the Nineteenth Century*, 19–20.

7. Pateman, *The Sexual Contract*; Scott, *Only Paradoxes to Offer*; Landes, *Women in the Public Sphere*; Reynolds, "Marianne's Citizens?" 102–22. See also

Patrice Higonnet, *Sister Republics: The Origins of French and American Republican-ism* (Cambridge, MA, and London: Harvard University Press, 1988).

8. Hunt, *The Family Romance of the French Revolution*; Hunt, "Reading the French Revolution"; Fraisse, *Reason's Muse*; Suzanne Desan, "'War between Brothers and Sisters': Inheritance Law and Gender Politics in Revolutionary France," *French Historical Studies* 20 (fall 1997): 597–634. See also William Rog-ers Brubaker, "The French Revolution and the Invention of Citizenship," *French Politics and Society* 7 (summer 1989): 30–49; Patrice Higonnet, *Class, Ideology, and the Rights of Nobles during the French Revolution* (Oxford: Clarendon Press, 1981); Lynn Hunt, ed., *The French Revolution and Human Rights: A Brief Documentary History* (Boston and New York: Bedford Books of St. Martin's Press, 1996), esp. 119–39.

9. Landes, *Women in the Public Sphere*, 129–38; Karen Offen, "Contextualiz-ing the Theory and Practice of Feminism in Nineteenth-Century Europe (1789–1914)," in *Becoming Visible: Women in European History*, 3d ed., ed. Renate Bri-denthal, Susan Mosher Stuard, and Merry E. Wiesner (Boston and New York: Houghton Mifflin, 1998), 327–55; Karen Offen, "Reclaiming the European En-lightenment for Feminism, or Prologomena to Any Future History of Eight-eenth-century Europe," in *Perspectives on Feminist Political Thought in European History from the Middle Ages to the Present*, ed. Tjitske Akkerman and Siep Stuurman (London and New York: Routledge, 1998), 85–103; Karen Offen, "Was Mary Wollstonecraft a Feminist? A Contextual Re-reading of *A Vindica-tion of the Rights of Woman, 1792–1992*," in *Quilting a New Canon: Stitching Women's Words*, ed. Uma Parameswaran (Toronto: Sister Vision, 1996), 3–24; Linda K. Kerber, *Toward an Intellectual History of Women* (Chapel Hill and Lon-don: University of North Carolina Press, 1997), esp. "The Republican Mother: Women and the Enlightenment—An American Perspective," 41–62; Linda K. Kerber, *Women of the Republic: Intellect and Ideology in Revolutionary America* (Chapel Hill: University of North Carolina Press, 1980).

10. Abensour, *Le Féminisme sous le règne de Louis-Philippe*, 14–23; Albistur and Armogathe, *Histoire du féminisme français*, 286–91; Moses, *French Feminism in the Nineteenth Century*, 98–107.

11. Abensour, *Le Féminisme sous le règne de Louis-Philippe*, 9–14; Albistur and Armogathe, *Histoire du féminisme français*, 270–91; Adler, *A l'Aube du féminisme*; Riot-Sarcey, *La Démocratie à l'épreuve des femmes*; Moses and Rabine, *Feminism, Socialism, and French Romanticism*; Scott, *Only Paradoxes to Offer*; Moses, *French Feminism in the Nineteenth Century*, chs. 3–4; Thibert, *Le Féminisme dans le social-isme français*. See also Laura S. Strumingher, "Looking Back: Women of 1848 and the Revolutionary Heritage of 1789," in *Women and Politics in the Age of the Democratic Revolution*, ed. Harriet B. Applewhite and Darline G. Levy (Ann Ar-bor: University of Michigan, 1990), 259–85; Felicia Gordon and Máire Cross, *Early French Feminisms, 1830–1940: A Passion for Liberty* (Cheltenham, UK, and Brookfield, VT: Edward Elgar, 1996), chs. on Deroin, Flora Tristan, and Pauline Roland.

12. Sand, *Lettres d'un voyageur*, 165–83. Thompson, "Creating Boundaries,"

102–27; Courtivron, "Weak Men and Fatal Women," 210–27. See Chapter 5, above.

13. Sand, *Story of My Life*, 1036, 1034.

14. Ibid., 1034–35.

15. Ibid., 1036–37.

16. For a sensitive analysis of Sand's mutable feminine identity and her complex, intermittent relationship to republicanism and to politics, see Perrot, "Présentation," 39–44.

17. D'Agoult, *Mémoires, souvenirs et journaux*, 2:22.

18. Ibid., 23–24.

19. Ibid., 25–26. In her journal d'Agoult went further in her analysis of Lamennais's limitations as a republican ("he is condemned to be an amateur republican"), in particular his failure to exploit Sand's willingness to work in partnership with him on the dissemination of his ideas. D'Agoult believed that Lamennais missed a golden opportunity to benefit from Sand's literary talent, from her offer to put her writing skills at his disposal, "to make herself in a sense the handtool [*le manoeuvre*] of his thought. He did not realize that he could have given his impetus to the writer most capable of popularizing his ideas and presenting them in a form that was less austere and more lively." D'Agoult maintains that Lamennais mishandled Sand, that he contradicted her beliefs (notably about the need to legalize divorce), and that he failed to convince her of his own position. But d'Agoult suggests that had their partnership actually worked out, Sand would have contributed more than just "translation" skills to this joint enterprise. "These two intelligences that, in modifying one another, would have approached the truth, perhaps as much as is humanly possible, will remain incomplete." Ibid., 120–21.

20. Ibid., 26. According to d'Agoult, Lamennais was also unable to sustain a leading role among male republicans. In 1848 d'Agoult claims that she brought together Lamennais and Lamartine, at Lamartine's request, in her home to discuss the constitution of the Second Republic. After Lamennais's proposed constitution met with indifference on the part of Lamartine, Lamennais resigned from the Constitutional Committee. Ibid., 25–27.

21. Saman, *Les Enchantements de Prudence*, 149, 205–6, 210, 216–17. Allart deplored the demise of the rotten boroughs because she thought that lords often put highly qualified men into office by this means: "I viewed with regret the destruction of the aristocratic boroughs to which on occasion great talents had been named, formed by the aristocracy and its supporters." Ibid., 217.

22. Letter from Allart to d'Agoult, 22 April 1851, in Bibliothèque Nationale, Manuscrits, N.A.F. 25185, 218. In her book on Staël, Allart assesses her contribution to French politics in this way: "To wish liberal institutions for France for its own happiness, to employ all the power of her work and reason to make France understand the importance of them and to prove that France is worthy of them … that we should have a larger number of citizens with her good faith!" Hortense Allart, *Lettres sur les ouvrages de Madame de Staël* (Paris: Bossange père, 1824), 137. Admiring references to Staël as a political theorist increase over time in Allart's letters to d'Agoult and to Sainte-Beuve.

23. Saman, *Les Enchantements de Prudence*, 255–56; Billy, *Hortense et ses amants*; Uffenbeck, *The Life and Writings of Hortense Allart*, 177–80, 200–201, 273–74. Letter from d'Agoult to Allart, 16 June 1851, in Bibliothèque Nationale, Manuscrits, N.A.F. 25181, 157. Letter from Allart to d'Agoult, 18 June 1851, in Bibliothèque Nationale, Manuscrits, N.A.F. 25185, 225; "We have lost that poor Madame Roland. . . . I am devastated by the death of this person." Letter from Allart to d'Agoult, 17 January 1853, in Bibliothèque Nationale, Manuscrits, N.A.F. 25185, 248.

24. Letter from Allart to Sainte-Beuve, 31 March 1845, in Allart, *Lettres inédites à Sainte-Beuve*, 95.

25. Girardin, *Lettres parisiennes*, 13 June 1841, in *Oeuvres complètes*, 5:174–77.

26. *Lettres parisiennes*, 11 July 1847, in ibid., 460.

27. *Lettres parisiennes*, 4 April 1847, in ibid., 438.

28. Cited in Séché, *Delphine Gay*, 177. Also quoted in Malo, *La Gloire du Vicomte de Launay*, 237.

29. George Sand, *Indiana*, 184.

30. Letter of Allart to Sainte-Beuve, 20 October 1843; and 2 March 1844; in *Lettres inédites à Sainte-Beuve*, 83, 86.

31. Saman, *Les Enchantements de Prudence*, 308, 311–12.

32. Séché, *Delphine Gay*, 72; Malo, *La Gloire du Vicomte de Launay*, 1–4, 15–17, 146; Martin-Fugier, *La Vie élégante*, 279.

33. Girardin, "Le vote," 1:431.

34. Gautier, "Madame Emile de Girardin," 1:v, xix; D'Heilly, *Madame E. de Girardin (Delphine Gay)*, 56–57; Martin-Fugier, *La Vie élégante*, 283; Malo, *La Gloire du Vicomte de Launay*, 111.

35. Emile de Girardin was most concerned about ending discrimination against illegitimate children by endowing mothers with more authority over children. He anticipates social peace and justice "when finally woman will have fully won equality, as she has already won liberty." Emile de Girardin, *La Liberté dans le mariage par l'égalité des enfants devant la mère* (Paris: Librairie nouvelle, 1854), 9.

36. Girardin et al., *La Croix de Berny*, 132–33.

37. Slama, "Femmes ecrivains," Albistur and Armogathe, *Histoire du féminisme français*, 279–88.

38. Sand wrote that Dudevant considered her "an idiot," and that "he managed to make [her] feel so strongly the superiority of his reason and intelligence, that for a long time [she] was overwhelmed by it and intimidated in front of others." Sand, *Story of My Life*, 841.

39. Letter to Michel de Bourges, 22 October 1835, in Sand, *Correspondance*, 3:75–90; "Procès de séparation de corps provoqué par Mme Dudevant," *Gazette des Tribunaux*, 11th year, no. 3391 (30–31 July 1836): 873–74; Edouard Maynial, "Le Procès en séparation de George Sand," *Mercure de France* (15 November 1906): 321–41.

40. Sand, *Story of My Life*, 1009.

41. Ibid., 1058.

42. Ibid., 1065.

43. D'Agoult, *Essai sur la liberté*, 71.

44. Ibid., 72.

45. Ibid., 95, 98.

46. Ibid., 98.

47. Ibid., 97, 99.

48. George Sand, *Lettres à Marcie*, in *Les Sept cordes de la lyre*, new ed. (Paris: Michel Lévy frères, 1869 [orig. 1837]), 228. I am deeply grateful to Frederick Kluck for sharing with me his copy of this text.

49. D'Agoult, *Essai sur la liberté*, 105.

50. George Sand, "Réponse à diverses objections," 6 December 1844, in *Questions politiques et sociales* (Paris: Editions d'Aujourd'hui, 1976), 94.

51. Sand, *Lettres à Marcie*, 229.

52. Ibid., 231.

53. D'Agoult, *Essai sur la liberté*, 104–5.

54. Albistur and Armogathe, *Histoire du féminisme français*, 289.

55. Allart, *La Femme et la démocratie de nos temps*, 12.

56. D'Agoult, *Essai sur la liberté*, 105.

57. Allart, *La Femme et la démocratie de nos temps*, 122.

58. D'Agoult, *Mémoires, souvenirs et journaux*, 1:177.

59. Sand, *Story of My Life*, 1010–11.

60. Mme Prudence de Saman, *Derniers enchantements: Gertrude. Harold. Le Jeune comte Henri. Lettres de Béranger* (Paris: Michel Lévy frères, 1874), 62.

61. Ibid., 190.

62. William Fortescue, "Divorce Debated and Deferred: The French Debate on Divorce and the Failure of the Crémieux Divorce Bill in 1848," *French History* 7 (1993): 137–62; Theresa McBride, "Public Authority and Private Lives: Divorce after the French Revolution," *French Historical Studies* 17 (spring 1992): 747–68. See also Roderick Phillips, *Putting Asunder: A History of Divorce in Western Society* (New York: Cambridge University Press, 1988), 422–28.

63. Moses and Rabine, *Feminism, Socialism, and French Romanticism*; Fortescue, "Divorce Debated and Deferred"; Riot-Sarcey, *La Démocratie à l'épreuve des femmes*, 218–20, 224–25.

64. D'Agoult, *Essai sur la liberté*, 124–25.

65. Sand, *Story of My Life*, 1067.

66. D'Agoult, *Esquisses morales*, 53.

67. Sand, *Story of My Life*, 378–79.

68. Riot-Sarcey, *La Démocratie à l'épreuve des femmes*, 70.

69. D'Agoult, *Esquisses morales*, 117.

70. Ibid., 121–22.

71. Sand, *Story of My Life*, 854.

72. George Sand, *Jacques*, in *Romans 1830* (Paris[?]: Presses de la Cité, 1991), 995.

73. D'Agoult, *Mémoires, souvenirs et journaux*, 1:317.

74. Saman, *Les Enchantements de Prudence*, 1.

75. Ibid., 269.

76. Letter from Allart to Sainte-Beuve, 20 October 1843, in Allart, *Lettres inédites à Sainte-Beuve*, 84.

77. Allart wrote to d'Agoult: "The day will come, after obtaining freedom of the press and individual freedom, when we will be accorded the freedom of giving birth." Letter of 7 May 1839, Bibliothèque Nationale, Fonds Daniel Ollivier, N.A.F. 25185, 83.

78. Saman, *Les Enchantements de Prudence*, 276.

79. Ibid., 302. For an analysis of the feminist and subversive narrative style of this story, see Rabine, "Feminist Writers in French Romanticism."

80. Sand, *Lettres à Marcie*, 176.

81. Saman, *Les Enchantements de Prudence*, 46. Allart uses the same line in her novel *Gertrude*, in Saman, *Derniers Enchantements*, 187.

82. Sand, *Story of My Life*, 1011. Sand's interpretation of sexual love is very similar to that of the socialist Pierre Leroux, who greatly influenced Sand's thinking. Fraisse, "A Philosophical History of Sexual Difference," 63.

83. Letter from Allart to Sainte-Beuve, 18 April 1844, in Allart, *Nouvelles Lettres à Sainte-Beuve*, 18.

84. Sand, *Horace*, 400, 402, 377.

85. Letter of Sand to François Buloz, 15 September 1841, in Sand, *Correspondance*, 5:418–23.

86. Girardin, *La Canne de M. de Balzac*, in *Oeuvres complètes*, 2:214, 223, 235, 243.

87. Ezdinli, "*La Canne de M. de Balzac.*"

88. Allart, *Settimia*, xxiv–xxv, 201.

89. Sand, *Lélia*, 479, 481, 509–10.

90. D'Agoult, *Nélida*, 207, 213, 251.

91. Allart, *Settimia*, 1:vi.

92. Sand, *Lettres à Marcie*, 173.

93. Whitney Walton, "Literary Production and the Rearticulation of Home Space in the Works of George Sand, Marie d'Agoult, and Hortense Allart," *Women's History Review* 6 (1997): 115–32.

94. Sand, *Story of My Life*, 1068–69.

95. Ibid., 1083.

96. Ibid.

97. Ibid.

98. Saman, *Les Enchantements de Prudence*, 103.

99. Ibid., 234.

100. Letter of 21 December 1841, in Allart, *Lettres inédites à Sainte-Beuve*, 34. Just two years later Allart's desire to share her life with a man led her into a brief marriage of one year's duration. Thereafter, she was scathing in her critique of the institution of marriage in terms of how it subordinated women. See, for example, Saman, *Les Enchantements de Prudence*, 311–12.

101. D'Agoult, *Mémoires, souvenirs et journaux*, 2:40.

102. Ibid., 41.

103. Ibid., 40.

104. Ibid., 1:202.

105. Sand, *Story of My Life*, 1081.

106. Ibid., 1020.

107. Ibid., 1018–21, 1073–74, 1082–83, 1098–99, 1101–2. Sand's letters, especially following the separation trial of 1836, often address her thoughts and actions regarding her children's education and their upbringing in general, to say nothing of the letters she wrote to Maurice and Solange.

108. D'Agoult, *Mèmoires, souvenirs et journaux*, 2:225–41.

109. Vier, *La Comtesse d'Agoult et son temps*, 2:15, 137–40.

110. Letter from Allart to d'Agoult, 1839 (no date), in Bibliothèque Nationale, Manuscrits, Fonds Daniel Ollivier, N.A.F. 25185, 92.

111. Séché, *Hortense Allart de Méritens*, 77.

112. Ibid., 63–67.

113. Letter from Allart to d'Agoult, 1844, in Bibliothèque Nationale, Manuscrits, N.A.F. 25185, 119.

114. Letter to Charlotte Marliani, 25 June 1844, in Sand, *Correspondance*, 6:571.

115. Dupêchez, *Marie d'Agoult*, 206–7, 230–36, 245–51, 259–60, 262, 267–68, 298; Vier, *La comtesse d'Agoult et son temps*.

116. Allart, *Histoire de la République d'Athènes*; Letter to Sainte-Beuve, 1 September 1863, and footnote 1, in Allart, *Nouvelles Lettres à Sainte-Beuve*, 155–56.

117. Malo, *Une Muse et sa mère*, 299.

118. Girardin, "La Fête de Noël," in *Oeuvres complètes*, 1:363.

119. Malo, *La Gloire du Vicomte de Launay*, 278; Malo, *Une Muse et sa mère*, 299; D'Heilly, *Madame E. de Girardin (Delphine Gay)*, 83.

120. *Esprit de Madame de Girardin* (Paris: Hetzel, 1863?), 349–50.

121. Sand, *Story of My Life*, 1087.

122. Scott, *Only Paradoxes to Offer*; Riot-Sarcey, *La Démocratie à l'épreuve des femmes*, 190–93, 202–3; Moses, *French Feminism in the Nineteenth Century*.

Chapter 7: Writing and Rewriting the Revolution

1. Letter from Sand to Charles Poncy, 8 March 1848, in Sand, *Correspondance*, 8:330.

2. Letter from Sand to Frédéric Girerd, 6 March 1848, in ibid., 324.

3. Letter from Sand to Charles Poncy, 28 March 1848, in ibid., 372.

4. Agulhon, *The Republican Experiment*.

5. Girardin, *Lettres parisiennes*, 11 July 1847, in *Oeuvres complètes*, 5:454–63.

6. Letter from Sand to Allart, 16 February 1848, in Sand, *Correspondance*, 8:292.

7. Letter from Sand to Maurice, 18 February 1848, in Sand, *Correspondance*, 8:299.

8. Vier, *La Comtesse d'Agoult et son temps*, 3:15; Saman, *Les Enchantements de Prudence*, 320–21; D'Heilly, *Madame E. de Girardin (Delphine Gay)*, 70; Malo, *La Gloire du Vicomte de Launay*, 213–14.

9. Malo, *La Gloire du Vicomte de Launay*, 214–16; Pierre Pellisier, *Emile de Girardin, Prince de la presse* (Paris: Denoel, 1985).

10. Letter to René Vallet de Villeneuve, 4 March 1848, in Sand, *Correspondance*, 8:316.

11. Letter to Adolphe Cremieux, 2[?] March 1848; letter to Frédéric Girerd, 6 March 1848; letter to Pauline Viardot, 17 March 1848; in Sand, *Correspondance*, 8:308–9, 325, 351.

12. Letters of 21 May 1848, (no date) 1848, and 15 March 1848, in Allart, *Lettres inédites à Sainte-Beuve*, 309, 300, 295; Saman, *Les Enchantements de Prudence*, 321–30.

13. Sand, *Politique et polémiques*, 221–413.

14. Vier, *La Comtesse d'Agoult et son temps*, 3:14–15, 24–25; Daniel Stern, *Lettres républicaines* (Paris: Imprimerie Edouard Proux et Cie, 1848), letter of 11 June to F. Lamennais, 3; letter of 4 June to Fanny Lewald, 15.

15. Sand, "Aux riches" and "Histoire de la France écrite sous la dictée de Blaise Bonnin," in *Politique et polémiques*, 230, 264.

16. Letter of 23 September to the workers of Paris, Stern, *Lettres républicaines*, 1.

17. Sand, "Hier et aujourd'hui," in *Politique et polémiques*, 241.

18. Letter from Sand to Charles Poncy, 8 March 1848, in Sand, *Correspondance*, 8:330.

19. Letter from Solange Clésinger to George Sand, 20 March 1848, in Sand, *Correspondance*, 8:345.

20. Letter from Sand to Maurice Dudevant-Sand, 16–17 April 1848, in Sand, *Correspondance*, 8:418–19; Sand, "Souvenirs de mars-avril 1848," in *Oeuvres autobiographiques*, 2:1187–89; Agulhon, *The Republican Experiment*, 42–43.

21. Letter from Sand to René Vallet de Villeneuve, 20 May 1848, in Sand, *Correspondance*, 8:464.

22. Letter from Sand to Maurice Dudevant-Sand, 23 March 1848, in Sand, *Correspondance*, 8:359; letter from Sand to Charles Duvernet, early March 1848; letter from Sand to Frédéric Girerd, 6 March 1848, in ibid., 315, 324.

23. Sand, "Bulletin de la République," in *Politique et polémiques*, 402.

24. Letter from Sand to Frédéric Girerd, 7 August 1848, in Sand, *Correspondance*, 8:589.

25. Letter from Sand to Marc Caussidière, 20 May 1848; and letter to René Vallet de Villeneuve, 20 May 1848; in Sand, *Correspondance*, 8:466–67.

26. Letter from Sand to Richard Monckton-Milnes, 9 June 1848, in Sand, *Correspondance*, 25:565.

27. Sand, *Story of My Life*, 375.

28. Girardin, *Lettres parisiennes*, 13 May 1848, in *Oeuvres complètes*, 5:464–73.

29. Ibid., 474–77.

30. *Lettres parisiennes*, 30 June 1848, in ibid., 5:477–83; Malo, *La Gloire du Vicomte de Launay*, 225–28.

31. Girardin, *Lettres parisiennes*, 3 September 1848, in *Oeuvres complètes*, 5:483–95.

32. Girardin, "1848. 24 juin–24 novembre," in ibid., 1:439–41.

33. Letter of 29 June 1848, in Allart, *Lettres inédites à Sainte-Beuve*, 313–15.

34. Letters of 22 August, 29 June, and of (no date) 1848, in ibid., 323, 315,

317, 320, 322; Allart, letters of 13 December 1848, 17 December 1848, *Nouvelles Lettres à Sainte-Beuve*, 64, 68.

35. Allart, *Second petit livre*, 6, 9, 27; Allart, *Essai sur l'histoire politique*, 2:335–40.

36. Marie d'Agoult, *Histoire de la Révolution de 1848* (Paris: Gustave Sandré, 1850), 1:vii. In the preface to the second edition of the book, published in 1862, d'Agoult makes a further claim to objectivity that is highly dubious and disingenuous. She asserts that as a woman she had no stake in the triumph of any faction or position, that she was not affiliated with republicans at the outset, and that she did not aspire to exercise power through influence: "Whatever the outcome of an imminent revolution, I had little to fear, and I had nothing to expect for myself. Under all regimes my sex prohibits me from having political ambitions; no more was permitted to me the feminine covetousness of power for my friends. If I was removed from the party that the revolution would overthrow, I neither belonged to the party that was preparing its triumph." D'Agoult, *Histoire de la Révolution de 1848*, 2d ed. (Paris: Charpentier, 1862), 1:ix.

37. D'Agoult, *Histoire de la Révolution*, 2d ed., 1:5.

38. *Histoire de la Révolution* (1850), 1:273.

39. Ibid., 2:13–14.

40. Ibid., 126.

41. Ibid., 388.

42. Ibid., 3:346.

43. Bergman-Carton focuses on the sources of caricatures of Sand and Girardin from representations by other artists, but much of the women's specific political and literary activity is absent from her analysis; Riot-Sarcey, *La Démocratie à l'épreuve des femmes*, 177, 204, 215–20, 235, 250. Riot-Sarcey mentions only caricatures of socialist women, including Niboyet and Deroin, which is consistent with her effort to present bourgeois republicans, such as Sand and d'Agoult, to be wholly antagonistic to socialist feminists. I see the relationship between the two different groups of women to be more nuanced, and evidence of greater affinity is the fact that Sand and Girardin were caricatured as were Niboyet and Deroin. Bergman-Carton, *The Woman of Ideas in French Art*, esp. 45–64. See also Powell and Childs, *Femmes d'esprit*.

44. This caricature appeared in *Le Monde illustré* in 1884 on the occasion of the inauguration of a statue to Sand in La Châtre near her home of Nohant. According to the accompanying article, the caricature had never before been published or even seen outside of the Berry region. "We owe receipt of it to M. Adolphe Jullien. It is a caricature *au lavis* [a technique using Chinese ink] done in 1848 at Bourges probably by one named Gaucher, and that makes fun of the illustrious writer regarding all the people, relatives or friends, that she was able to place [in positions] after the Revolution of 1848 in Cher, in Indre, and even beyond. From under her skirts emerge all her political children, in the dress or with the insignias of the function they were to exercise." *Le Monde illustré*, 28e année, no. 1429 (16 August 1884): 112.

45. Le Rat, "Silhouette bibliographique: *Lettres au Peuple* par George Sand,"

La Silhouette 5 (9 April 1848): 1–2; Ahasverus, "Profils républicains: George Sand," *La Mode* 19 (November 1848): 979–88.

46. Malo, *La Gloire du Vicomte de Launay*, 230–31; the caricatures are reproduced on 225, 241, 257.

47. Alexandre Dufai, "A Madame Delphine Gay de Girardin," *L'Illustration, journal universel* 12 (2 December 1848): 210–11. See also Anonymous, "A Madame Delphine Gay de Girardin," *Revue comique* 15 (1848–49): 31.

48. Reddy, "Condottieri of the Pen."

49. Thomas, *Les Femmes de 1848*, 40, 68, 78; Riot-Sarcey, *La Démocratie à l'épreuve des femmes*, 204–5; Moses, *French Feminism in the Nineteenth Century*, 140–41.

50. Sand, "Au Rédacteur de *La Réforme*: Au Rédacteur de *La Vraie République*," in *Politique et polémiques*, 532.

51. Sand, "Bulletin de la République" and "Aux membres du Comité Central," in ibid., 392–94, 534, 536–39.

52. Sand, "Revue politique et morale de la semaine" and "Aux membres du comité central," in ibid., 448, 541.

53. Ibid., 448, 541–42. See also Georges Lubin, "George Sand en 1848," in *George Sand Papers: Conference Proceedings, 1976* (New York: AMS Press, 1980), 28–41; Louis Devance, "Femme, famille, travail et morale sexuelle dans l'idéologie de 1848," *Romantisme* 13–14 (1976): 79–103.

54. D'Agoult, *Histoire de la Révolution*, 2:190.

55. Ibid., 192.

56. Girardin, *Lettres parisiennes*, 13 May 1848, in *Oeuvres complètes*, 5:468–69.

57. *Lettres parisiennes*, 4 April 1847; 13 May 1848, in ibid., 443, 470.

58. D'Agoult, *Histoire de la Révolution*, 2:187.

59. Allart, *La Femme et la démocratie de nos temps*, 122–23.

60. Letter from Allart to d'Agoult, 23 December 1869, Bibliothèque Nationale, Manuscrits, Fonds Daniel Ollivier, N.A.F. 25185, 434.

61. Letter of 13 February 1850, in Allart, *Nouvelles Lettres à Sainte-Beuve*, 91.

62. Girardin, *Lettres parisiennes*, 13 May 1848, in *Oeuvres complètes*, 5:470.

63. Letter from Sand to Théophile Thoré, 28 May 1848, in Sand, *Correspondance*, 8:481.

64. Letter from Sand to Hortense Allart, 12 June 1848, in ibid., 8:507.

65. Letter from Sand to Jean Dessoliaire, 2 November 1848, in ibid., 8:685.

66. On another level, however, Schor argues that Sand used historical context to show that sexual identity is constructed, and therefore mutable, and that sexual difference has both natural and historical origins; Schor, "Reading Double," 248–69.

67. Margaret Cohen, "A Woman's Place: *La Petite Fadette* vs. *La Voix des Femmes*," *L'Esprit créateur* 29 (summer 1989): 26–38.

68. George Sand, *La Petite Fadette* (Paris: Flammarion, 1967), 239, 241.

69. George Sand, *Nanon* (Meylan: Les Editions de l'Aurore, 1987), 189–90, 233, 154.

70. Letter from Sand to Allart, 12 June 1848, in *Correspondance*, 8:508.

71. D'Agoult, *Histoire de la Révolution de 1848*, 2d ed., 1:viii–ix.

72. Rice, "Masculin/Féminin"; Vier, *La Comtesse d'Agoult et son temps*, 3:12–18.

73. D'Agoult, *Histoire de la Révolution de 1848*, 1st ed., 1:188.

74. Ibid., 1:204. D'Agoult's sympathetic portrayal of even the most demeaned of women in the revolution contrasts sharply with the demonizations of revolutionary females by men in 1848, as well as in the first French Revolution and in the Commune of 1871. Neil Hertz, "Medusa's Head: Male Hysteria under Political Pressure," *Representations* 4 (fall 1983): 27–54; Lynn Hunt, "The Many Bodies of Marie Antoinette: Political Pornography and the Problem of the Feminine in the French Revolution," in *Eroticism and the Body Politic*, ed. Lynn Hunt (Baltimore, MD, and London: Johns Hopkins University Press, 1991), 108–30; Gay L. Gullickson, "La Pétroleuse: Representing Revolution," *Feminist Studies* 17 (summer 1991): 241–65.

75. Letter from d'Agoult to Allart, 5 April 1853, in Bibliothèque Nationale, Manuscrits, Fonds Daniel Olliver, N.A.F. 25181, 171.

76. Girardin, *C'est la Faute du mari*, in *Oeuvres complètes*, 6:249–50.

77. Girardin, *Lettres parisiennes*, 13 May 1848, in ibid., 5:469.

78. Girardin, *C'est la Faute du mari*, in ibid., 6:249–50.

79. Girardin, *Une Femme qui déteste son mari*, in ibid., 6:468, 470, 485.

80. Allart, *Essai sur l'histoire politique*, 1:vi; 2:349.

81. Ibid., 351–54.

82. Allart, *Histoire de la République d'Athènes*, 24–25, 29, 50, 410.

83. Ibid., 190–91, 193.

84. Ibid., 357, 374, 367, 369.

Chapter 8: Conclusion

1. Malo, *La Gloire du Vicomte de Launay*, 232–77; D'Heilly, *Madame E. de Girardin (Delphine Gay)*, 71–77, 84–88; Séché, *Delphine Gay*, 176–96; Lamartine, "Madame de Girardin," 182–87.

2. Letter from Sand to Edmond Plauchut, 24 March 1871, in Sand, *Correspondance*, 22:350. Three months later, to Plauchut again, she exclaimed, "Don't defend me when I am accused of not being *sufficiently republican*; to the contrary, tell them that I am not [republican] in their manner. They have lost and they will always lose the republic. . . . They are arrogant, narrow, pedantic, and never question what they can or cannot do." The same themes of 1848 appear in Sand's interpretation of 1871; Sand abhors violence as a means of establishing a republic, and she thinks that republican leaders need to be more consultative with their constituents and less prone to factionalism. Letter from Sand to Edmond Plauchut, 16 June 1871, in Sand, *Correspondance*, 22:424. Karénine, *George Sand*, 4:350–556.

3. Vier, *La Comtesse d'Agoult et son temps*, vols. 4–6; Phyllis Stock-Morton, "Daniel Stern, Historian," *History of European Ideas* 8 (1987): 489–501; Dupêchez, *Marie d'Agoult*, chs. 9–11; Letter from d'Agoult to Allart, 1854 (no date), Bibliothèque Nationale, Manuscrits, Fonds Daniel Ollivier, N.A.F. 25181, 183.

4. Uffenbeck, *The Life and Writings of Hortense Allart*, chs. 10–11; Eloge to d'Agoult by Allart, Bibliothèque Nationale, Manuscrits, Fonds Daniel Ollivier, N.A.F. 25181, 500; Séché, *Hortense Allart de Méritens*, 25–30.

5. Scott, *Only Paradoxes to Offer*; Moses, *French Feminism in the Nineteenth Century*; Riot-Sarcey, *La Démocratie à l'épreuve des femmes*.

☞ Selected Bibliography

Primary Sources

Correspondence between Marie d'Agoult and Hortense Allart, Bibliothèque Nationale. Manuscrits. Fonds Daniel Ollivier. N.A.F. 25181 and 25185.

Book reviews in various newspapers:
L'Artiste, Le Charivari, Le Constitutionnel, Le Courrier de Paris, Le Figaro, Le Globe, Journal littéraire, L'Illustration, Journal des Débats politiques et littéraires, La Mode, La Presse, Revue de Paris, La Revue des deux mondes, La Revue Indépendante, Le Semeur, Le Temps

Ahasverus. "Profils républicains: George Sand." La Mode 19 (November 1848): 979–88.

Allart, Hortense [Mlle A. H.]. Conjuration d'Amboise. Paris: A. Marc, 1822.

——— [Mme Prudence de Saman]. Derniers enchantements: Gertrude. Harold. Le Jeune comte Henri. Lettres de Béranger. Paris: Michel Lévy frères, 1874.

——— [Mme P. de Saman]. Les Enchantements de Prudence. 3d ed. Paris: Michel Lévy frères, 1873.

———. Essai sur l'histoire politique depuis l'invasion des barbares jusqu'en 1848. 2 vols. Paris: Just Rouvier, 1857.

———. La Femme et la démocratie de nos temps. Paris: Delaunay, 1836.

———. Histoire de la République d'Athènes. Paris: n.p., 1866.

———. Histoire de la République de Florence. Part 1. Paris: Moutardier, 1837.

———. Histoire de la République de Florence. 2 vols. Paris: Garnier, 1843.

———. Lettres inédites à Sainte-Beuve (1841–1848). Edited by Léon Séché. 2d ed. Paris: Société du Mercure de France, 1908.

———. Lettres sur les ouvrages de Madame de Staël. Paris: Bossange père, 1824.

———. Les Nouveaux Enchantements. Paris: Michel Lévy frères, 1873.

———. Nouvelles Lettres à Sainte-Beuve (1832–1864). Edited by Lorin A. Uffenbeck. Geneva: Droz, 1965.

———. Novum Organum, ou sainteté philosophique. Paris: Garnier frères, 1857.

———. Premier petit livre: Etudes diverses. Paris: Renault, 1850.

———. Second petit livre: Etudes diverses. Paris: Renault, 1850.

———. Settimia. 2 vols. Brussels: Ad. Wahlen et Cie, 1836.

———. Troisième petit livre: Etudes diverses. Paris: Renault, 1851.

Anonymous. "Feuilleton du Journal des Débats. Théâtre-français: *Judith*, tragé-die en trois actes." *Journal des Débats politiques et littéraires* (1 May 1843): 1–2.

———. "Galerie de Portraits: Lélia." *Revue critique* 4 (March 1840): 2–3.

———. "A Madame Delphine Gay de Girardin." *Revue comique* 15 (1848–49): 31.

Balzac, Honoré. *Béatrix*. Paris: Gallimard, 1979 [orig. 1839].

———. *Illusions perdues*. Paris: Librairie Générale Française / Le Livre de po-che, 1972 [orig. 1843].

Barbey d'Aurévilly, Jules. *Les Bas-bleus*. Genève: Slatkine Reprints, 1968 [orig. 1878].

Blanc, Louis. *The History of Ten Years, 1830–1840*. 2 vols. London: Chapman and Hall, 1845.

Code Napoleon, or the French Civil Code. Literally translated from the original and offi-cial edition. Published at Paris in 1804. Reprint, Baton Rouge, LA: Claitor's Book Store, 1960.

d'Agoult, Marie [Daniel Stern]. *Dante et Goethe: Dialogues*. Paris: Didier, 1866.

———. "Ecrivains modernes de l'Allemagne: Mme d'Arnim." *Revue des deux mondes* 6 (1844): 265–97.

———. *Esquisses morales: Pensées, réflexions et maximes*. 3d ed. Paris: J. Techener, 1859.

———. *Essai sur la liberté*. Paris: Aymot, 1847.

———. *Histoire de la Révolution de 1848*. 3 vols. Paris: Gustave Sandré, 1850–53.

———. *Histoire de la Révolution de 1848*. 2d ed. 3 vols. Paris: Charpentier, 1862.

———. *Histoire des commencements de la République aux Pays-bas, 1581–1625*. Paris: Michel Lévy, 1872.

———. *Lettres républicaines*. Paris: Imprimerie Edouard Proux et Cie., 1848.

———. [Daniel Stern] *Lettres républicaines du Second Empire*. Edited by Jacques Vier. Paris: Les Editions du Cèdre, 1951 [orig. 1850–64].

———. *Mémoires 1833–1854*. Paris: Calmann Lévy, 1927.

———. *Mémoires, souvenirs et journaux de la Comtesse d'Agoult (Daniel Stern)*. Edited by Charles F. Dupêchez. 2 vols. Paris: Mercure de France, 1990.

———. *Mes souvenirs, 1806–1833*. Paris: Calmann Lévy, 1877.

———. *Nélida*. Paris: Calmann-Lévy, 1987 [orig. 1846].

———. *Valentia. Hervé. Julien. La Boite aux lettres: Ninon au couvent*. Paris: Cal-mann Lévy, 1883.

———. "Variétés." *La Presse* (9 January 1841): 3 [review of Sand, *Le Compagnon du Tour de France*].

Dufai, Alexandre. "A Madame Delphine Gay de Girardin." *L'Illustration, jour-nal universel* 12 (2 December 1848): 210–11.

Esprit de Mme. de Girardin. Paris: Hetzel, 1863.

"Femmes de lettres françaises contemporaines." *L'Illustration* 69 (22 June 1844): 264–67.

Feuillide, C. "Les Bas-bleus: Fragment." *L'Europe littéraire* 69 (9 August 1833):4.

Girardin, Delphine Gay de. *Oeuvres complètes de Madame Emile de Girardin*. 6 vols. Paris: Henri Plon, 1860–61.

Girardin, Emile de. *La Liberté dans le mariage par l'égalité des enfants devant la mère*. Paris: Librairie nouvelle, 1854.

Girardin, Mme Emile de, Théophile Gautier, Jules Sandeau, and Méry. *La Croix de Berny*. New ed. Paris: Calmann Lévy, 1882 [orig. 1846].

Janin, Jules. "Le Bas-bleu." In *Les Français peints par eux-mêmes: Encyclopédie morale du dix-neuvième siècle*, vol. 5, 201–31. Paris: L. Curmer, 1842.

———. "Galerie contemporaine. George Sand." *La Mode* 24 (September 1835): 177–83.

———. "Mme George Sand." In *Les Femmes célèbres contemporaines françaises*, 439–55. Paris: Le Bailly, 1843.

Lagenevais. F. de. "Simples Essais d'histoire littéraire. III: Le Feuilleton—Lettres parisiennes." *Revue des deux mondes*, sér. 2, no. 4 (1843): 133–50.

Lamartine, Alphonse de. "Madame de Girardin." In *Portraits et salons romantiques*, 153–87. Paris: Le Goupy, 1927.

Latour, Antoine de. "Les Femmes poètes au XIXe siècle. II: Madame Emile de Girardin." *Revue de Paris* 25 (1835): 191–202.

Lerminier. "Poètes et romanciers contemporains. Seconde phase. I: Mme. Sand." *Revue des deux mondes*, nouv. sér. 6, no. 14 (1844): 84–117.

Liszt, Franz. *Correspondance de Liszt et de la Comtesse d'Agoult, 1833–1840*. Edited by Daniel Ollivier. 2 vols. Paris: Bernard Grasset, 1933–34.

Molènes, G. de. "Simples Essais d'histoire littéraire. I: Les femmes poètes." *Revue des deux mondes* 31, no. 3 (1842): 48–76.

"National Convention Outlaws Clubs and Popular Societies of Women." In *Women in Revolutionary Paris, 1789–1795*, edited by Darline Gay Levy, Harriet Branson Applewhite, and Mary Durham Johnson, 215–17. Urbana: University of Illinois Press, 1979.

Rat, Le. "Silhouette bibliographique: *Lettres au Peuple* par George Sand." *La Silhouette* 5 (9 April 1848): 1–2.

Ronchaud, L. de. "Du génie au dix-neuvième siècle: Daniel Stern." *La Libre Recherche: Revue universelle*, 2e année, 6 (1857): 396–416.

Sainte-Beuve, C. A. "Madame Emile de Girardin." In *Causeries du lundi*, 3d ed., 3:384–406. Paris: Garnier frères, no date.

Sand, George. *Le Compagnon du tour de France*. Grenoble: Presses universitaires de Grenoble, 1988 [orig. 1840].

———. *Consuelo: La Comtesse de Rudolstadt*. 3 vols. Grenoble: Les Editions de l'Aurore, 1991 [orig. 1842–43; 1844].

———. *Correspondance*. Edited by Georges Lubin. 25 vols. Paris: Garnier frères, 1964–91.

———. *Horace*. In *Vies d'artistes*. Paris[?]: Presses de la Cité, 1992 [orig. 1841].

———. *Indiana*. Translated by Eleanor Hochman. New York: Penguin Books, 1993 [orig. 1832].

———. *Jacques*. In *Romans 1830*. Paris[?]: Presses de la Cité, 1991 [orig. 1834].

———. *Lélia*. rev. ed. Paris: Garnier, 1960 [orig. 1839].

———. *Lettres à Marcie*. In *Les Sept cordes de la lyre*, 165–234. New ed. Paris: Michel Lévy frères, 1869 [orig. 1837].

———. *Lettres d'un voyageur*. New ed. Paris: Calmann-Lévy, 1927 [orig. 1834–36; 1837].

——. *The Miller of Angibault*. Translated by Donna Dickenson. Oxford and New York: Oxford University Press, 1995 [orig. 1845].

——. *Nanon*. Meylan: Les Editions de l'Aurore, 1987 [orig. 1871].

——. *Oeuvres autobiographiques*. Edited by Georges Lubin. 2 vols. Paris: Gallimard, 1971.

——. *Le Péché de Monsieur Antoine*. Meylan: Les Editions de l'Aurore, 1982 [orig. 1847].

——. *La Petite Fadette*. Paris: Flammarion, 1967 [orig. 1848–1849].

——. *Politique et polémiques (1843–1850)*. Paris. Imprimerie nationale, 1997.

——. *Questions politiques et sociales*. Paris: Editions d'Aujourd'hui, 1976.

——. *Story of My Life: The Autobiography of George Sand*. A group translation. Edited by Thelma Jurgrau. Albany: State University of New York Press, 1991 [orig. 1854–55].

——. *Valentine*. Meylan: Les Editions de l'Aurore, 1988 [orig. 1832].

——. "Variétés: Madame Hortense Allart." *Le Courrier de Paris* 255 (23 December 1857): 3–4.

Scherer, Ed. "Variétés: Daniel Stern." *Le Temps*, 6e année (18 September 1866): 3.

Simon-Viennot, Mme. "Célébrités contemporaines: Influence de Georges [sic] Sand." *Journal des mères et des jeunes filles* (août 1844): 200–211.

Soulié, Frédéric. *Physiologie du bas-bleu*. Paris: Aubert, 1841.

Tocqueville, Alexis de. *The Recollections of Alexis de Tocqueville*. Translated by Alexander Teixeira de Mattos. London: Harville Press, 1948.

Walsh, Cte. Théobald. *George Sand*. Paris: Hivert, 1837.

Secondary Sources

Abensour, Léon. *Le Féminisme sous le règne de Louis-Philippe et en 1848*. 2d ed. Paris: Plon, 1913.

Adler, Laure. *A l'Aube du féminisme: Les Premières journalistes (1830–1850)*. Paris: Payot, 1979.

Agulhon, Maurice. *The Republican Experiment, 1848–1852*. Translated by Janet Lloyd. Cambridge and Paris: Cambridge University Press, 1983.

Albistur, Maïté, and Daniel Armogathe. *Histoire du féminisme français du moyen âge à nos jours*. Paris: des femmes, 1977.

Allen, James Smith. *Popular French Romanticism: Authors, Readers and Books in the Nineteenth Century*. Syracuse, NY: Syracuse University Press, 1981.

Aminzade, Ronald. *Ballots and Barricades: Class Formation and Republican Politics in France, 1830–1871*. Princeton, NJ: Princeton University Press, 1993.

Ariès, Philippe. *Centuries of Childhood: A Social History of Family Life*. Translated by Robert Baldick. New York: Vintage Books, 1962.

Barry, Joseph. *Infamous Woman: The Life of George Sand*. Garden City, NY: Doubleday, 1977.

Bell, Susan Groag, and Karen M. Offen, eds. *Women, the Family, and Freedom: The Debate in Documents*. Vol. 1. Stanford, CA: Stanford University Press, 1983.

Bellet, Roger, ed. *Femmes de lettres au XIXe siècle: Autour de Louise Colet*. Lyon: Presses universitaires de Lyon, 1982.

Bénichou, Paul. *Le Temps des prophètes: Doctrines de l'âge romantique*. Paris: Gallimard, 1977.

Bergman-Carton, Janis. *The Woman of Ideas in French Art, 1830–1848*. New Haven, CT, and London: Yale University Press, 1995.

Bertholet, Denis. *Les Français par eux-mêmes, 1815–1885*. Paris: Olivier Orban, 1991.

Billy, André. *Hortense et ses amants*. Paris: Flammarion, 1961.

Bricard, Isabelle. *Saintes ou pouliches: L'Éducation des jeunes filles au XIXe siècle*. Paris: Albin Michel, 1985.

Canning, Kathleen. "Feminist History after the Linguistic Turn: Historicizing Discourse and Experience." *Signs* 19 (winter 1994): 368–404.

Cate, Curtis. *George Sand*. Boston: Houghton Mifflin, 1975.

Clark, Priscilla Parkhurst. *Literary France: The Making of a Culture*. Berkeley: University of California Press, 1987.

Cohen, Margaret. "A Woman's Place: *La Petite Fadette* vs. *La Voix des Femmes*." *L'Esprit créateur* 29 (summer 1989): 26–38.

Copley, Antony. *Sexual Moralities in France, 1780–1980: New Ideas on the Family, Divorce and Homosexuality*. London and New York: Routledge, 1992.

Courtivron, Isabelle de. "Weak Men and Fatal Women: The Sand Image." In *Homosexualities and French Literature: Cultural Contexts/Critical Texts*, edited by George Stambolian and Elaine Marks, 210–27. Ithaca, NY, and London: Cornell University Press, 1979.

Crecilius, Kathryn J. *Family Romances: George Sand's Early Novels*. Bloomington and Indianapolis: Indiana University Press, 1987.

Crossley, Ceri. *French Historians and Romanticism: Thierry, Guizot, the Saint-Simonians, Quinet, Michelet*. London and New York: Routledge, 1993.

Crubellier, Maurice. *L'Enfance et la jeunesse dans la société française, 1800–1950*. Paris: Armand Colin, 1979.

Darrow, Margaret H. "French Noblewomen and the New Domesticity, 1750–1850." *Feminist Studies* 5 (spring 1979): 41–65.

———. *Revolution in the House: Family, Class, and Inheritance in Southern France, 1775–1825*. Princeton, NJ: Princeton University Press, 1989.

Decreus, Juliette. *Henry Bulwer-Lytton et Hortense Allart*. Paris: M. J. Minard, 1961.

Desan, Suzanne. "Rewriting Family and Nation: Women's Political Pamphlets in the Early Revolution." Paper presented at the 23d annual meeting of the Western Society for French History, Las Vegas, Nevada, 1995.

———. "War between Brothers and Sisters: Inheritance Law and Gender Politics in Revolutionary France." *French Historical Studies* 20 (fall 1997): 597–634.

Desanti, Dominique. *Daniel, ou le visage secret d'une comtesse romantique, Marie d'Agoult*. Paris: Stock, 1980.

Devance, Louis. "Femme, famille, travail et morale sexuelle dans l'idéologie de 1848." *Romantisme* 13–14 (1976): 79–103.

D'Heilly, Georges. *Madame E. de Girardin (Delphine Gay): Sa Vie et ses oeuvres*. Paris: Bachelin-Deflorenne, 1869.

Dupêchez, Charles. *Marie d'Agoult 1805–1876*. Paris: Perrin, 1989.

Ezdinli, Leyla. "*La Canne de M. de Balzac*: Parody at the Intersection of Politics and Literature." *Esprit créateur* 33 (fall 1993): 95–103.

Fortescue, William. "Divorce Debated and Deferred: The French Debate on Divorce and the Failure of the Crémieux Divorce Bill in 1848." *French History* 7 (1993): 137–62.

Foucault, Michel. *An Introduction*. Vol. 1 of *The History of Sexuality*. Translated by Robert Hurley. New York: Vintage Books, 1980.

Fraisse, Geneviève. *Reason's Muse: Sexual Difference and the Birth of Democracy*. Translated by Jane Marie Todd. Chicago and London: University of Chicago Press, 1994.

Fraisse, Geneviève, and Michelle Perrot, eds. *Emerging Feminism from Revolution to World War*. Vol. 4 of *A History of Women in the West*, edited by Georges Duby and Michelle Perrot. Cambridge, MA, and London: Belknap Press of Harvard University Press, 1993.

Friedman, Susan Stanford. "Women's Autobiographical Selves: Theory and Practice." In *The Private Self: Theory and Practice of Women's Autobiographical Writings*, edited by Shari Benstock, 34–62. Chapel Hill and London: University of North Carolina Press, 1988.

Garnett, Mary Anne. "Marie d'Agoult and the 'Anxiety of Authorship.'" In *Continental, Latin American and Francophone Women Writers*, vol. 2, edited by Ginette Adamson and Eunice Myers, 123–30. Lanham, MD: University Press of America, 1990.

———. "La Reine noire et la reine blanche: George Sand et Hortense Allart." In *George Sand Today: Proceedings of the 8th International George Sand Conference—Tours 1989*, edited by David A. Powell, 255–68. Lanham, MD, New York, and London: University Press of America, 1992.

Gay, Peter. *The Tender Passion*. Vol. 2 of *The Bourgeois Experience from Victoria to Freud*. New York and Oxford: Oxford University Press, 1986.

Guiot-Lauret, Jacqueline. "Amour et taboux linguistiques dans quelques romans et nouvelles des années 1833–1836." In *Aimer en France, 1760–1860*, edited by Paul Viallaneix and Jean Ehrand, 1:205–15. Clermont-Ferrand: Association des Publications de la Faculté des Lettres et Sciences Humaines de Clermont-Ferrand, 1980.

Gullickson, Gay L. "La Pétroleuse: Representing Revolution." *Feminist Studies* 17 (summer 1991): 241–65.

Hertz, Neil. "Medusa's Head: Male Hysteria under Political Pressure." *Representations* 4 (fall 1983): 27–54.

Hesse, Carla. "Reading Signatures: Female Authorship and Revolutionary Law in France, 1750–1850." *Eighteenth-Century Studies* 22 (spring 1989): 469–87.

Hovey, Tamara. *A Mind of Her Own: A Life of the Writer George Sand*. New York: Harper & Row, 1977.

Hunt, Lynn. *The Family Romance of the French Revolution*. Berkeley: University of California Press, 1992.

———. "The Many Bodies of Marie Antoinette: Political Pornography and the Problem of the Feminine in the French Revolution." In *Eroticism and the Body*

Politic, edited by Lynn Hunt, 108–30. Baltimore, MD, and London: Johns Hopkins University Press, 1991.

———. "Reading the French Revolution: A Reply." *French Historical Studies* 19 (fall 1995): 289–98.

Israel, Kali A. K. "Writing inside the Kaleidoscope: Re-Representing Victorian Women Public Figures." *Gender & History* 2 (spring 1990): 40–48.

Jardin, A., and A. J. Tudesq. *La France des Notables: L'Évolution générale, 1815–1848.* Paris: Seuil, 1973.

Jordan, Ruth. *George Sand: A Biographical Portrait.* New York: Taplinger Publishing Company, 1976.

Karénine, Wladimir [Komorova, Varvara Dmitriëvna]. *George Sand: Sa Vie et ses oeuvres, 1804–1876.* 4 vols. 2d ed. Paris: Paul Ollendorff, 1899, and Plon, 1926.

Kerber, Linda K. *Toward an Intellectual History of Women.* Chapel Hill and London: University of North Carolina Press, 1997.

———. *Women of the Republic: Intellect and Ideology in Revolutionary America.* Chapel Hill: University of North Carolina Press, 1980.

Landes, Joan B. *Women and the Public Sphere in the Age of the French Revolution.* Ithaca, NY, and London: Cornell University Press, 1988.

Lubin, Georges. "George Sand en 1848." In *George Sand Papers: Conference Proceedings, 1976,* 28–41. New York: AMS Press, 1980.

Lyons, Martyn. *Le Triomph du livre: Une Histoire sociologique de la lecture dans la France du XIXe siècle.* Paris: Editions du Cercle de la Librairie, 1987.

McBride, Theresa. "Public Authority and Private Lives: Divorce after the French Revolution." *French Historical Studies* 17 (spring 1992): 747–68.

MacCallum-Schwartz, Lucy. "Sensibilité et sensualité: Rapports sexuels dans les premiers romans de George Sand (1831–1843)." In *George Sand,* edited by Simone Vierne, 171–77. Paris: CDU et SEDES Réunis, 1983.

Magraw, Roger. *France 1814–1914: The Bourgeois Century.* New York and Oxford: Oxford University Press, 1986.

Malo, Henri. *La Gloire du Vicomte de Launay: Delphine Gay de Girardin.* Paris: Emile-Paul frères, 1925.

———. *Une Muse et sa mère: Delphine Gay de Girardin.* Paris: Emile-Paul frères, 1924.

Margadant, Jo Burr. "Introduction: Constructing Selves in Historical Perspective." In *The New Biography: Performing Femininity in Nineteenth-Century France,* edited by Jo Burr Margadant. Berkeley: University of California Press, forthcoming.

Martin-Fugier, Anne. *La Vie élégante, ou la formation du Tout-Paris 1815–1848.* Paris: Fayard, 1990.

Maurois. André. "George Sand et Marie d'Agoult: Mort d'une amitié." *Revue de Paris* 58 (July–December 1951): 3–15.

———. *Lélia: The Life of George Sand.* Translated by Gerard Hopkins. New York: Harper & Row, 1953.

Mayeur, Francoise. *L'Education des filles en France au XIXe siècle.* Paris: Hachette, 1979.

Miller, Nancy K. *Subject to Change: Reading Feminist Writing.* New York: Columbia University Press, 1988.

———. "Writing Fictions: Women's Autobiography in France." In *Life/Lines: Theorizing Women's Autobiography,* edited by Bella Brodzki and Celeste Schenck, 45–61. Ithaca, NY: Cornell University Press, 1988.

Moses, Claire Goldberg. *French Feminism in the Nineteenth Century.* Albany: State University of New York Press, 1984.

Moses, Claire Goldberg, and Leslie Wahl Rabine, eds. *Feminism, Socialism, and French Romanticism.* Bloomington and Indianapolis: Indiana University Press, 1993.

Nicolet, Claude. *L'Idée républicaine en France (1789–1924): Essai d'histoire critique.* Paris: Gallimard, 1982.

Nord, Philip. "Republican Politics and the Bourgeois Interior in Mid-Nineteenth-Century France." In *Home and Its Dislocations in Nineteenth-Century France,* edited by Suzanne Nash, 193–214. Albany: State University of New York Press, 1993.

Offen, Karen. "Contextualizing the Theory and Practice of Feminism in Nineteenth-Century Europe (1789–1914)." In *Becoming Visible: Women in European History,* 3d ed., edited by Renate Bridenthal, Susan Mosher Stuard, and Merry E. Wiesner, 327–55. Boston and New York: Houghton Mifflin, 1998.

———. "Defining Feminism: A Comparative Historical Approach." *Signs* 14 (1988): 119–57.

———. "Ernest Legouvé and the Doctrine of 'Equality in Difference' for Women: A Case Study of Male Feminism in Nineteenth-Century French Thought." *Journal of Modern History* 58 (June 1986): 452–84.

———. "Reclaiming the European Enlightenment for Feminism, or Prologomena to Any Future History of Eighteenth-century Europe." In *Perspectives on Feminist Thought in European History from the Middle Ages to the Present,* edited by Tjitske Akkerman and Siep Stuurman, 85–103. London and New York: Routledge, 1998.

———. "Was Mary Wollstonecraft a Feminist? A Contextual Re-reading of *A Vindication of the Rights of Woman,* 1792–1991." In *Quilting a New Canon: Stitching Women's Words,* edited by Uma Parameswaran, 3–24. Toronto: Sister Vision, 1996.

Ozouf, Mona. *Les Mots des femmes: Essai sur la singularité française.* Paris: Fayard, 1995.

Pateman, Carole. *The Sexual Contract.* Stanford, CA: Stanford University Press, 1988.

Pellissier, Pierre. *Emile de Girardin, Prince de la presse.* Paris: Denoel, 1985.

Perreux, Gabriel. *Au Temps des Sociétés secrètes: La Propagande républicaine au début de la Monarchie de Juillet (1830–1835).* Paris: Rieder, 1931.

Perrot, Michelle. "Presentation." In George Sand, *Politique et polémiques (1843–1850),* 7–57. Paris: Imprimerie nationale, 1997.

———, ed. *From the Fires of the Revolution to the Great War.* Vol. 4 of *A History of Private Life,* edited by Philippe Ariès and Georges Duby. Cambridge, MA, and London: Belknap Press of Harvard University Press, 1990.

Personal Narratives Group. *Interpreting Women's Lives: Feminist Theory and Personal Narratives*. Bloomington and Indianapolis: Indiana University Press, 1989.

Phillips, Roderick. *Family Breakdown in Late Eighteenth-Century France: Divorces in Rouen, 1792–1803*. Oxford: Clarendon Press, 1980.

———. *Putting Asunder: A History of Divorce in Western Society*. New York: Cambridge University Press, 1988.

Pilbeam, Pamela M. *Republicanism in Nineteenth-Century France, 1814–1871*. New York: St. Martin's Press, 1995.

Planté, Christine. *La Petite Soeur de Balzac: Essai sur la femme auteur*. Paris: Seuil, 1989.

Poli, Annarosa. "George Sand devant la critique, 1831–1833." In *George Sand*, edited by Simone Vierne, 95–100. Paris: CDU et SEDES Réunis, 1983.

Powell, Kirsten, and Elizabeth C. Childs. *Femmes d'esprit: Women in Daumier's Caricature*. Hanover, NH: University Press of New England, 1990.

Prassoloff, Annie. "Le Statut juridique de la femme auteur." *Romantisme* 77 (1992): 9–14.

Price, Roger. *The French Second Republic: A Social History*. Ithaca, NY: Cornell University Press, 1972.

Rabine, Leslie. "Feminist Writers in French Romanticism." *Studies in Romanticism* 16 (fall 1977): 491–507.

Reddy, William M. "Condottieri of the Pen: Journalists and the Public Sphere in Postrevolutionary France (1815–1850)." *American Historical Review* 99 (December 1994): 1546–70.

———. *The Invisible Code: Honor and Sentiment in Postrevolutionary France, 1814–1848*. Berkeley: University of California Press, 1997.

Reynolds, Siân. "Marianne's Citizens? Women, the Republic and Universal Suffrage in France." In *Women, State and Revolution: Essays on Power and Gender in Europe since 1789*, edited by Siân Reynolds, 102–22. Amherst: University of Massachusetts Press, 1987.

Rheinstein, Max. "The Code and the Family." In *The Code Napoleon and the Common-Law World*, edited by Bernard Schwartz, 139–61. New York: New York University Press, 1956.

Rice, Mary. "Masculin/Féminin: Daniel Stern's *Histoire de la Révolution de 1848*." *L'Esprit créateur* 29 (fall 1989): 84–91.

Riot-Sarcey, Michèle. *La Démocratie à l'épreuve des femmes: Trois figures critiques du pouvoir, 1830–1848*. Paris: Albin Michel, 1994.

Rocheblave, S. "Une Amitié romanesque: George Sand et Madame d'Agoult." *Revue de Paris* 6 (November–December 1894): 792–836.

Rosanvallon, Pierre. *Le Moment Guizot*. Paris: Gallimard, 1985.

Saint-Saëns, Ann MacCall. "Du bas-bleuisme et des correspondantes: Marie d'Agoult, Hortense Allart et la surenchère épistolaire." *Romantisme* 90 (1995): 77–88.

Schor, Naomi. *George Sand and Idealism*. New York: Columbia University Press, 1993.

———. "Reading Double: Sand's Difference." In *The Poetics of Gender*, edited by Nancy K. Miller, 248–69. New York: Columbia University Press, 1986.

Scott, Joan Wallach. *Only Paradoxes to Offer: French Feminists and the Rights of Man*. Cambridge, MA, and London: Harvard University Press, 1996.

Séché, Léon. "Les Correspondants d'Hortense Allart de Méritens: Sainte-Beuve—Madame d'Agoult." *La Revue de Paris* 14, no. 5 (September–October 1907): 289–330.

———. *Delphine Gay*. Paris: Mercure de France, 1910.

———. *Hortense Allart de Méritens*. Paris: Société du Mercure de France, 1908.

Slama, Béatrice. "Femmes écrivains." In *Misérable et glorieuse: La Femme du XIXe siècle*, edited by Jean-Paul Aron, 213–48. Bruxelles: Editions Complexe, 1984.

Steedman, Carolyn. *Childhood, Culture and Class in Britain: Margaret McMillan, 1860–1931*. New Brunswick, NJ: Rutgers University Press, 1990.

Stock-Morton, Phyllis. "Daniel Stern, Historian." *History of European Ideas* 8 (1987): 489–501.

Terdiman, Richard. *Discourse/Counter-Discourse: The Theory and Practice of Symbolic Resistance in Nineteenth-Century France*. Ithaca, NY, and London: Cornell University Press, 1985.

Thibert, Marguerite. *Le Féminisme dans le socialisme français de 1830 à 1850*. Paris: Marcel Giard, 1926.

Thomas, Edith. *Les Femmes de 1848*. Paris: Presses universitaires de France, 1948.

Thompson, Victoria. "Creating Boundaries: Homosexuality and the Changing Social Order in France, 1830–1870." In *Homosexuality in Modern France*, edited by Jeffrey Merrick and Bryant T. Ragan, Jr., 102–27. New York and Oxford: Oxford University Press, 1996.

Uffenbeck, Lorin A. *The Life and Writings of Hortense Allart (1801–1879)*. Ph.D. dissertation, University of Wisconsin-Madison, 1957.

Vier, Jacques. *La Comtesse d'Agoult et Hortense Allart de Méritens sous le Second Empire*. Paris: Archives des Lettres modernes (no. 33), 1960.

———. *La Comtesse d'Agoult et son temps*. 6 vols. Paris: Armand Colin, 1955–63.

Vigier, Philippe. *La Monarchie de Juillet*. Paris: Presses universitaires de France, 1962.

Waller, Margaret. *The Male Malady: Fictions of Impotence in the French Romantic Novel*. New Brunswick, NJ: Rutgers University Press, 1993.

Walton, Whitney. "Literary Production and the Rearticulation of Home Space in the Works of George Sand, Marie d'Agoult, and Hortense Allart." *Women's History Review* 6 (1997): 115–32.

———. "Republican Families and Republican Women in the Personal Narratives of George Sand, Marie d'Agoult, and Hortense Allart." In *The New Biography: Performing Femininity in Nineteenth-Century France*, edited by Jo Burr Margadant. Berkeley: University of California Press, forthcoming.

———. "Sailing a Fragile Bark: Rewriting the Family and the Individual in Nineteenth-Century France." *Journal of Family History* 22 (April 1997): 150–75.

———. "Writing the 1848 Revolution: Politics, Gender, and Feminism in the Works of French Women of Letters." *French Historical Studies* 18 (fall 1994): 1001–24.

Winegarten, Renée. *The Double Life of George Sand: Woman and Writer. A Critical Biography*. New York: Basic Books, 1978.

Yalom, Marilyn. "Towards a History of Female Adolescence: The Contributions of George Sand." In *George Sand: Collected Essays*, edited by Janis Glasgow, 204–15. Troy, NY: Whitston Publishing Company, 1985.

☞ Index

In this index an "f" after a number indicates a separate reference on the next page, and an "ff" indicates separate references on the next two pages. A continuous discussion over two or more pages is indicated by a span of page numbers, e.g., "57–59." *Passim* is used for a cluster of references in close but not consecutive sequence.

Library of Congress Cataloging-in-Publication Data

Walton, Whitney
   Eve's Proud Descendants : Four Women Writers and Republican
Politics in Nineteenth-Century France / Whitney Walton.
      p.   cm.
   Includes bibliographical references and index.
   ISBN 0-8047-3754-1 (alk. paper).
      1. Women—France—Social conditions—19th century.   2. Authors,
French—19th century—Political activity.   3. France—Politics and
government—19th century.   4. Social reformers—France—Political
activity.   5. Feminism and literature—France—History—19th century—
Political aspects.   6. Sand, George, 1804–1876—Political and social
views.   7. Stern, Daniel, 1805–1876—Political and social views.
8. Allart de Mâritens, Hortense, 1801–1879—Political and social views.
9. Girardin, Emile de, Mme, 1804–1855—Political and social views.
10. Women's rights—France—History—19th century.   I. Title.

HQ1611.W34   2000
305.42'0944 21—dc21   99-045418

This book is printed on acid-free, archival-quality paper.

Original printing 2000
Last figure below indicates year of this printing:
09   08   07   06   05   04   03   02   01   00

Typeset by John Feneron in 10/13 Palatino